P9-CKO-547

S·A
Special A

satoru&hikari 16years old

Volume 12

Story & Art by
Maki Minami

STORY

★At the tender age of 6, carpenter's daughter Hikari Hanazono suffered her first loss to the wealthy Kei Takishima in a wrestling match. Now the hardworking Hikari has followed Kei to the most elite school for the rich just to beat him! I call this story "Overthrow Takishima! Rise Above Perpetual Second Place!!" It's the story of Hikari's sweat, tears and passion, with a little bit of love thrown in!

★ Hikari finally admitted her feelings to Kei, so now they're dating. ♥ Even with Kei's mother and grandfather butting in, Hikari and Kei manage to have a lot of fun together. Meanwhile, Ryu, Megumi and Jun spot Kei walking with another girl…

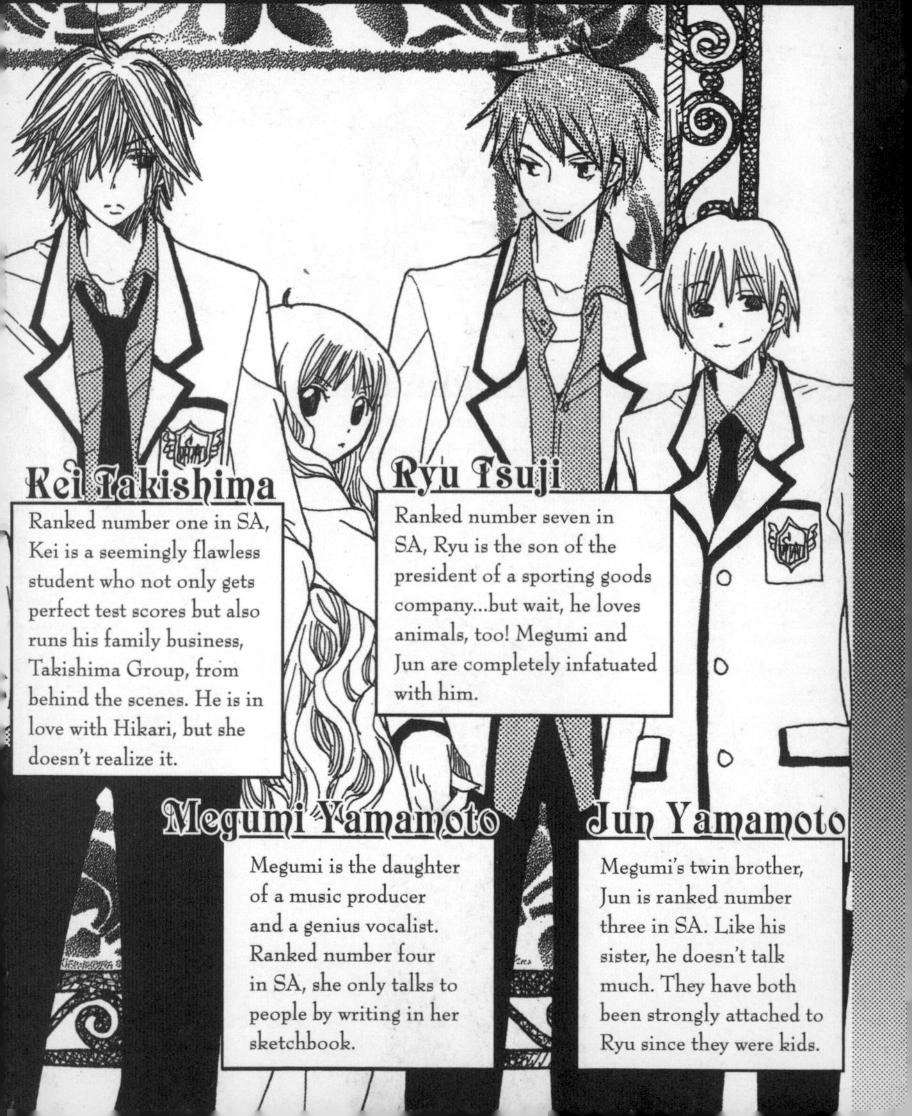
Kei Takishima
Ranked number one in SA, Kei is a seemingly flawless student who not only gets perfect test scores but also runs his family business, Takishima Group, from behind the scenes. He is in love with Hikari, but she doesn't realize it.
Ryu Tsuji
Ranked number seven in SA, Ryu is the son of the president of a sporting goods company...but wait, he loves animals, too! Megumi and Jun are completely infatuated with him.
Megumi Yamamoto
Megumi is the daughter of a music producer and a genius vocalist. Ranked number four in SA, she only talks to people by writing in her sketchbook.
Jun Yamamoto
Megumi's twin brother, Jun is ranked number three in SA. Like his sister, he doesn't talk much. They have both been strongly attached to Ryu since they were kids.

S·A CHARACTERS

Hikari goes to an elite school called Hakusenkan High School. This school divides each grade level into groups A through F, according to the students' test scores. Group A includes only the top seven students in each class. Then the top seven students from all grades' A groups are put into a group called Special A, which is considered much higher than all others. Known as SA, they are "the elite among the elite."

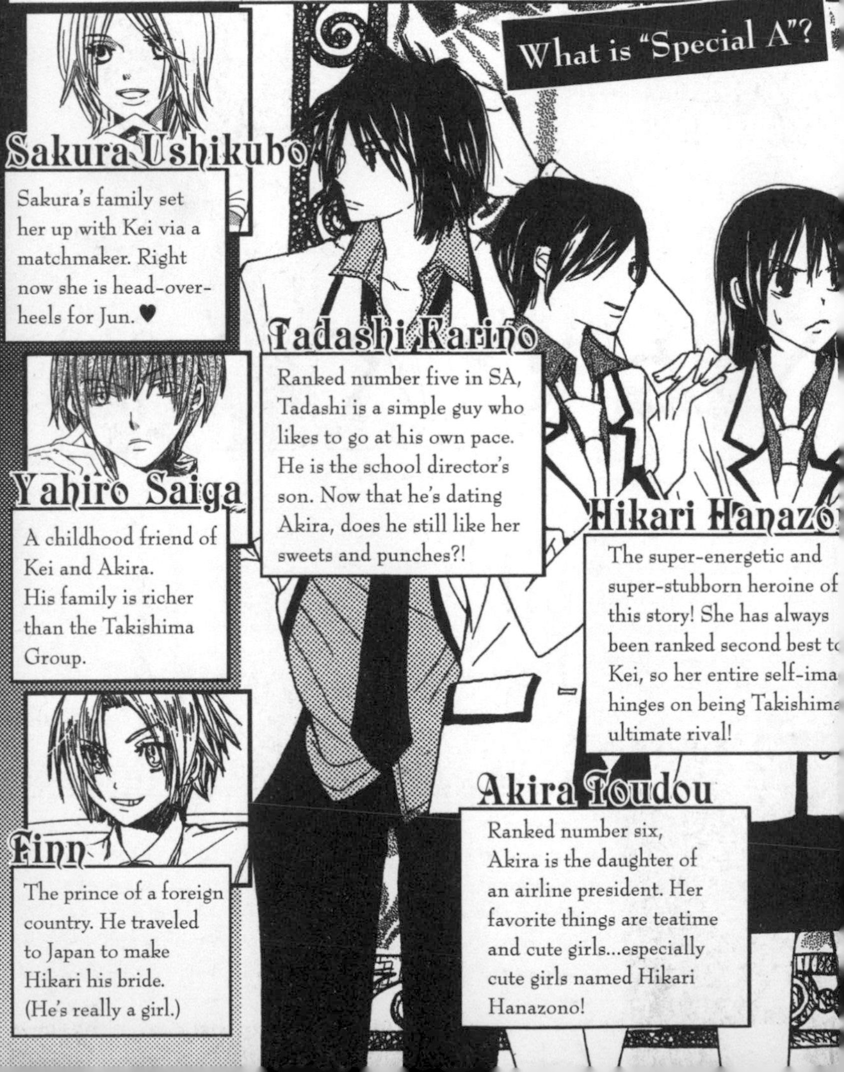

What is "Special A"?

Sakura Ushikubo

Sakura's family set her up with Kei via a matchmaker. Right now she is head-over-heels for Jun. ♥

Yahiro Saiga

A childhood friend of Kei and Akira. His family is richer than the Takishima Group.

Finn

The prince of a foreign country. He traveled to Japan to make Hikari his bride. (He's really a girl.)

Tadashi Karino

Ranked number five in SA, Tadashi is a simple guy who likes to go at his own pace. He is the school director's son. Now that he's dating Akira, does he still like her sweets and punches?!

Hikari Hanazo

The super-energetic and super-stubborn heroine of this story! She has always been ranked second best to Kei, so her entire self-ima hinges on being Takishima ultimate rival!

Akira Toudou

Ranked number six, Akira is the daughter of an airline president. Her favorite things are teatime and cute girls...especially cute girls named Hikari Hanazono!

Contents

High school Coed Company President
What kind of stupid thing is she doing now...?

Chapter 64

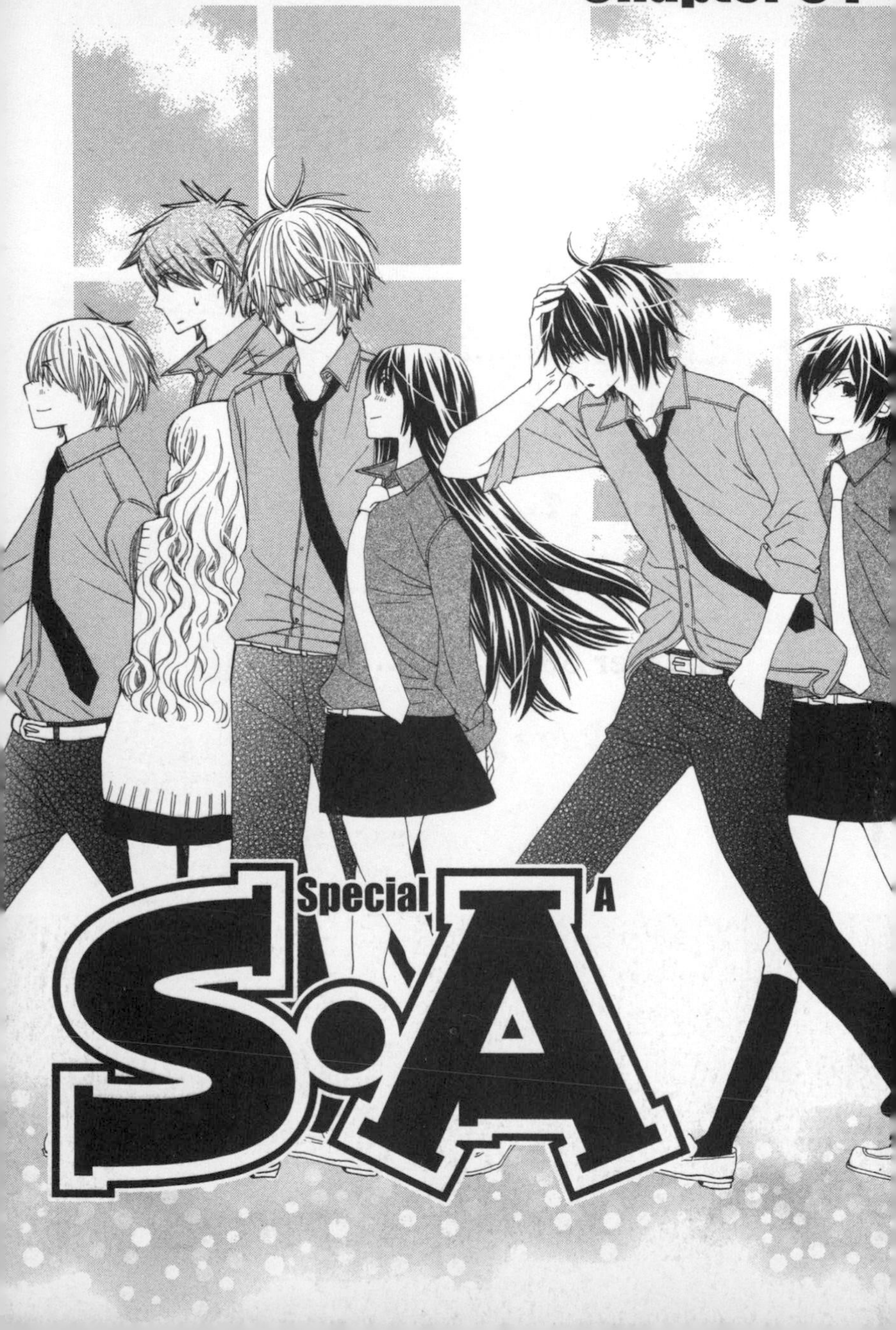
S.A
Special A

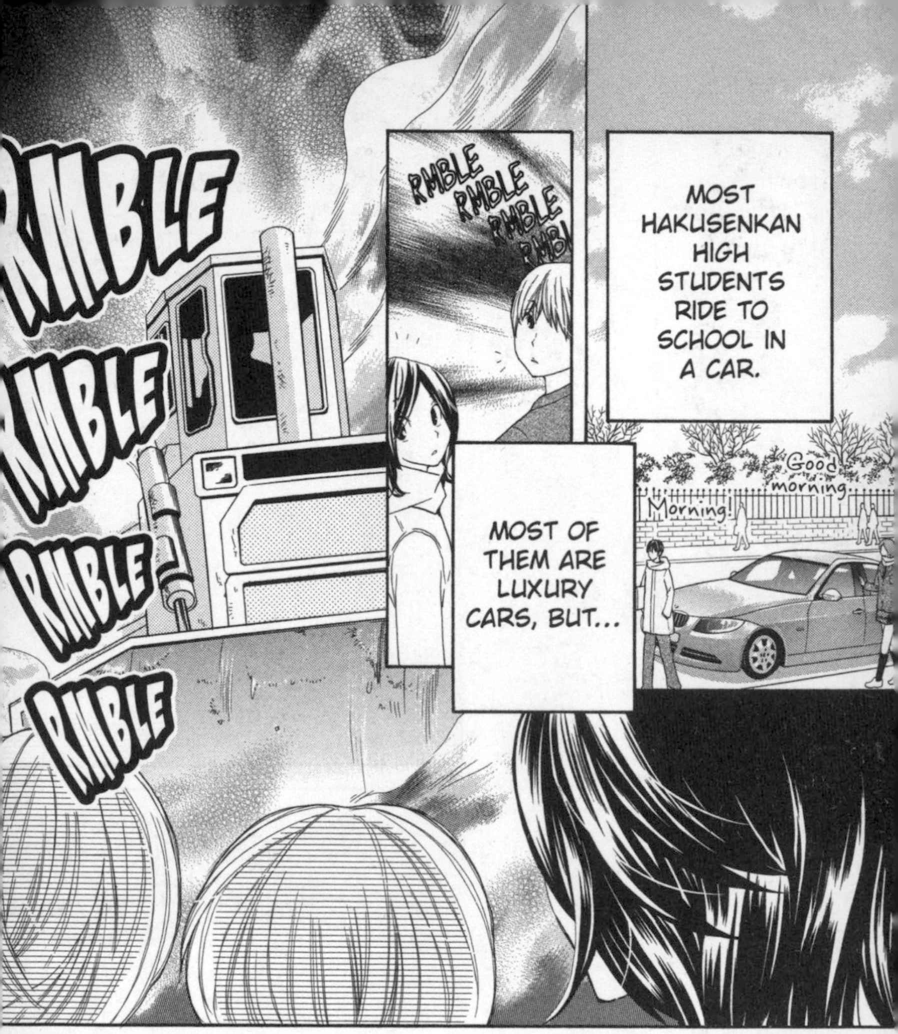
MOST HAKUSENKAN HIGH STUDENTS RIDE TO SCHOOL IN A CAR.
Good morning
Morning!
MOST OF THEM ARE LUXURY CARS, BUT...
RMBLE RMBLE RMBLE
RMBLE RMBLE RMBLE RMBLE

• COVER AND THIS AND THAT •

• THE COVER ART SHOWS HIKARI WITH KEI'S DAD THIS TIME. IT WAS REALLY FUN TO DRAW HIS DAD AS A 16-YEAR-OLD. AND DRAWING THE FRUIT WAS REALLY FUN TOO!!!

• I JUST FOUND OUT THAT A FRIEND OF A FRIEND (TOTAL STRANGER) WHO'S AN AUTHOR CAN DO CALLIGRAPHY AND TALK ON THE PHONE AT THE SAME TIME. IT GOES TO SHOW HOW MUCH TALENT SOME PEOPLE HAVE OUT THERE...

AH... TALENT...

And on the phone...

Unbelievable.

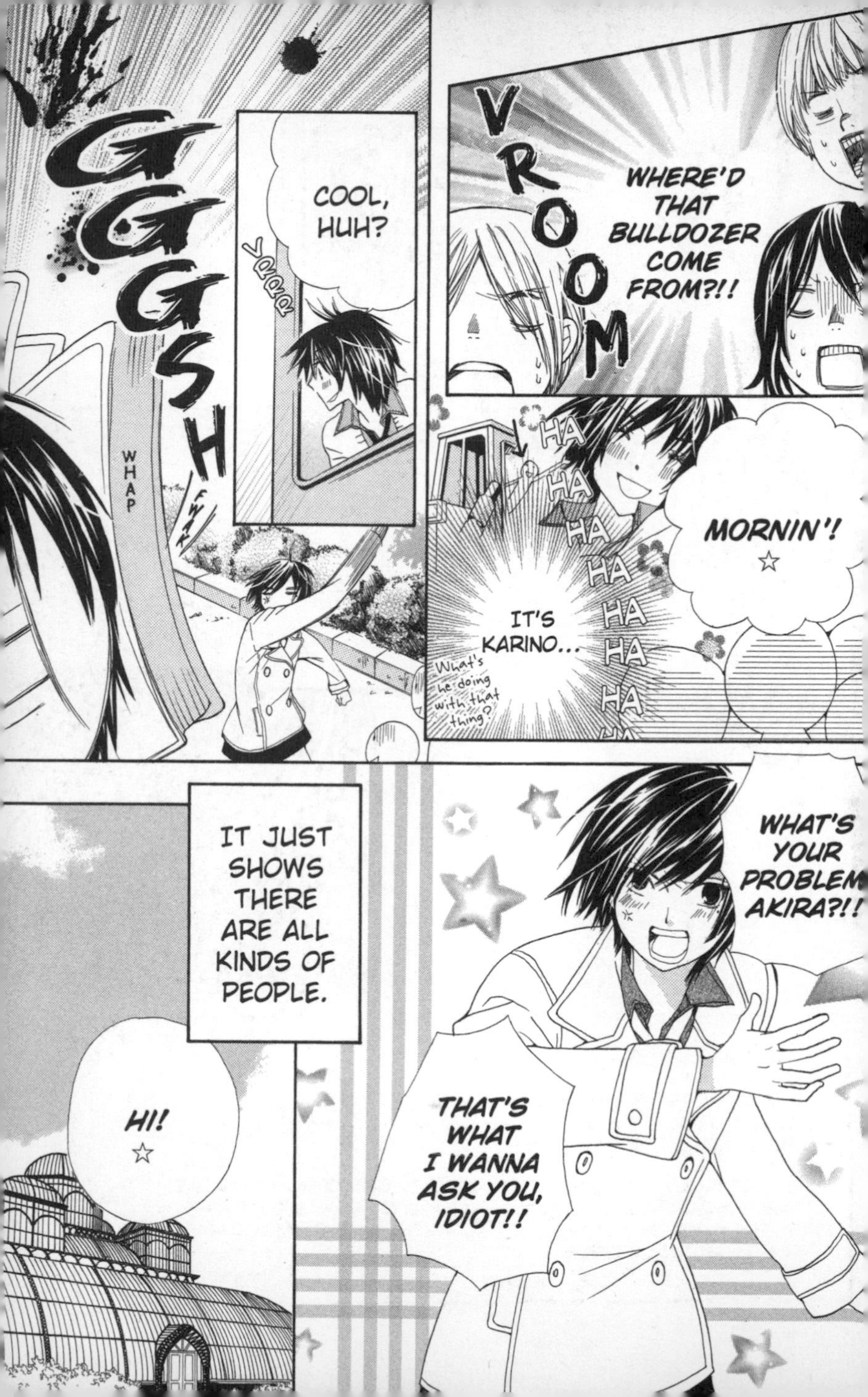
VROOM
WHERE'D THAT BULLDOZER COME FROM?!!
HA HA HA HA HA HA HA
MORNIN'! ☆
IT'S KARINO...
What's he doing with that thing?
COOL, HUH?
GGGSH
WHAP
IT JUST SHOWS THERE ARE ALL KINDS OF PEOPLE.
HI! ☆
WHAT'S YOUR PROBLEM AKIRA?!!
THAT'S WHAT I WANNA ASK YOU, IDIOT!!

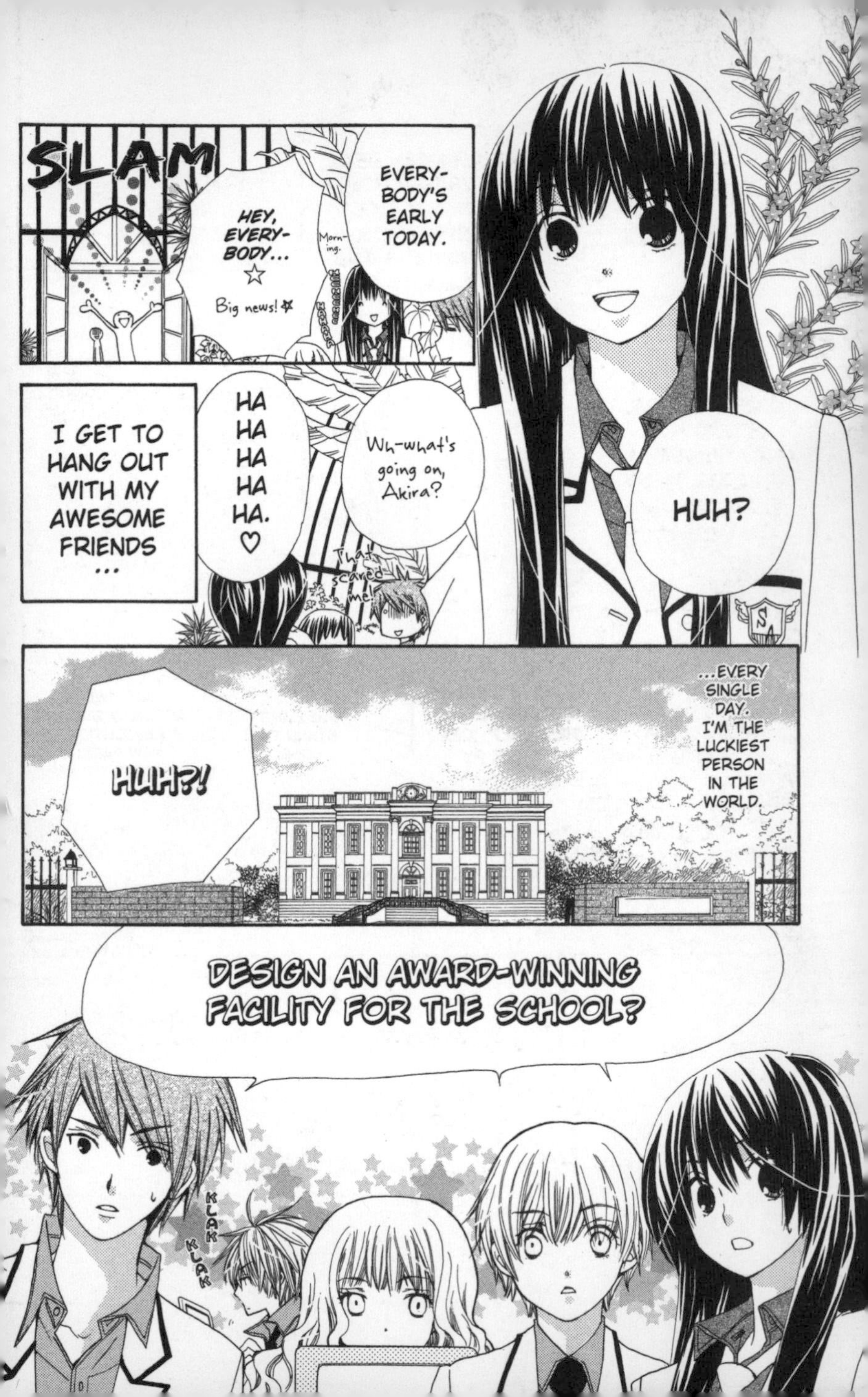
HUH?
EVERY-BODY'S EARLY TODAY.
Morn-ing.
HEY, EVERY-BODY... ☆
Big news! ☆
SLAM
Wh-what's going on, Akira?
That scared me!
HA HA HA HA HA. ♡
I GET TO HANG OUT WITH MY AWESOME FRIENDS ...
...EVERY SINGLE DAY. I'M THE LUCKIEST PERSON IN THE WORLD.
HUH?!
DESIGN AN AWARD-WINNING FACILITY FOR THE SCHOOL?
KLAK KLAK

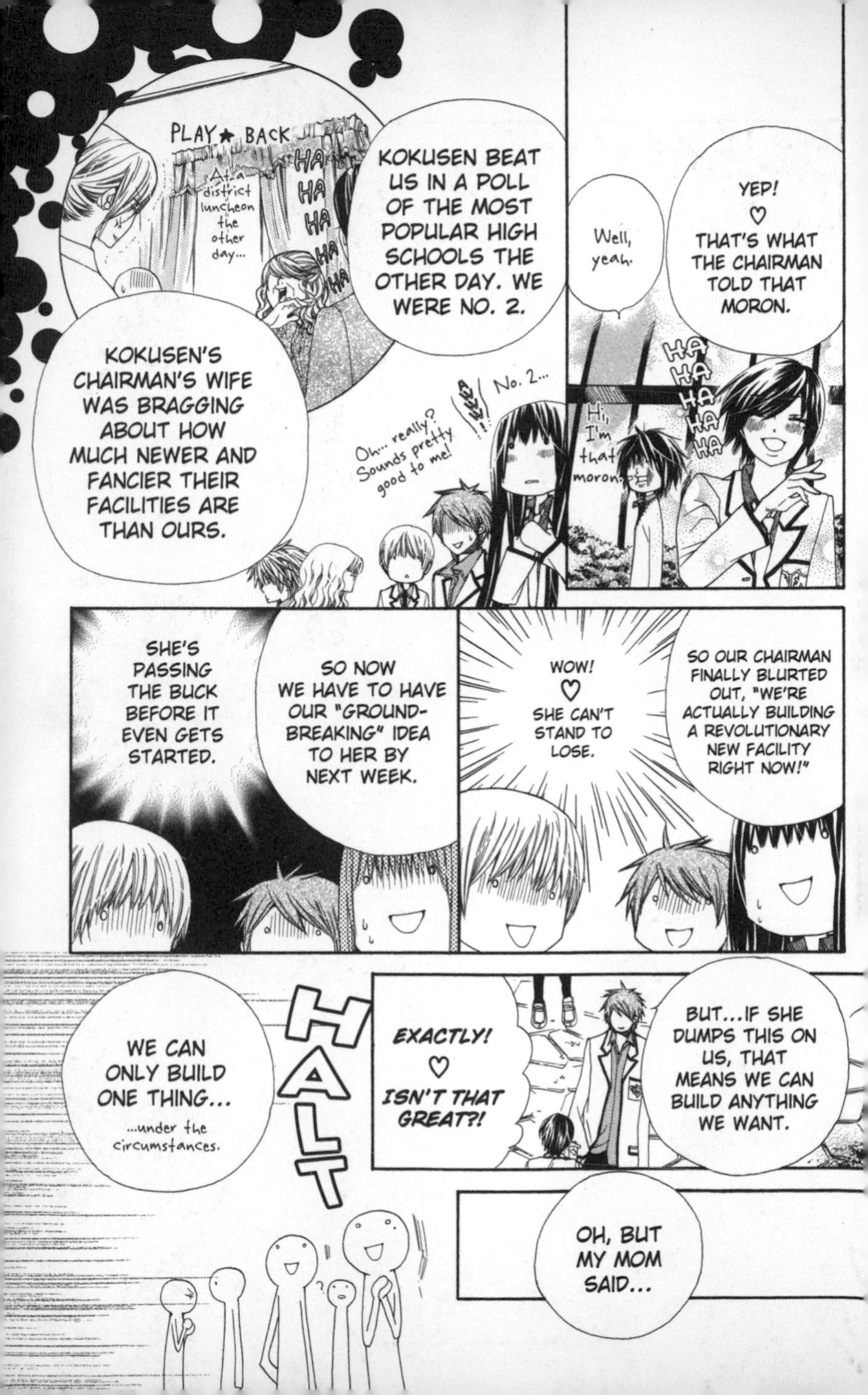
Well, yeah.
YEP! ♡ THAT'S WHAT THE CHAIRMAN TOLD THAT MORON.
HA HA HA HA HA HA
Hi, I'm that moron.
PLAY★BACK
At a district luncheon the other day...
HA HA HA HA HA
KOKUSEN BEAT US IN A POLL OF THE MOST POPULAR HIGH SCHOOLS THE OTHER DAY. WE WERE NO. 2.
KOKUSEN'S CHAIRMAN'S WIFE WAS BRAGGING ABOUT HOW MUCH NEWER AND FANCIER THEIR FACILITIES ARE THAN OURS.
No. 2...
AWW
Oh... really? Sounds pretty good to me!
SO OUR CHAIRMAN FINALLY BLURTED OUT, "WE'RE ACTUALLY BUILDING A REVOLUTIONARY NEW FACILITY RIGHT NOW!"
WOW! ♡ SHE CAN'T STAND TO LOSE.
SO NOW WE HAVE TO HAVE OUR "GROUND-BREAKING" IDEA TO HER BY NEXT WEEK.
SHE'S PASSING THE BUCK BEFORE IT EVEN GETS STARTED.
BUT...IF SHE DUMPS THIS ON US, THAT MEANS WE CAN BUILD ANYTHING WE WANT.
EXACTLY! ♡ ISN'T THAT GREAT?!
HALT
WE CAN ONLY BUILD ONE THING...
...under the circumstances.
OH, BUT MY MOM SAID...

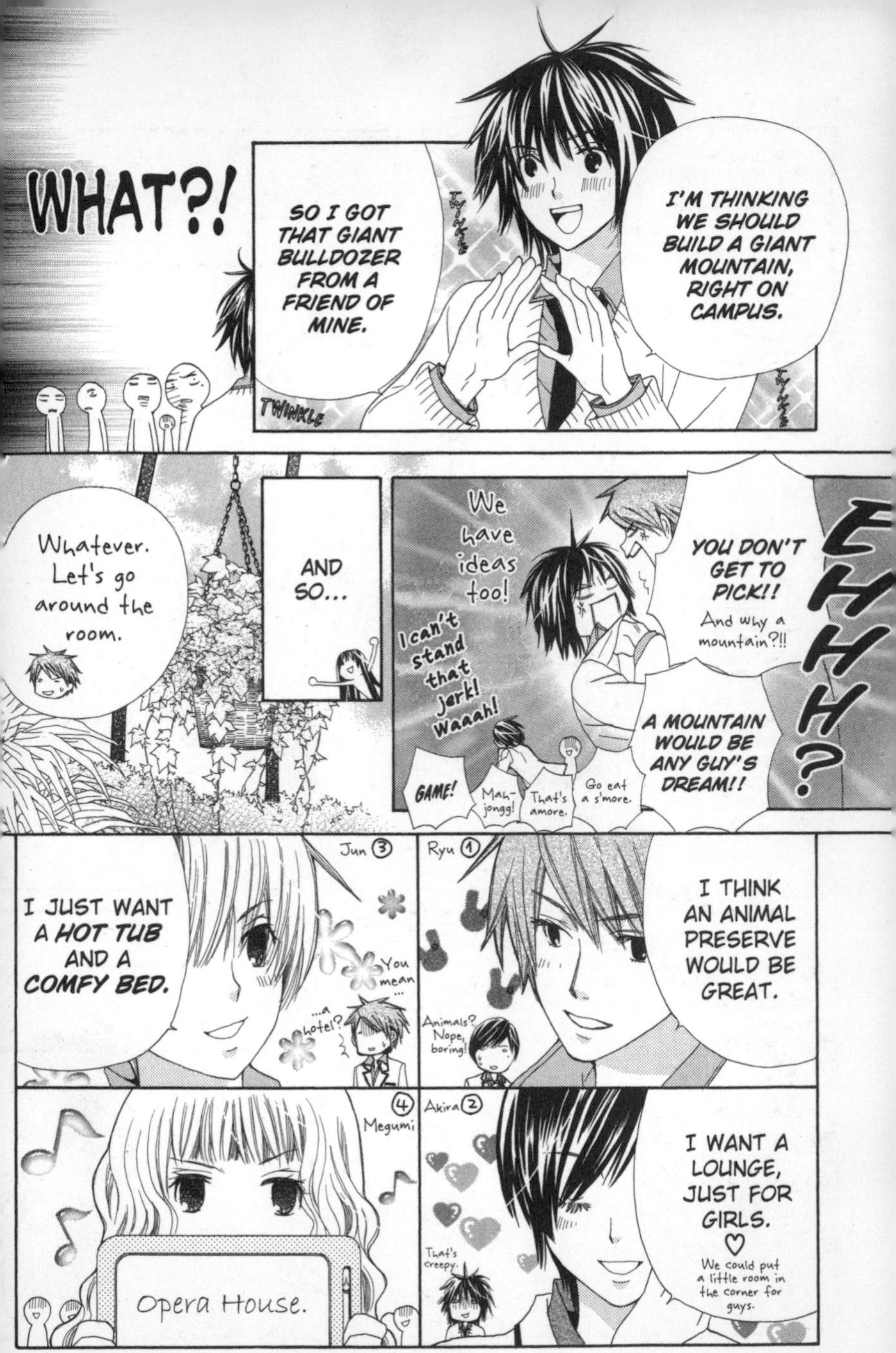

TWINKLE
I'M THINKING WE SHOULD BUILD A GIANT MOUNTAIN, RIGHT ON CAMPUS.
SO I GOT THAT GIANT BULLDOZER FROM A FRIEND OF MINE.
TWINKLE
WHAT?!
EHHHH?
YOU DON'T GET TO PICK!!
And why a mountain?!!
We have ideas too!
A MOUNTAIN WOULD BE ANY GUY'S DREAM!!
I can't stand that jerk! Waaah!
Go eat a s'more.
That's amore.
Mah-jongg!
GAME!
AND SO...
Whatever. Let's go around the room.
Ryu ①
I THINK AN ANIMAL PRESERVE WOULD BE GREAT.
Animals? Nope, boring!
Jun ③
I JUST WANT A HOT TUB AND A COMFY BED.
You mean ...
...a hotel?
Akira ②
I WANT A LOUNGE, JUST FOR GIRLS. ♡
We could put a little room in the corner for guys.
That's creepy.
④ Megumi
Opera House.

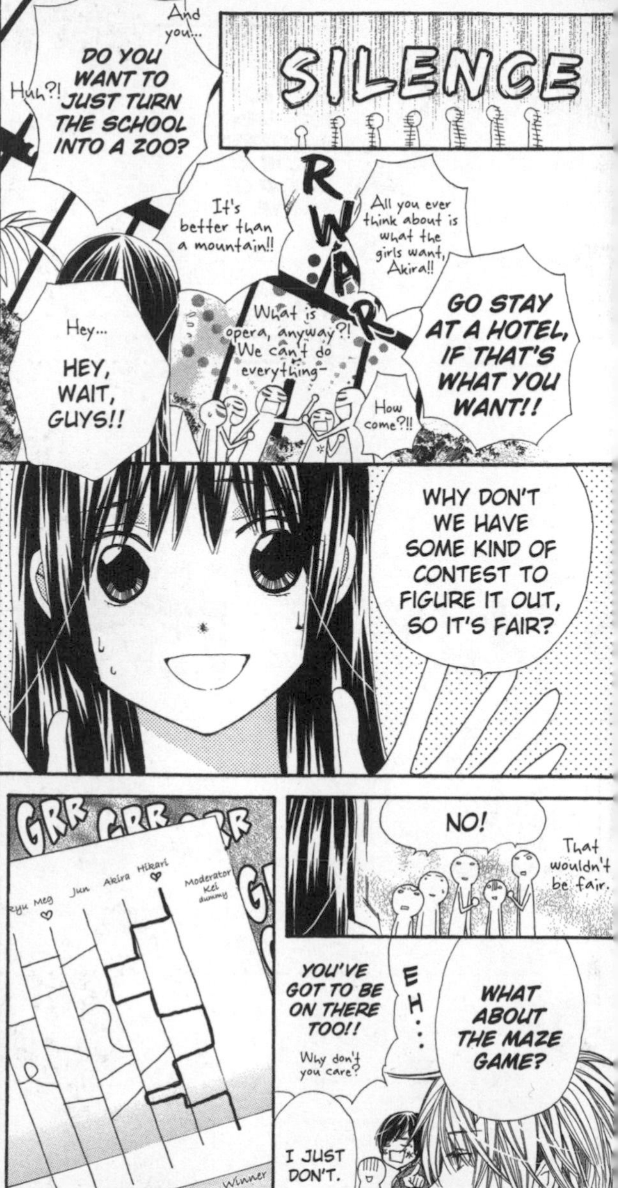
SILENCE
And you...
DO YOU WANT TO JUST TURN THE SCHOOL INTO A ZOO?
Huh?!
All you ever think about is what the girls want, Akira!!
GO STAY AT A HOTEL, IF THAT'S WHAT YOU WANT!!
RWAR
It's better than a mountain!!
What is opera, anyway?! We can't do everything-
How come?!!
Hey...
HEY, WAIT, GUYS!!
WHY DON'T WE HAVE SOME KIND OF CONTEST TO FIGURE IT OUT, SO IT'S FAIR?
NO!
That wouldn't be fair.
WHAT ABOUT THE MAZE GAME?
EH...
YOU'VE GOT TO BE ON THERE TOO!!
Why don't you care?
I JUST DON'T.
GRR GRR GRR
Ryu
Meg
Jun
Akira
Hikari
Moderator Kei dummy
Winner

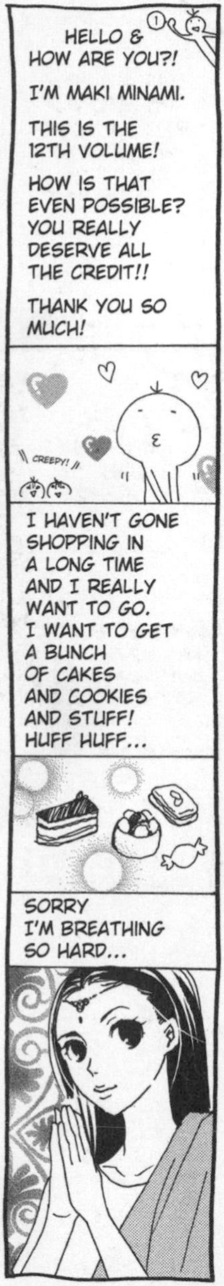
①
HELLO & HOW ARE YOU?!
I'M MAKI MINAMI.
THIS IS THE 12TH VOLUME!
HOW IS THAT EVEN POSSIBLE? YOU REALLY DESERVE ALL THE CREDIT!!
THANK YOU SO MUCH!
CREEPY!
I HAVEN'T GONE SHOPPING IN A LONG TIME AND I REALLY WANT TO GO. I WANT TO GET A BUNCH OF CAKES AND COOKIES AND STUFF! HUFF HUFF...
SORRY I'M BREATHING SO HARD...

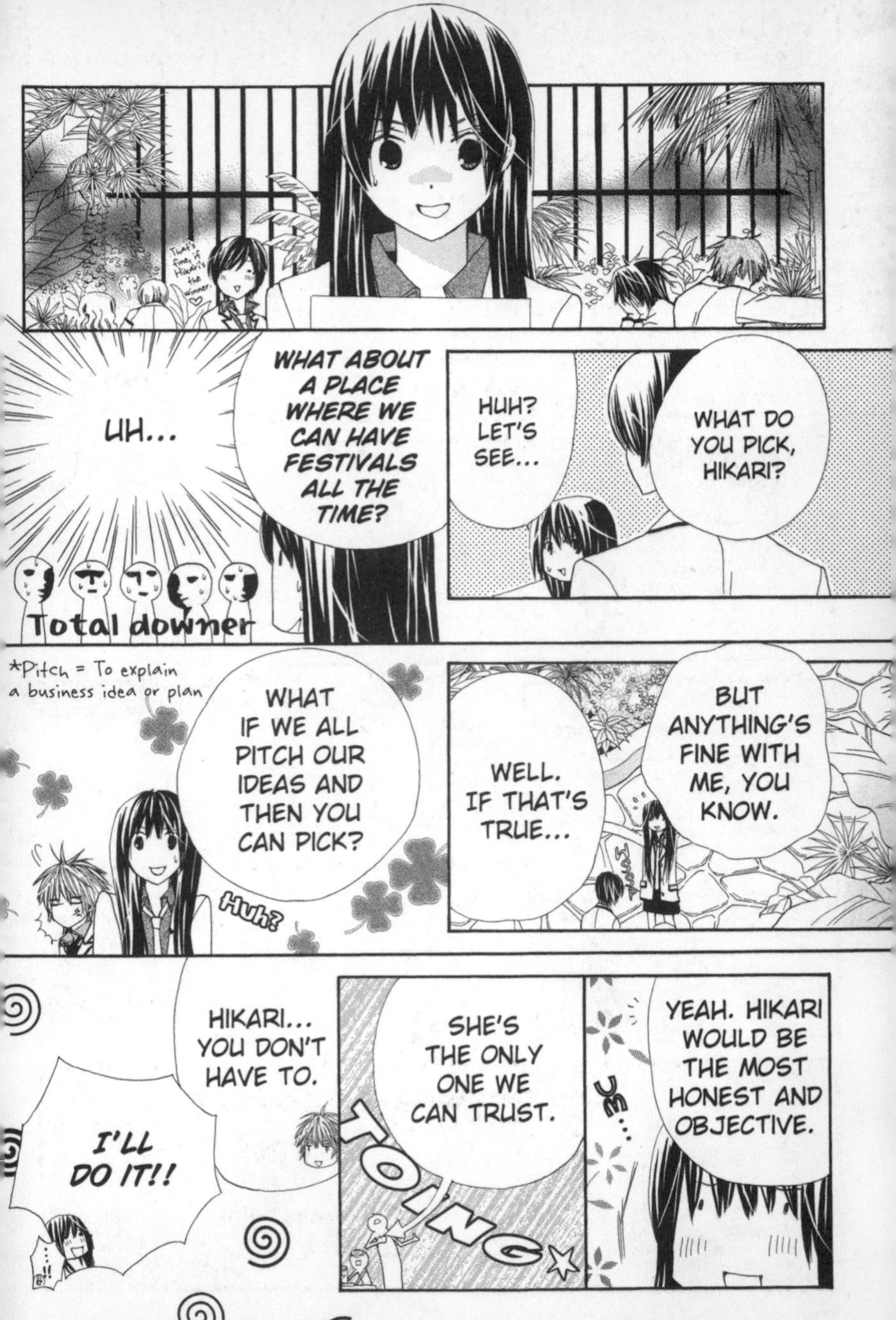
That's fine, if Hikari's the winner.
WHAT DO YOU PICK, HIKARI?
HUH? LET'S SEE...
WHAT ABOUT A PLACE WHERE WE CAN HAVE FESTIVALS ALL THE TIME?
UH...
Total downer
BUT ANYTHING'S FINE WITH ME, YOU KNOW.
WELL. IF THAT'S TRUE...
WHAT IF WE ALL PITCH OUR IDEAS AND THEN YOU CAN PICK?
Huh?
*Pitch = To explain a business idea or plan
UM...
YEAH. HIKARI WOULD BE THE MOST HONEST AND OBJECTIVE.
SHE'S THE ONLY ONE WE CAN TRUST.
TOING☆
HIKARI... YOU DON'T HAVE TO.
I'LL DO IT!!

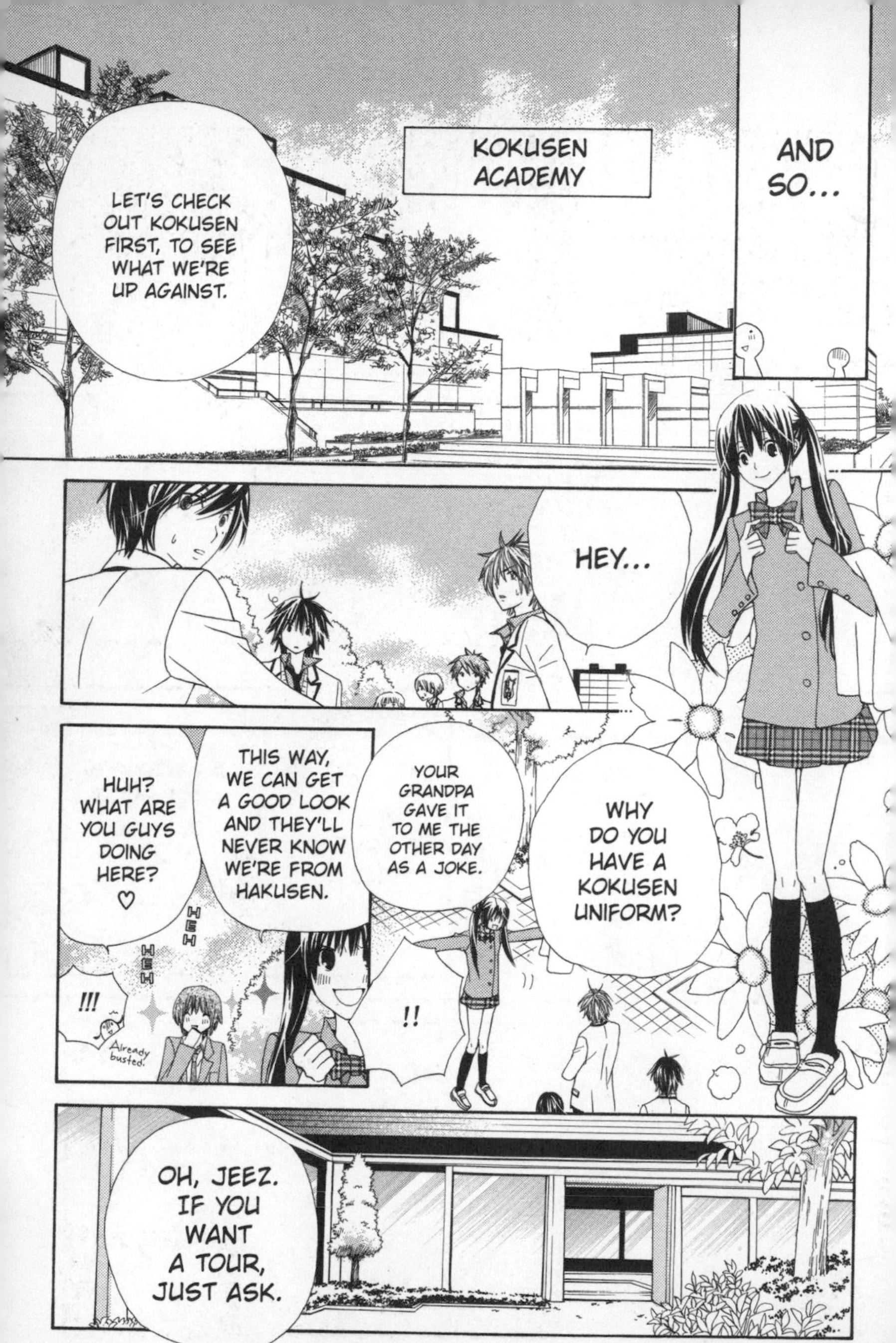

AND SO...
KOKUSEN ACADEMY
LET'S CHECK OUT KOKUSEN FIRST, TO SEE WHAT WE'RE UP AGAINST.
HEY...
WHY DO YOU HAVE A KOKUSEN UNIFORM?
YOUR GRANDPA GAVE IT TO ME THE OTHER DAY AS A JOKE.
THIS WAY, WE CAN GET A GOOD LOOK AND THEY'LL NEVER KNOW WE'RE FROM HAKUSEN.
!!
HUH? WHAT ARE YOU GUYS DOING HERE? ♡
HEH HEH
!!!
Already busted.
OH, JEEZ. IF YOU WANT A TOUR, JUST ASK.

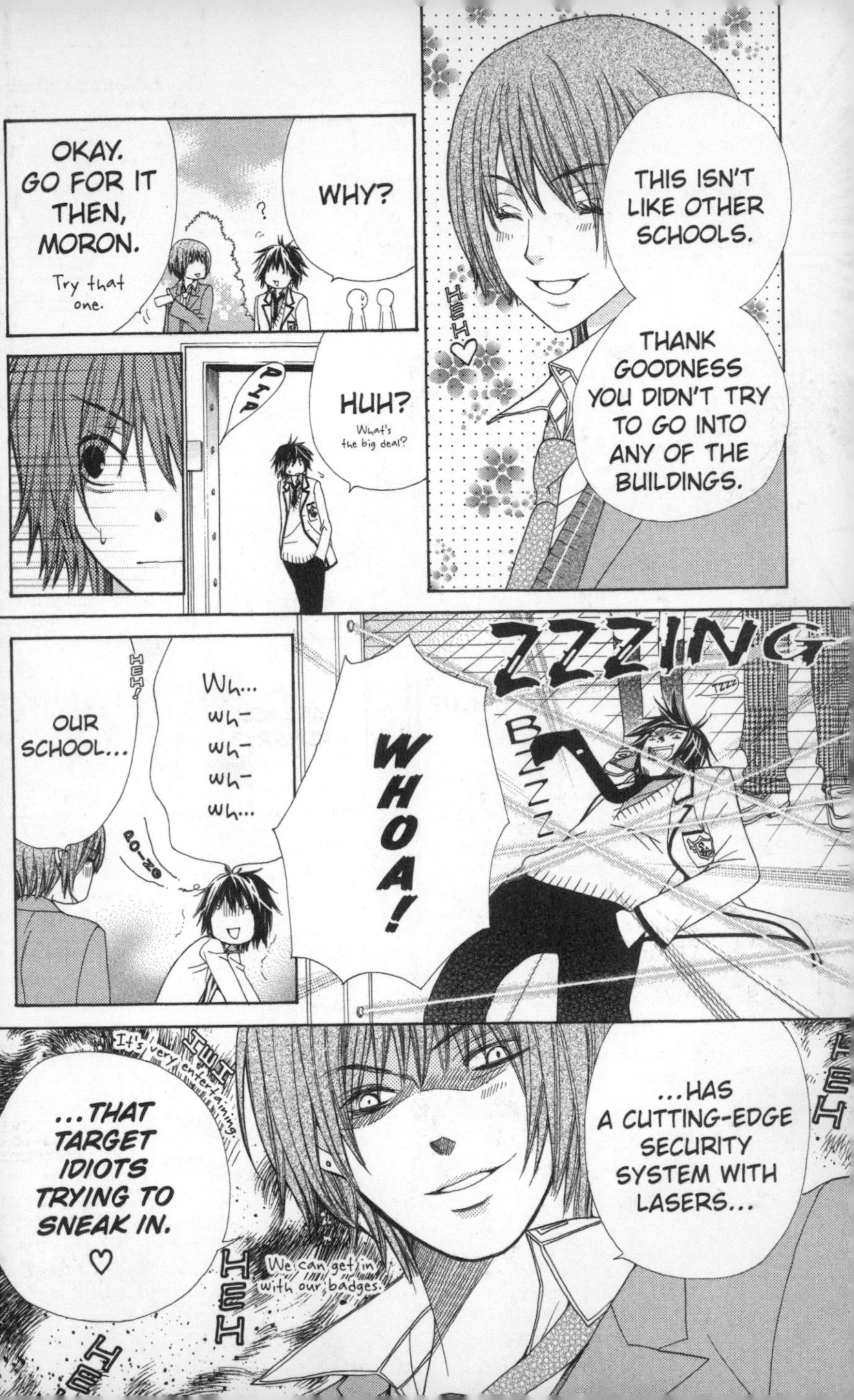
THIS ISN'T LIKE OTHER SCHOOLS.
HEH♥
THANK GOODNESS YOU DIDN'T TRY TO GO INTO ANY OF THE BUILDINGS.
WHY?
?
OKAY. GO FOR IT THEN, MORON.
Try that one.
HUH?
What's the big deal?
ZZZING
TZZZ
BZZZ
WHOA!
Wh... wh- wh- wh- wh...
HEH!
OUR SCHOOL...
...HAS A CUTTING-EDGE SECURITY SYSTEM WITH LASERS...
HEH
...THAT TARGET IDIOTS TRYING TO SNEAK IN. ♡
It's very entertaining.
We can get in with our badges.
HEH

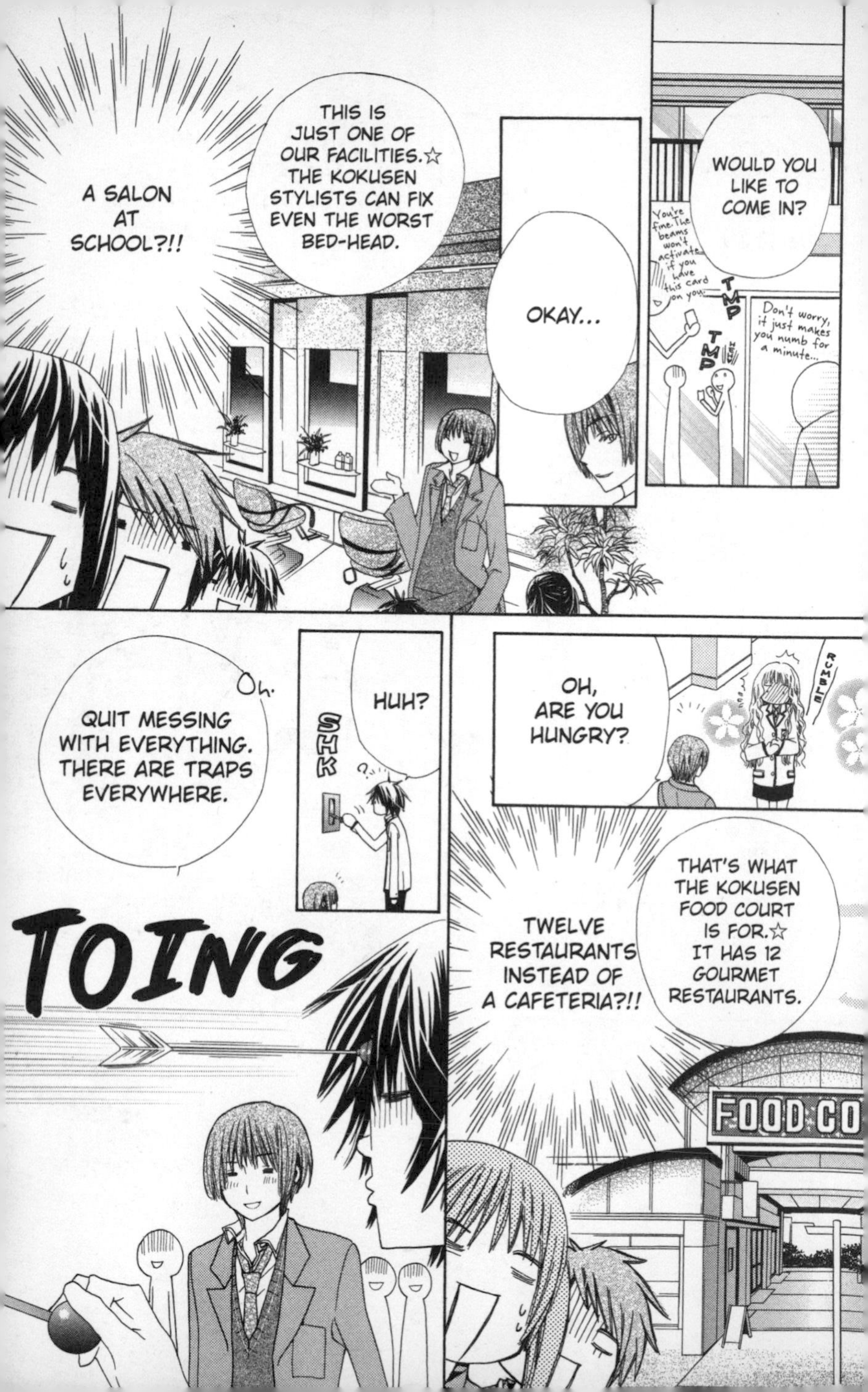
WOULD YOU LIKE TO COME IN?
You're fine. The beams won't activate if you have this card on you.
TMP
TMP
HEY
Don't worry, it just makes you numb for a minute...
OKAY...
THIS IS JUST ONE OF OUR FACILITIES.☆ THE KOKUSEN STYLISTS CAN FIX EVEN THE WORST BED-HEAD.
A SALON AT SCHOOL?!!
RUMBLE
OH, ARE YOU HUNGRY?
THAT'S WHAT THE KOKUSEN FOOD COURT IS FOR.☆ IT HAS 12 GOURMET RESTAURANTS.
TWELVE RESTAURANTS INSTEAD OF A CAFETERIA?!!
FOOD CO
HUH?
SHK
Oh.
QUIT MESSING WITH EVERYTHING. THERE ARE TRAPS EVERYWHERE.
TOING

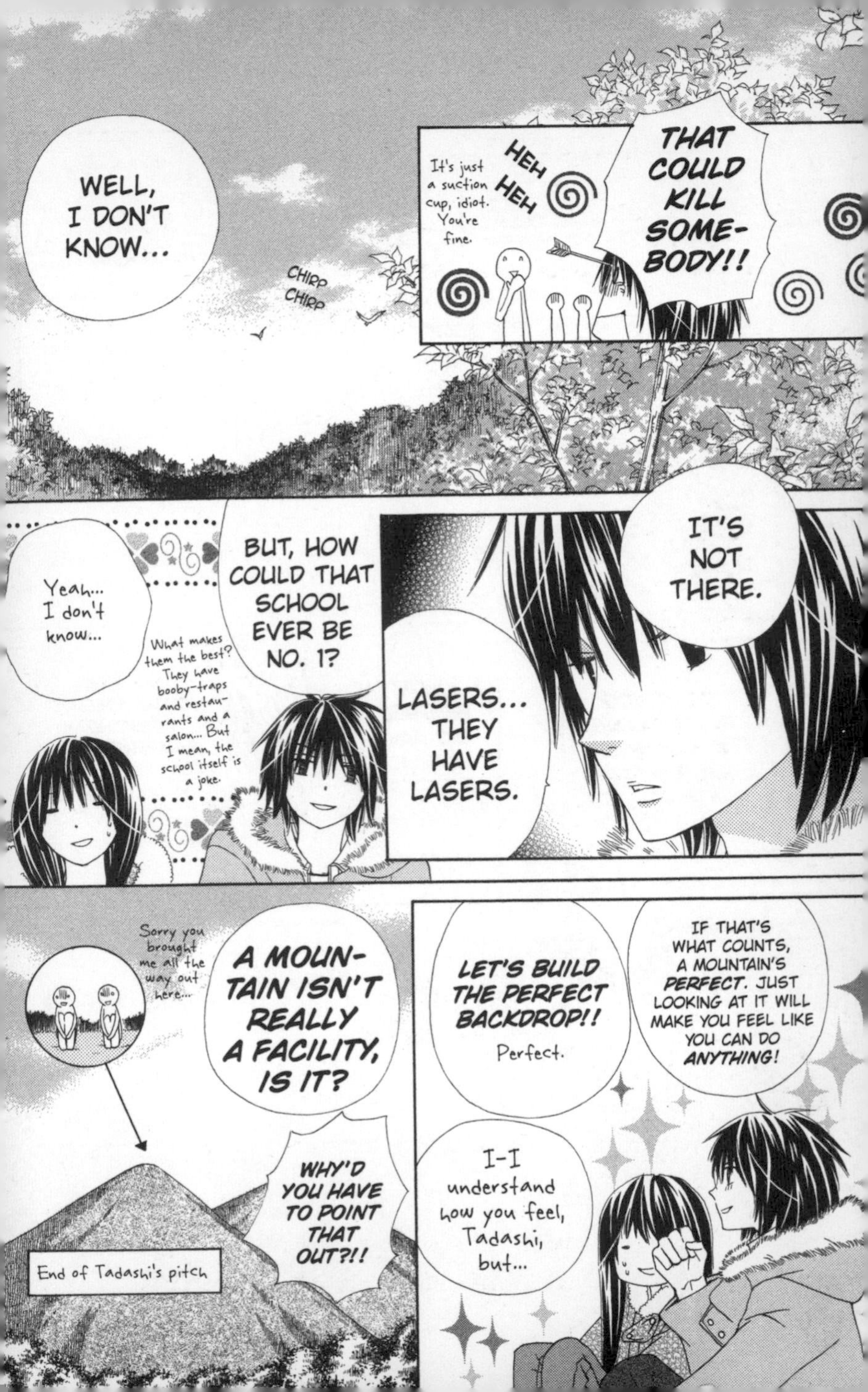
THAT COULD KILL SOMEBODY!!
HEH HEH
It's just a suction cup, idiot. You're fine.
WELL, I DON'T KNOW...
CHIRP CHIRP
IT'S NOT THERE.
LASERS... THEY HAVE LASERS.
BUT, HOW COULD THAT SCHOOL EVER BE NO. 1?
What makes them the best? They have booby-traps and restaurants and a salon... But I mean, the school itself is a joke.
Yeah... I don't know...
IF THAT'S WHAT COUNTS, A MOUNTAIN'S PERFECT. JUST LOOKING AT IT WILL MAKE YOU FEEL LIKE YOU CAN DO ANYTHING!
LET'S BUILD THE PERFECT BACKDROP!!
Perfect.
I-I understand how you feel, Tadashi, but...
A MOUNTAIN ISN'T REALLY A FACILITY, IS IT?
WHY'D YOU HAVE TO POINT THAT OUT?!!
Sorry you brought me all the way out here...
End of Tadashi's pitch

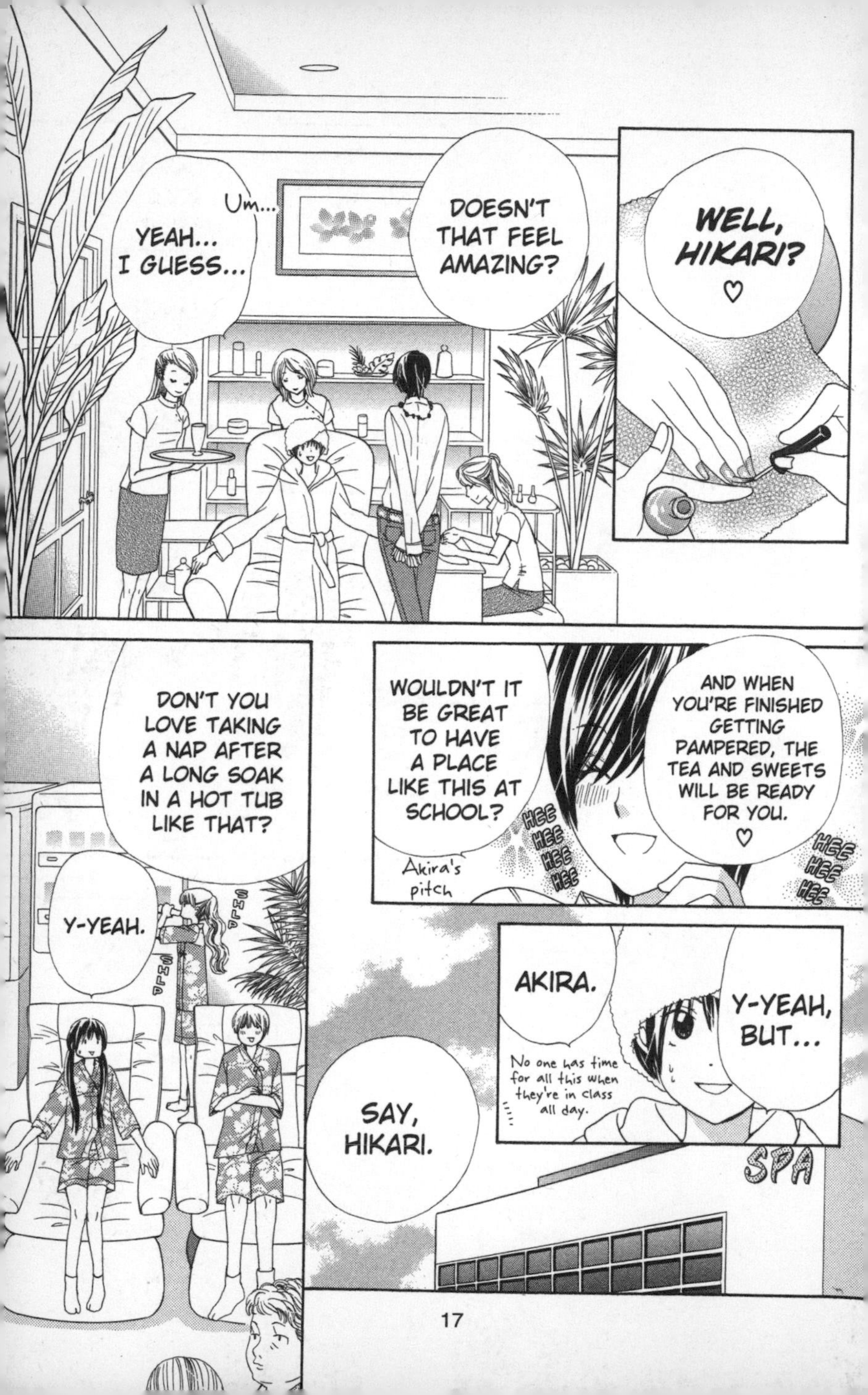
WELL, HIKARI? ♡
DOESN'T THAT FEEL AMAZING?
Um...
YEAH... I GUESS...
AND WHEN YOU'RE FINISHED GETTING PAMPERED, THE TEA AND SWEETS WILL BE READY FOR YOU. ♡
HEE HEE HEE
WOULDN'T IT BE GREAT TO HAVE A PLACE LIKE THIS AT SCHOOL?
HEE HEE HEE HEE
Akira's pitch
Y-YEAH, BUT...
AKIRA.
No one has time for all this when they're in class all day.
SPA
SAY, HIKARI.
DON'T YOU LOVE TAKING A NAP AFTER A LONG SOAK IN A HOT TUB LIKE THAT?
SHLP
Y-YEAH.
SHLP

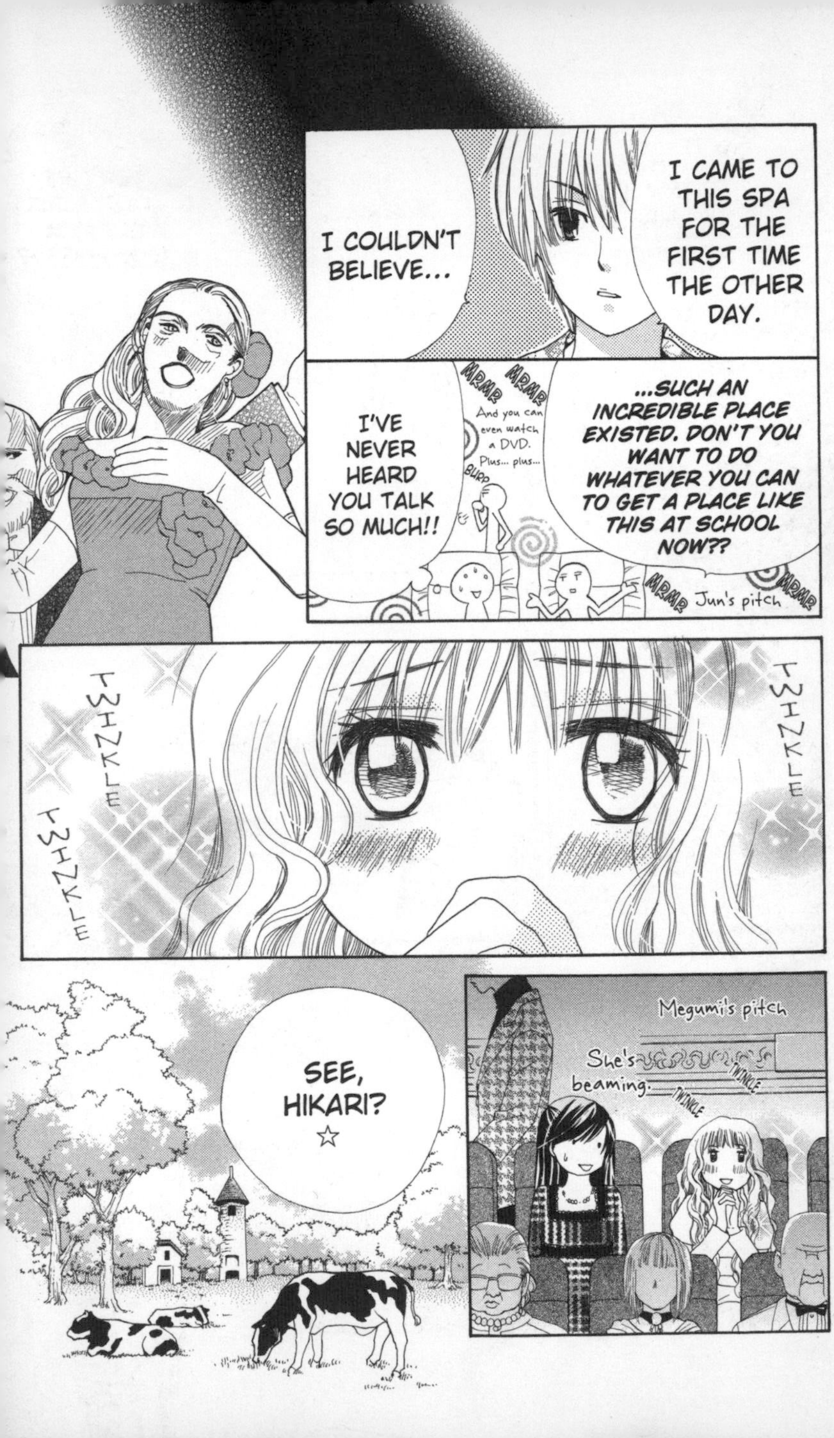

I CAME TO THIS SPA FOR THE FIRST TIME THE OTHER DAY.
I COULDN'T BELIEVE...
...SUCH AN INCREDIBLE PLACE EXISTED. DON'T YOU WANT TO DO WHATEVER YOU CAN TO GET A PLACE LIKE THIS AT SCHOOL NOW??
MRMR
MRMR
Jun's pitch
MRMR
MRMR
And you can even watch a DVD. Plus... plus...
BURP
I'VE NEVER HEARD YOU TALK SO MUCH!!
TWINKLE
TWINKLE
TWINKLE
Megumi's pitch
She's beaming.
TWINKLE
TWINKLE
SEE, HIKARI? ☆

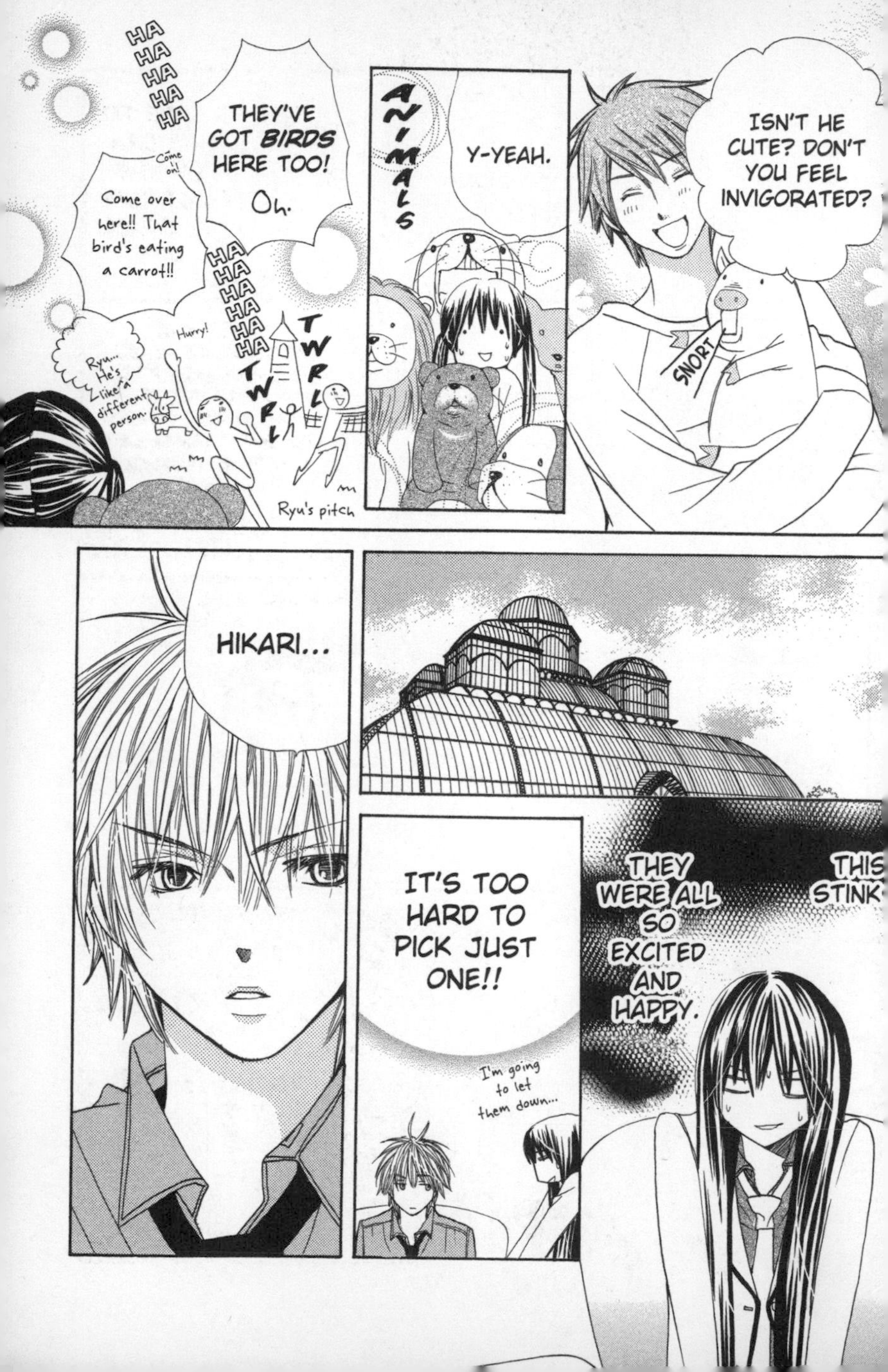
ISN'T HE CUTE? DON'T YOU FEEL INVIGORATED?
SNORT
ANIMALS
Y-YEAH.
HA HA HA HA HA
THEY'VE GOT BIRDS HERE TOO!
Come on!
Oh.
Come over here!! That bird's eating a carrot!!
HA HA HA HA HA HA HA
TWRL TWRL
Hurry!
Ryu... He's like a different person.
Ryu's pitch
THIS STINK
THEY WERE ALL SO EXCITED AND HAPPY.
IT'S TOO HARD TO PICK JUST ONE!!
I'm going to let them down...
HIKARI...

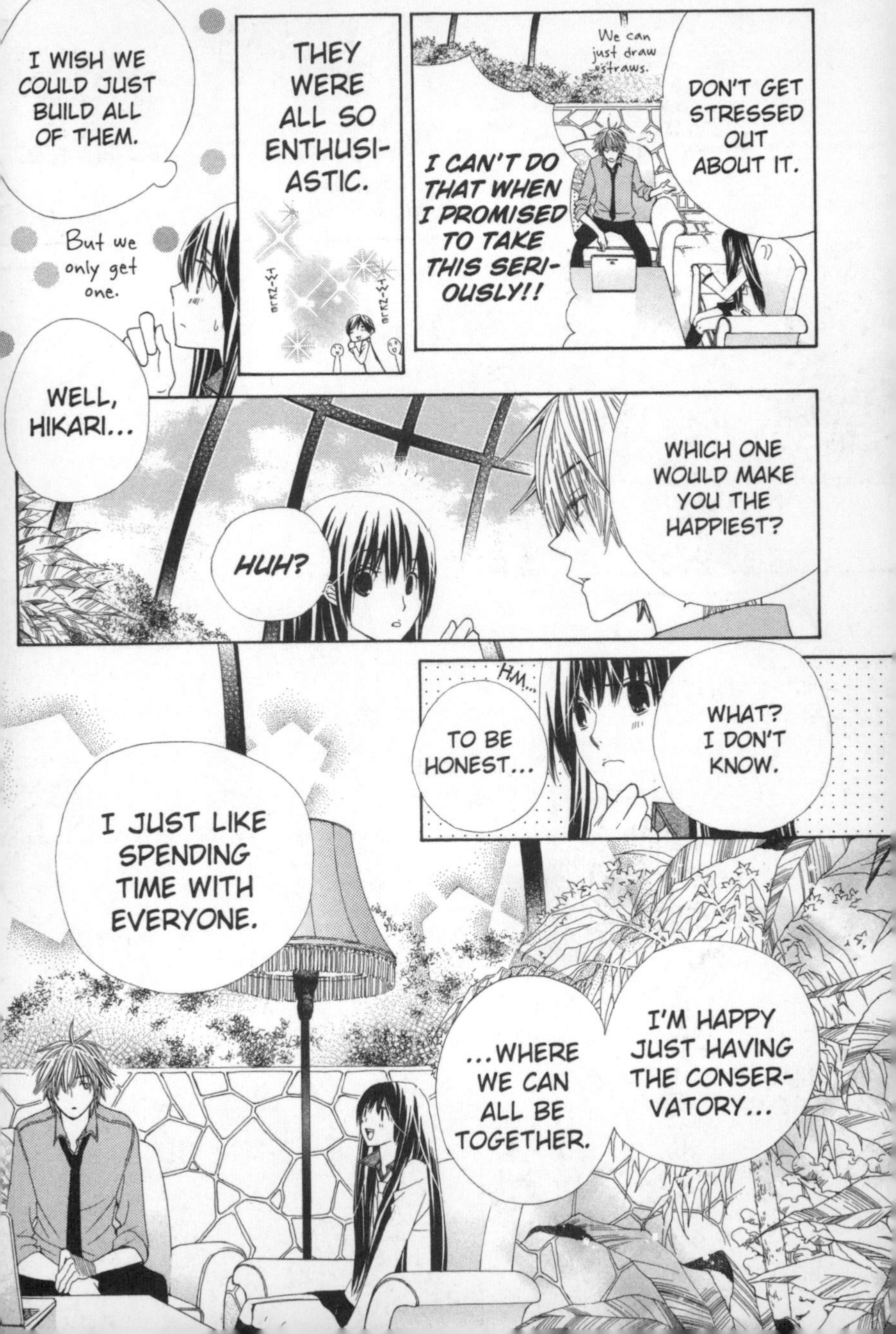
DON'T GET STRESSED OUT ABOUT IT.
We can just draw straws.
I CAN'T DO THAT WHEN I PROMISED TO TAKE THIS SERIOUSLY!!
THEY WERE ALL SO ENTHUSIASTIC.
I WISH WE COULD JUST BUILD ALL OF THEM.
But we only get one.
WELL, HIKARI...
WHICH ONE WOULD MAKE YOU THE HAPPIEST?
HUH?
WHAT? I DON'T KNOW.
HM...
TO BE HONEST...
I JUST LIKE SPENDING TIME WITH EVERYONE.
I'M HAPPY JUST HAVING THE CONSERVATORY...
...WHERE WE CAN ALL BE TOGETHER.

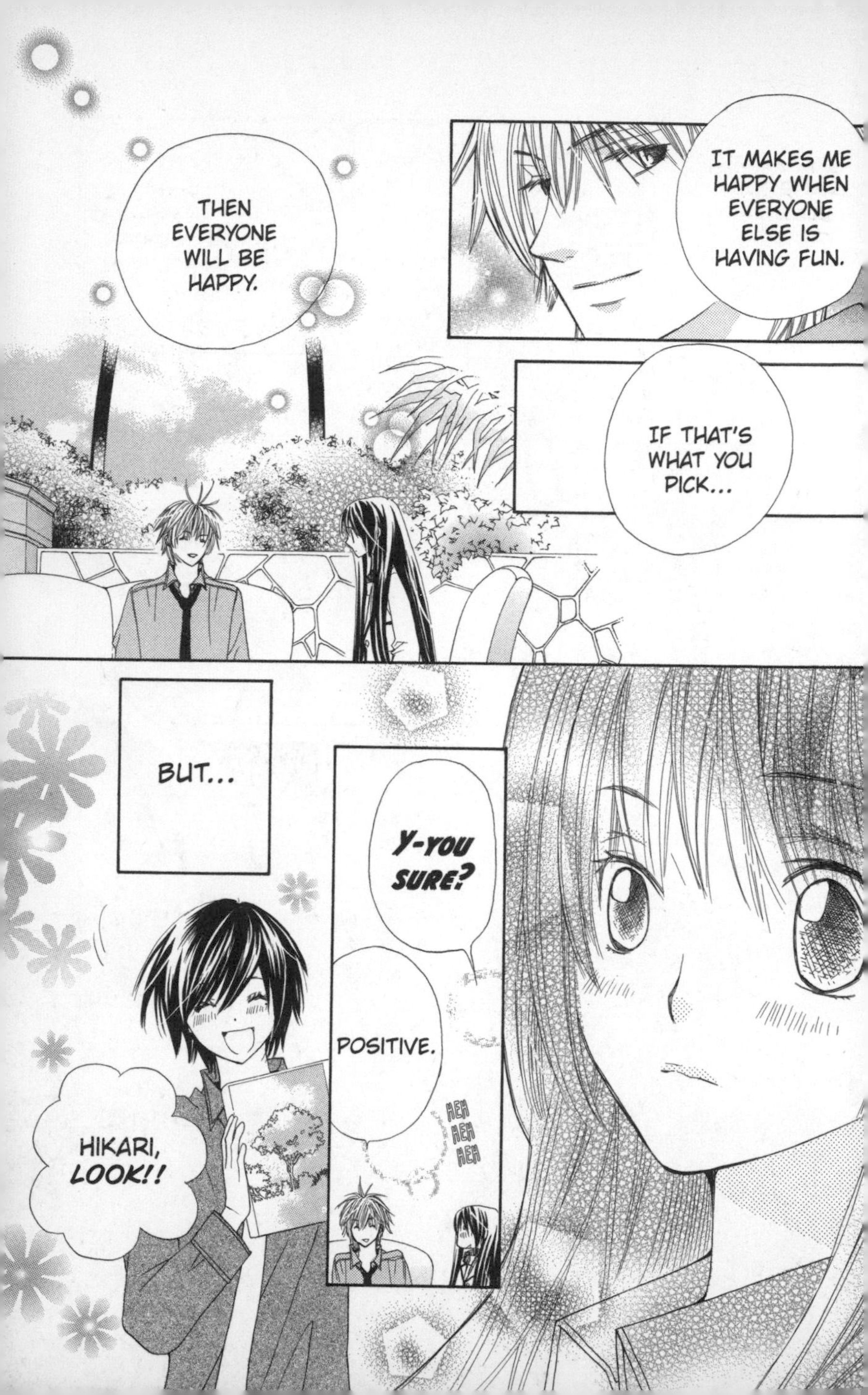
IT MAKES ME HAPPY WHEN EVERYONE ELSE IS HAVING FUN.
THEN EVERYONE WILL BE HAPPY.
IF THAT'S WHAT YOU PICK...
Y-YOU SURE?
POSITIVE.
HEH HEH HEH
BUT...
HIKARI, LOOK!!

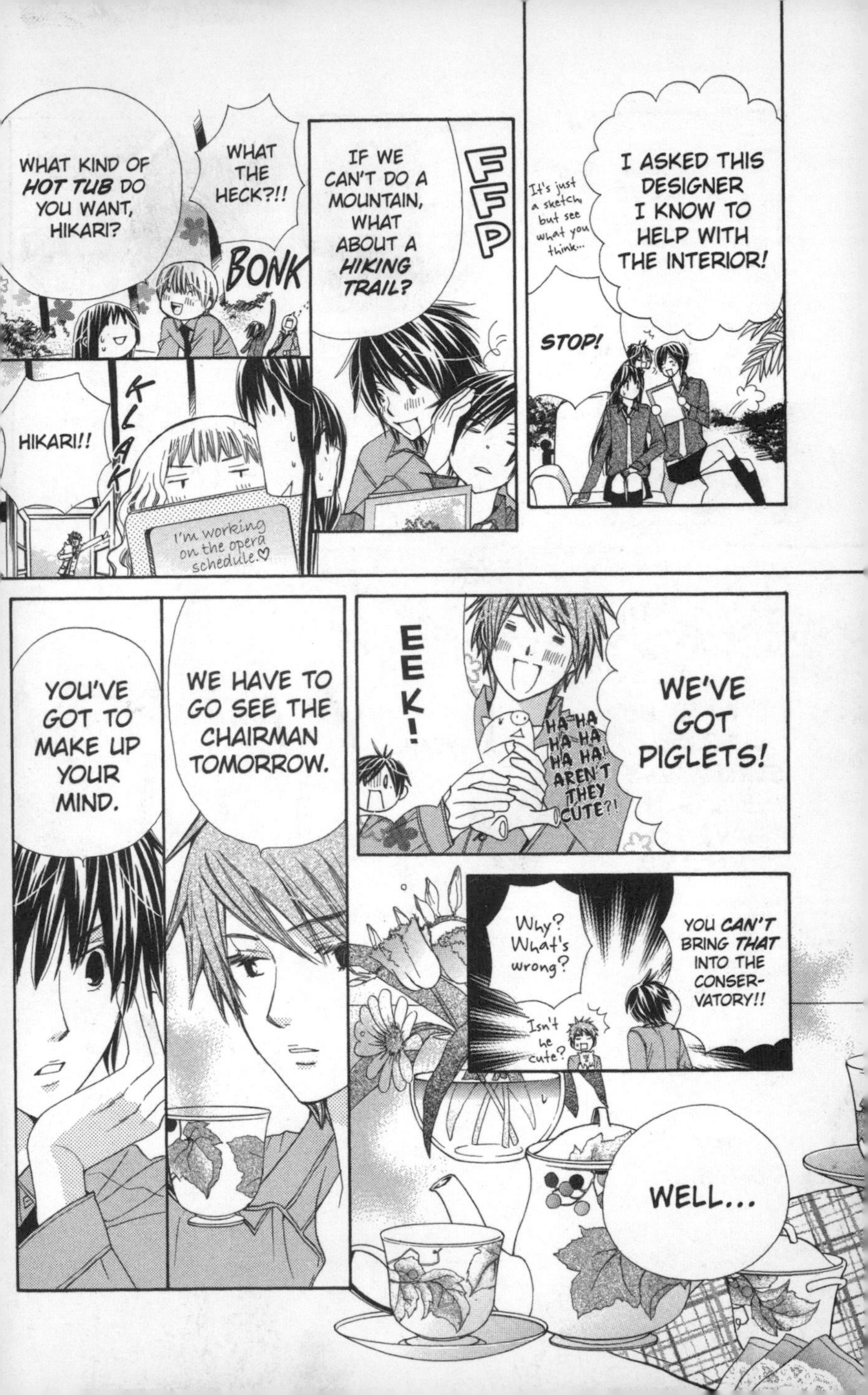
I ASKED THIS DESIGNER I KNOW TO HELP WITH THE INTERIOR!
It's just a sketch, but see what you think...
STOP!
FFP
IF WE CAN'T DO A MOUNTAIN, WHAT ABOUT A *HIKING TRAIL*?
WHAT THE HECK?!!
BONK
WHAT KIND OF *HOT TUB* DO YOU WANT, HIKARI?
KLAK
HIKARI!!
I'm working on the opera schedule.♡
WE'VE GOT PIGLETS!
HA HA HA HA HA HA! AREN'T THEY CUTE?!
EEK!
YOU *CAN'T* BRING *THAT* INTO THE CONSERVATORY!!
Why? What's wrong?
Isn't he cute?
WE HAVE TO GO SEE THE CHAIRMAN TOMORROW.
YOU'VE GOT TO MAKE UP YOUR MIND.
WELL...

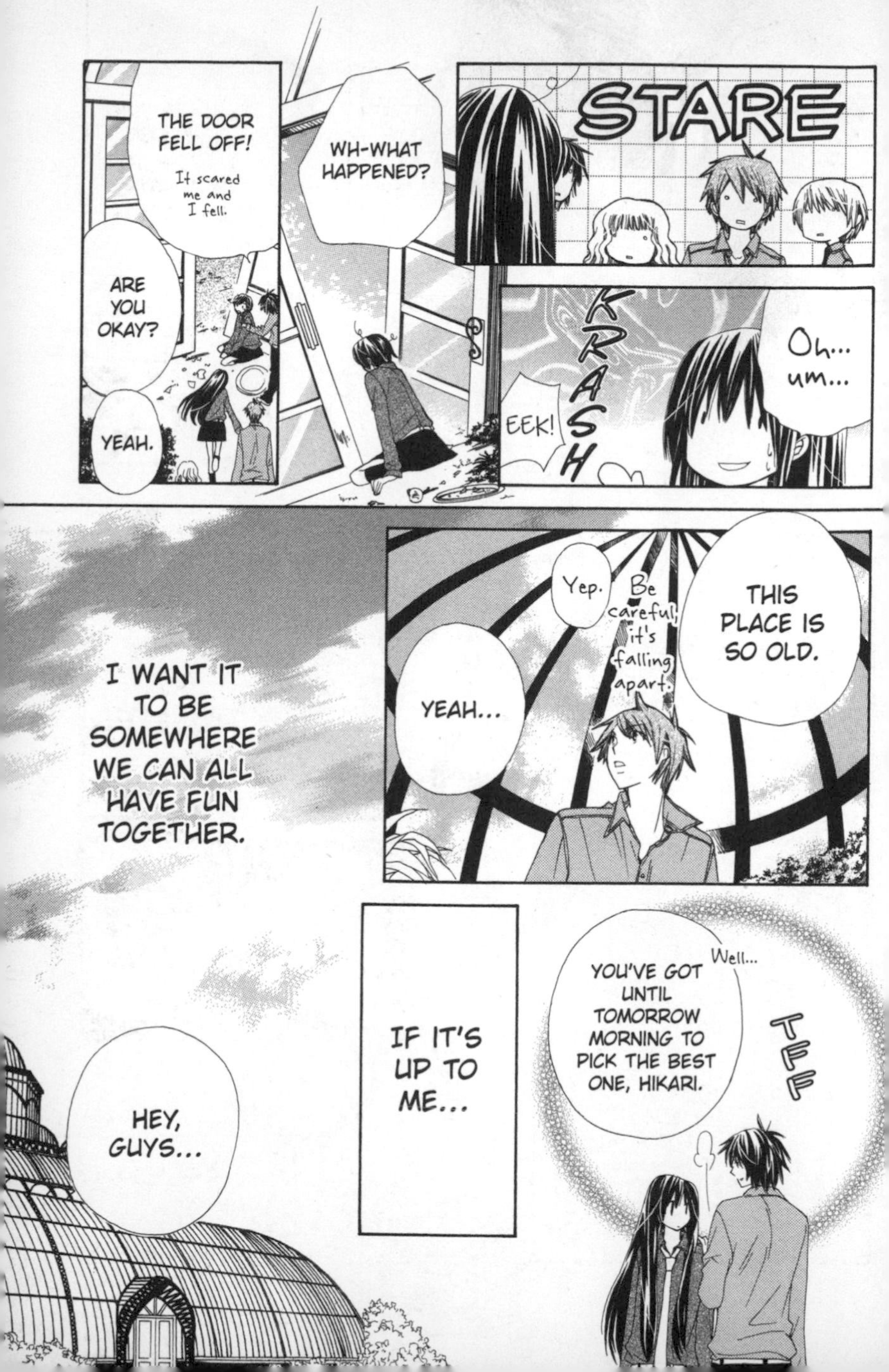
STARE
Oh... um...
KRASH
EEK!
WH-WHAT HAPPENED?
THE DOOR FELL OFF!
It scared me and I fell.
ARE YOU OKAY?
YEAH.
THIS PLACE IS SO OLD.
Be careful, it's falling apart.
Yep.
YEAH...
I WANT IT TO BE SOMEWHERE WE CAN ALL HAVE FUN TOGETHER.
TFF
Well...
YOU'VE GOT UNTIL TOMORROW MORNING TO PICK THE BEST ONE, HIKARI.
IF IT'S UP TO ME...
HEY, GUYS...

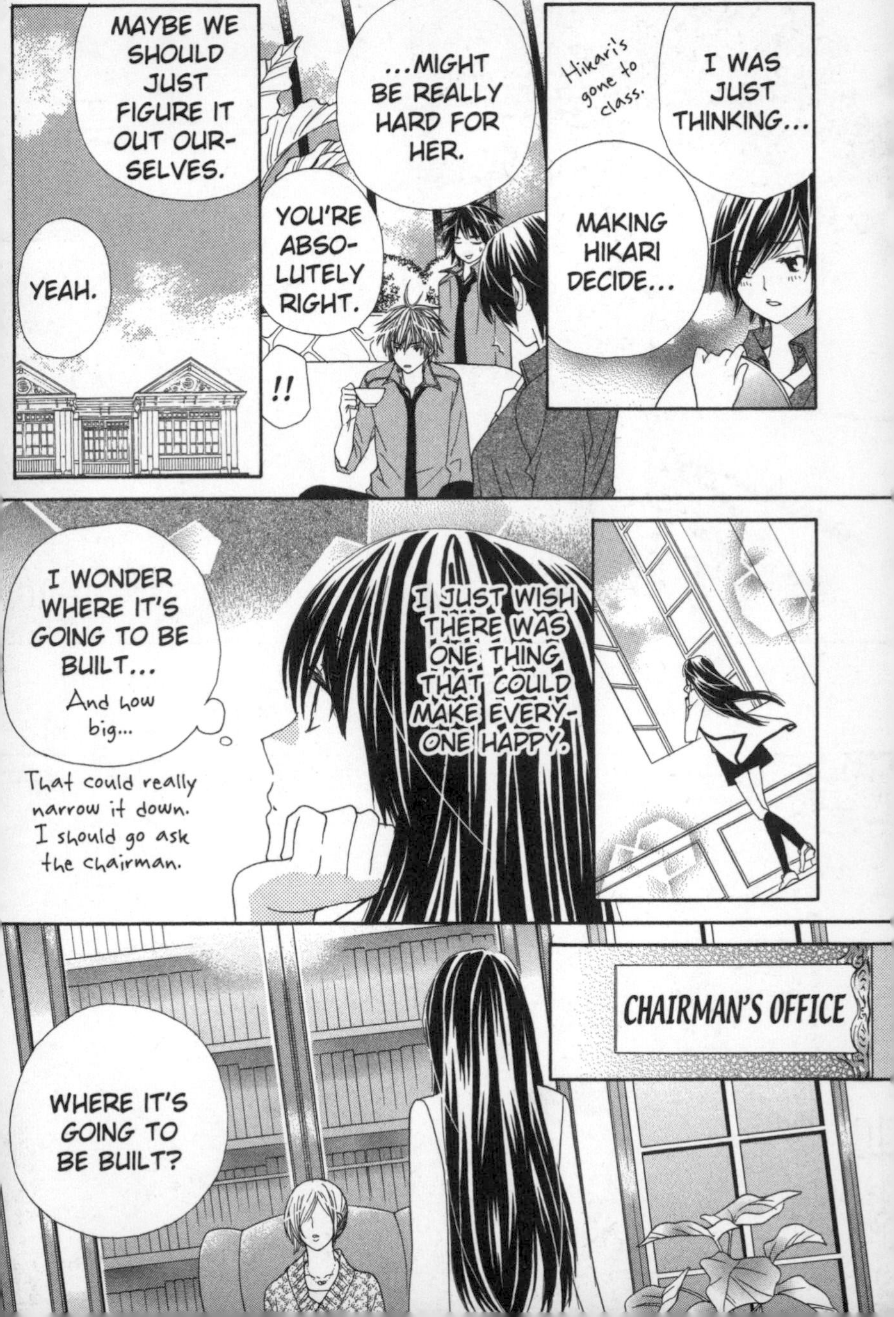

Hikari's gone to class.
I WAS JUST THINKING...
MAKING HIKARI DECIDE...
...MIGHT BE REALLY HARD FOR HER.
YOU'RE ABSOLUTELY RIGHT.
!!
MAYBE WE SHOULD JUST FIGURE IT OUT OURSELVES.
YEAH.
I JUST WISH THERE WAS ONE THING THAT COULD MAKE EVERYONE HAPPY.
I WONDER WHERE IT'S GOING TO BE BUILT...
And how big...
That could really narrow it down. I should go ask the chairman.
CHAIRMAN'S OFFICE
WHERE IT'S GOING TO BE BUILT?

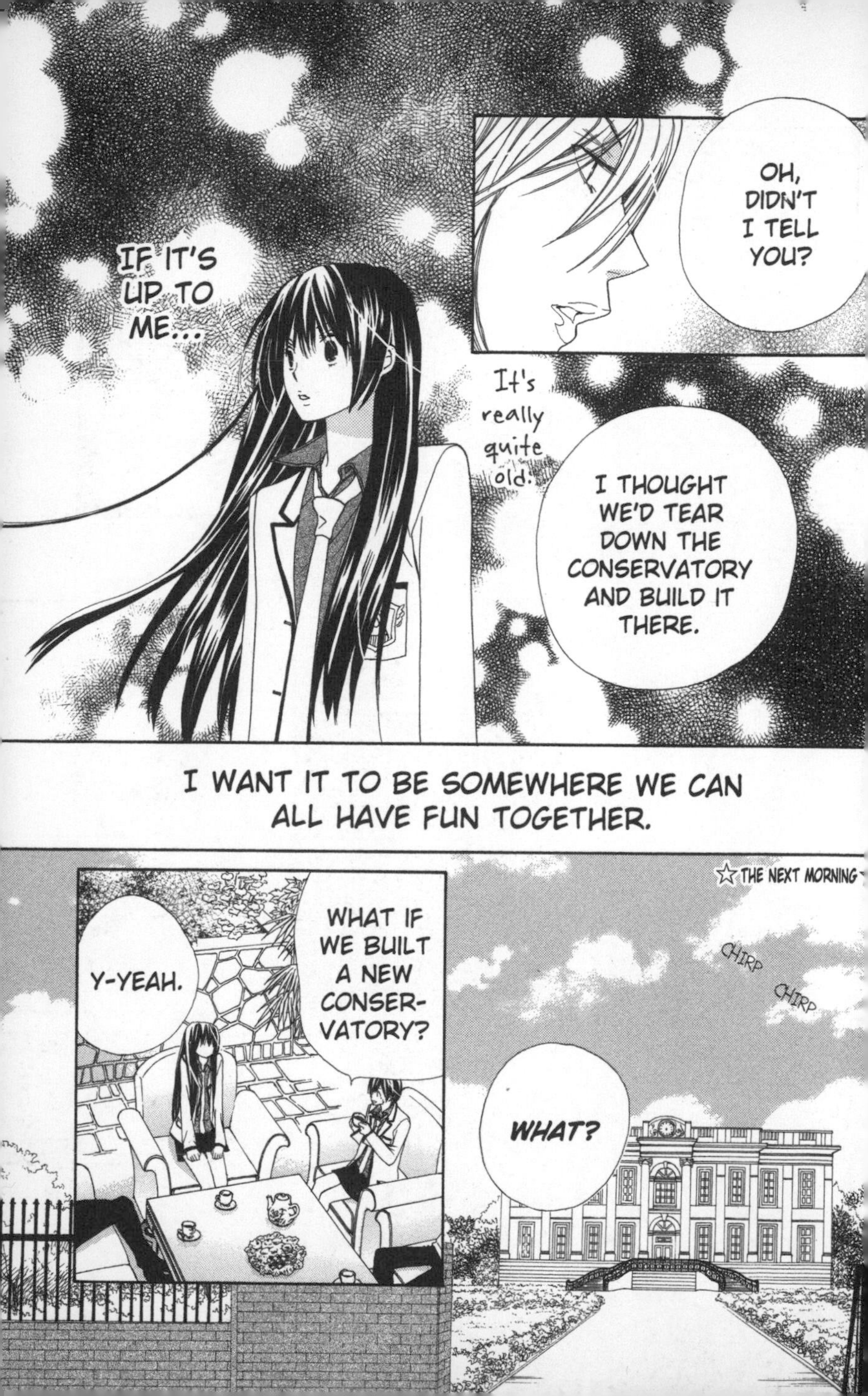
OH, DIDN'T I TELL YOU?
I THOUGHT WE'D TEAR DOWN THE CONSERVATORY AND BUILD IT THERE.
It's really quite old.
IF IT'S UP TO ME...
I WANT IT TO BE SOMEWHERE WE CAN ALL HAVE FUN TOGETHER.
☆THE NEXT MORNING
CHIRP
CHIRP
WHAT?
WHAT IF WE BUILT A NEW CONSERVATORY?
Y-YEAH.

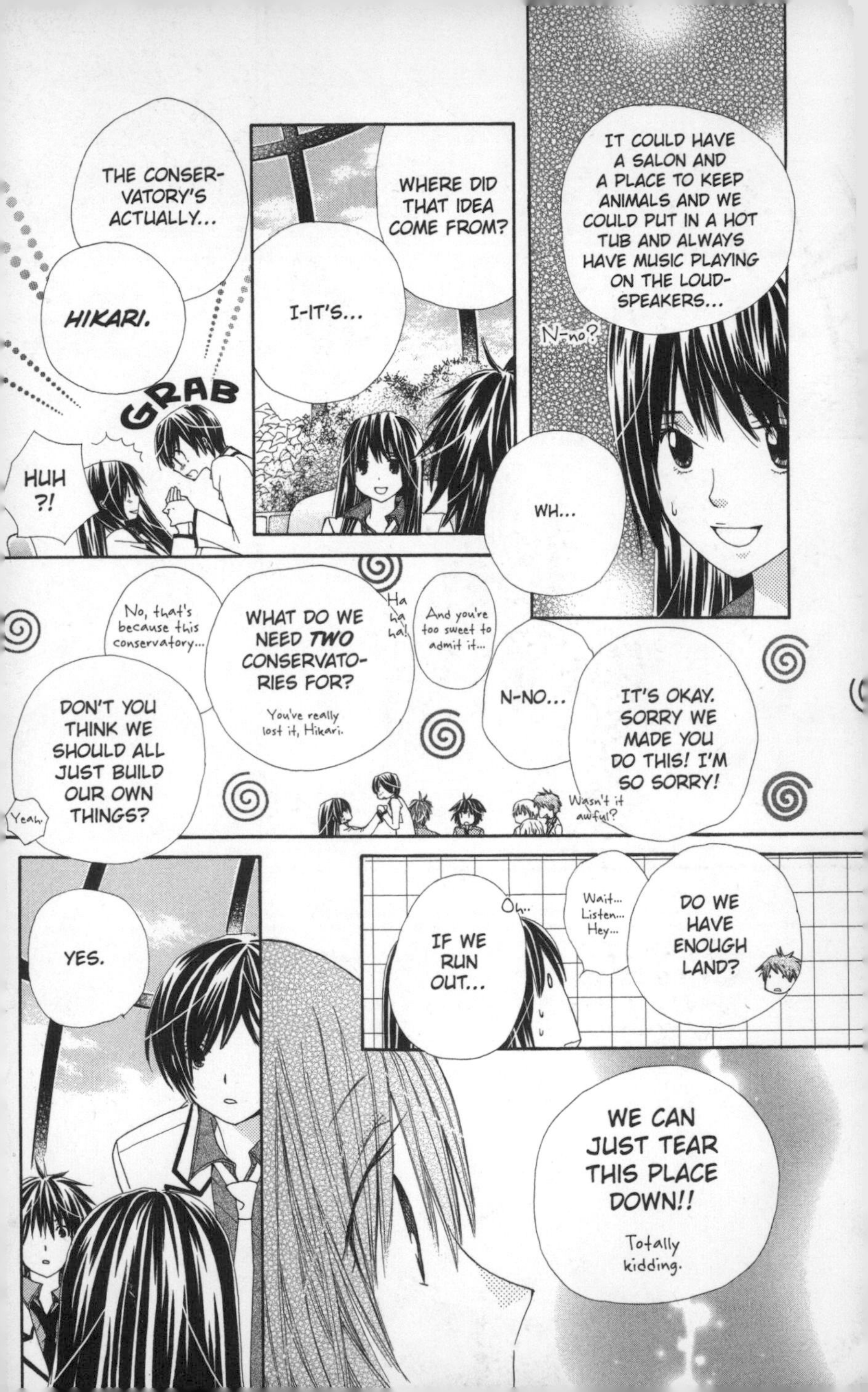
IT COULD HAVE A SALON AND A PLACE TO KEEP ANIMALS AND WE COULD PUT IN A HOT TUB AND ALWAYS HAVE MUSIC PLAYING ON THE LOUD-SPEAKERS...
N-no?
WH...
WHERE DID THAT IDEA COME FROM?
I-IT'S...
THE CONSER-VATORY'S ACTUALLY...
HIKARI.
GRAB
HUH ?!
IT'S OKAY. SORRY WE MADE YOU DO THIS! I'M SO SORRY!
Wasn't it awful?
N-NO...
And you're too sweet to admit it...
Ha ha ha!
WHAT DO WE NEED TWO CONSERVATO-RIES FOR?
You've really lost it, Hikari.
No, that's because this conservatory...
DON'T YOU THINK WE SHOULD ALL JUST BUILD OUR OWN THINGS?
Yeah.
DO WE HAVE ENOUGH LAND?
Wait... Listen... Hey...
Oh..
IF WE RUN OUT...
WE CAN JUST TEAR THIS PLACE DOWN!!
Totally kidding.
YES.

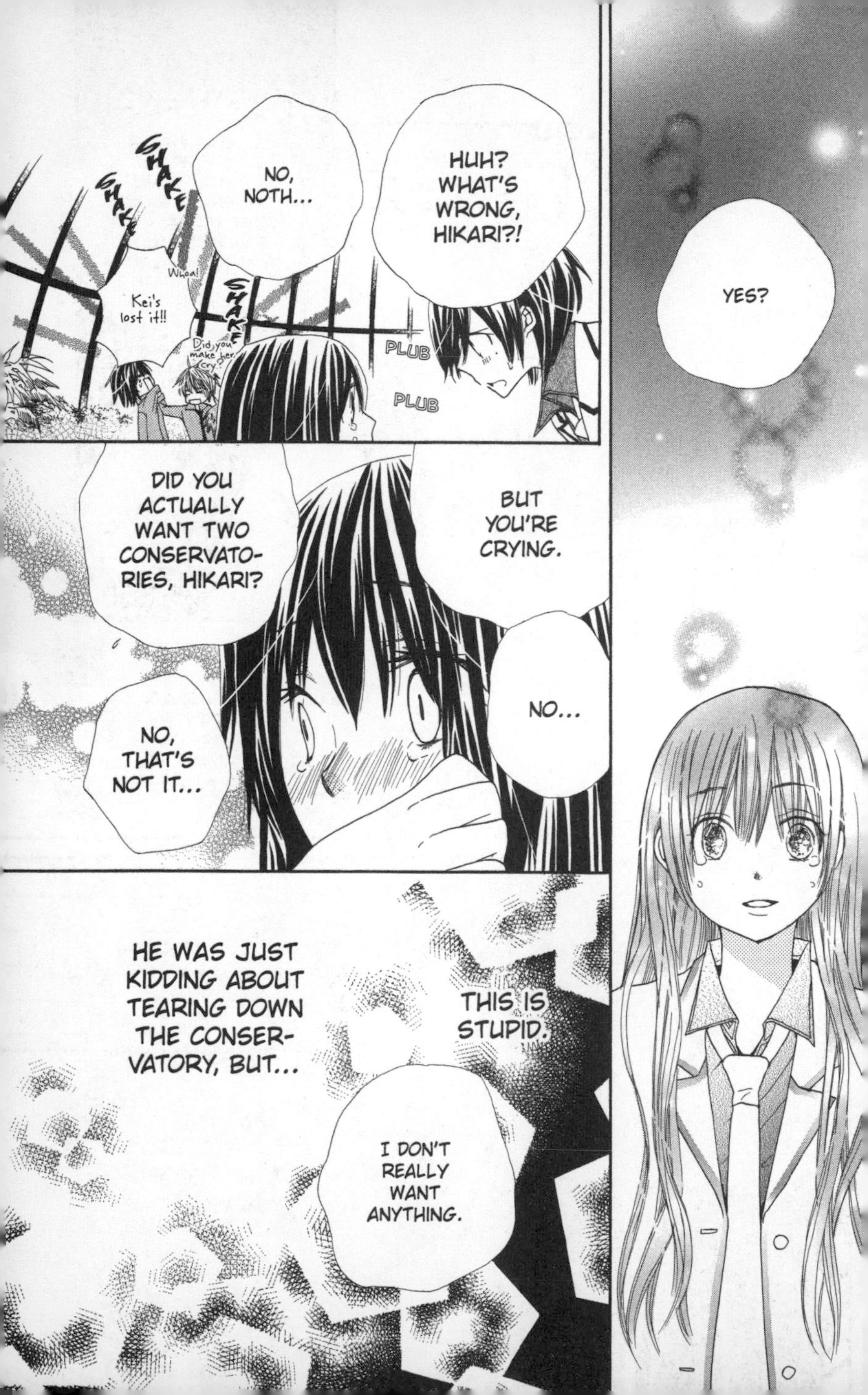
YES?
HUH? WHAT'S WRONG, HIKARI?!
NO, NOTH...
SHAKE
SHAKE
Whoa!
SHAKE
Kei's lost it!!
Did you make her cry
PLUB
PLUB
BUT YOU'RE CRYING.
DID YOU ACTUALLY WANT TWO CONSERVATO-RIES, HIKARI?
NO...
NO, THAT'S NOT IT...
THIS IS STUPID.
HE WAS JUST KIDDING ABOUT TEARING DOWN THE CONSER-VATORY, BUT...
I DON'T REALLY WANT ANYTHING.

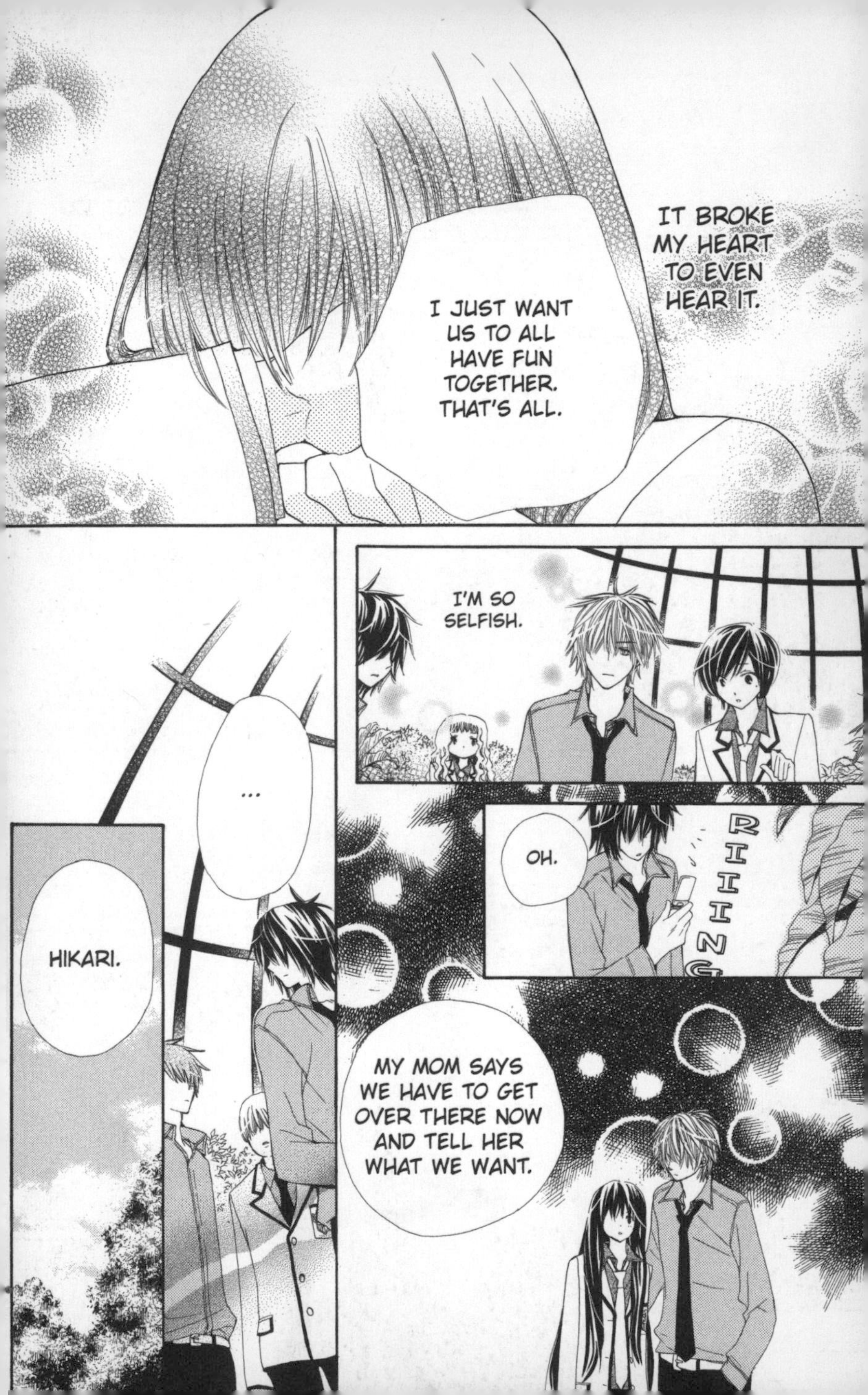
IT BROKE MY HEART TO EVEN HEAR IT.
I JUST WANT US TO ALL HAVE FUN TOGETHER. THAT'S ALL.
I'M SO SELFISH.
OH.
RIIING
MY MOM SAYS WE HAVE TO GET OVER THERE NOW AND TELL HER WHAT WE WANT.
...
HIKARI.

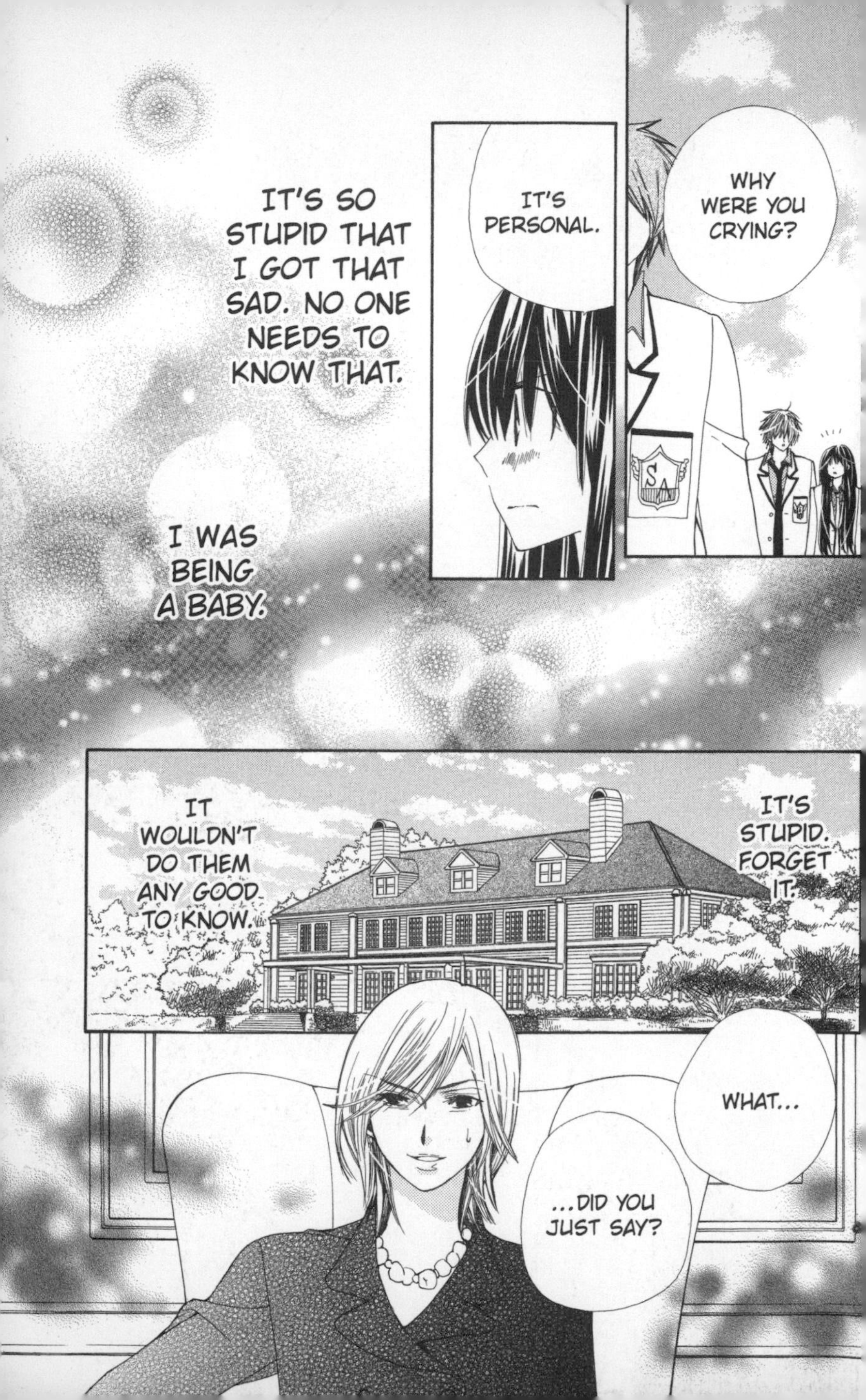
WHY WERE YOU CRYING?
IT'S PERSONAL.
IT'S SO STUPID THAT I GOT THAT SAD. NO ONE NEEDS TO KNOW THAT.
I WAS BEING A BABY.
IT'S STUPID. FORGET IT.
IT WOULDN'T DO THEM ANY GOOD TO KNOW.
WHAT...
...DID YOU JUST SAY?

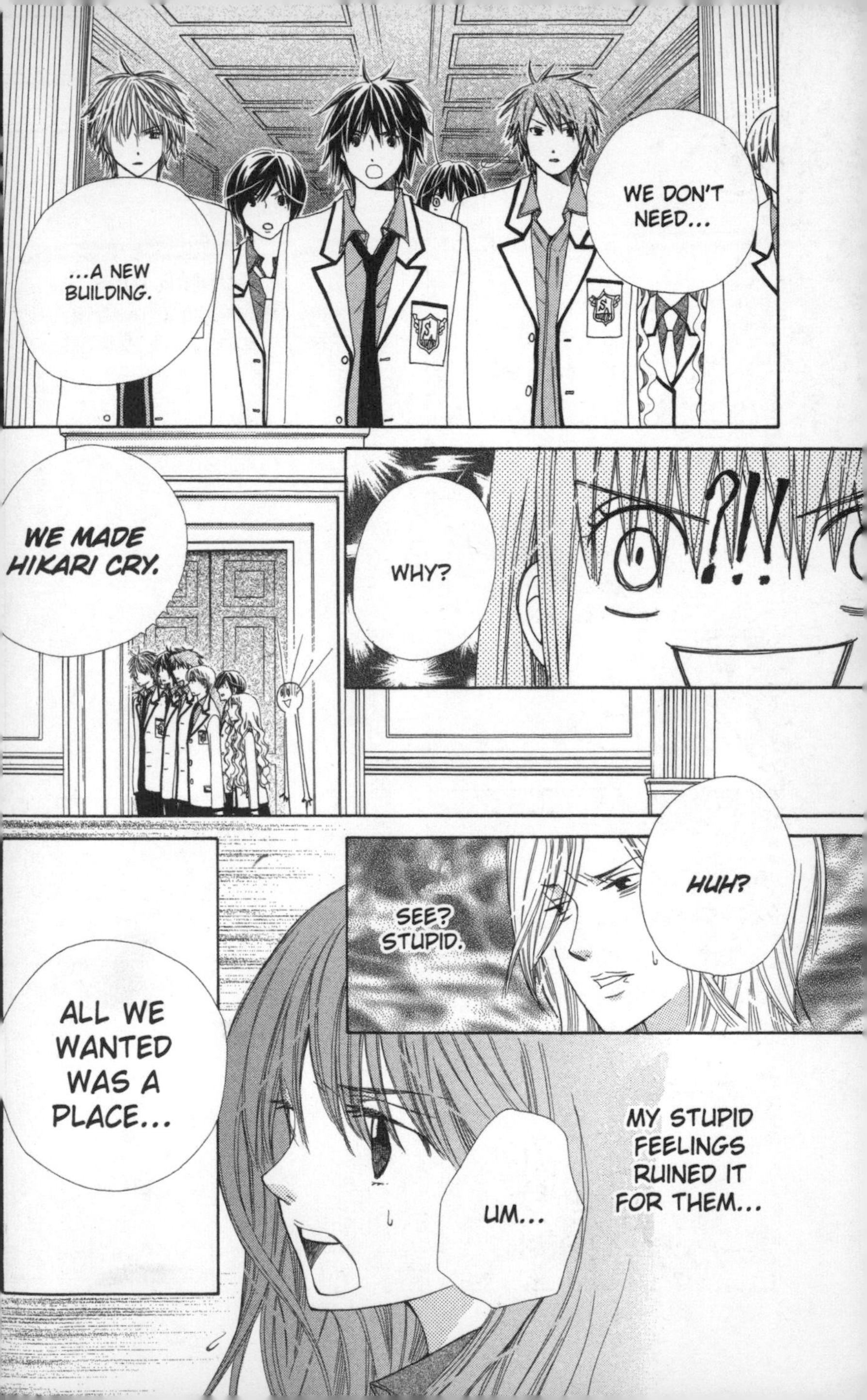
WE DON'T NEED...
...A NEW BUILDING.
?!!!
WHY?
WE MADE HIKARI CRY.
HUH?
SEE? STUPID.
MY STUPID FEELINGS RUINED IT FOR THEM...
UM...
ALL WE WANTED WAS A PLACE...

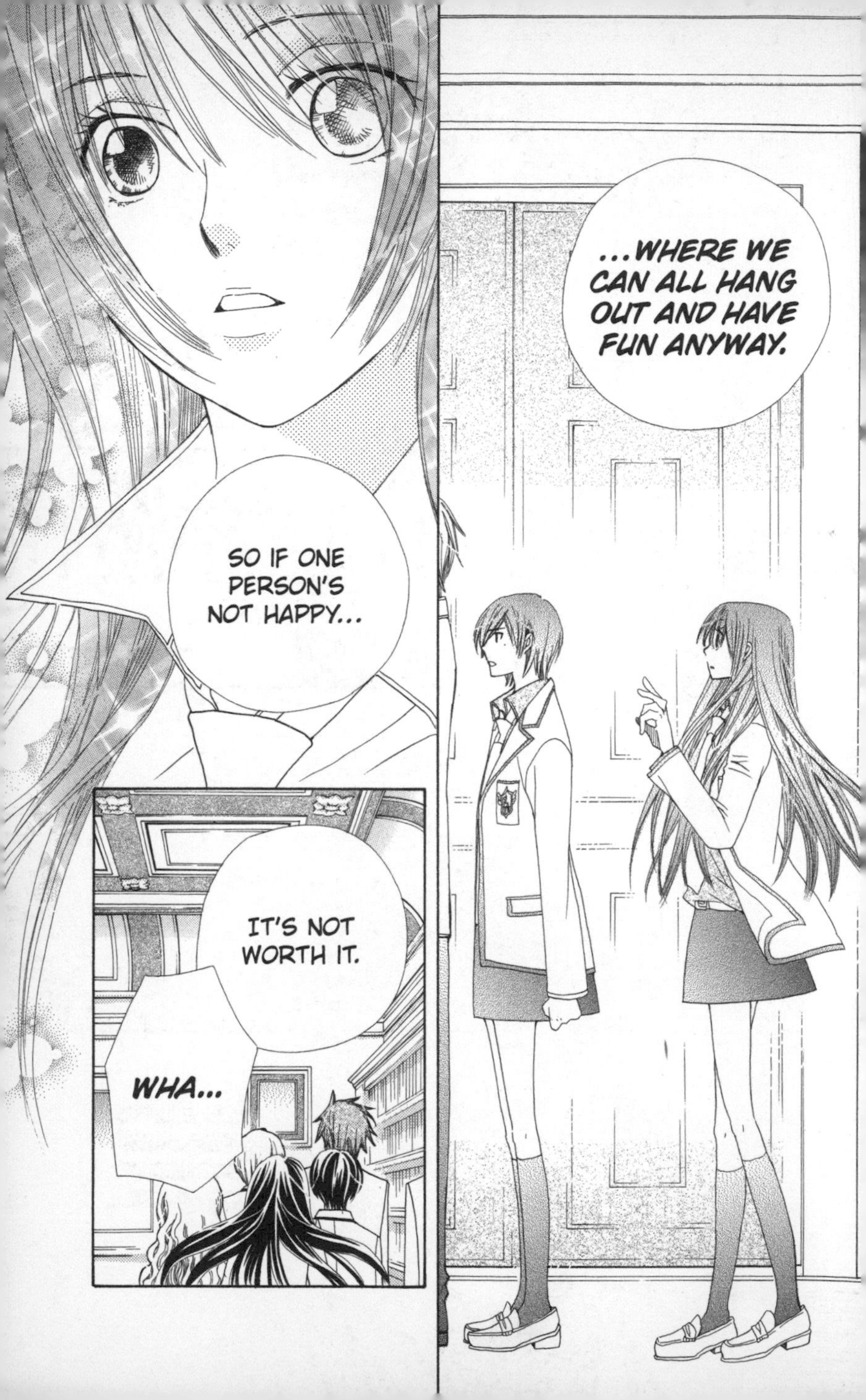
...WHERE WE CAN ALL HANG OUT AND HAVE FUN ANYWAY.
SO IF ONE PERSON'S NOT HAPPY...
IT'S NOT WORTH IT.
WHA...

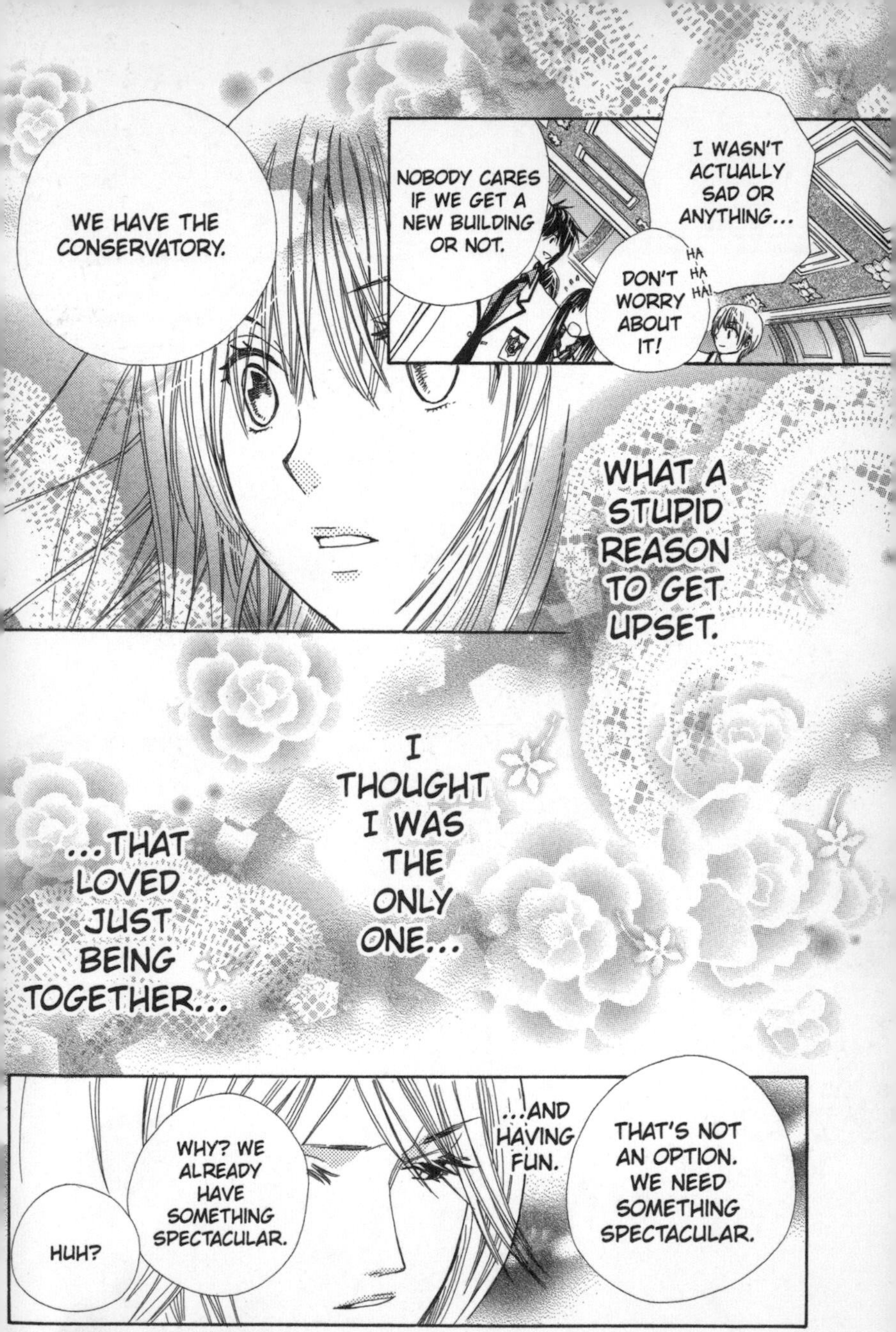
I WASN'T ACTUALLY SAD OR ANYTHING...
HA HA HA!
DON'T WORRY ABOUT IT!
NOBODY CARES IF WE GET A NEW BUILDING OR NOT.
WE HAVE THE CONSERVATORY.
WHAT A STUPID REASON TO GET UPSET.
I THOUGHT I WAS THE ONLY ONE...
...THAT LOVED JUST BEING TOGETHER...
...AND HAVING FUN.
THAT'S NOT AN OPTION. WE NEED SOMETHING SPECTACULAR.
WHY? WE ALREADY HAVE SOMETHING SPECTACULAR.
HUH?

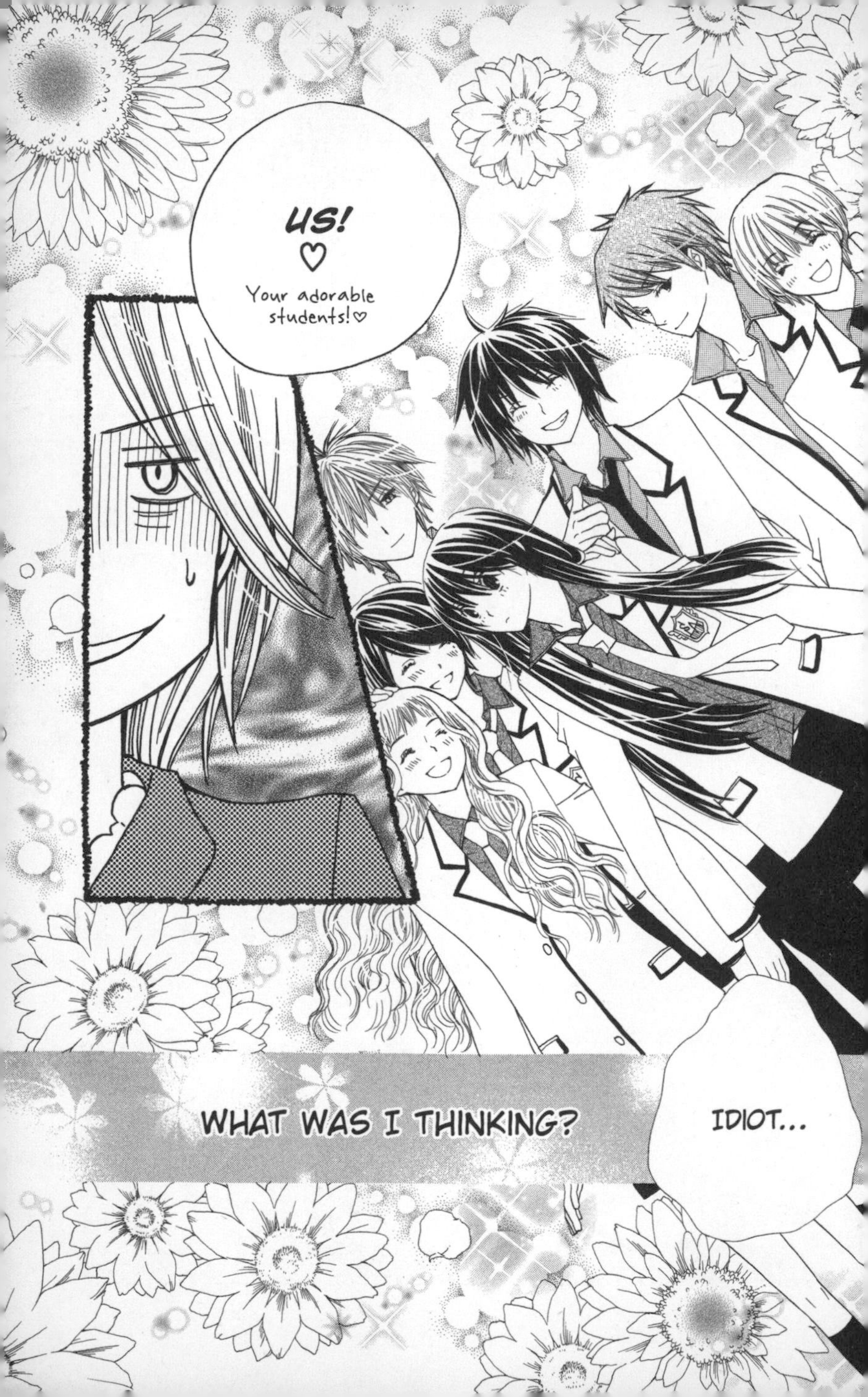
US! ♡
Your adorable students! ♡
IDIOT...
WHAT WAS I THINKING?

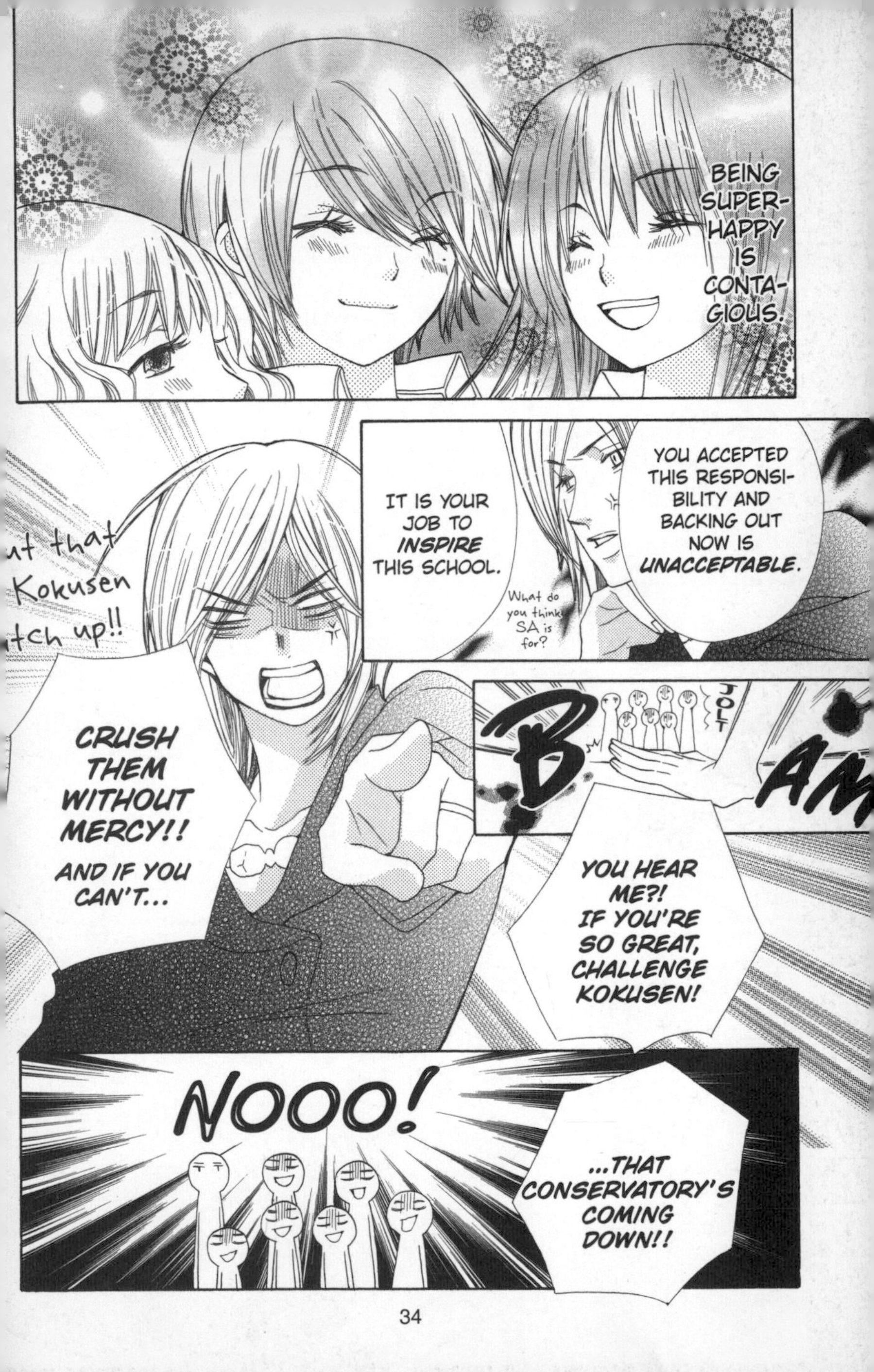
BEING SUPER-HAPPY IS CONTAGIOUS.
YOU ACCEPTED THIS RESPONSIBILITY AND BACKING OUT NOW IS UNACCEPTABLE.
IT IS YOUR JOB TO INSPIRE THIS SCHOOL.
What do you think SA is for?
JOLT
BAM
YOU HEAR ME?! IF YOU'RE SO GREAT, CHALLENGE KOKUSEN!
CRUSH THEM WITHOUT MERCY!!
AND IF YOU CAN'T...
ut that Kokusen tch up!!
NOOO!
...THAT CONSERVATORY'S COMING DOWN!!

Chapter 65

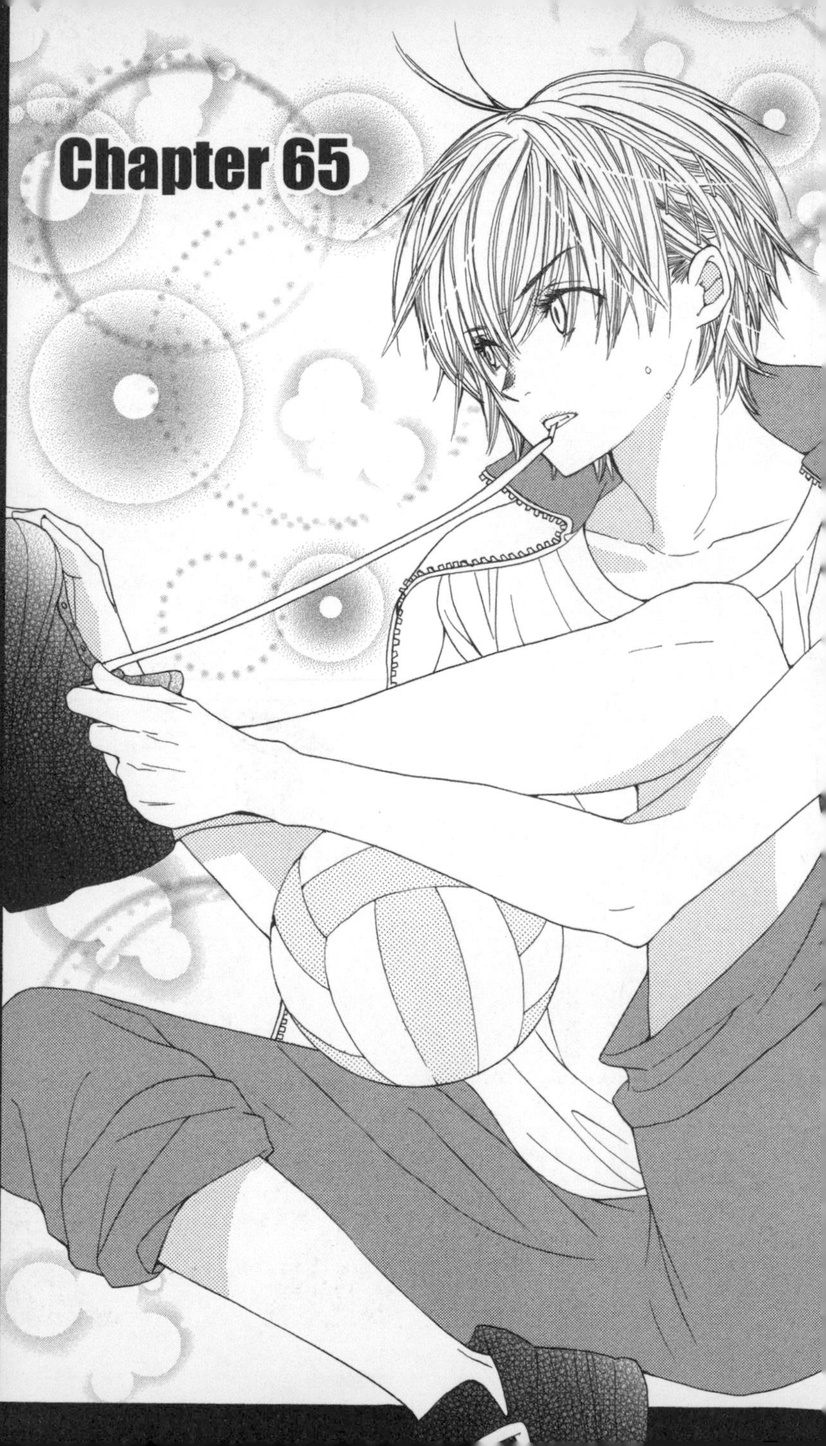

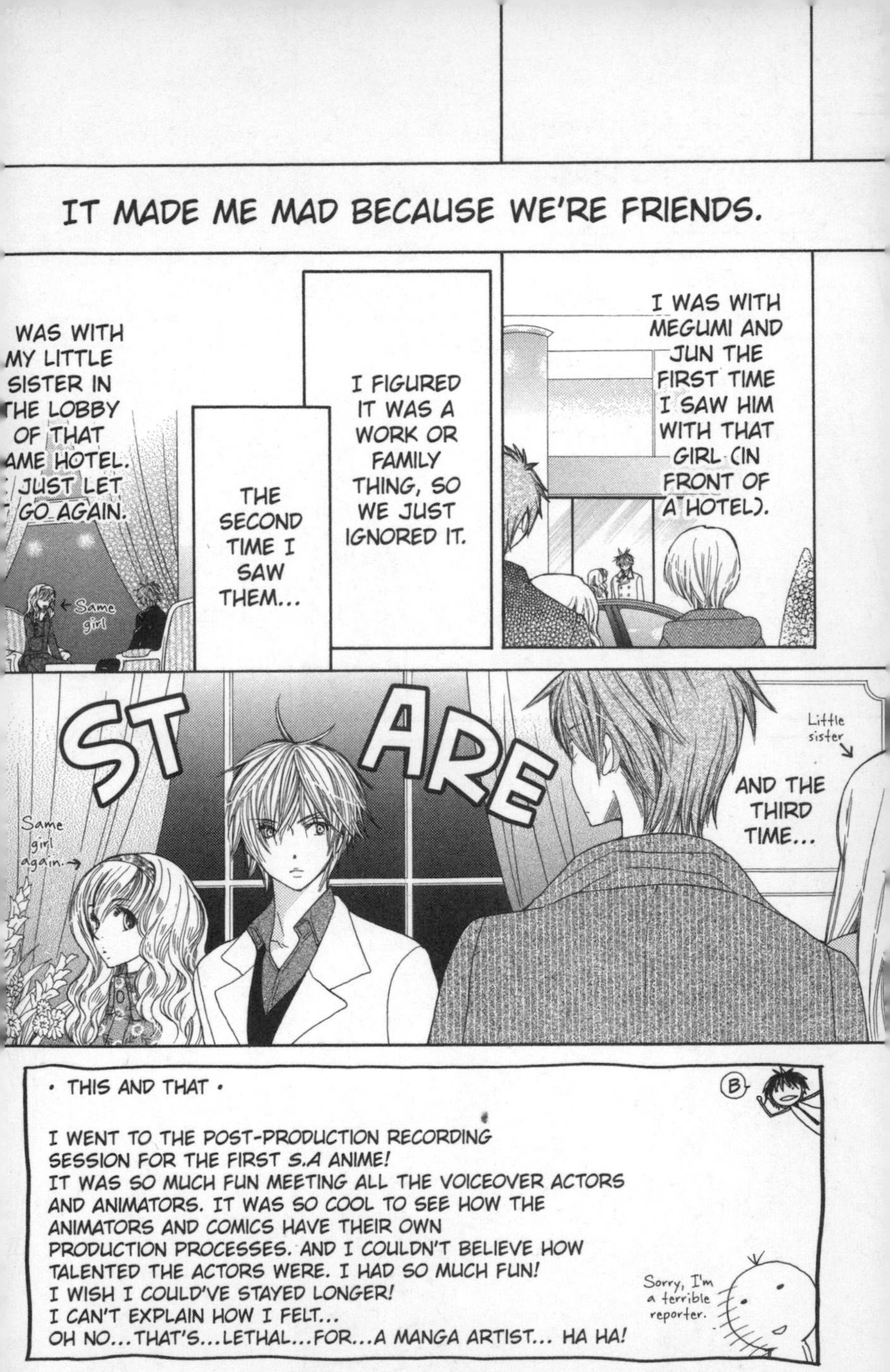
IT MADE ME MAD BECAUSE WE'RE FRIENDS.
I WAS WITH MEGUMI AND JUN THE FIRST TIME I SAW HIM WITH THAT GIRL (IN FRONT OF A HOTEL).
I FIGURED IT WAS A WORK OR FAMILY THING, SO WE JUST IGNORED IT.
THE SECOND TIME I SAW THEM...
WAS WITH MY LITTLE SISTER IN THE LOBBY OF THAT AME HOTEL. JUST LET GO AGAIN.
← Same girl
Little sister
AND THE THIRD TIME...
STARE
Same girl again. →

• THIS AND THAT •

I WENT TO THE POST-PRODUCTION RECORDING SESSION FOR THE FIRST *S.A* ANIME!
IT WAS SO MUCH FUN MEETING ALL THE VOICEOVER ACTORS AND ANIMATORS. IT WAS SO COOL TO SEE HOW THE ANIMATORS AND COMICS HAVE THEIR OWN PRODUCTION PROCESSES. AND I COULDN'T BELIEVE HOW TALENTED THE ACTORS WERE. I HAD SO MUCH FUN!
I WISH I COULD'VE STAYED LONGER!
I CAN'T EXPLAIN HOW I FELT...
OH NO...THAT'S...LETHAL...FOR...A MANGA ARTIST... HA HA!

Sorry, I'm a terrible reporter.

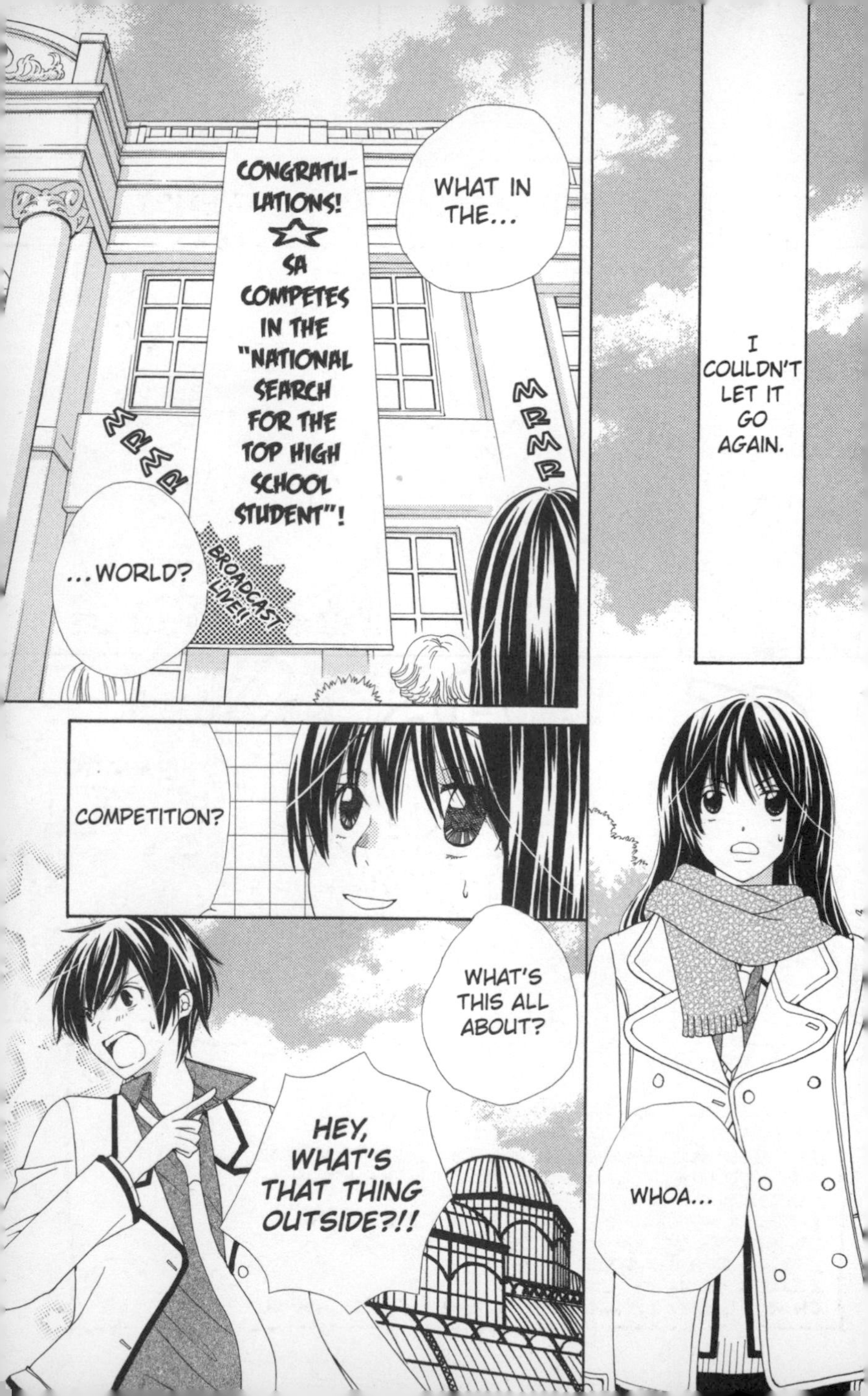
I COULDN'T LET IT GO AGAIN.
WHAT IN THE...
CONGRATULATIONS! ☆ SA COMPETES IN THE "NATIONAL SEARCH FOR THE TOP HIGH SCHOOL STUDENT"!
MRMR
MRMR
...WORLD?
BROADCAST LIVE!!
WHOA...
COMPETITION?
WHAT'S THIS ALL ABOUT?
HEY, WHAT'S THAT THING OUTSIDE?!!

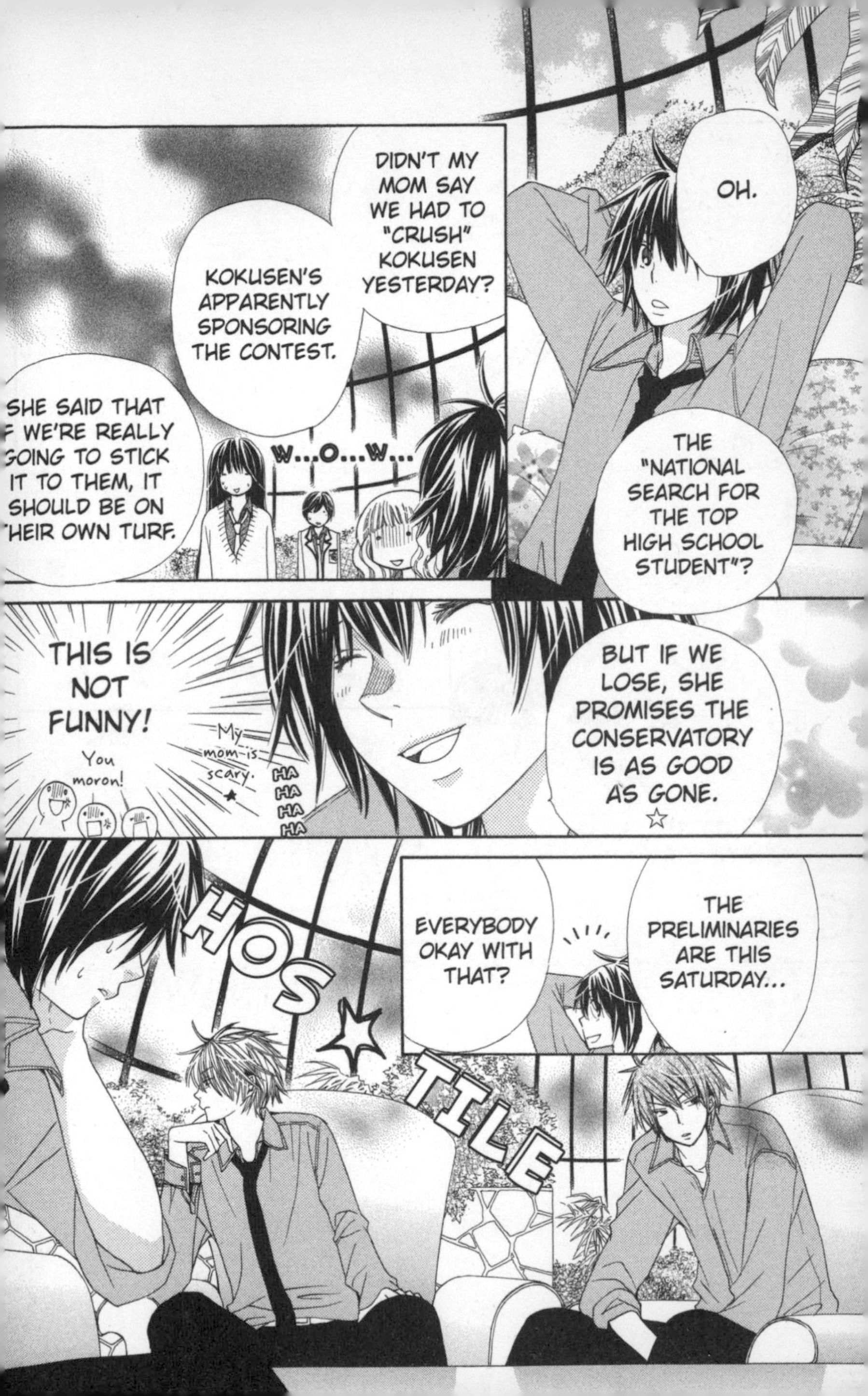
OH.
THE "NATIONAL SEARCH FOR THE TOP HIGH SCHOOL STUDENT"?
DIDN'T MY MOM SAY WE HAD TO "CRUSH" KOKUSEN YESTERDAY?
KOKUSEN'S APPARENTLY SPONSORING THE CONTEST.
SHE SAID THAT F WE'RE REALLY GOING TO STICK IT TO THEM, IT SHOULD BE ON HEIR OWN TURF.
W...O...W...
BUT IF WE LOSE, SHE PROMISES THE CONSERVATORY IS AS GOOD AS GONE. ☆
HA HA HA HA
My mom is scary. ★
THIS IS NOT FUNNY!
You moron!
THE PRELIMINARIES ARE THIS SATURDAY...
EVERYBODY OKAY WITH THAT?
HOS☆TILE

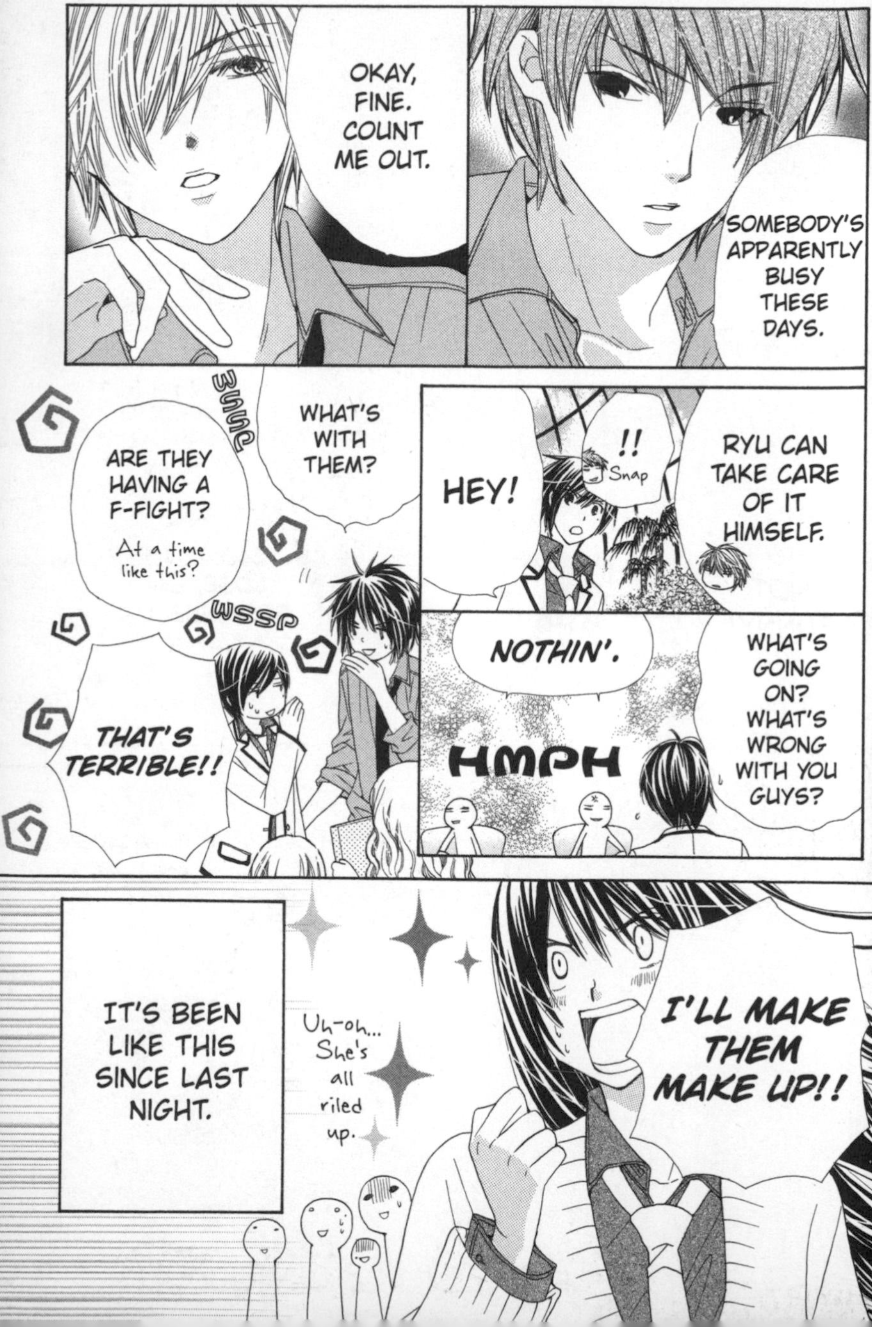
SOMEBODY'S APPARENTLY BUSY THESE DAYS.
OKAY, FINE. COUNT ME OUT.
RYU CAN TAKE CARE OF IT HIMSELF.
!!
Snap
HEY!
WHAT'S GOING ON? WHAT'S WRONG WITH YOU GUYS?
NOTHIN'.
HMPH
WHAT'S WITH THEM?
ARE THEY HAVING A F-FIGHT?
At a time like this?
WSSP
THAT'S TERRIBLE!!
I'LL MAKE THEM MAKE UP!!
Uh-oh... She's all riled up.
IT'S BEEN LIKE THIS SINCE LAST NIGHT.

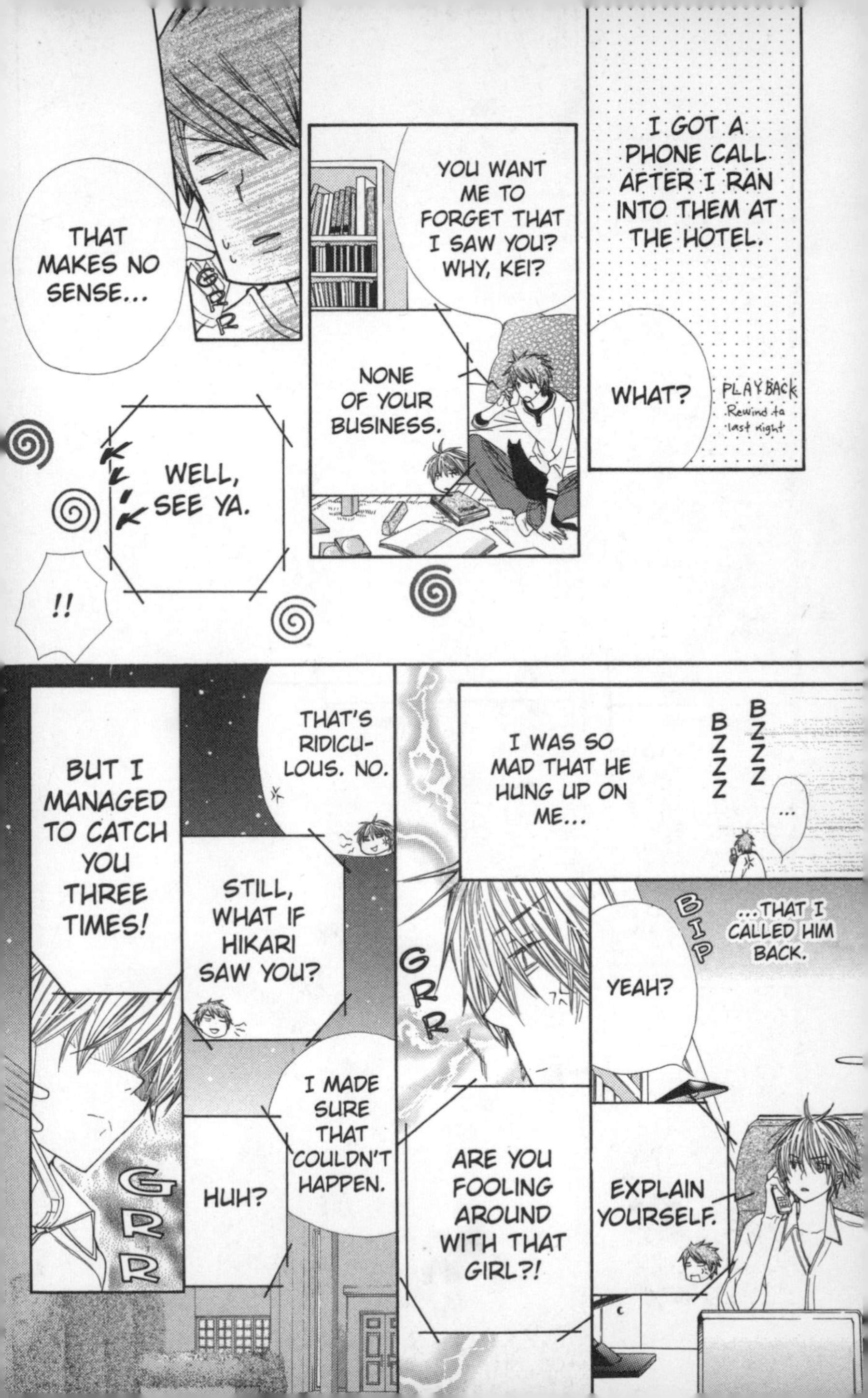
I GOT A PHONE CALL AFTER I RAN INTO THEM AT THE HOTEL.
WHAT?
PLAY BACK
Rewind to last night
YOU WANT ME TO FORGET THAT I SAW YOU? WHY, KEI?
NONE OF YOUR BUSINESS.
THAT MAKES NO SENSE...
GRR
WELL, SEE YA.
!!
I WAS SO MAD THAT HE HUNG UP ON ME...
BZZZ
BZZZ
...
...THAT I CALLED HIM BACK.
BIP
YEAH?
EXPLAIN YOURSELF.
GRR
ARE YOU FOOLING AROUND WITH THAT GIRL?!
THAT'S RIDICULOUS. NO.
STILL, WHAT IF HIKARI SAW YOU?
I MADE SURE THAT COULDN'T HAPPEN.
HUH?
BUT I MANAGED TO CATCH YOU THREE TIMES!
GRR

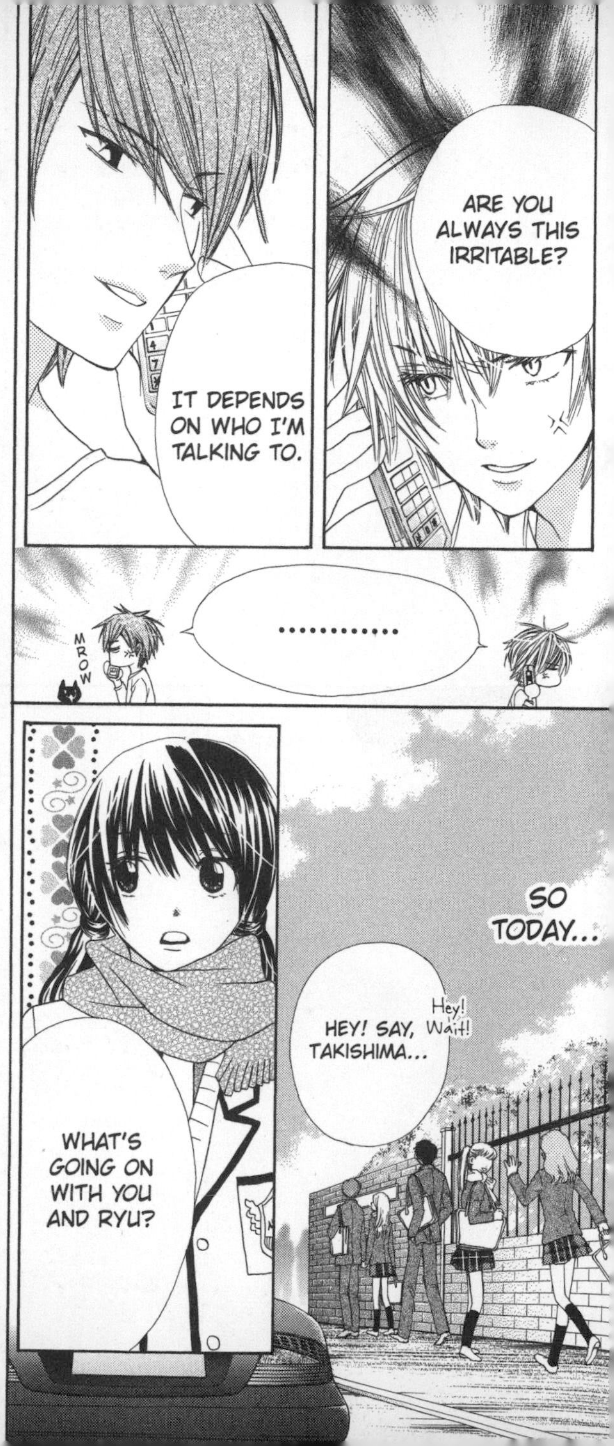
ARE YOU ALWAYS THIS IRRITABLE?
IT DEPENDS ON WHO I'M TALKING TO.
MROW
....
SO TODAY...
HEY! SAY, TAKISHIMA...
Hey! Wait!
WHAT'S GOING ON WITH YOU AND RYU?

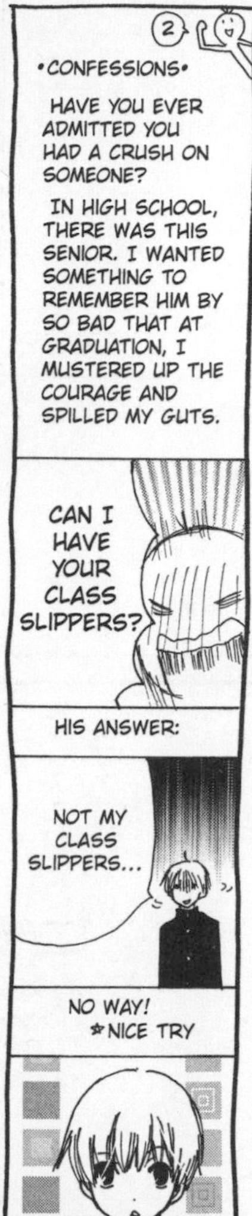
2
•CONFESSIONS•
HAVE YOU EVER ADMITTED YOU HAD A CRUSH ON SOMEONE?
IN HIGH SCHOOL, THERE WAS THIS SENIOR. I WANTED SOMETHING TO REMEMBER HIM BY SO BAD THAT AT GRADUATION, I MUSTERED UP THE COURAGE AND SPILLED MY GUTS.
CAN I HAVE YOUR CLASS SLIPPERS?
HIS ANSWER:
NOT MY CLASS SLIPPERS...
NO WAY! ☆NICE TRY

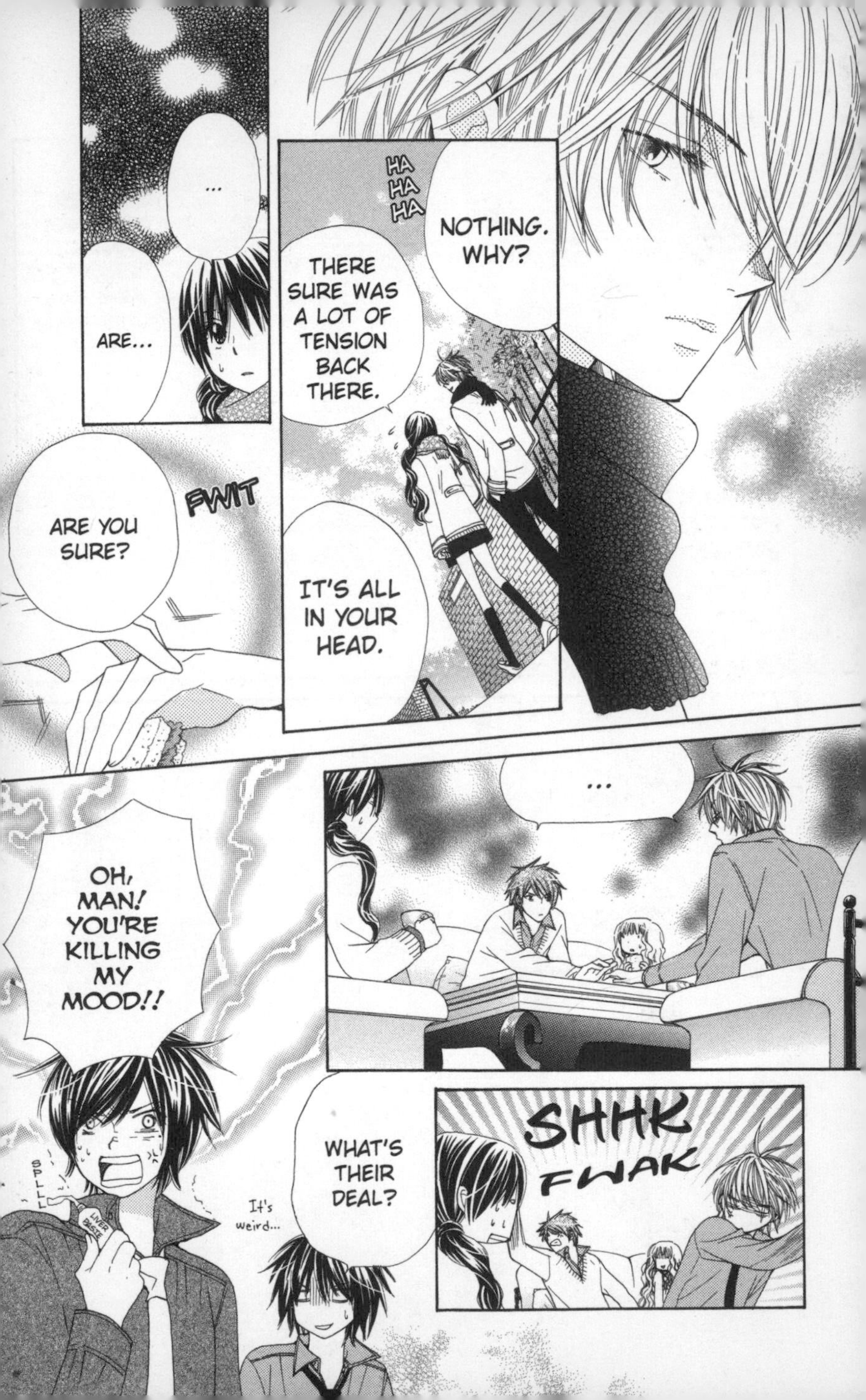
HA HA HA
NOTHING. WHY?
THERE SURE WAS A LOT OF TENSION BACK THERE.
IT'S ALL IN YOUR HEAD.
...
ARE...
FWIT
ARE YOU SURE?
...
OH, MAN! YOU'RE KILLING MY MOOD!!
SHHK
FWAK
WHAT'S THEIR DEAL?
It's weird...
LIVER PASTE
SPLLL

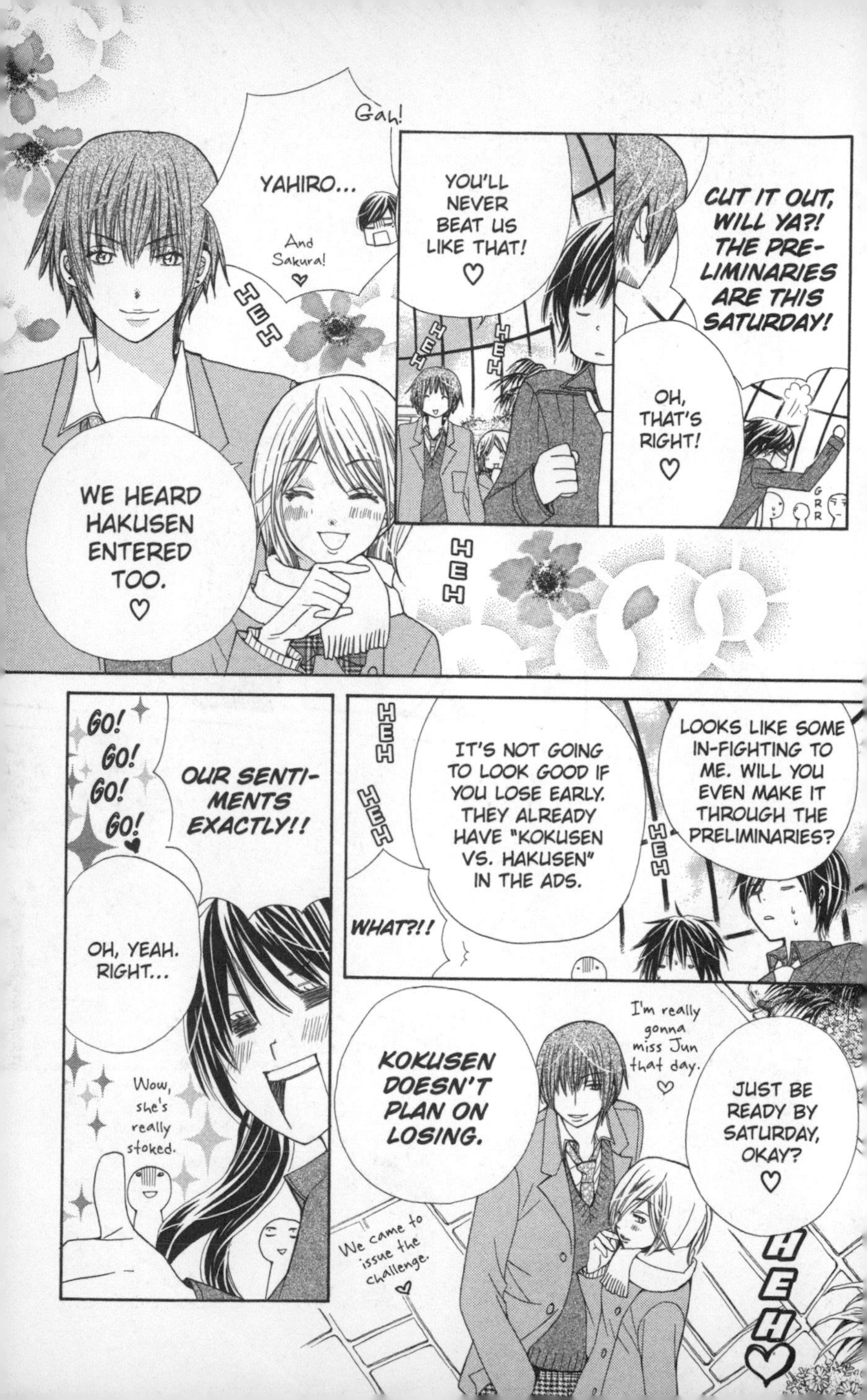
Gah!
YAHIRO...
And Sakura! ♡
HEH HEH
CUT IT OUT, WILL YA?! THE PRE-LIMINARIES ARE THIS SATURDAY!
OH, THAT'S RIGHT! ♡
GRR
YOU'LL NEVER BEAT US LIKE THAT! ♡
HEH HEH
HEH HEH
WE HEARD HAKUSEN ENTERED TOO. ♡
HEH HEH
LOOKS LIKE SOME IN-FIGHTING TO ME. WILL YOU EVEN MAKE IT THROUGH THE PRELIMINARIES?
HEH HEH
IT'S NOT GOING TO LOOK GOOD IF YOU LOSE EARLY. THEY ALREADY HAVE "KOKUSEN VS. HAKUSEN" IN THE ADS.
HEH HEH
HEH HEH
WHAT?!!
JUST BE READY BY SATURDAY, OKAY? ♡
I'm really gonna miss Jun that day. ♡
KOKUSEN DOESN'T PLAN ON LOSING.
We came to issue the challenge. ♡
HEH ♡
OUR SENTI-MENTS EXACTLY!!
GO! GO! GO! GO! ♥
OH, YEAH. RIGHT...
Wow, she's really stoked.

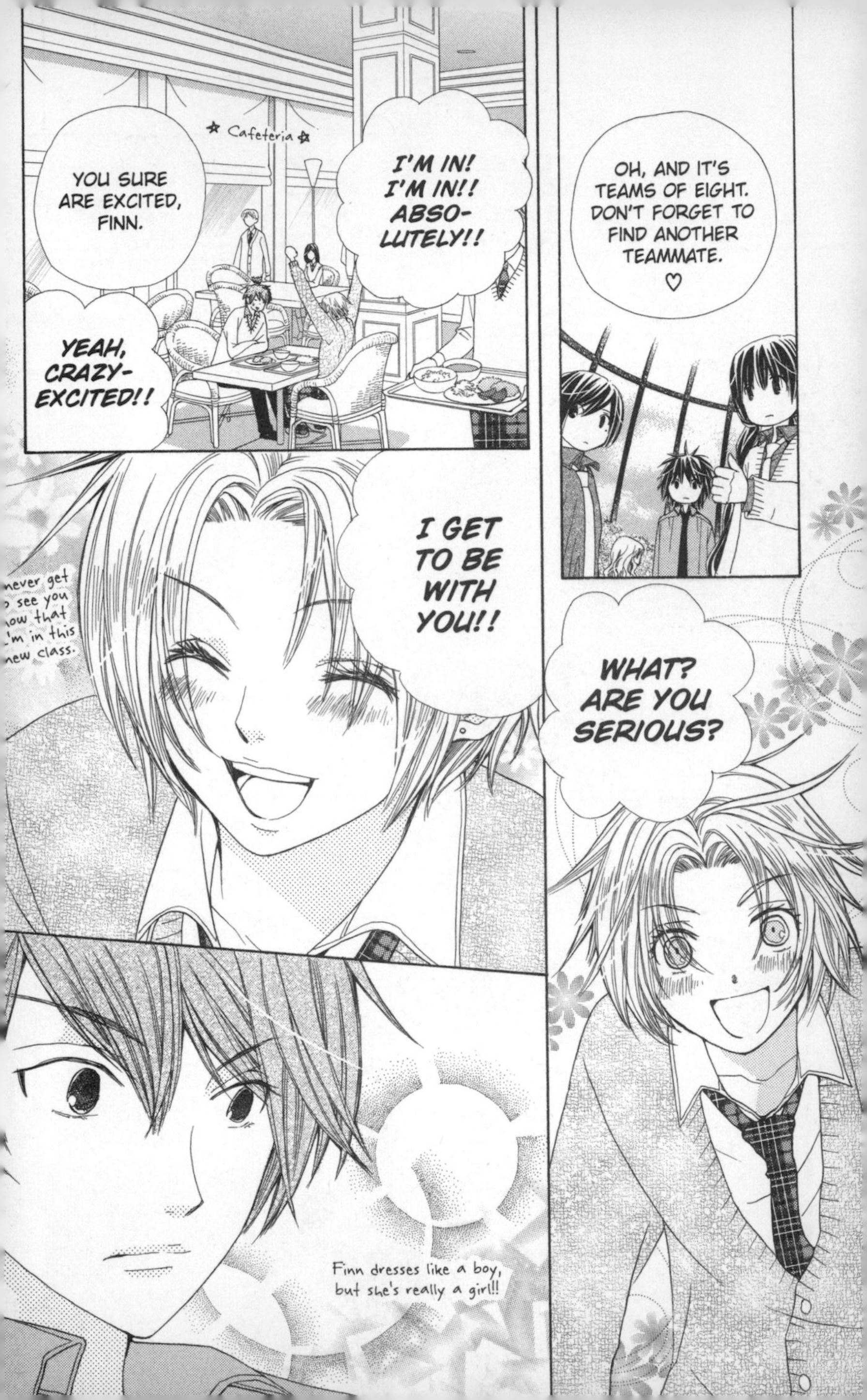
OH, AND IT'S TEAMS OF EIGHT. DON'T FORGET TO FIND ANOTHER TEAMMATE. ♡
WHAT? ARE YOU SERIOUS?
I'M IN! I'M IN!! ABSO-LUTELY!!
☆ Cafeteria ☆
YOU SURE ARE EXCITED, FINN.
YEAH, CRAZY-EXCITED!!
I GET TO BE WITH YOU!!
never get
o see you
ow that
'm in this
new class.
Finn dresses like a boy, but she's really a girl!!

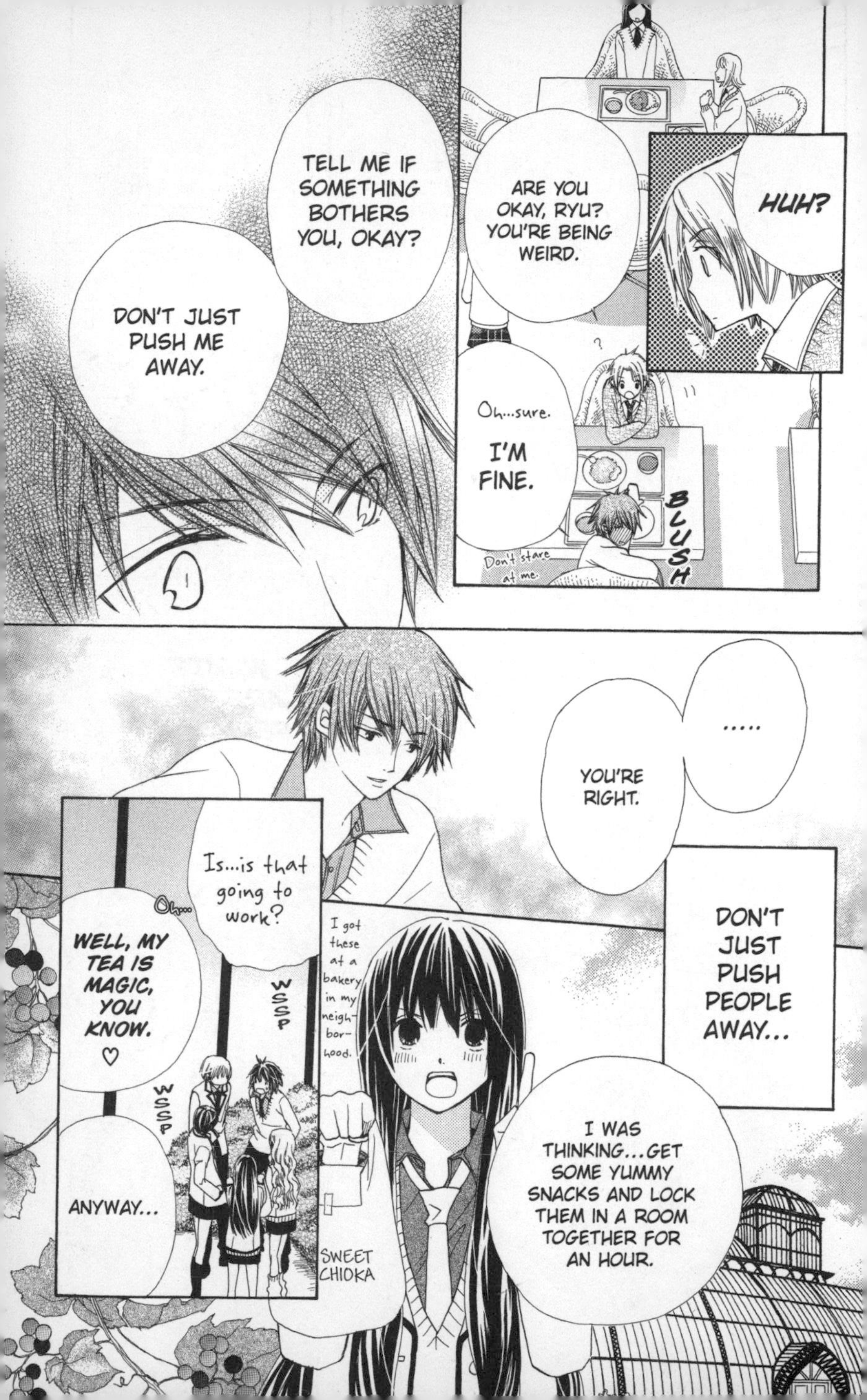
ARE YOU OKAY, RYU? YOU'RE BEING WEIRD.
HUH?
Oh...sure.
I'M FINE.
BLUSH
Don't stare at me.
TELL ME IF SOMETHING BOTHERS YOU, OKAY?
DON'T JUST PUSH ME AWAY.
.....
YOU'RE RIGHT.
DON'T JUST PUSH PEOPLE AWAY...
I got these at a bakery in my neighborhood.
I WAS THINKING...GET SOME YUMMY SNACKS AND LOCK THEM IN A ROOM TOGETHER FOR AN HOUR.
SWEET CHIOKA
Is...is that going to work?
Oh...
WELL, MY TEA IS MAGIC, YOU KNOW. ♡
WSSP
WSSP
ANYWAY...

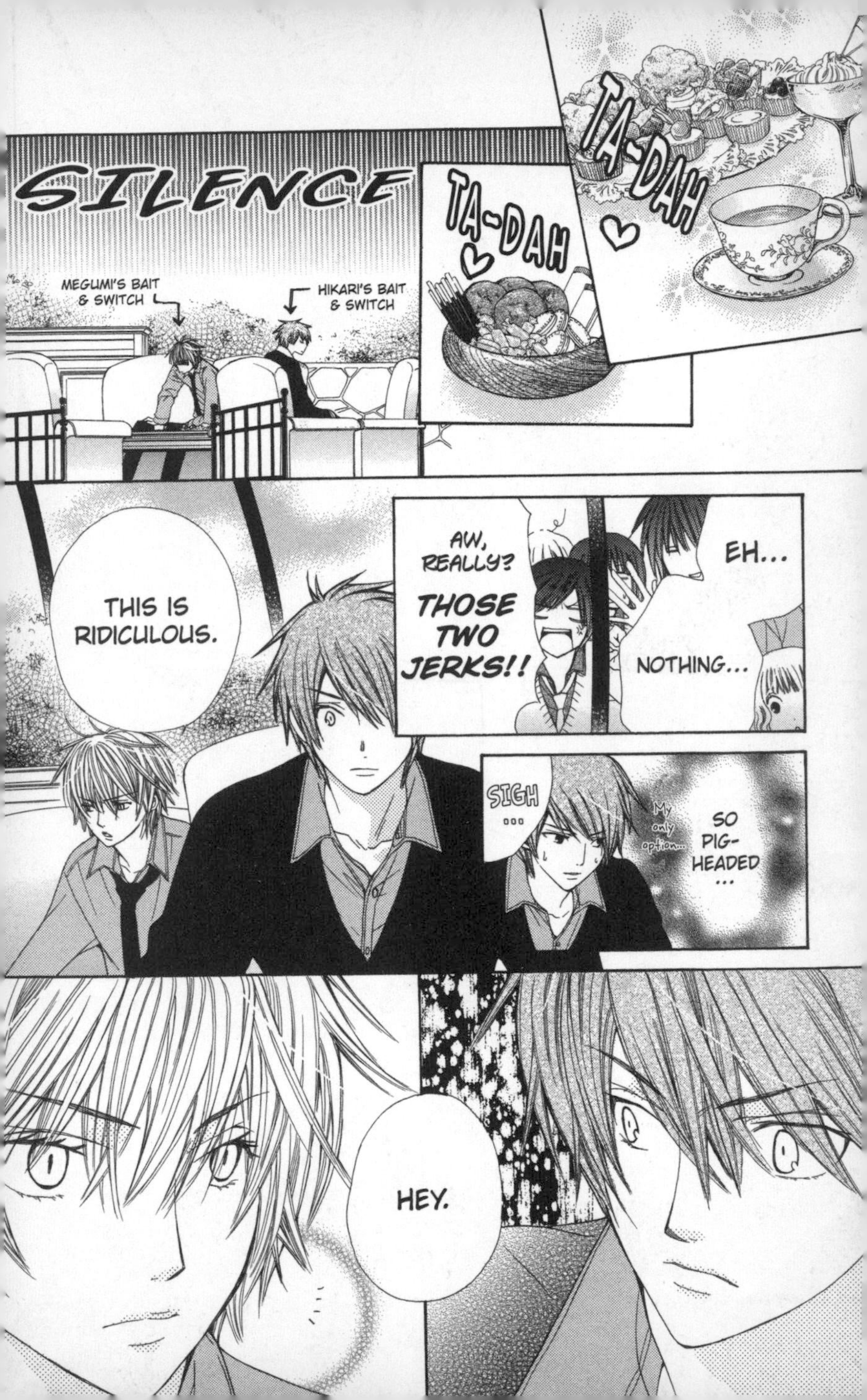
TA-DAH
TA-DAH
SILENCE
HIKARI'S BAIT & SWITCH
MEGUMI'S BAIT & SWITCH
EH...
NOTHING...
AW, REALLY?
THOSE TWO JERKS!!
SIGH...
My only option...
SO PIG-HEADED...
THIS IS RIDICULOUS.
HEY.

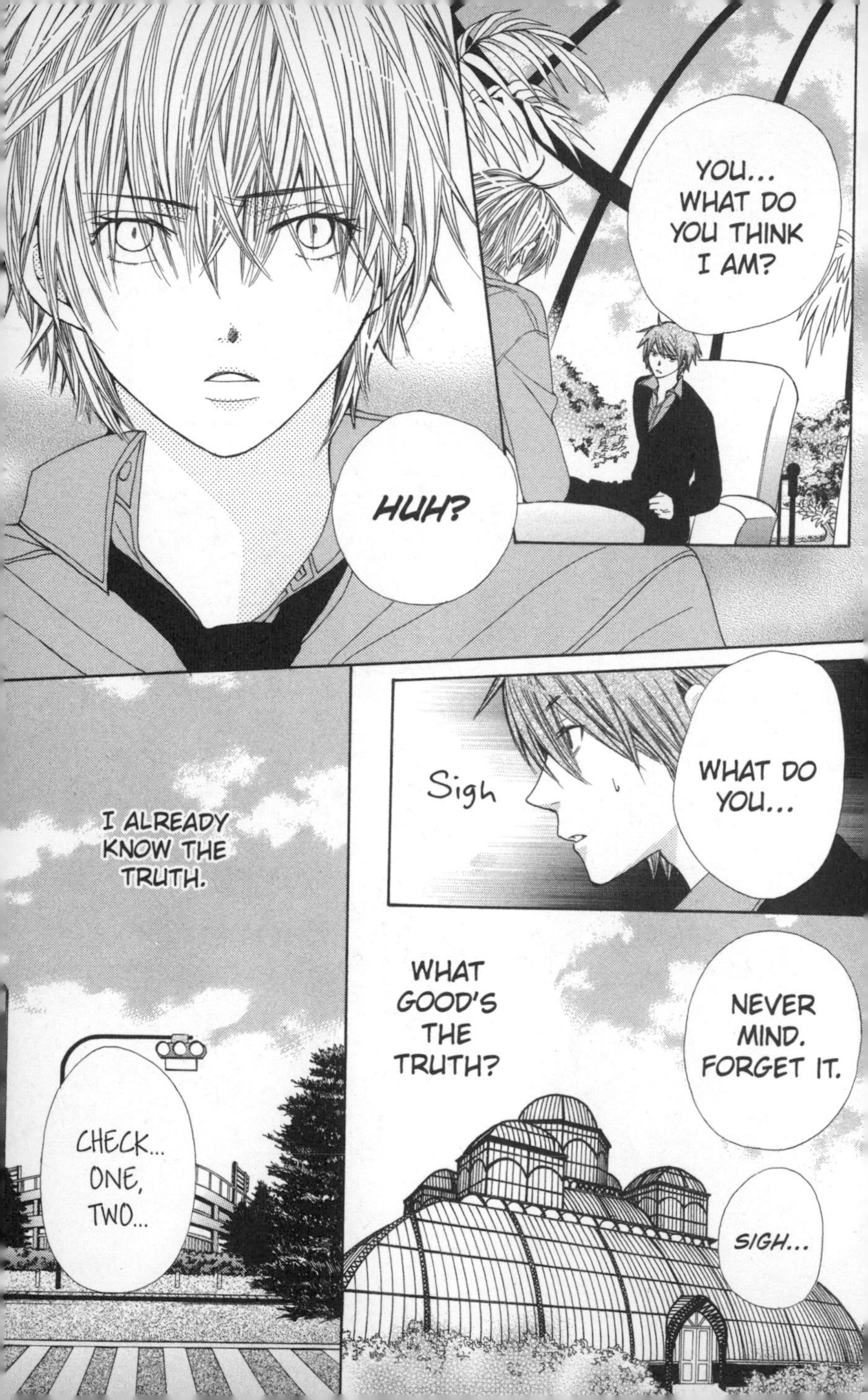
YOU... WHAT DO YOU THINK I AM?
HUH?
WHAT DO YOU...
Sigh
NEVER MIND. FORGET IT.
WHAT GOOD'S THE TRUTH?
SIGH...
I ALREADY KNOW THE TRUTH.
CHECK... ONE, TWO...

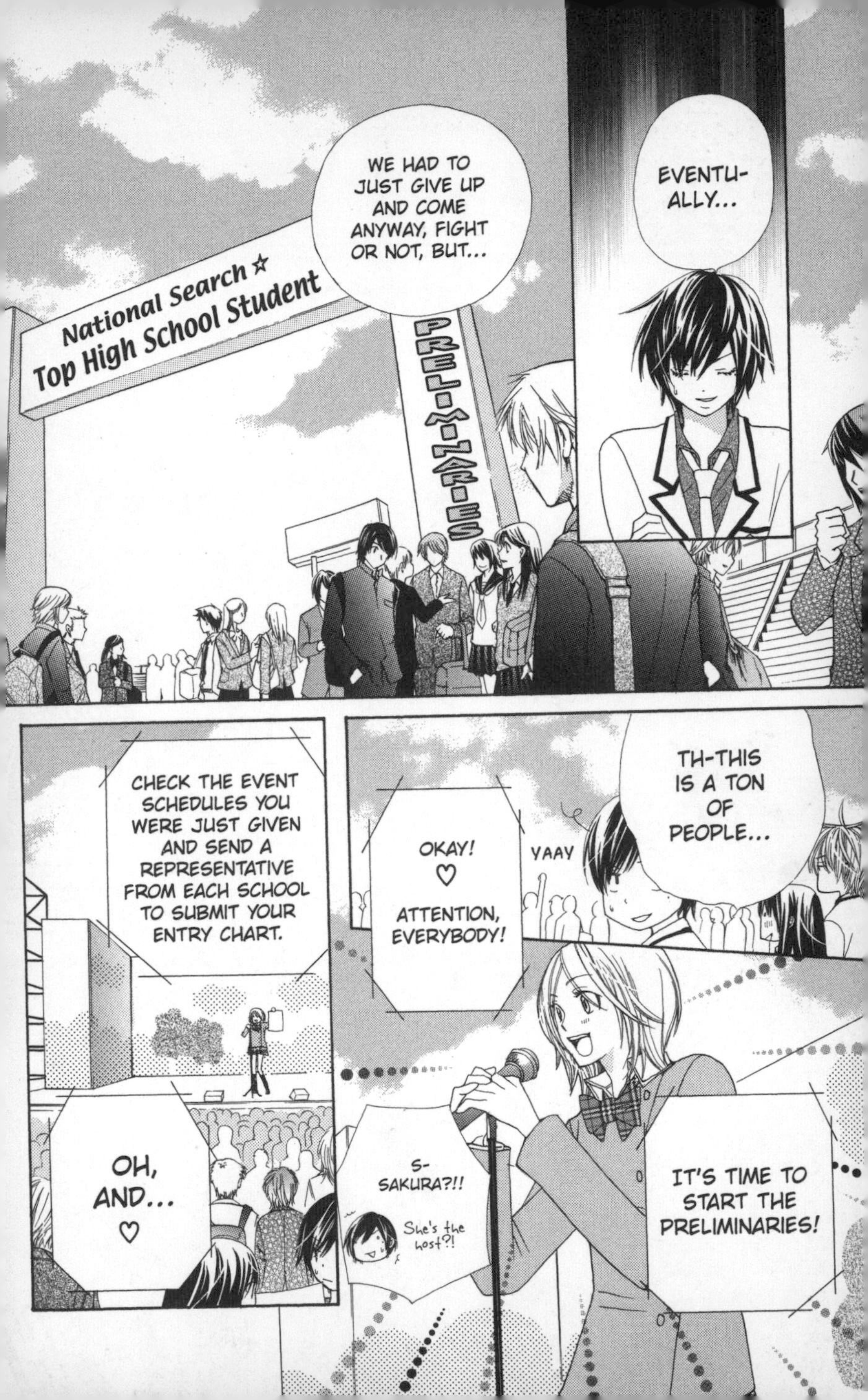
EVENTU-ALLY...
WE HAD TO JUST GIVE UP AND COME ANYWAY, FIGHT OR NOT, BUT...
National Search ☆ Top High School Student
PRELIMINARIES
TH-THIS IS A TON OF PEOPLE...
OKAY! ♡ ATTENTION, EVERYBODY!
YAAY
CHECK THE EVENT SCHEDULES YOU WERE JUST GIVEN AND SEND A REPRESENTATIVE FROM EACH SCHOOL TO SUBMIT YOUR ENTRY CHART.
OH, AND... ♡
IT'S TIME TO START THE PRELIMINARIES!
S-SAKURA?!!
She's the host?!

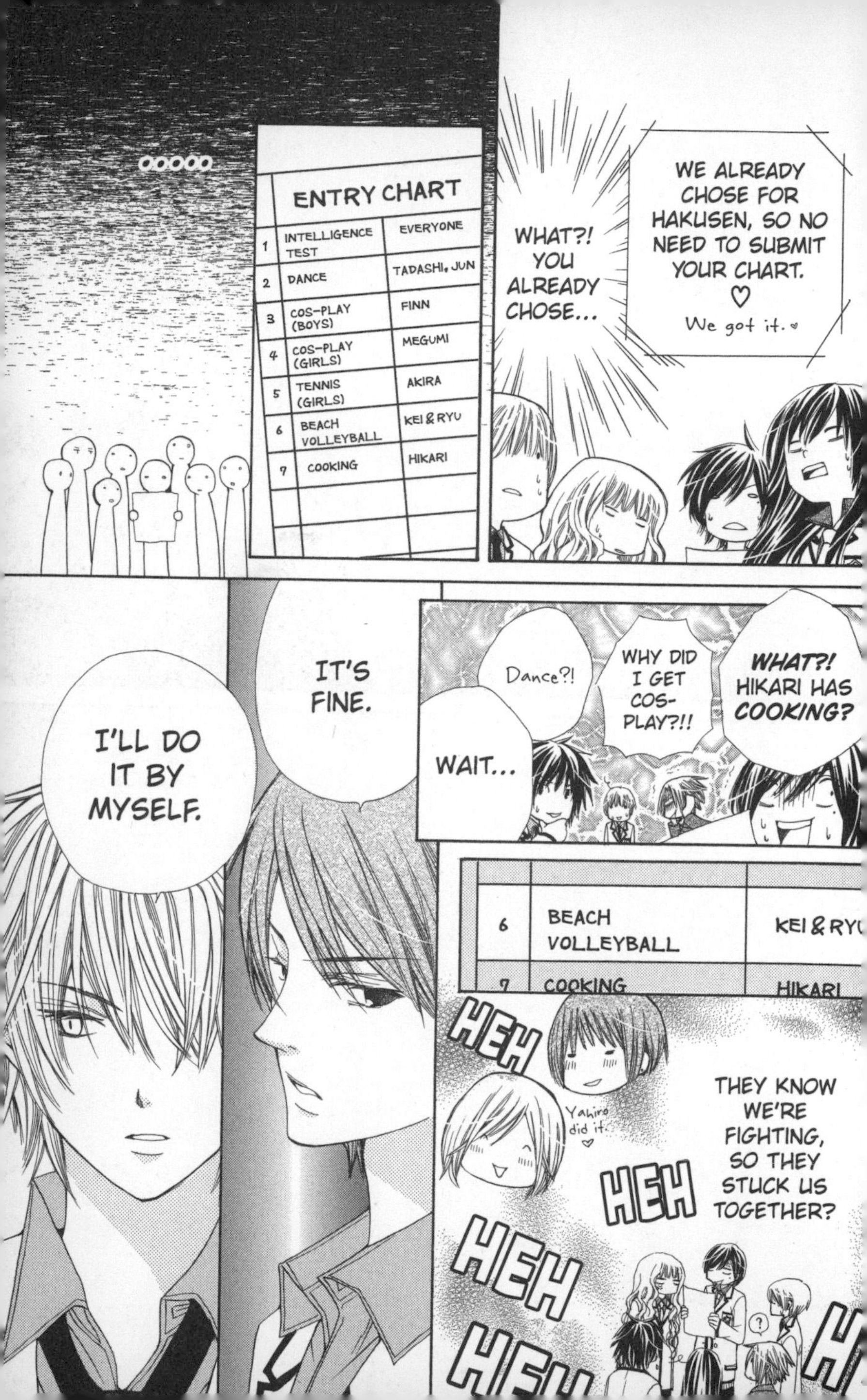
WE ALREADY CHOSE FOR HAKUSEN, SO NO NEED TO SUBMIT YOUR CHART. ♡
We got it. ♥
WHAT?! YOU ALREADY CHOSE...
ENTRY CHART
1 INTELLIGENCE TEST EVERYONE
2 DANCE TADASHI, JUN
3 COS-PLAY (BOYS) FINN
4 COS-PLAY (GIRLS) MEGUMI
5 TENNIS (GIRLS) AKIRA
6 BEACH VOLLEYBALL KEI & RYU
7 COOKING HIKARI
ooooo
WHAT?! HIKARI HAS COOKING?
WHY DID I GET COS-PLAY?!!
Dance?!
WAIT...
6 BEACH VOLLEYBALL KEI & RYU
7 COOKING HIKARI
HEH
THEY KNOW WE'RE FIGHTING, SO THEY STUCK US TOGETHER?
Yahiro did it. ♡
HEH
HEH
HEH
?
IT'S FINE.
I'LL DO IT BY MYSELF.

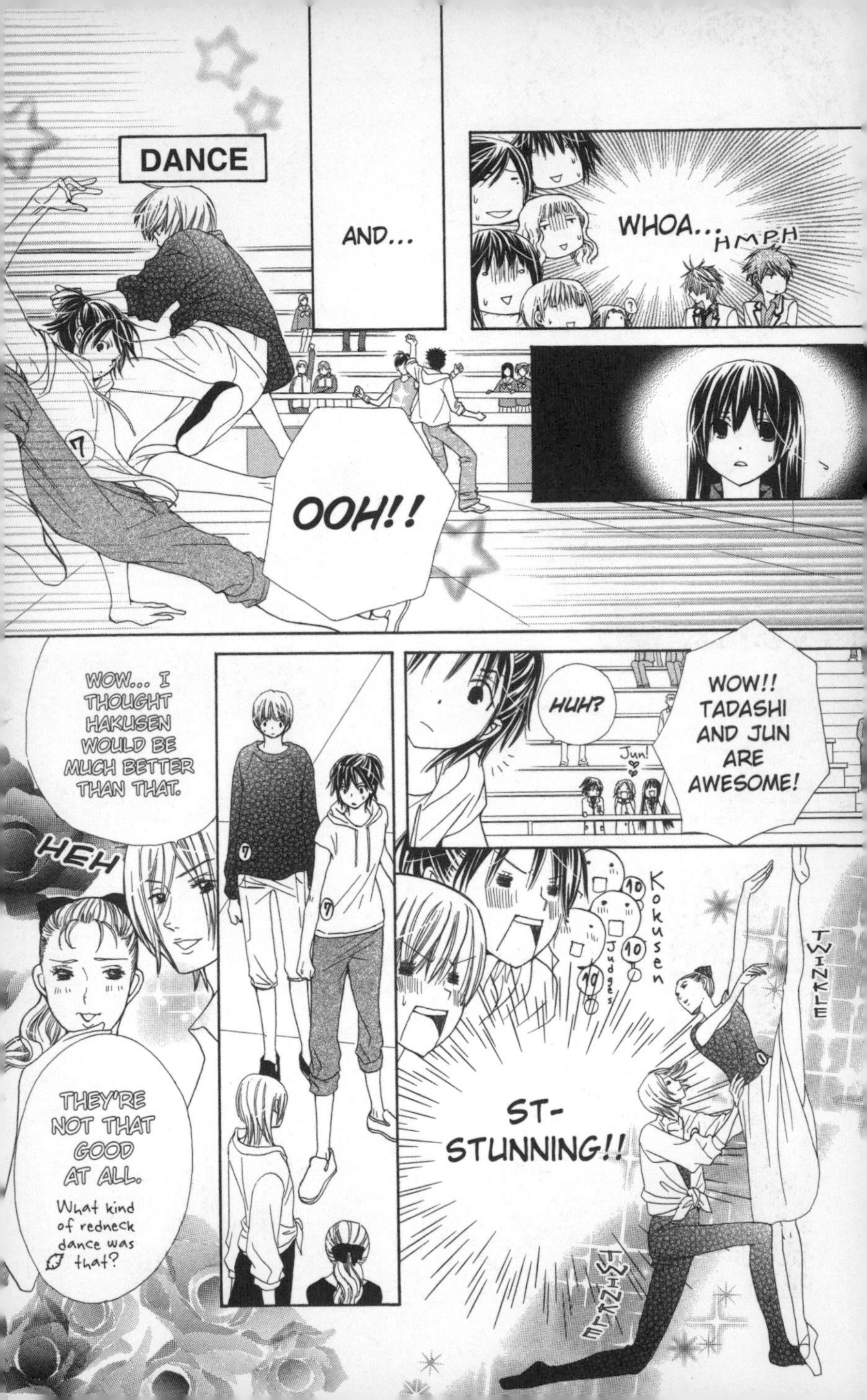
WHOA...
HMPH
AND...
DANCE
OOH!!
WOW!! TADASHI AND JUN ARE AWESOME!
HUH?
Jun!
TWINKLE
Kokusen Judges
10
10
10
10
ST-STUNNING!!
TWINKLE
WOW... I THOUGHT HAKUSEN WOULD BE MUCH BETTER THAN THAT.
HEH
THEY'RE NOT THAT GOOD AT ALL.
What kind of redneck dance was that?

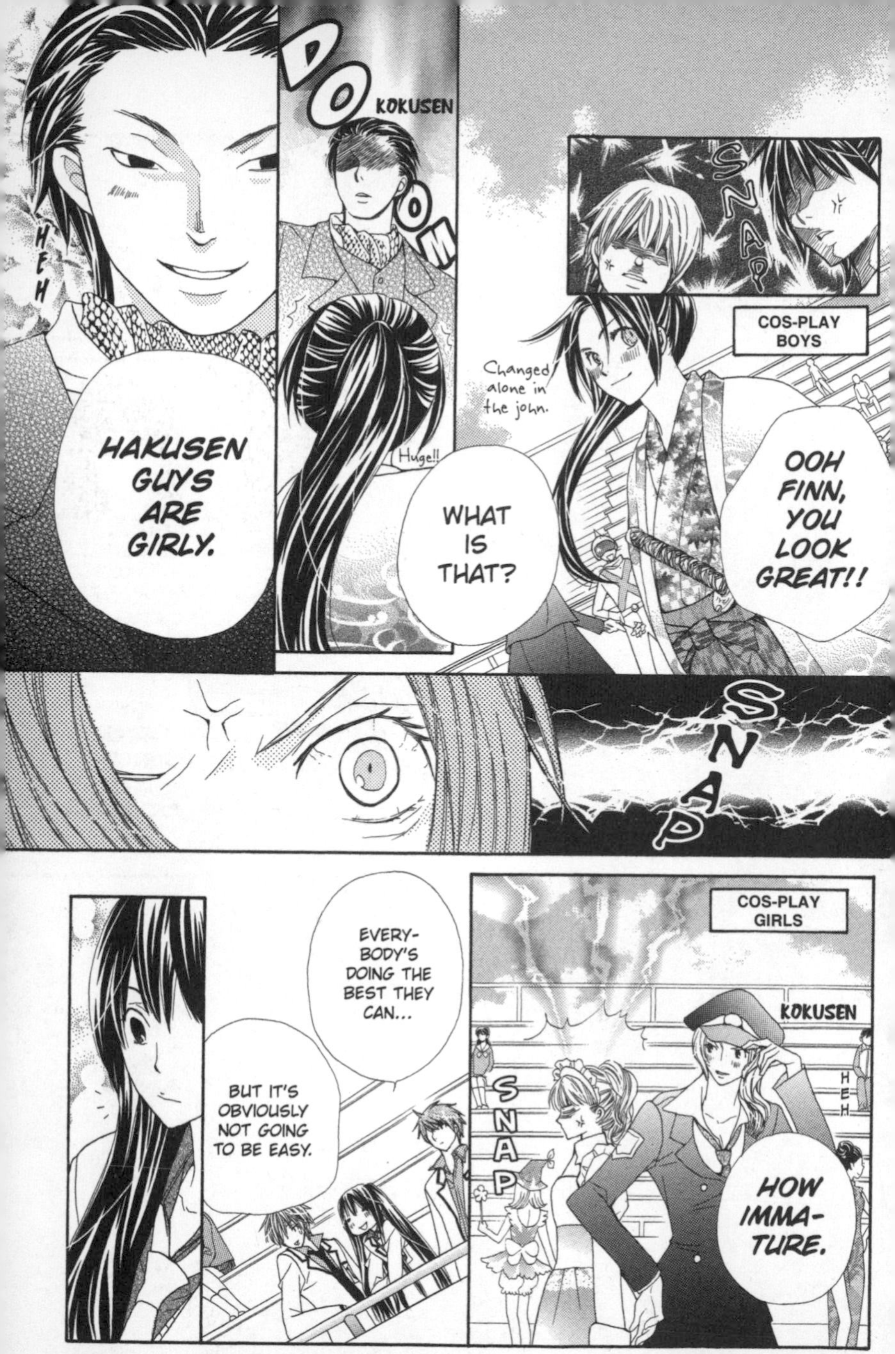
SNAP
COS-PLAY BOYS
OOH FINN, YOU LOOK GREAT!!
Changed alone in the john.
WHAT IS THAT?
Huge!!
DOOM
KOKUSEN
HEH
HAKUSEN GUYS ARE GIRLY.
SNAP
COS-PLAY GIRLS
KOKUSEN
HEH
HOW IMMA-TURE.
SNAP
EVERY-BODY'S DOING THE BEST THEY CAN...
BUT IT'S OBVIOUSLY NOT GOING TO BE EASY.

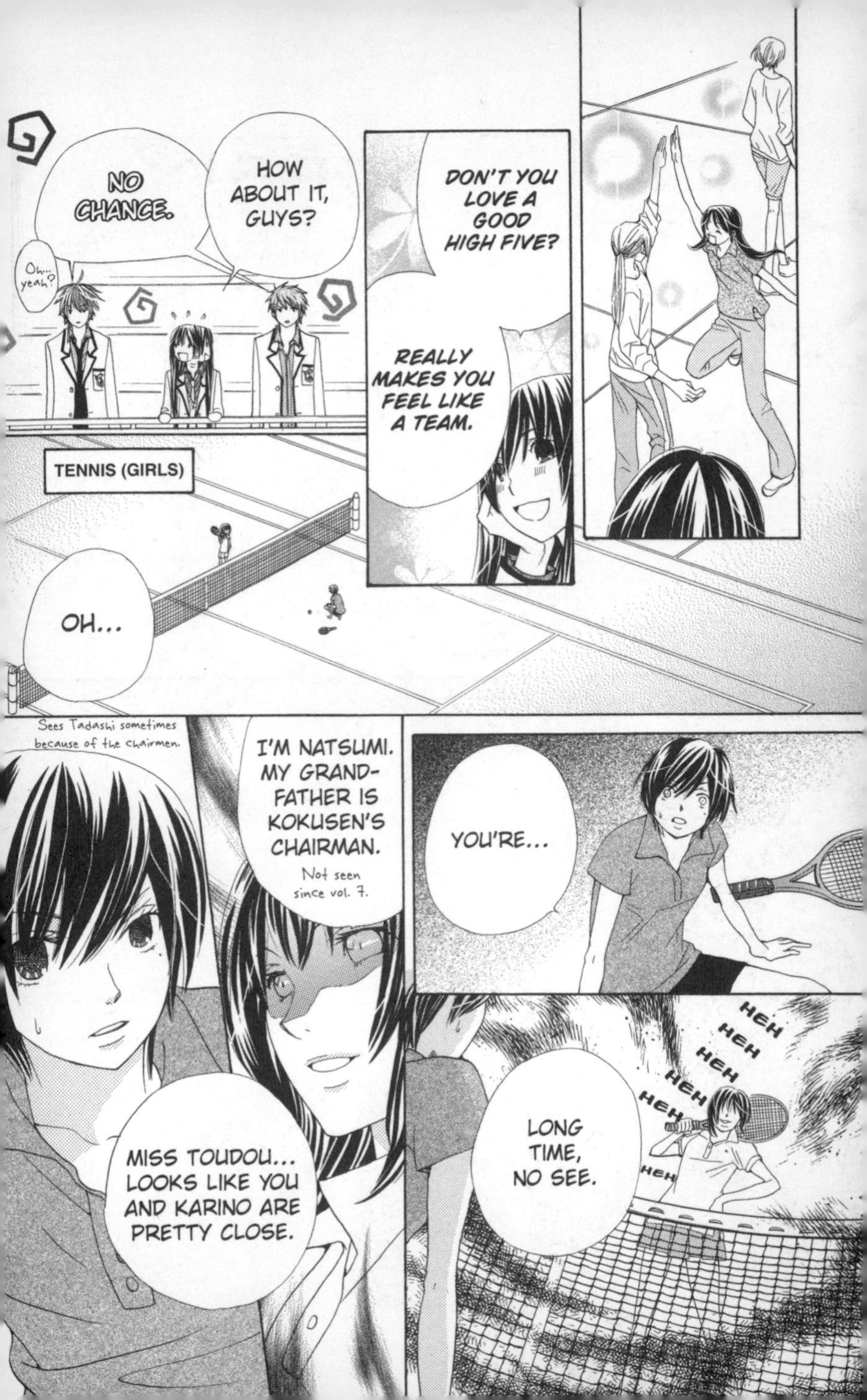
DON'T YOU LOVE A GOOD HIGH FIVE?
REALLY MAKES YOU FEEL LIKE A TEAM.
HOW ABOUT IT, GUYS?
NO CHANCE.
Oh... yeah?
TENNIS (GIRLS)
OH...
YOU'RE...
HEH HEH HEH HEH HEH HEH
LONG TIME, NO SEE.
Sees Tadashi sometimes because of the chairmen.
I'M NATSUMI. MY GRAND-FATHER IS KOKUSEN'S CHAIRMAN.
Not seen since vol. 7.
MISS TOUDOU... LOOKS LIKE YOU AND KARINO ARE PRETTY CLOSE.

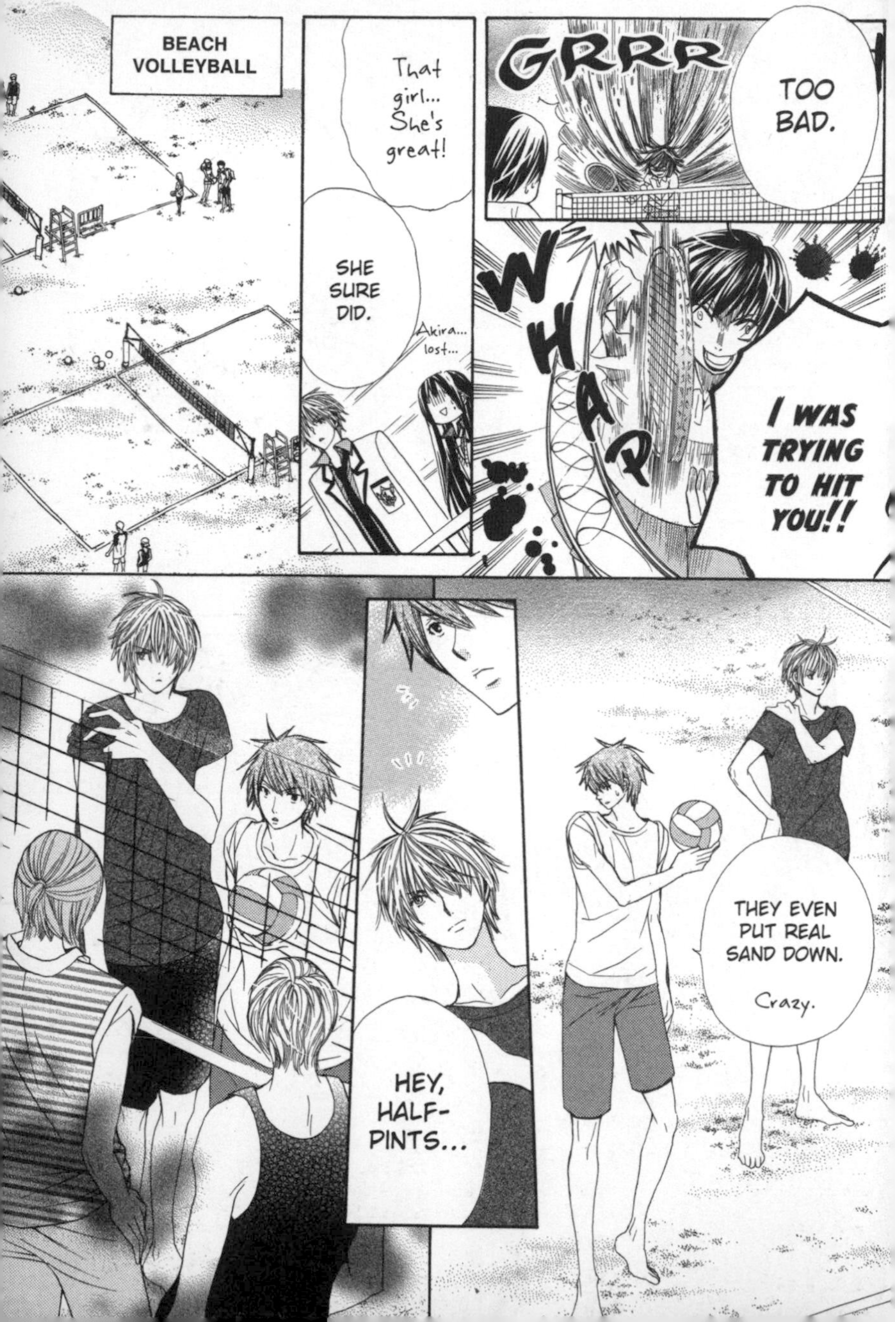
GRRR
TOO BAD.
WHAP
I WAS TRYING TO HIT YOU!!
That girl... She's great!
SHE SURE DID.
Akira... lost...
BEACH VOLLEYBALL
THEY EVEN PUT REAL SAND DOWN.
Crazy.
HEY, HALF-PINTS...

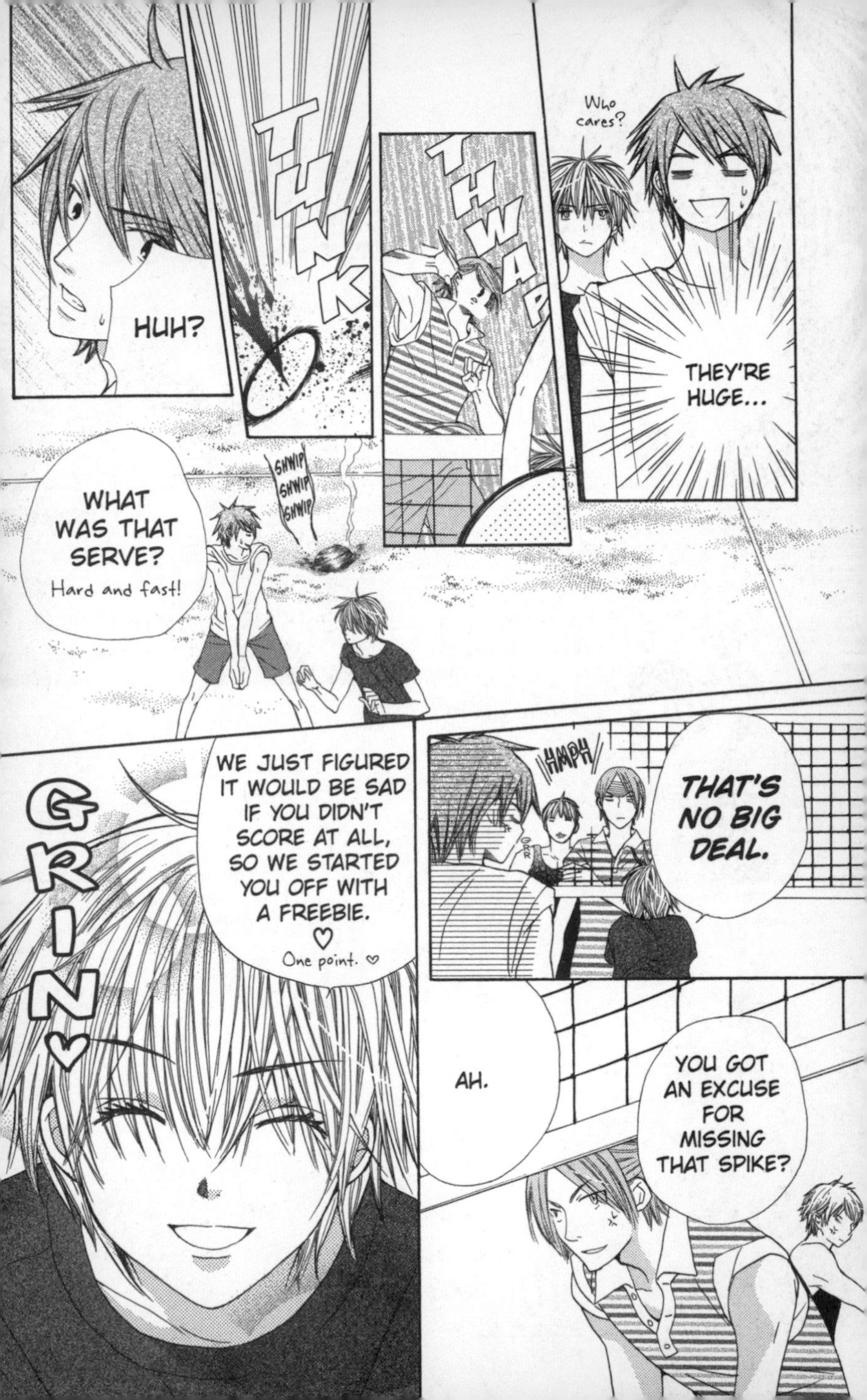
Who cares?
THEY'RE HUGE...
THWAP
THUNK
HUH?
SHWIP SHWIP SHWIP
WHAT WAS THAT SERVE?
Hard and fast!
THAT'S NO BIG DEAL.
HMPH
GRR
YOU GOT AN EXCUSE FOR MISSING THAT SPIKE?
AH.
WE JUST FIGURED IT WOULD BE SAD IF YOU DIDN'T SCORE AT ALL, SO WE STARTED YOU OFF WITH A FREEBIE. ♡
One point. ♡
GRIN♥

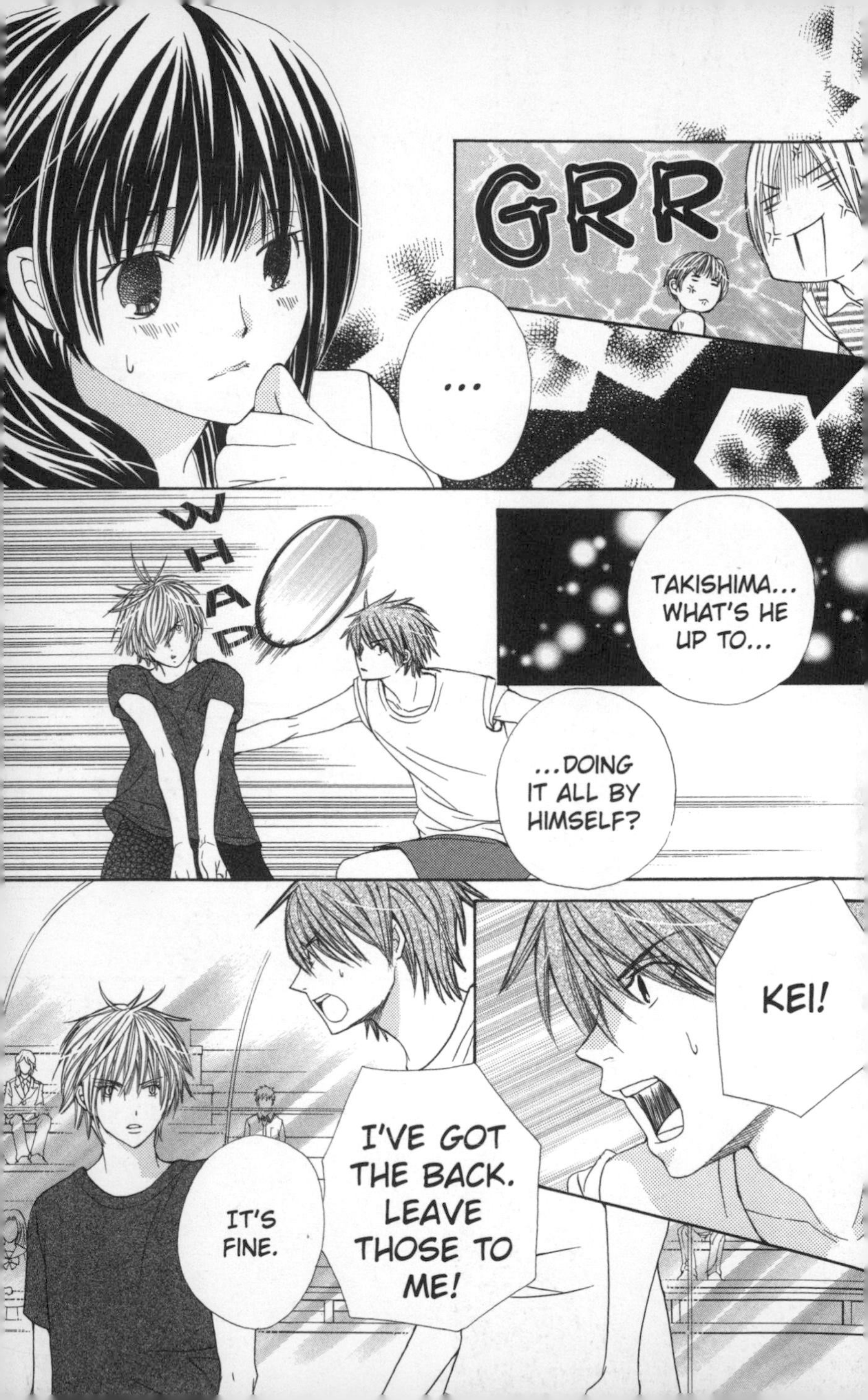
GRR
...
TAKISHIMA... WHAT'S HE UP TO...
...DOING IT ALL BY HIMSELF?
WHAP
KEI!
I'VE GOT THE BACK. LEAVE THOSE TO ME!
IT'S FINE.

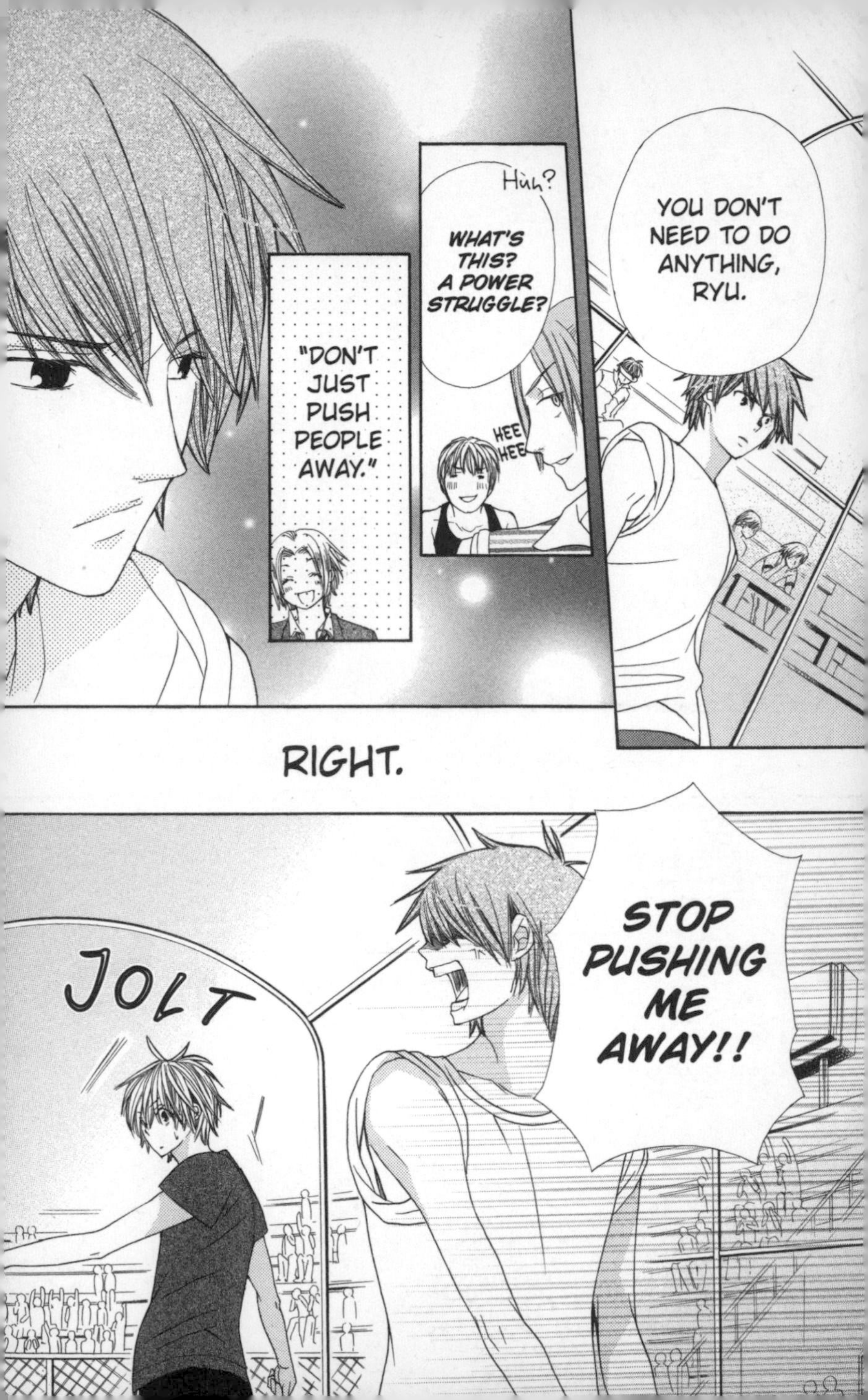
YOU DON'T NEED TO DO ANYTHING, RYU.
Huh?
WHAT'S THIS? A POWER STRUGGLE?
HEE HEE
"DON'T JUST PUSH PEOPLE AWAY."
RIGHT.
STOP PUSHING ME AWAY!!
JOLT

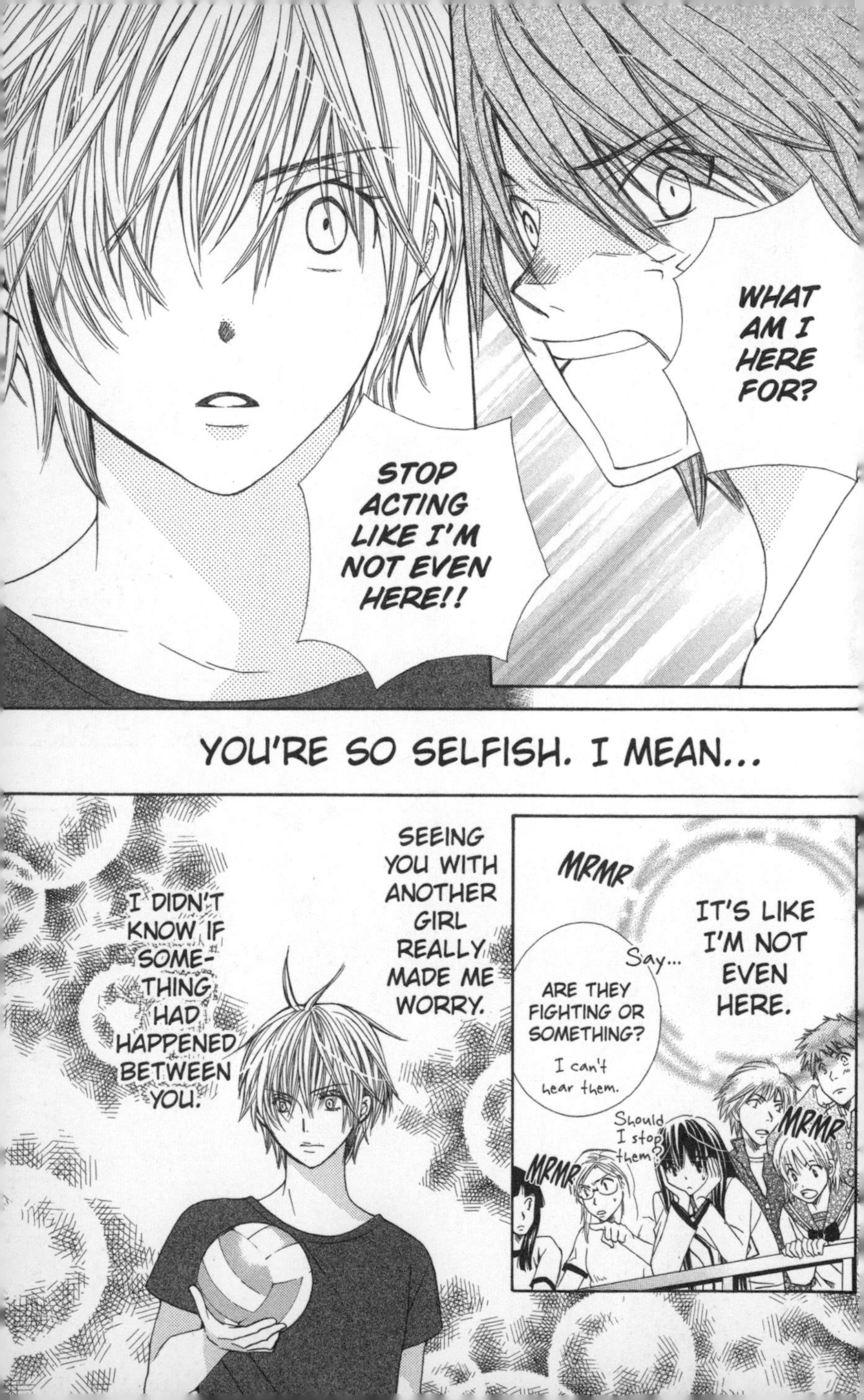
WHAT AM I HERE FOR?
STOP ACTING LIKE I'M NOT EVEN HERE!!
YOU'RE SO SELFISH. I MEAN...
IT'S LIKE I'M NOT EVEN HERE.
MRMR
Say...
ARE THEY FIGHTING OR SOMETHING?
I can't hear them.
Should I stop them?
MRMR
MRMR
SEEING YOU WITH ANOTHER GIRL REALLY MADE ME WORRY.
I DIDN'T KNOW IF SOME-THING HAD HAPPENED BETWEEN YOU.

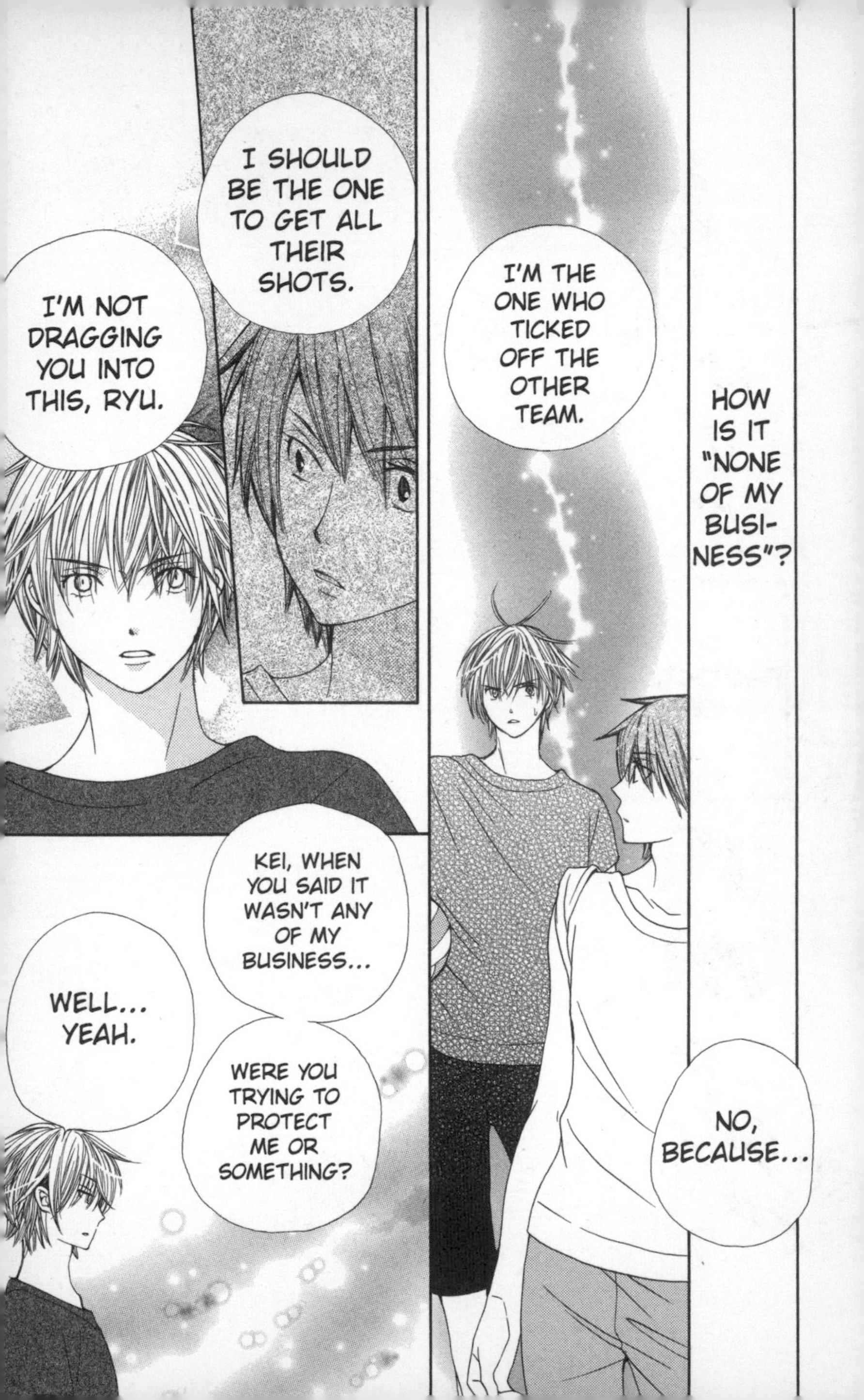
HOW IS IT "NONE OF MY BUSINESS"?
I'M THE ONE WHO TICKED OFF THE OTHER TEAM.
NO, BECAUSE...
I SHOULD BE THE ONE TO GET ALL THEIR SHOTS.
I'M NOT DRAGGING YOU INTO THIS, RYU.
KEI, WHEN YOU SAID IT WASN'T ANY OF MY BUSINESS...
WERE YOU TRYING TO PROTECT ME OR SOMETHING?
WELL... YEAH.

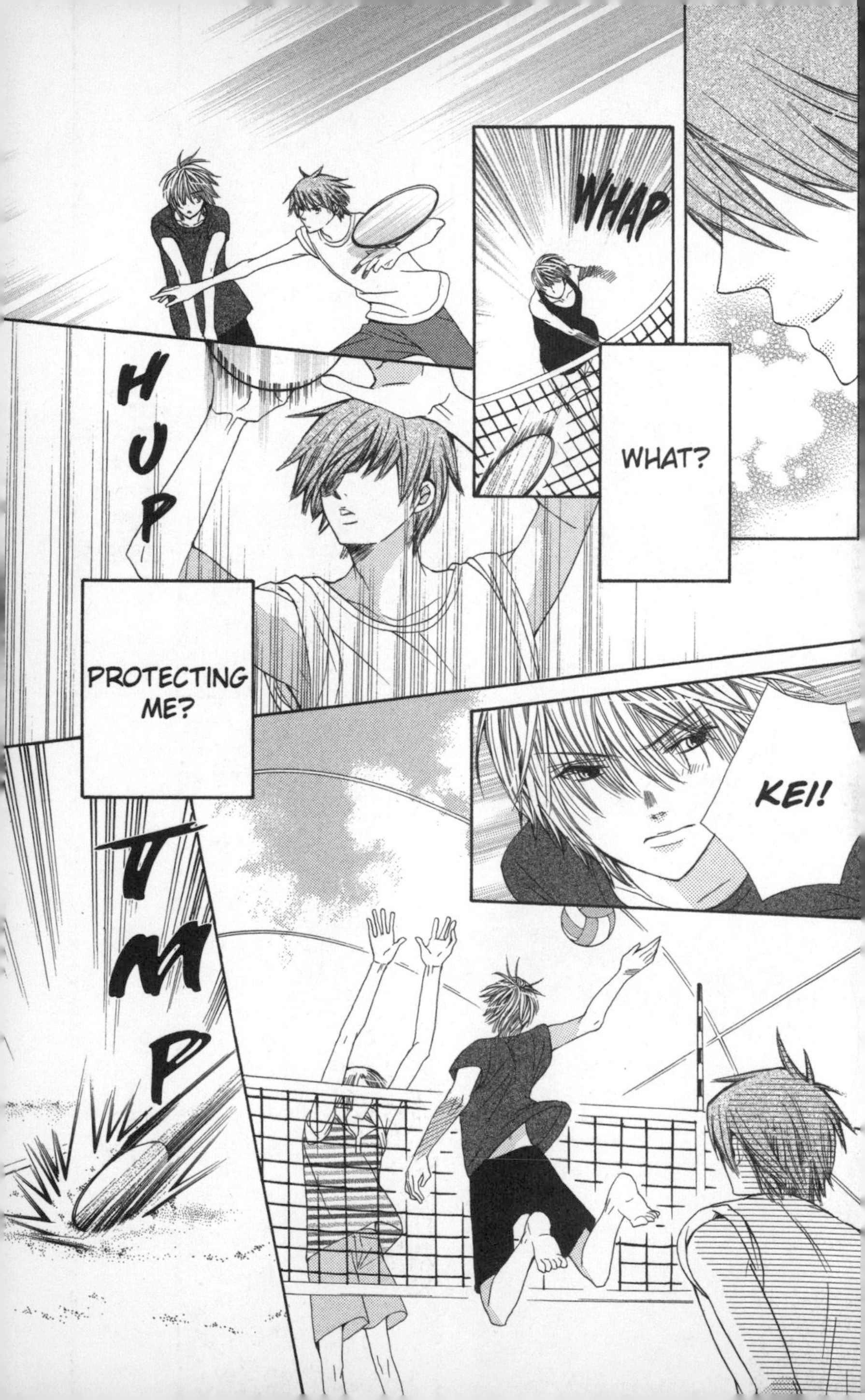
WHAT?
WHAP
HUP
PROTECTING ME?
KEI!
TMP

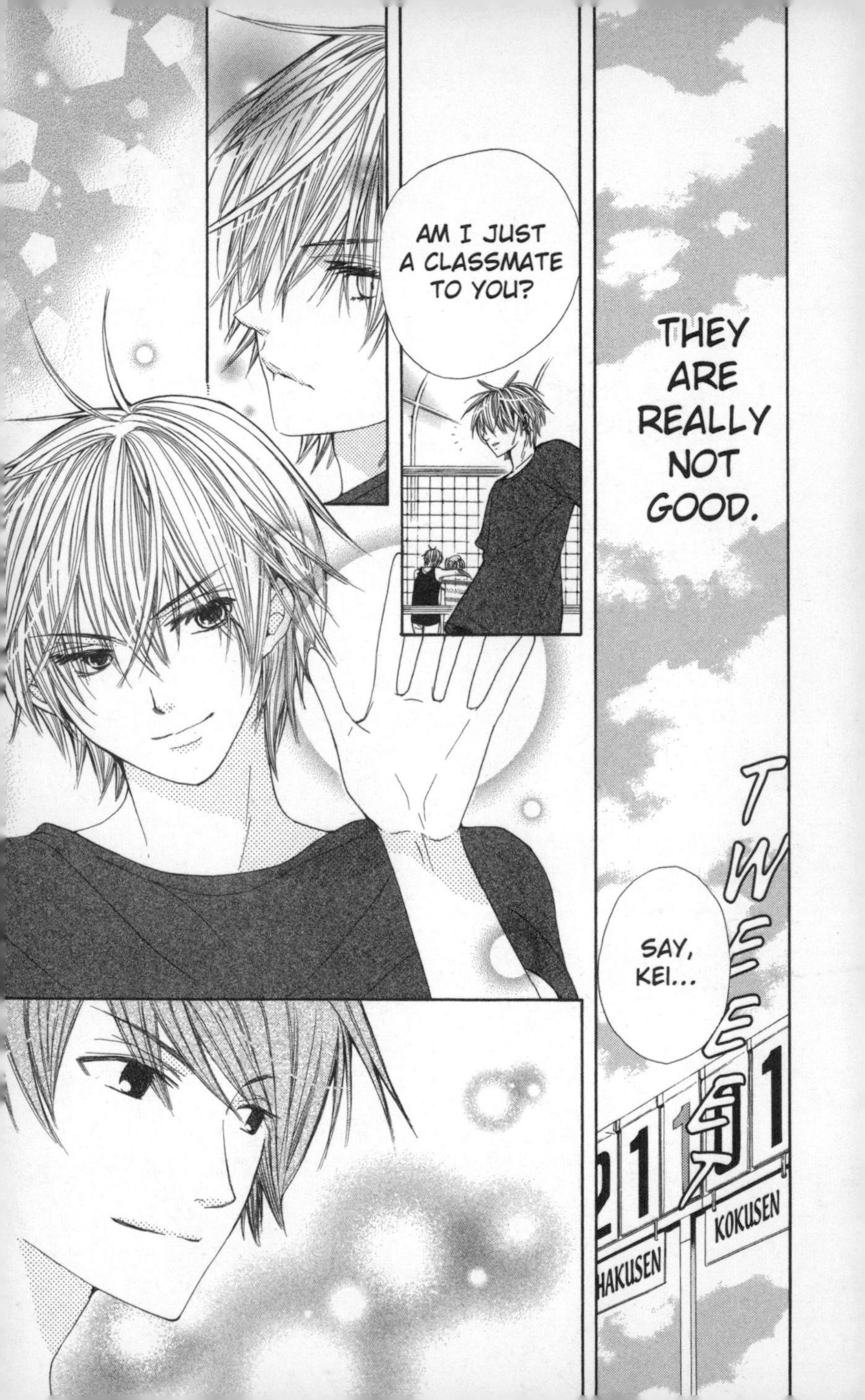
THEY ARE REALLY NOT GOOD.
TWEEE
SAY, KEI...
HAKUSEN
KOKUSEN
AM I JUST A CLASSMATE TO YOU?

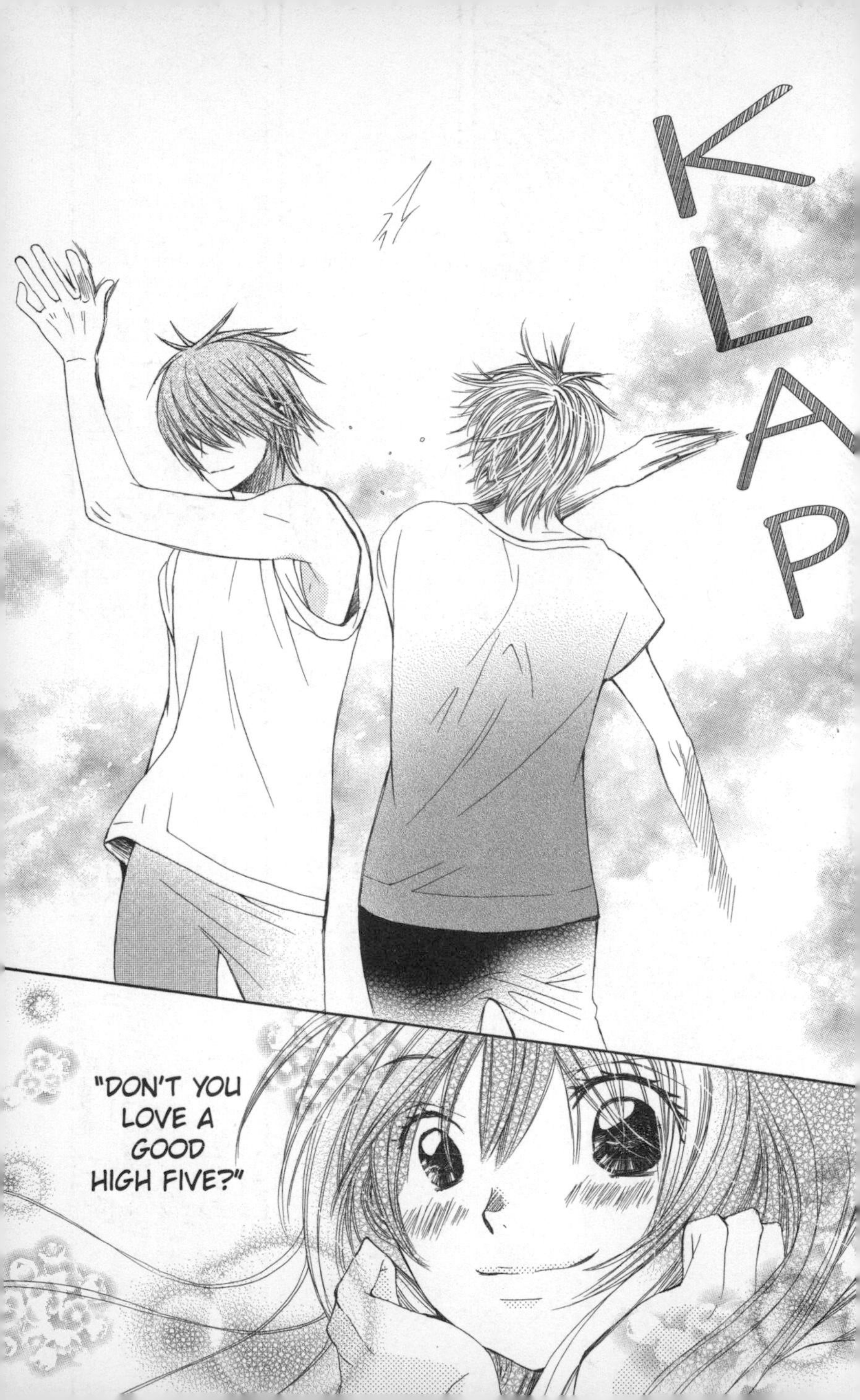
KLAP
"DON'T YOU LOVE A GOOD HIGH FIVE?"

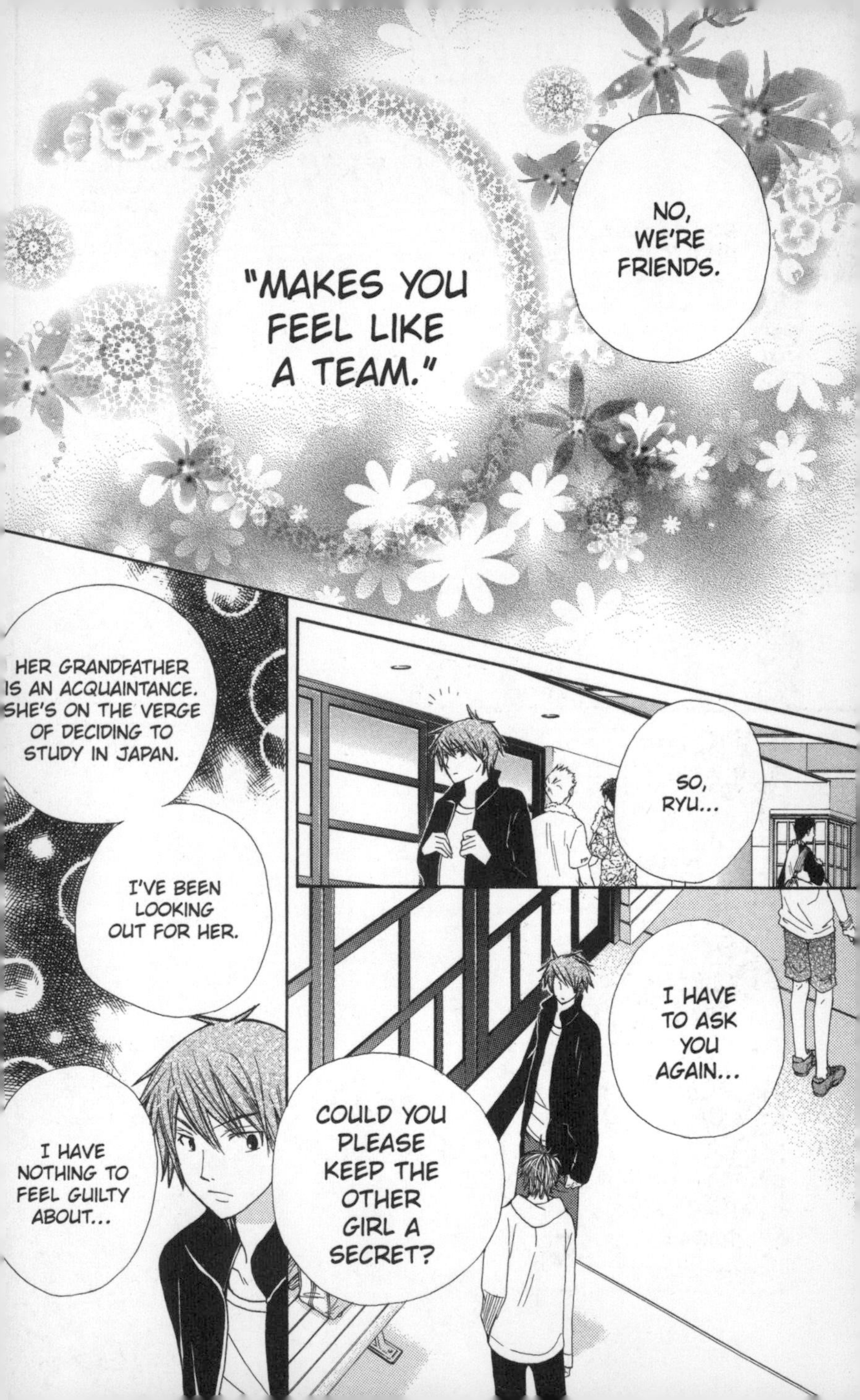
NO, WE'RE FRIENDS.
"MAKES YOU FEEL LIKE A TEAM."
SO, RYU...
I HAVE TO ASK YOU AGAIN...
COULD YOU PLEASE KEEP THE OTHER GIRL A SECRET?
HER GRANDFATHER IS AN ACQUAINTANCE. SHE'S ON THE VERGE OF DECIDING TO STUDY IN JAPAN.
I'VE BEEN LOOKING OUT FOR HER.
I HAVE NOTHING TO FEEL GUILTY ABOUT...

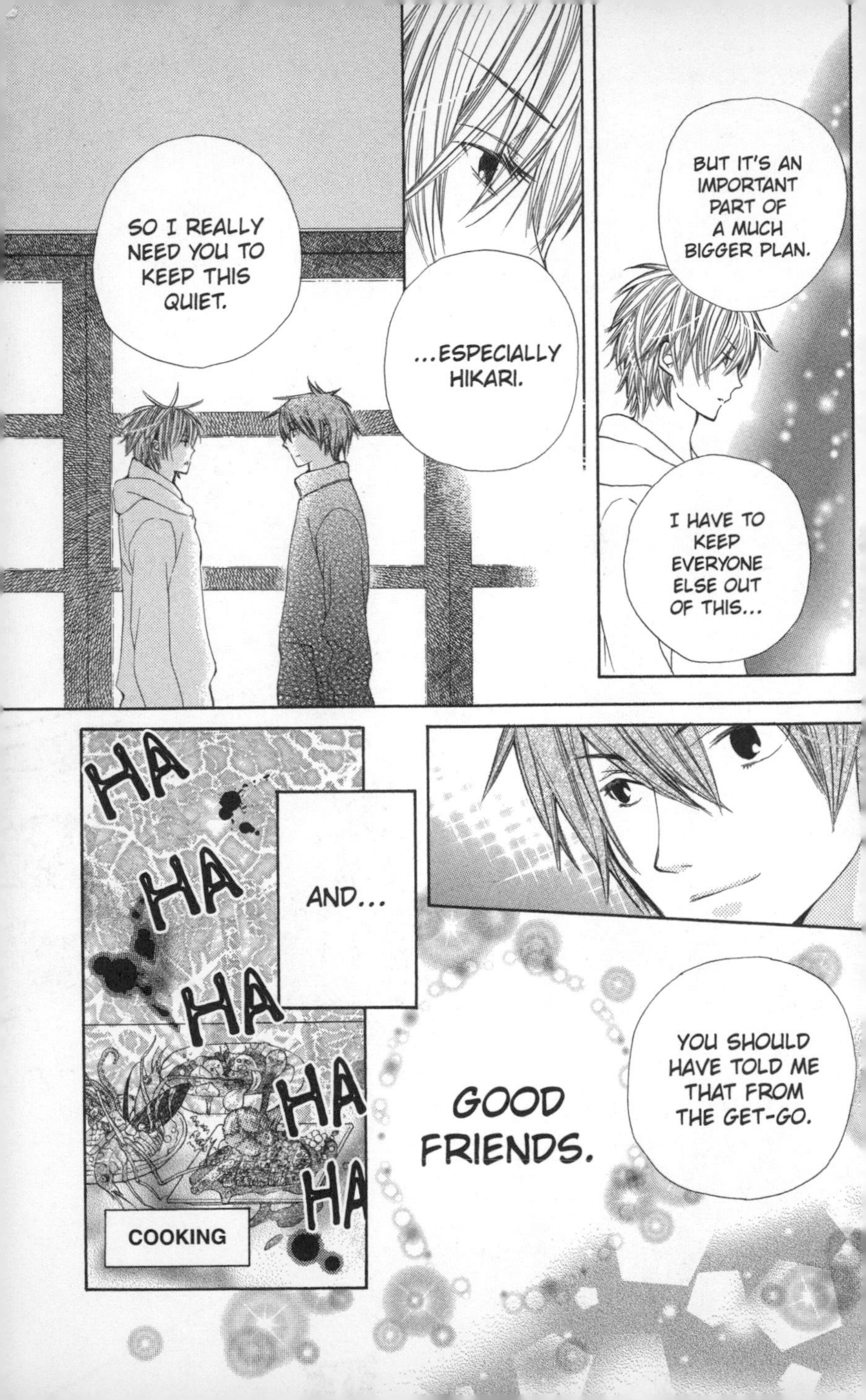
BUT IT'S AN IMPORTANT PART OF A MUCH BIGGER PLAN.
I HAVE TO KEEP EVERYONE ELSE OUT OF THIS...
...ESPECIALLY HIKARI.
SO I REALLY NEED YOU TO KEEP THIS QUIET.
YOU SHOULD HAVE TOLD ME THAT FROM THE GET-GO.
AND...
HA HA HA HA HA
COOKING
GOOD FRIENDS.

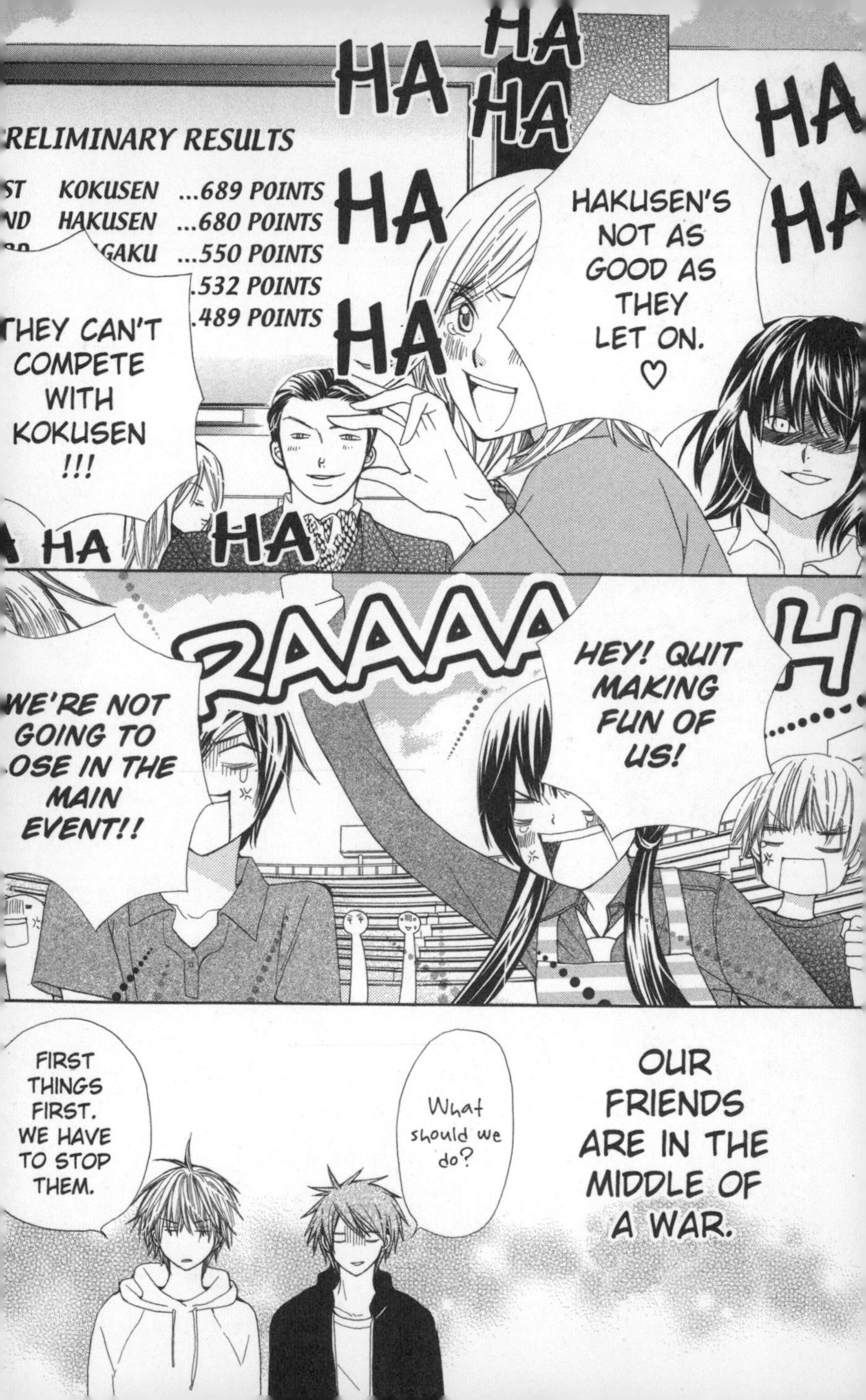
HA HA
HAKUSEN'S NOT AS GOOD AS THEY LET ON. ♡
HA HA HA HA HA
RELIMINARY RESULTS
ST KOKUSEN ...689 POINTS
ND HAKUSEN ...680 POINTS
GAKU ...550 POINTS
.532 POINTS
.489 POINTS
THEY CAN'T COMPETE WITH KOKUSEN !!!
HA HA
H
HEY! QUIT MAKING FUN OF US!
RAAAA
WE'RE NOT GOING TO OSE IN THE MAIN EVENT!!
OUR FRIENDS ARE IN THE MIDDLE OF A WAR.
What should we do?
FIRST THINGS FIRST. WE HAVE TO STOP THEM.

Chapter 66

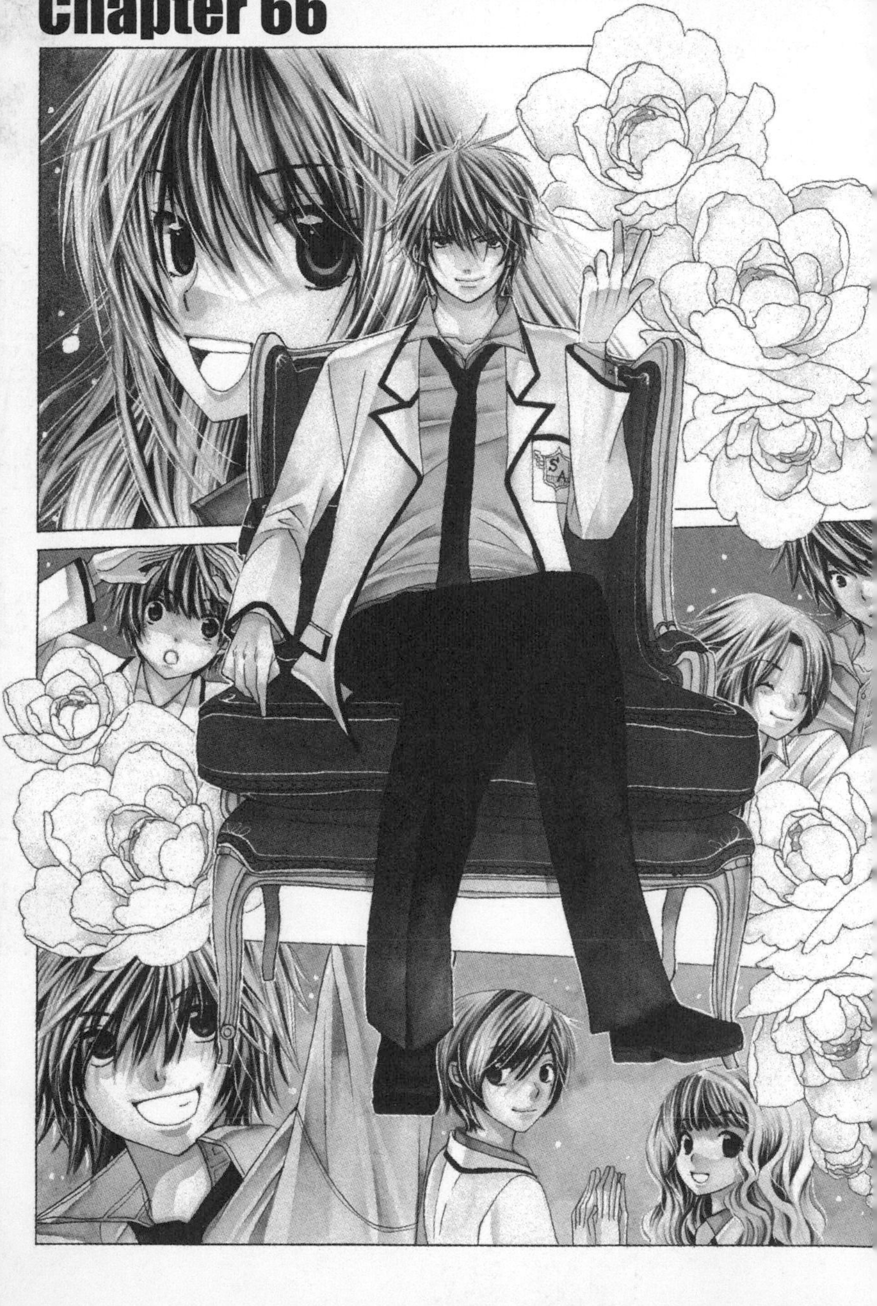

Special

A!

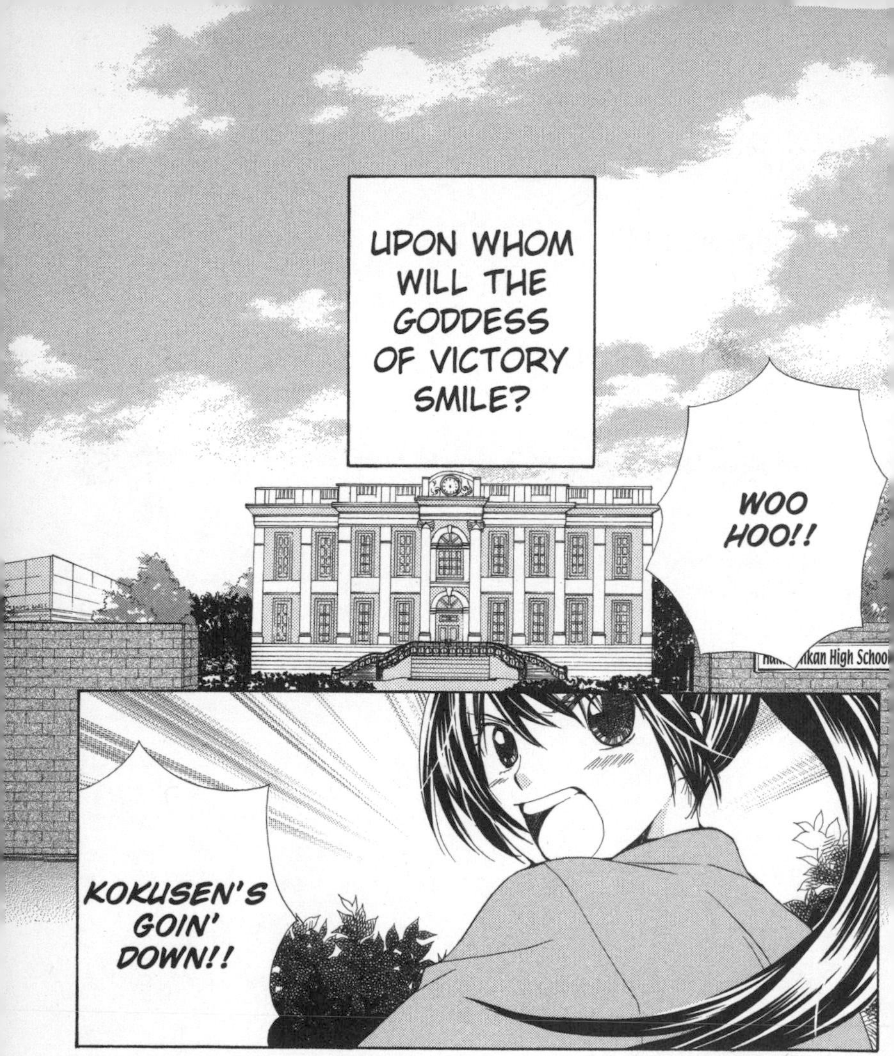
UPON WHOM WILL THE GODDESS OF VICTORY SMILE?
WOO HOO!!
KOKUSEN'S GOIN' DOWN!!

•COLOR INKS•

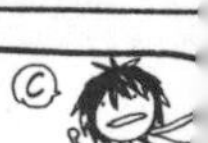

I USE IC COPY FILM A LOT WHEN I'M DRAWING IN COLOR AND I LIKE IT FOR MASKING. I'M NOT GREAT WITH REGULAR MASKING SHEETS, BUT THE FILM'S REALLY EASY TO USE BECAUSE THE TONE IS THE SAME.

I LIKE TO TRY STUFF LIKE STICKING LACE SEALS ALL OVER IT AND COLORING ON TOP OF THEM. DRAWING BY HAND IS A LOT OF FUN.

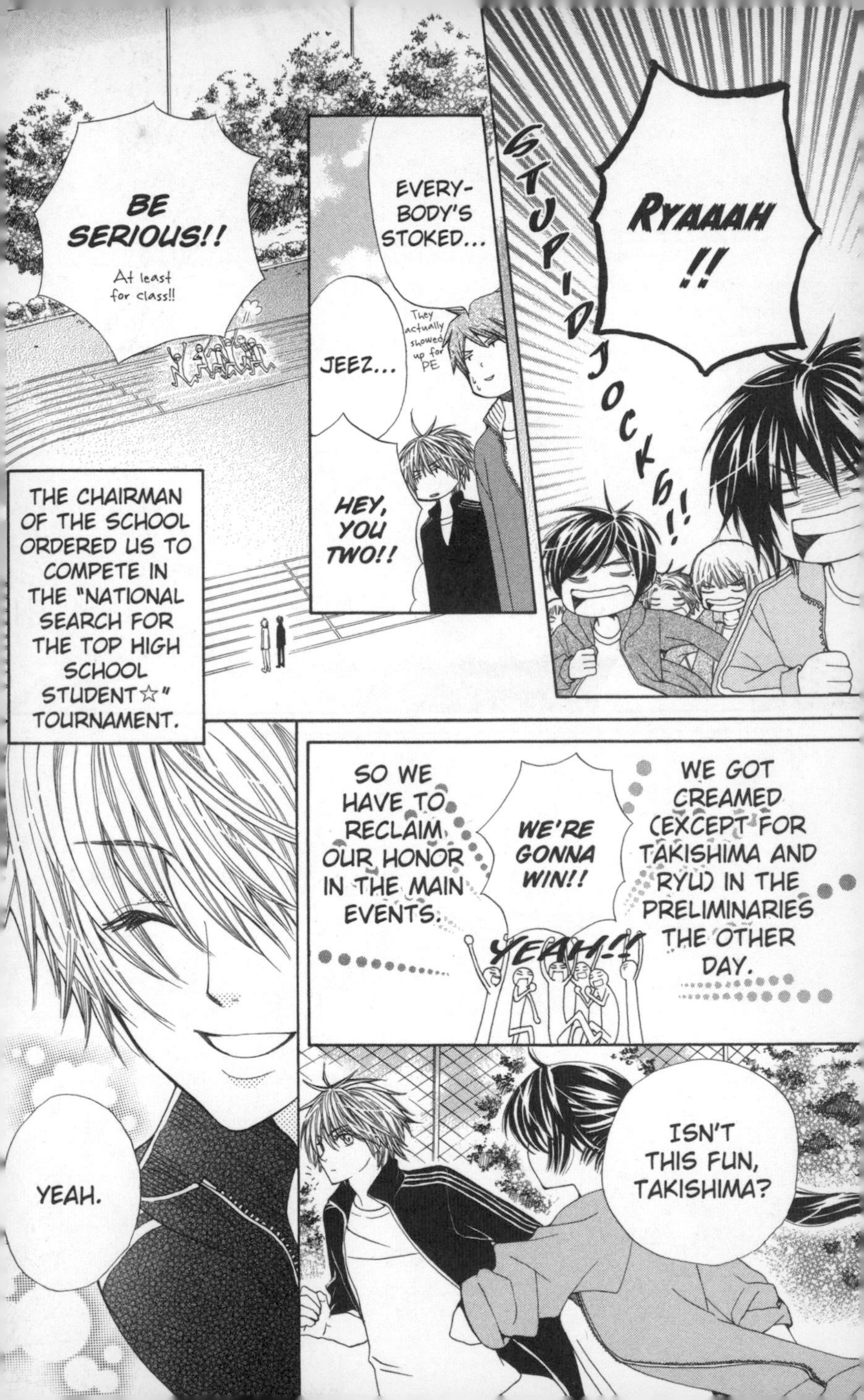
RYAAAH!!
STUPID JOCKS!!
EVERY-BODY'S STOKED...
They actually showed up for PE.
JEEZ...
HEY, YOU TWO!!
BE SERIOUS!!
At least for class!!
THE CHAIRMAN OF THE SCHOOL ORDERED US TO COMPETE IN THE "NATIONAL SEARCH FOR THE TOP HIGH SCHOOL STUDENT☆" TOURNAMENT.
WE GOT CREAMED (EXCEPT FOR TAKISHIMA AND RYU) IN THE PRELIMINARIES THE OTHER DAY.
WE'RE GONNA WIN!!
SO WE HAVE TO RECLAIM OUR HONOR IN THE MAIN EVENTS.
YEAH!!
ISN'T THIS FUN, TAKISHIMA?
YEAH.

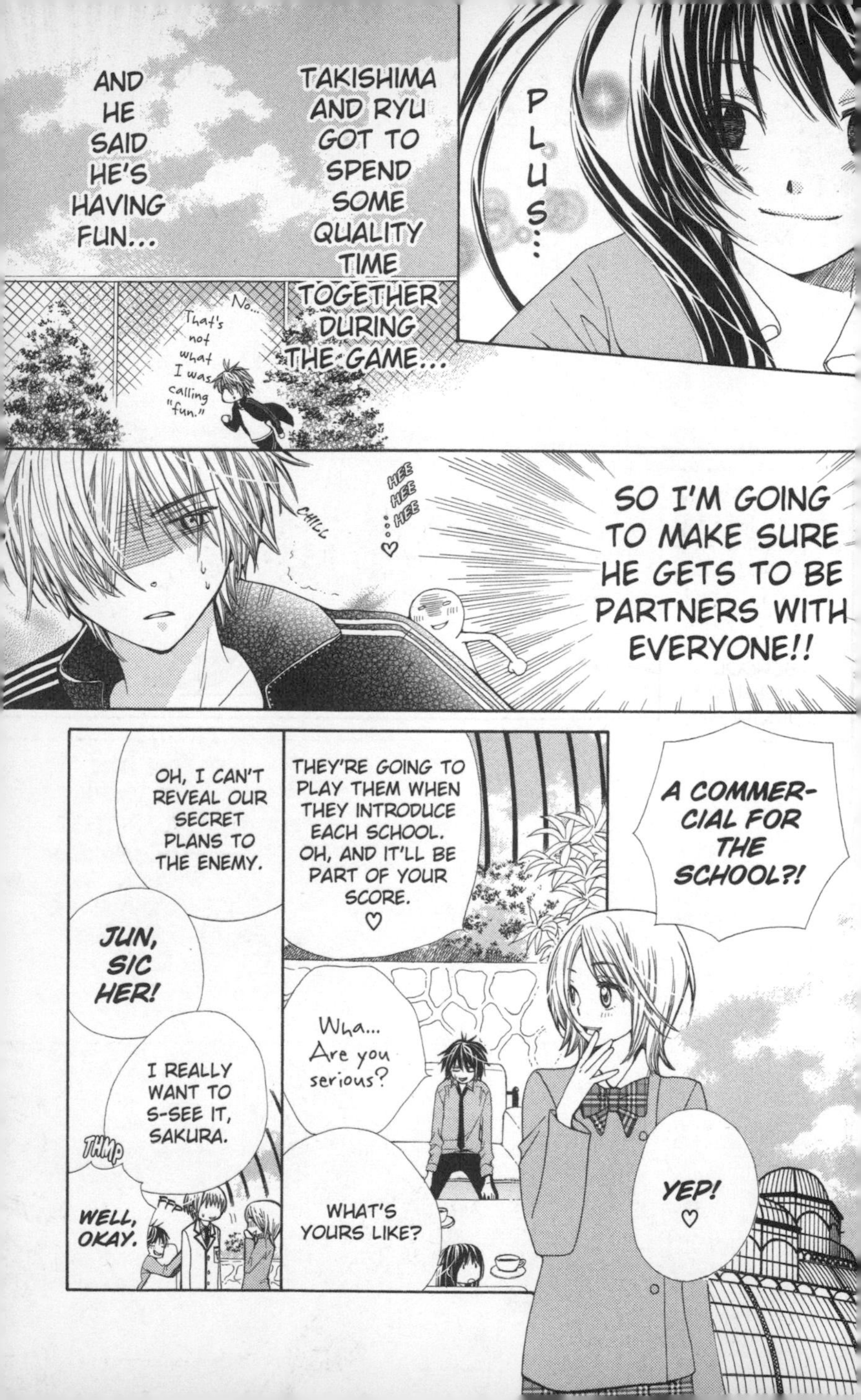
PLUS...
TAKISHIMA AND RYU GOT TO SPEND SOME QUALITY TIME TOGETHER DURING THE GAME...
AND HE SAID HE'S HAVING FUN...
No... That's not what I was calling "fun."
SO I'M GOING TO MAKE SURE HE GETS TO BE PARTNERS WITH EVERYONE!!
HEE HEE HEE ♡
CHILL
A COMMERCIAL FOR THE SCHOOL?!
YEP! ♡
THEY'RE GOING TO PLAY THEM WHEN THEY INTRODUCE EACH SCHOOL. OH, AND IT'LL BE PART OF YOUR SCORE. ♡
Wha... Are you serious?
WHAT'S YOURS LIKE?
OH, I CAN'T REVEAL OUR SECRET PLANS TO THE ENEMY.
JUN, SIC HER!
I REALLY WANT TO S-SEE IT, SAKURA.
THMP
WELL, OKAY.

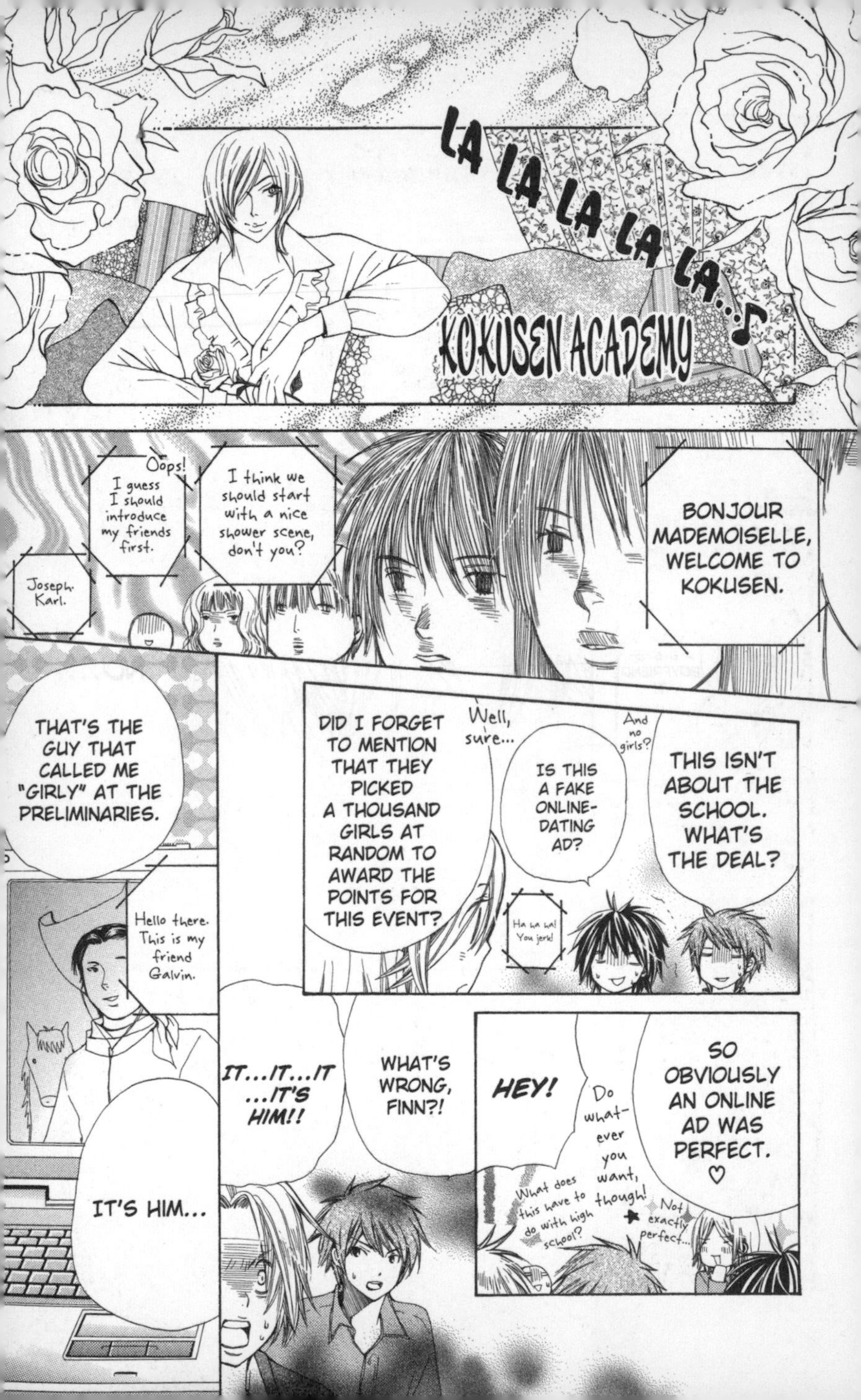

LA LA LA LA LA...♪
KOKUSEN ACADEMY
BONJOUR MADEMOISELLE, WELCOME TO KOKUSEN.
I think we should start with a nice shower scene, don't you?
Oops! I guess I should introduce my friends first.
Joseph. Karl.
THIS ISN'T ABOUT THE SCHOOL. WHAT'S THE DEAL?
And no girls?
IS THIS A FAKE ONLINE-DATING AD?
Well, sure...
DID I FORGET TO MENTION THAT THEY PICKED A THOUSAND GIRLS AT RANDOM TO AWARD THE POINTS FOR THIS EVENT?
Ha ha ha! You jerk!
SO OBVIOUSLY AN ONLINE AD WAS PERFECT. ♡
Not exactly perfect...
Do whatever you want, though!
What does this have to do with high school?
HEY!
WHAT'S WRONG, FINN?!
IT...IT...IT ...IT'S HIM!!
THAT'S THE GUY THAT CALLED ME "GIRLY" AT THE PRELIMINARIES.
Hello there. This is my friend Galvin.
IT'S HIM...

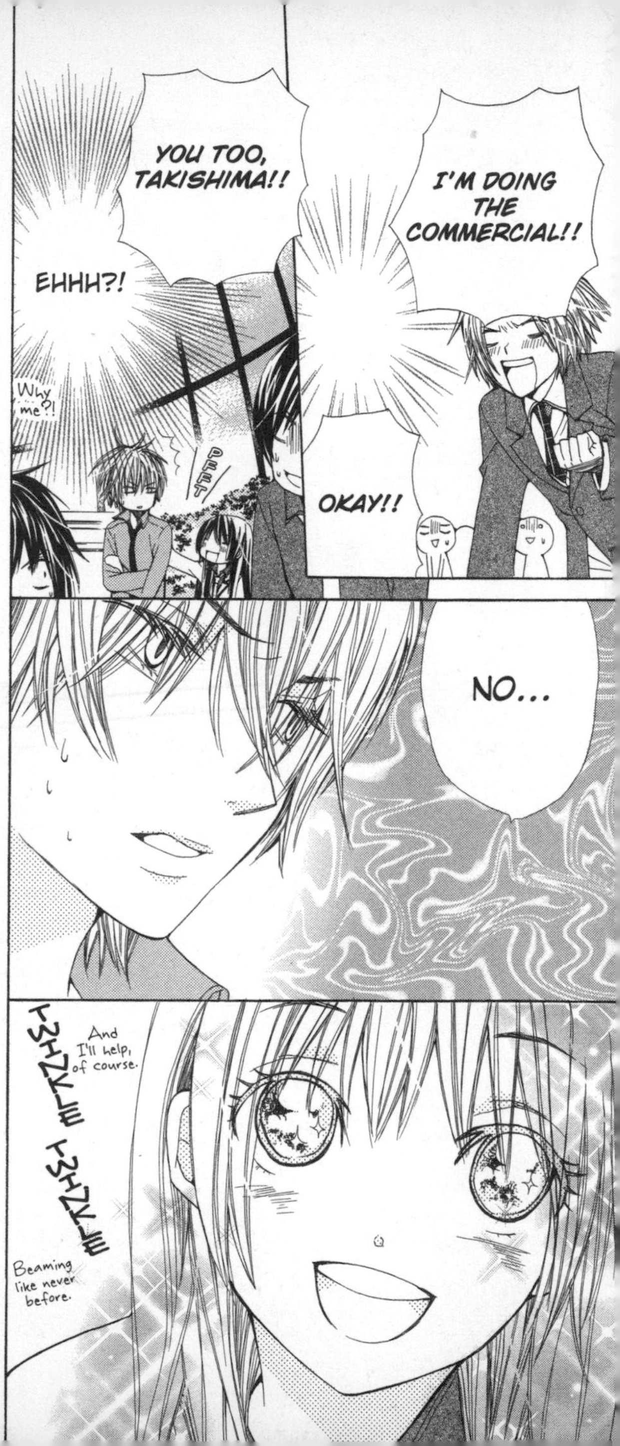
I'M DOING THE COMMERCIAL!!
OKAY!!
YOU TOO, TAKISHIMA!!
EHHH?!
Why me?!
PFFT
NO...
And I'll help, of course.
TWINKLE TWINKLE
Beaming like never before.

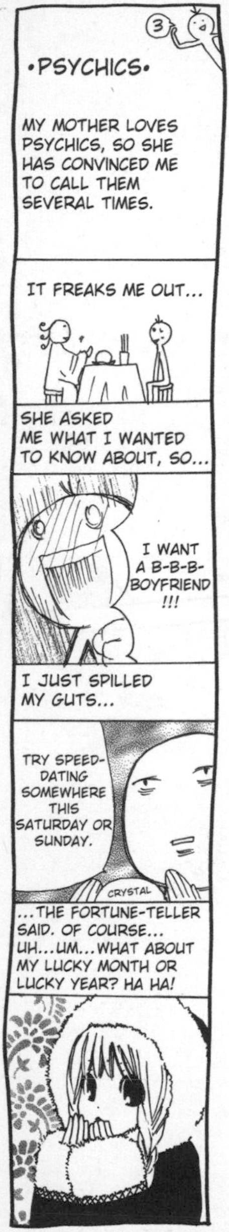
3
•PSYCHICS•
MY MOTHER LOVES PSYCHICS, SO SHE HAS CONVINCED ME TO CALL THEM SEVERAL TIMES.
IT FREAKS ME OUT...
SHE ASKED ME WHAT I WANTED TO KNOW ABOUT, SO...
I WANT A B-B-B-BOYFRIEND!!!
I JUST SPILLED MY GUTS...
TRY SPEED-DATING SOMEWHERE THIS SATURDAY OR SUNDAY.
CRYSTAL
...THE FORTUNE-TELLER SAID. OF COURSE... UH...UM...WHAT ABOUT MY LUCKY MONTH OR LUCKY YEAR? HA HA!

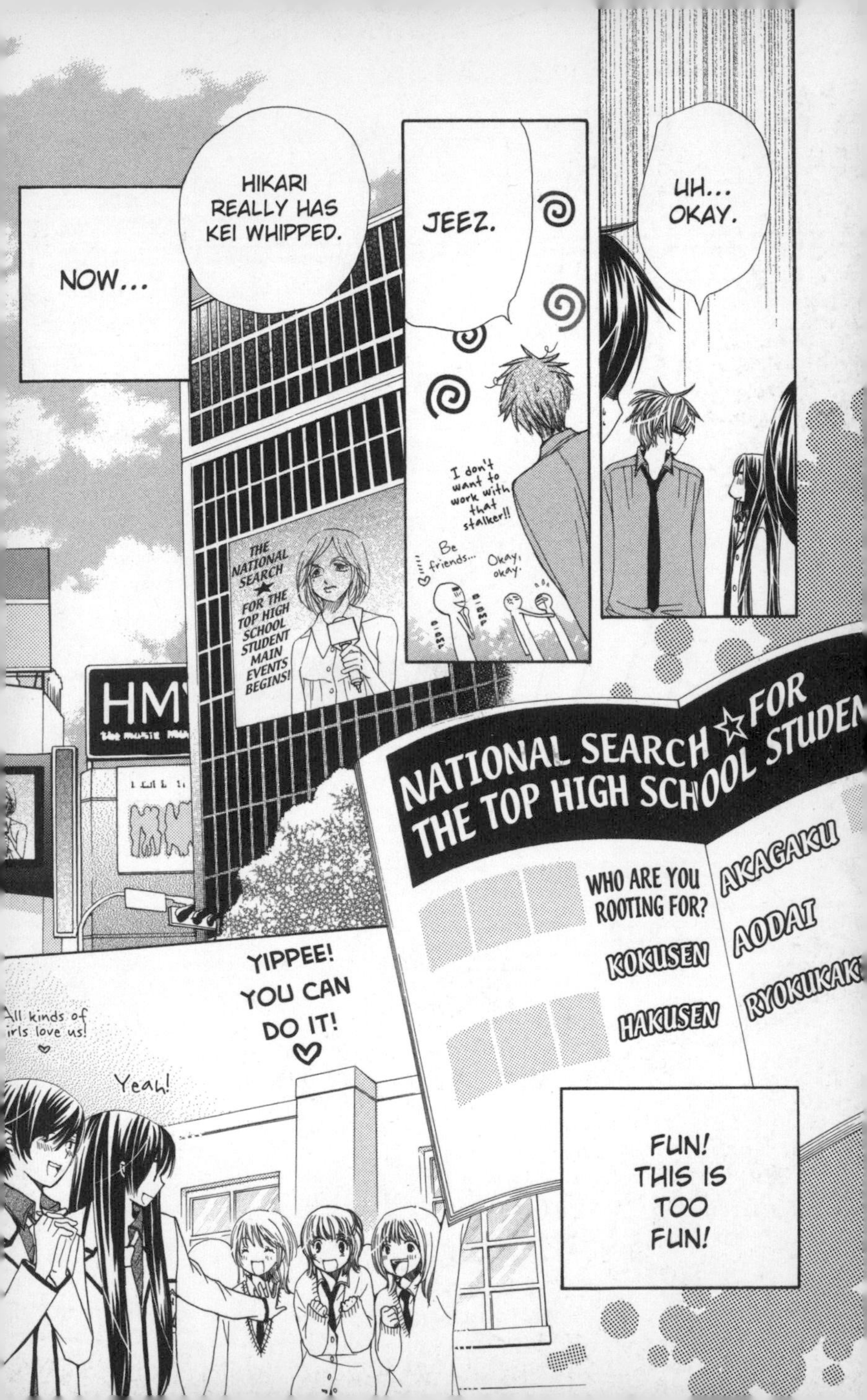
UH... OKAY.
JEEZ.
I don't want to work with that stalker!!
Be friends...
Okay, okay.
HIKARI REALLY HAS KEI WHIPPED.
NOW...
THE NATIONAL SEARCH ★ FOR THE TOP HIGH SCHOOL STUDENT MAIN EVENTS BEGINS!
HMV
NATIONAL SEARCH ☆ FOR THE TOP HIGH SCHOOL STUDEN
WHO ARE YOU ROOTING FOR?
AKAGAKU
AODAI
RYOKUKAKU
KOKUSEN
HAKUSEN
FUN! THIS IS TOO FUN!
YIPPEE! YOU CAN DO IT!
All kinds of irls love us!
Yeah!

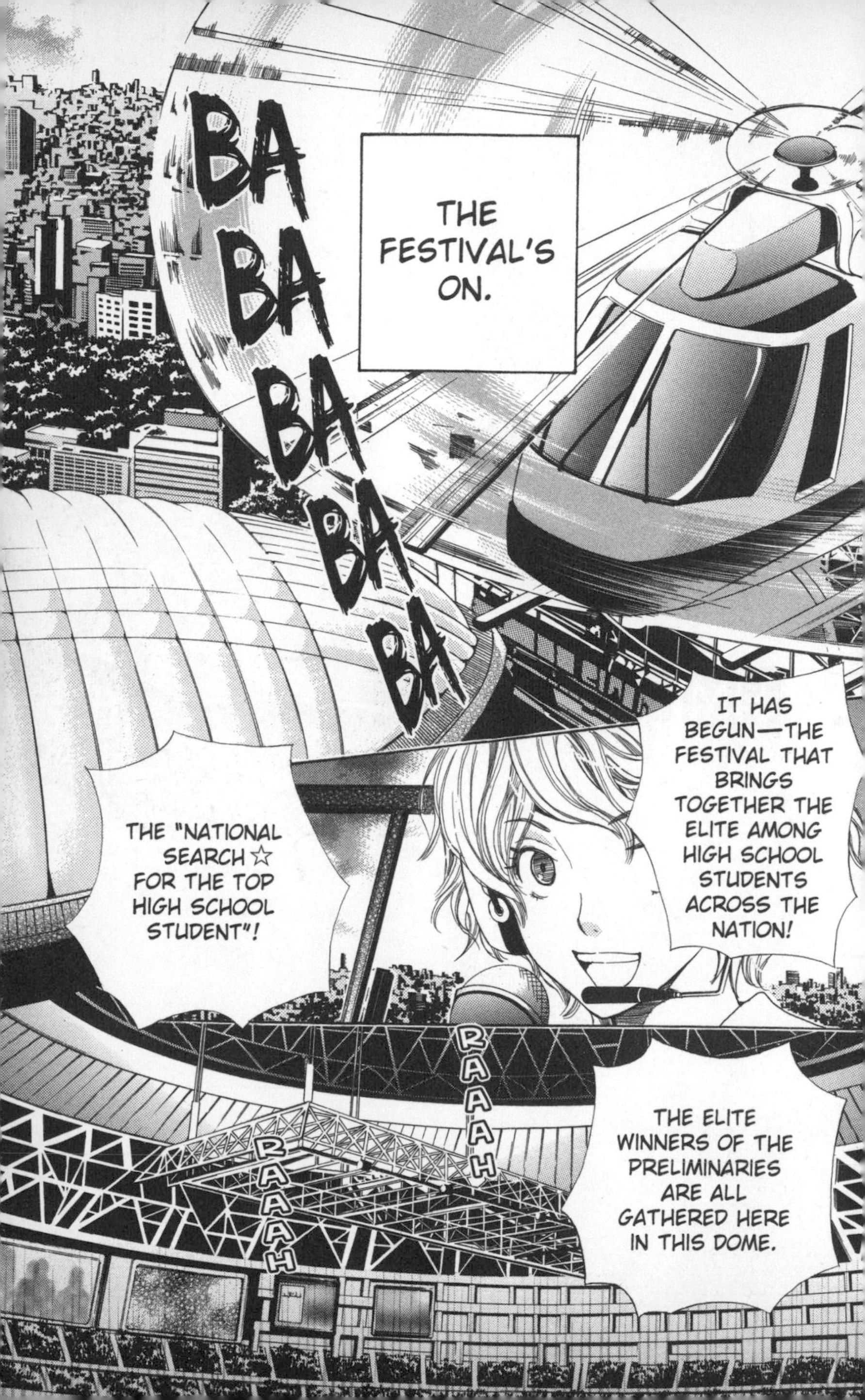
THE FESTIVAL'S ON.
BA BA BA BA BA BA
IT HAS BEGUN—THE FESTIVAL THAT BRINGS TOGETHER THE ELITE AMONG HIGH SCHOOL STUDENTS ACROSS THE NATION!
THE "NATIONAL SEARCH☆ FOR THE TOP HIGH SCHOOL STUDENT"!
THE ELITE WINNERS OF THE PRELIMINARIES ARE ALL GATHERED HERE IN THIS DOME.
RAAAAH
RAAAAH

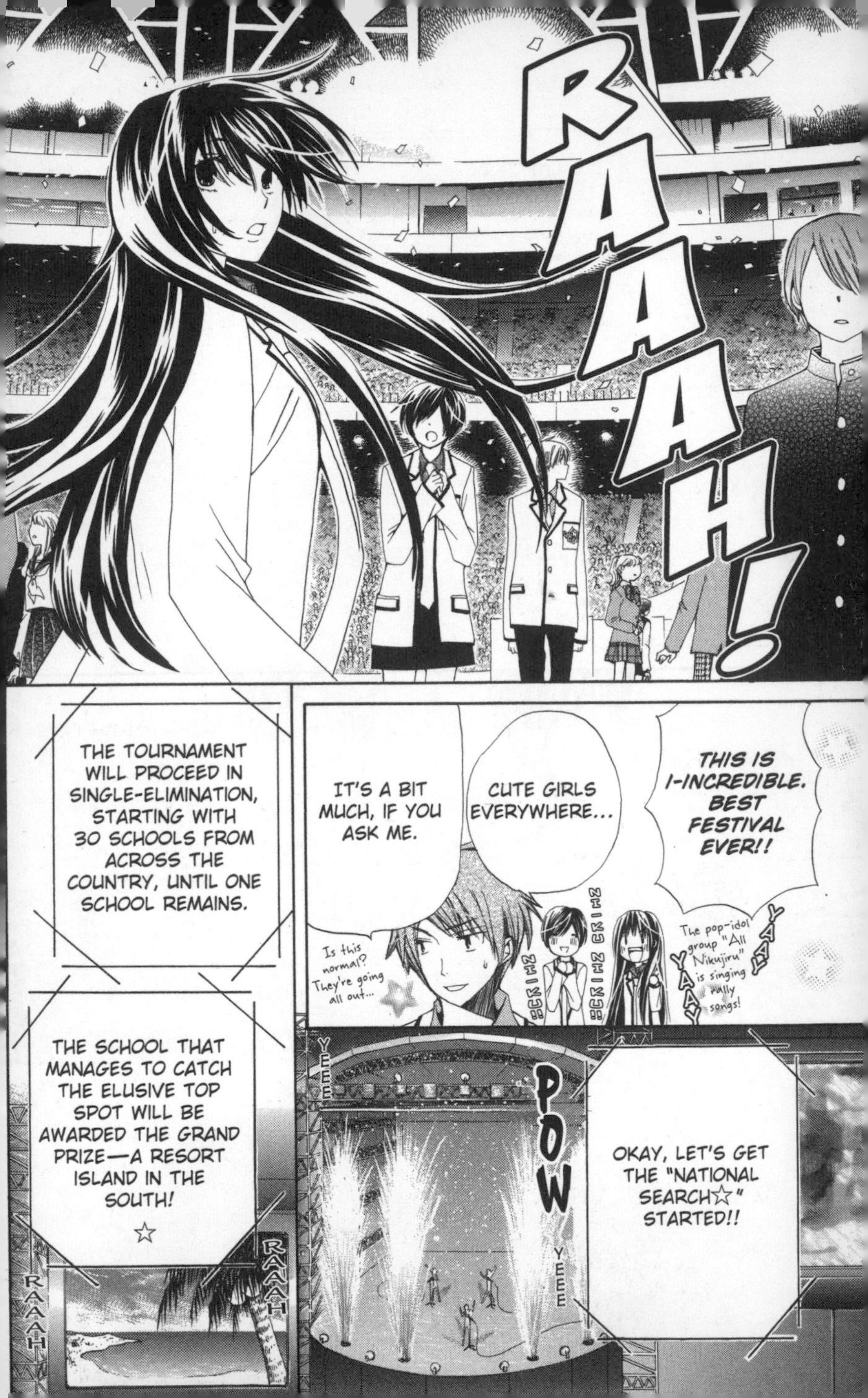

RAAAAH!
THIS IS I-INCREDIBLE. BEST FESTIVAL EVER!!
YAAAY
YAAAY
The pop-idol group "All Nikujiru" is singing rally songs!
NIKU NIKU!!
NIKU!!
CUTE GIRLS EVERYWHERE...
IT'S A BIT MUCH, IF YOU ASK ME.
Is this normal? They're going all out...
THE TOURNAMENT WILL PROCEED IN SINGLE-ELIMINATION, STARTING WITH 30 SCHOOLS FROM ACROSS THE COUNTRY, UNTIL ONE SCHOOL REMAINS.
OKAY, LET'S GET THE "NATIONAL SEARCH☆" STARTED!!
POW
YEEE
YEEE
THE SCHOOL THAT MANAGES TO CATCH THE ELUSIVE TOP SPOT WILL BE AWARDED THE GRAND PRIZE—A RESORT ISLAND IN THE SOUTH! ☆
RAAAAH
RAAAAH

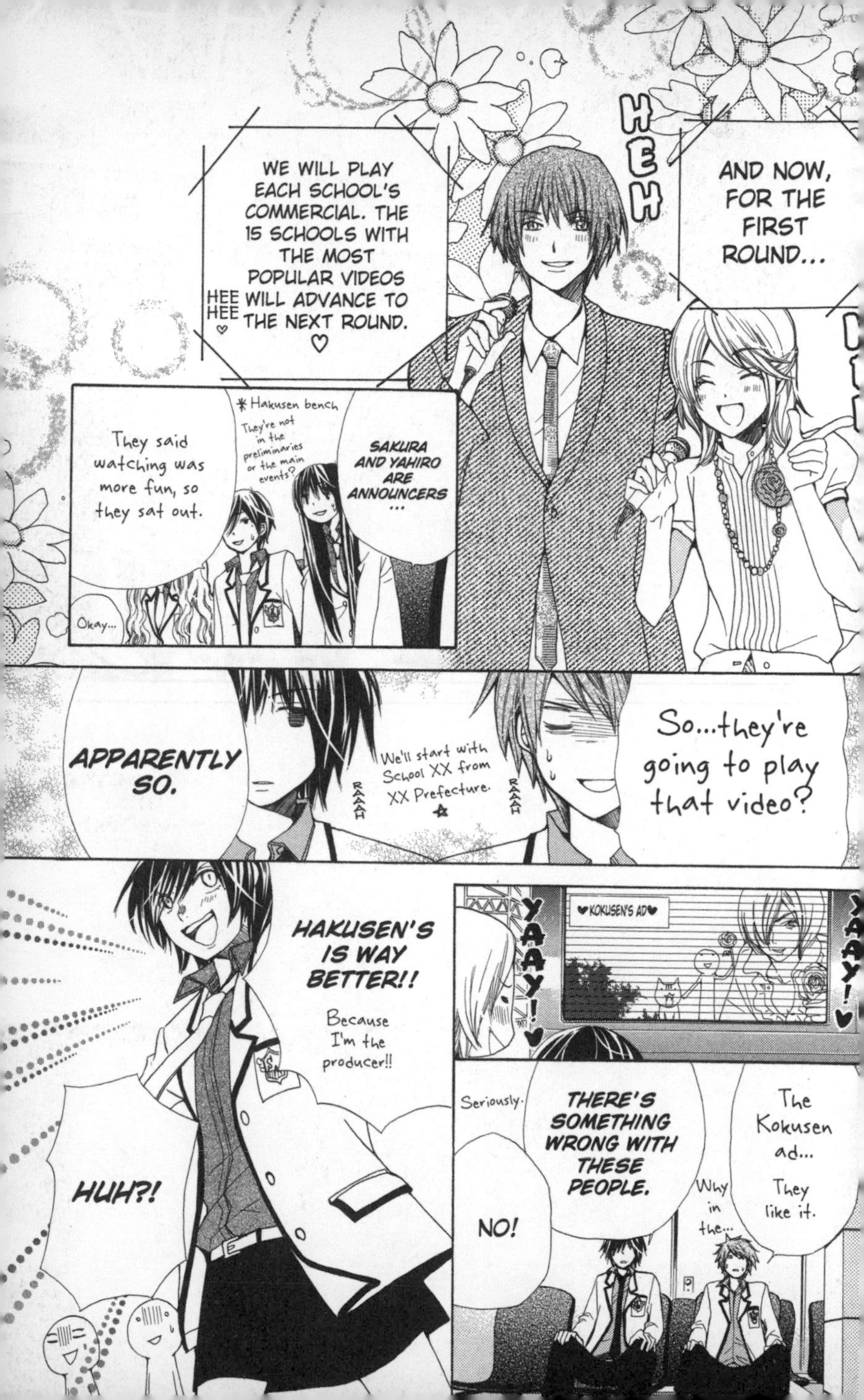
HEH
AND NOW, FOR THE FIRST ROUND...
WE WILL PLAY EACH SCHOOL'S COMMERCIAL. THE 15 SCHOOLS WITH THE MOST POPULAR VIDEOS WILL ADVANCE TO THE NEXT ROUND. ♡
HEE HEE ♡
SAKURA AND YAHIRO ARE ANNOUNCERS...
✱Hakusen bench
They're not in the preliminaries or the main events?
They said watching was more fun, so they sat out.
Okay...
So...they're going to play that video?
RAAAH
We'll start with School XX from XX Prefecture. ☆
RAAAH
APPARENTLY SO.
♥KOKUSEN'S AD♥
YAAAY!♥
YAAAY!♥
The Kokusen ad... They like it.
Why in the...
THERE'S SOMETHING WRONG WITH THESE PEOPLE.
Seriously.
NO!
HAKUSEN'S IS WAY BETTER!!
Because I'm the producer!!
HUH?!

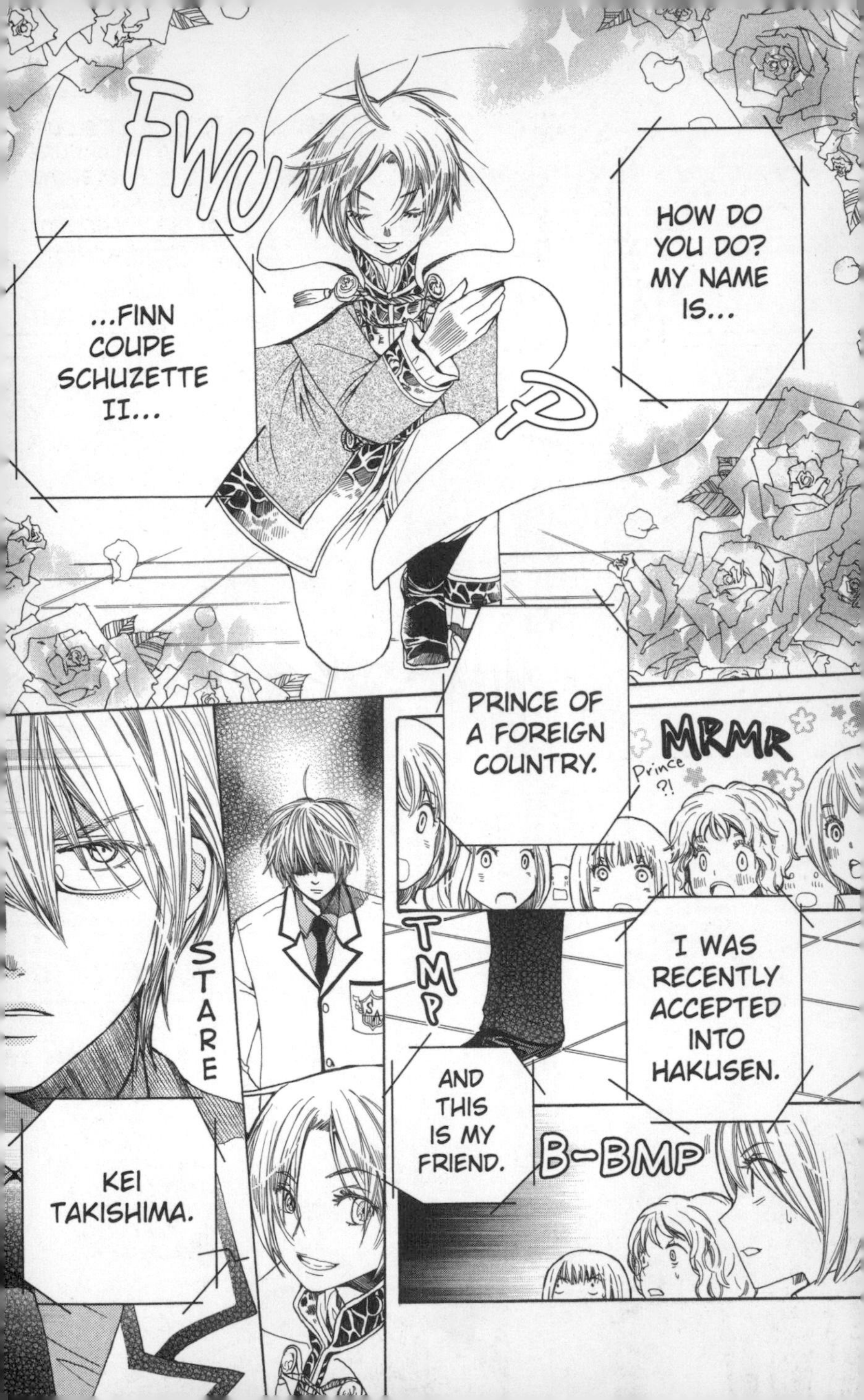
HOW DO YOU DO? MY NAME IS...
FWU
...FINN COUPE SCHUZETTE II...
PRINCE OF A FOREIGN COUNTRY.
MRMR
Prince ?!
I WAS RECENTLY ACCEPTED INTO HAKUSEN.
TMP
AND THIS IS MY FRIEND.
B-BMP
STARE
KEI TAKISHIMA.

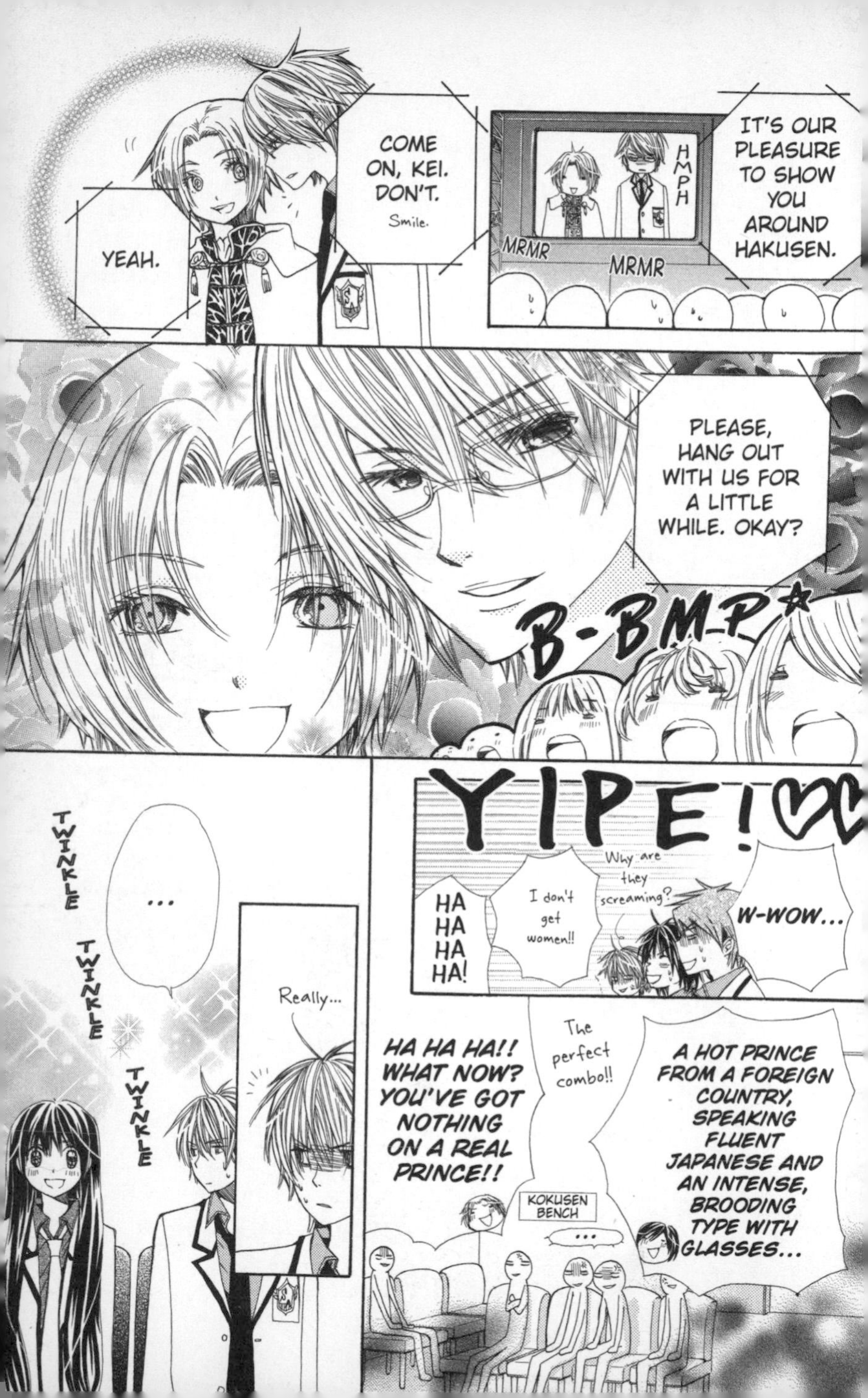
IT'S OUR PLEASURE TO SHOW YOU AROUND HAKUSEN.
HMPH
MRMR
MRMR
COME ON, KEI. DON'T.
Smile.
YEAH.
PLEASE, HANG OUT WITH US FOR A LITTLE WHILE. OKAY?
B-BMP☆
YIPE!
W-WOW...
Why are they screaming?
I don't get women!!
HA HA HA HA HA!
A HOT PRINCE FROM A FOREIGN COUNTRY, SPEAKING FLUENT JAPANESE AND AN INTENSE, BROODING TYPE WITH GLASSES...
The perfect combo!!
HA HA HA!! WHAT NOW? YOU'VE GOT NOTHING ON A REAL PRINCE!!
KOKUSEN BENCH
...
Really...
...
TWINKLE
TWINKLE
TWINKLE

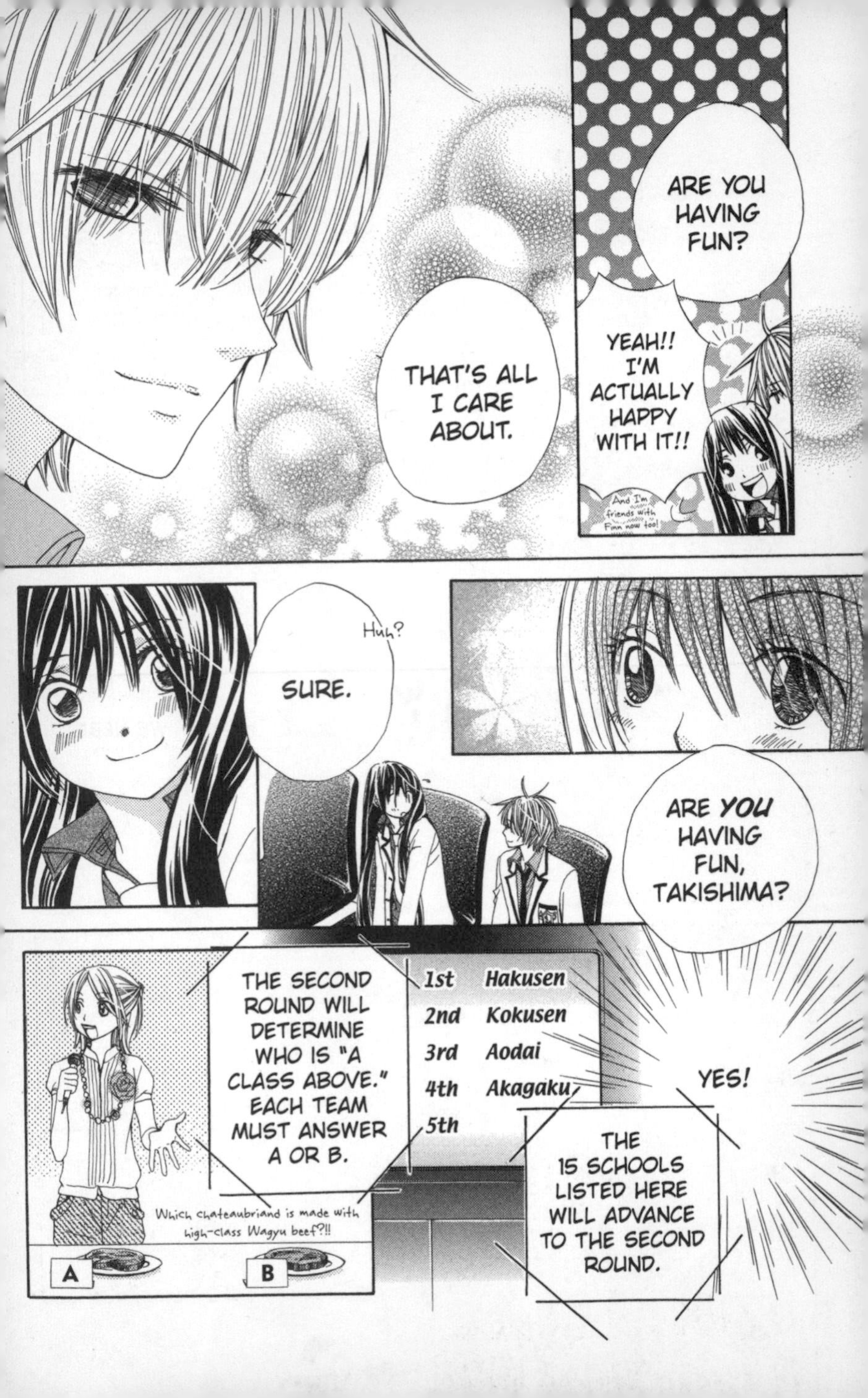
ARE YOU HAVING FUN?
YEAH!! I'M ACTUALLY HAPPY WITH IT!!
And I'm friends with Finn now too!
THAT'S ALL I CARE ABOUT.
ARE YOU HAVING FUN, TAKISHIMA?
Huh?
SURE.
YES!
THE 15 SCHOOLS LISTED HERE WILL ADVANCE TO THE SECOND ROUND.
1st Hakusen
2nd Kokusen
3rd Aodai
4th Akagaku
5th
THE SECOND ROUND WILL DETERMINE WHO IS "A CLASS ABOVE." EACH TEAM MUST ANSWER A OR B.
Which chateaubriand is made with high-class Wagyu beef?!!
A
B

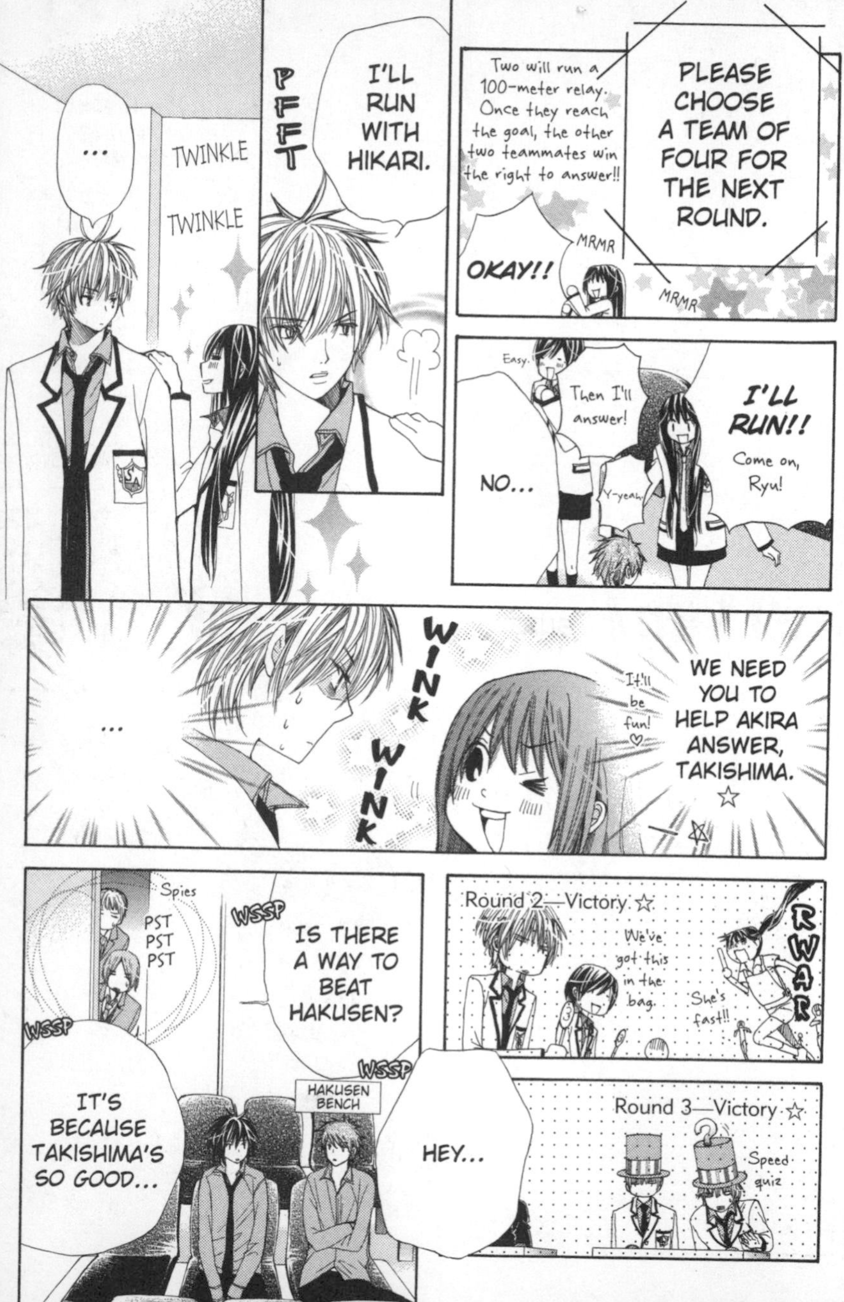
PLEASE CHOOSE A TEAM OF FOUR FOR THE NEXT ROUND.
Two will run a 100-meter relay. Once they reach the goal, the other two teammates win the right to answer!!
MRMR
MRMR
OKAY!!
I'LL RUN!!
Come on, Ryu!
Easy.
Then I'll answer!
Y-yeah.
NO...
I'LL RUN WITH HIKARI.
PFFT
...
TWINKLE
TWINKLE
WE NEED YOU TO HELP AKIRA ANSWER, TAKISHIMA. ☆
It'll be fun! ♡
WINK
WINK
...
Round 2—Victory ☆
RWAR
She's fast!!
We've got this in the bag.
Round 3—Victory ☆
Speed quiz
HEY...
WSSP
IS THERE A WAY TO BEAT HAKUSEN?
WSSP
HAKUSEN BENCH
WSSP
IT'S BECAUSE TAKISHIMA'S SO GOOD...
Spies
PST
PST
PST

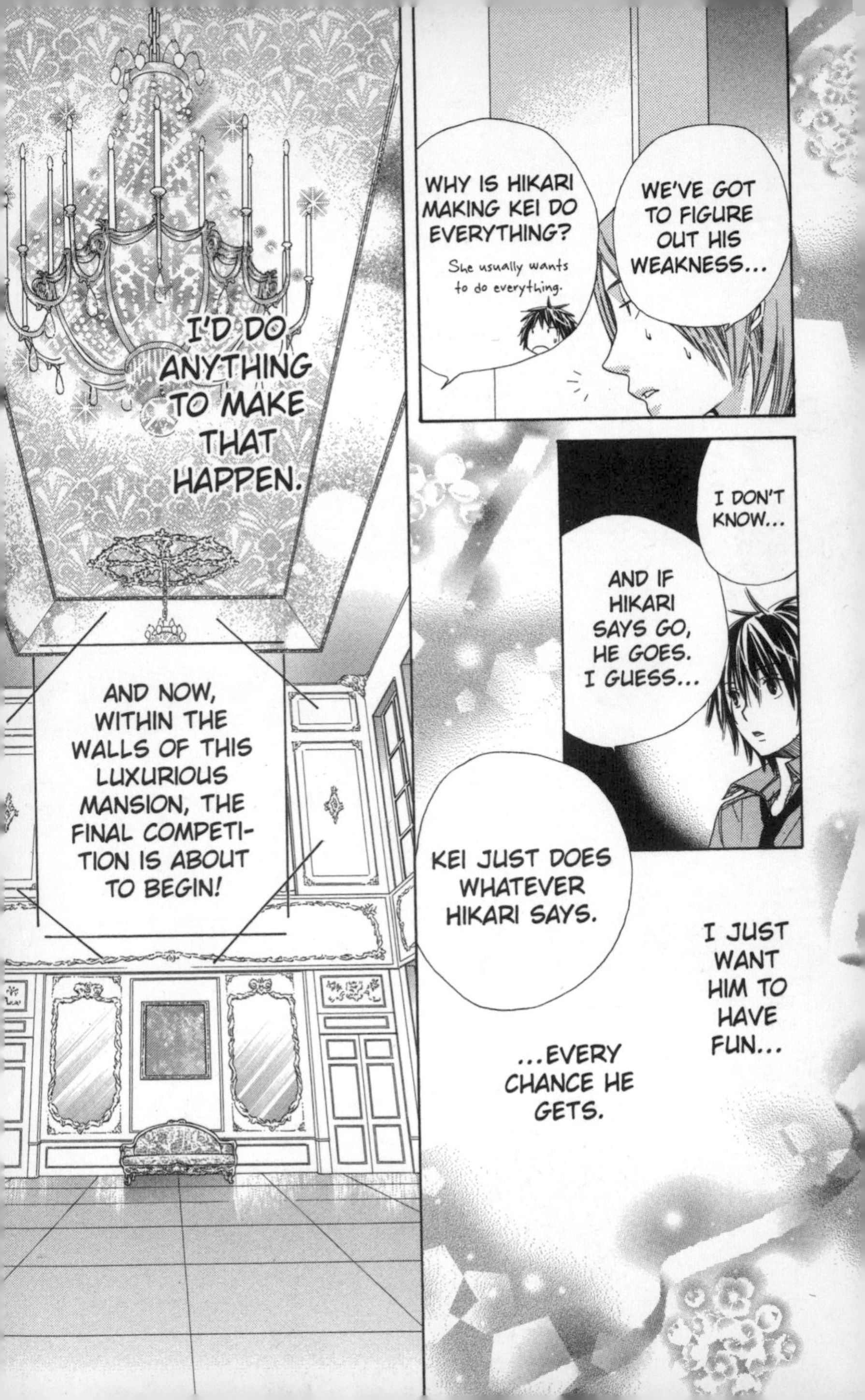
WE'VE GOT TO FIGURE OUT HIS WEAKNESS...
WHY IS HIKARI MAKING KEI DO EVERYTHING?
She usually wants to do everything.
I DON'T KNOW...
AND IF HIKARI SAYS GO, HE GOES. I GUESS...
KEI JUST DOES WHATEVER HIKARI SAYS.
I JUST WANT HIM TO HAVE FUN...
...EVERY CHANCE HE GETS.
I'D DO ANYTHING TO MAKE THAT HAPPEN.
AND NOW, WITHIN THE WALLS OF THIS LUXURIOUS MANSION, THE FINAL COMPETITION IS ABOUT TO BEGIN!

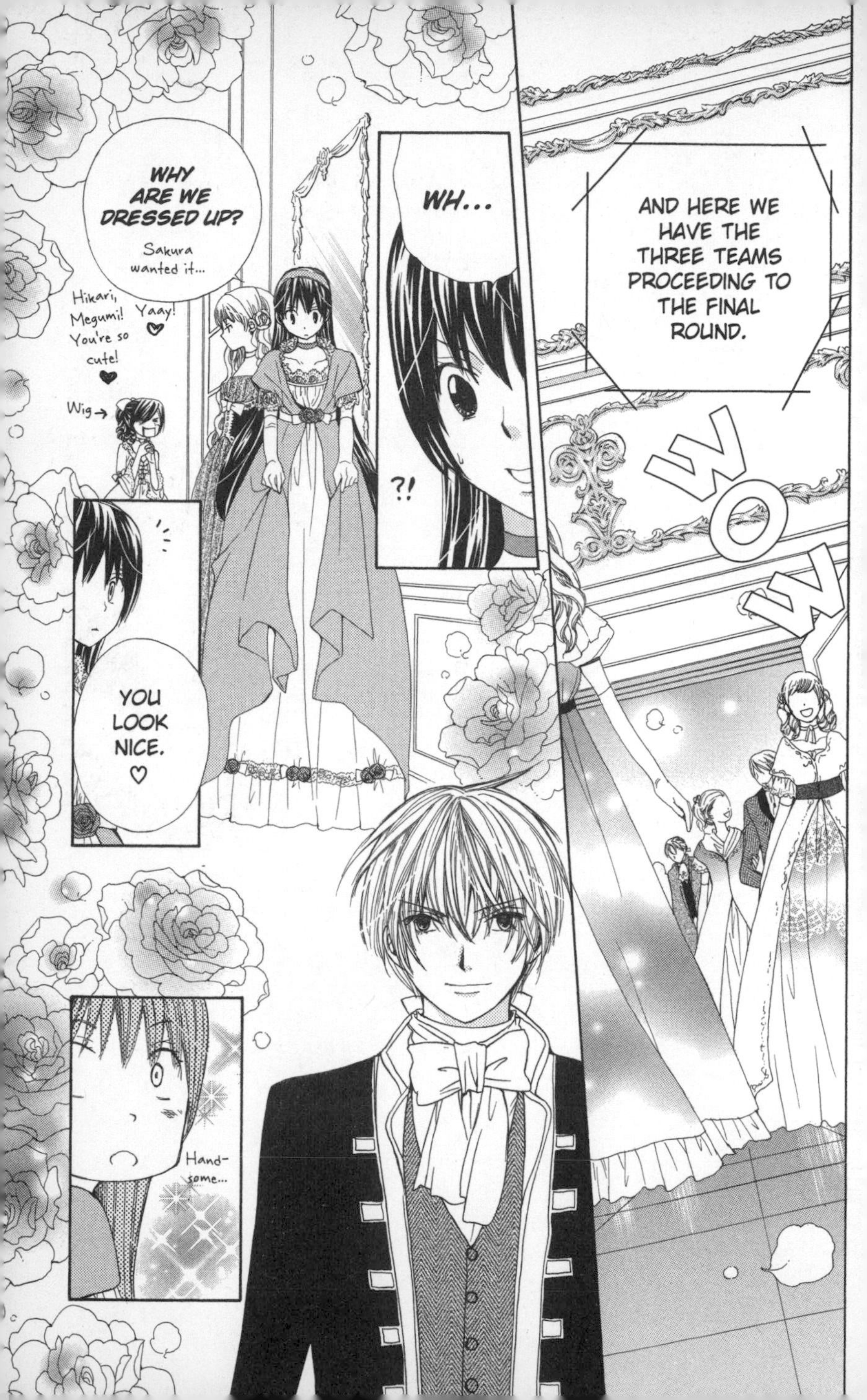
AND HERE WE HAVE THE THREE TEAMS PROCEEDING TO THE FINAL ROUND.
WOW
WH...
?!
WHY ARE WE DRESSED UP?
Sakura wanted it...
Yaay! ♡
Hikari, Megumi! You're so cute! ♥
Wig→
YOU LOOK NICE. ♡
Hand-some...

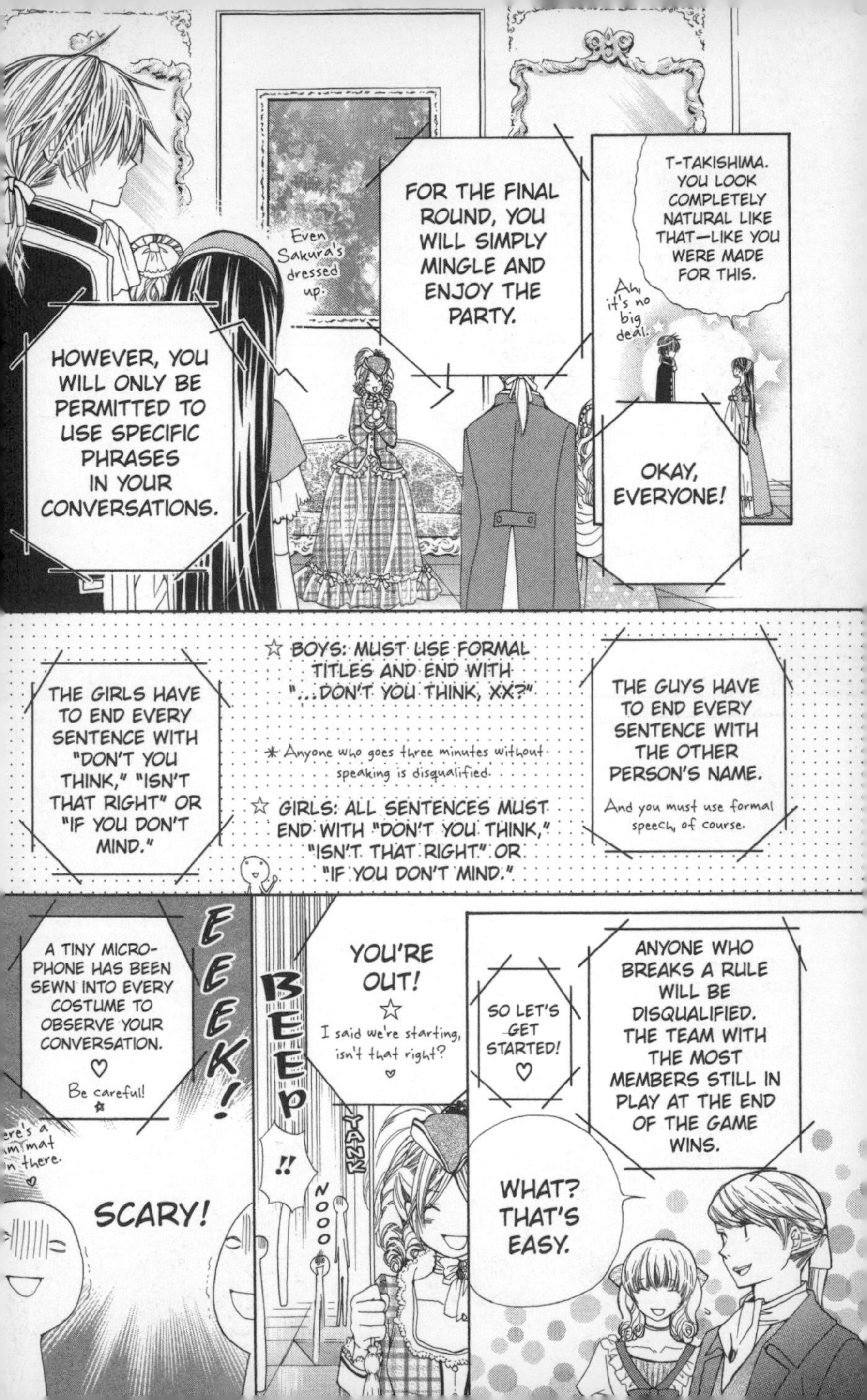

T-TAKISHIMA. YOU LOOK COMPLETELY NATURAL LIKE THAT—LIKE YOU WERE MADE FOR THIS.
Ah, it's no big deal.
OKAY, EVERYONE!
FOR THE FINAL ROUND, YOU WILL SIMPLY MINGLE AND ENJOY THE PARTY.
Even Sakura's dressed up.
HOWEVER, YOU WILL ONLY BE PERMITTED TO USE SPECIFIC PHRASES IN YOUR CONVERSATIONS.
THE GUYS HAVE TO END EVERY SENTENCE WITH THE OTHER PERSON'S NAME.
And you must use formal speech, of course.
☆ BOYS: MUST USE FORMAL TITLES AND END WITH "...DON'T YOU THINK, XX?"
* Anyone who goes three minutes without speaking is disqualified.
☆ GIRLS: ALL SENTENCES MUST END WITH "DON'T YOU THINK," "ISN'T THAT RIGHT" OR "IF YOU DON'T MIND."
THE GIRLS HAVE TO END EVERY SENTENCE WITH "DON'T YOU THINK," "ISN'T THAT RIGHT" OR "IF YOU DON'T MIND."
ANYONE WHO BREAKS A RULE WILL BE DISQUALIFIED. THE TEAM WITH THE MOST MEMBERS STILL IN PLAY AT THE END OF THE GAME WINS.
SO LET'S GET STARTED! ♡
WHAT? THAT'S EASY.
YOU'RE OUT! ☆
I said we're starting, isn't that right? ♡
BEEEP
YANK
!!
NOOO
A TINY MICRO-PHONE HAS BEEN SEWN INTO EVERY COSTUME TO OBSERVE YOUR CONVERSATION. ♡
Be careful! ☆
EEEEK!
SCARY!

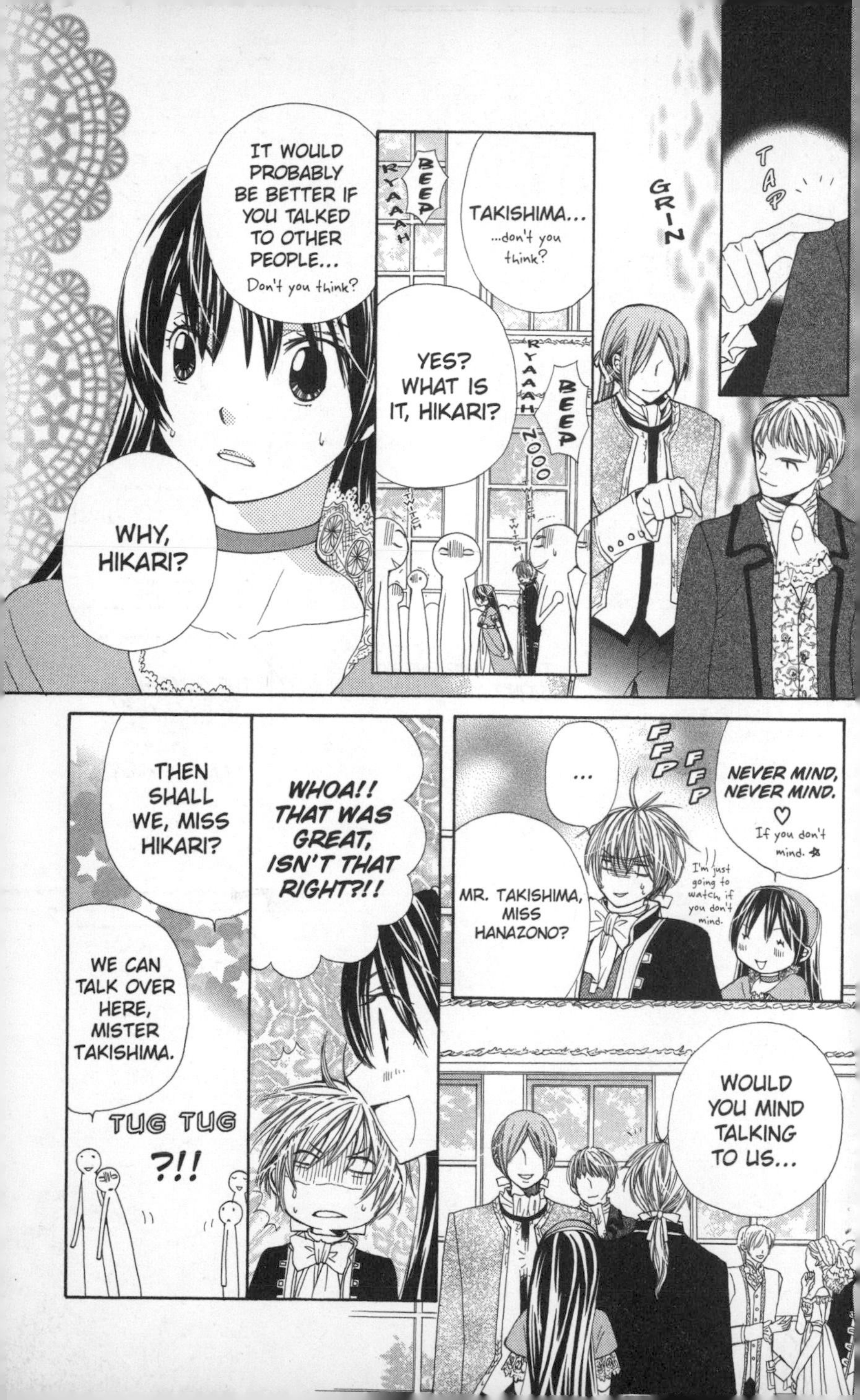
TAP
GRIN
TAKISHIMA... ...don't you think?
BEEP
RYAAAH
YES? WHAT IS IT, HIKARI?
BEEP
RYAAAH
NOOO
TWITCH
TWITCH
IT WOULD PROBABLY BE BETTER IF YOU TALKED TO OTHER PEOPLE... Don't you think?
WHY, HIKARI?
NEVER MIND, NEVER MIND. ♡ If you don't mind.
FFF
FFF
...
I'm just going to watch, if you don't mind.
MR. TAKISHIMA, MISS HANAZONO?
WOULD YOU MIND TALKING TO US...
WHOA!! THAT WAS GREAT, ISN'T THAT RIGHT?!!
THEN SHALL WE, MISS HIKARI?
WE CAN TALK OVER HERE, MISTER TAKISHIMA.
TUG TUG
?!!

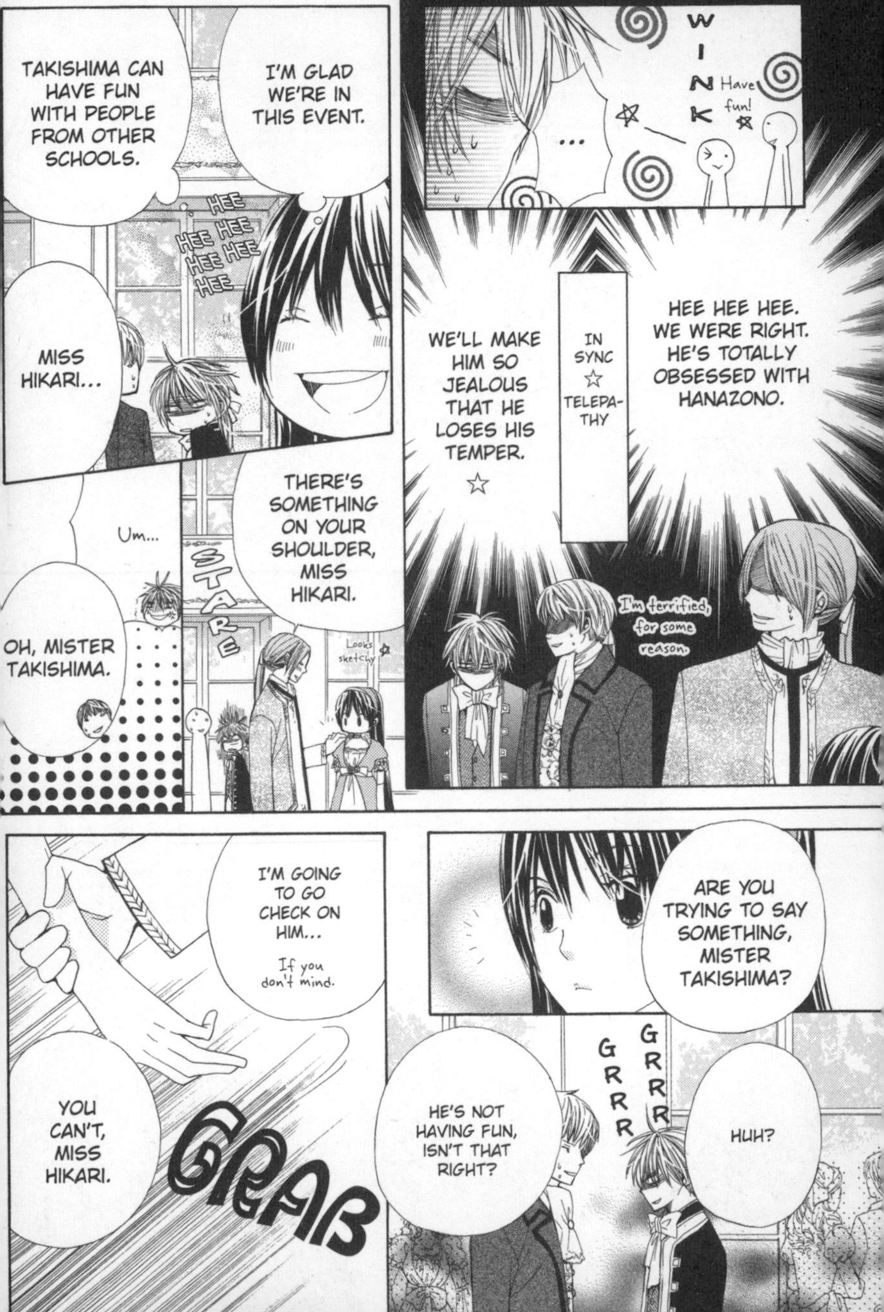
WINK
Have fun! ☆
...
HEE HEE HEE. WE WERE RIGHT. HE'S TOTALLY OBSESSED WITH HANAZONO.
IN SYNC ☆ TELEPATHY
WE'LL MAKE HIM SO JEALOUS THAT HE LOSES HIS TEMPER. ☆
I'm terrified, for some reason.
I'M GLAD WE'RE IN THIS EVENT.
TAKISHIMA CAN HAVE FUN WITH PEOPLE FROM OTHER SCHOOLS.
HEE HEE HEE HEE HEE HEE
MISS HIKARI...
THERE'S SOMETHING ON YOUR SHOULDER, MISS HIKARI.
STARE
Looks sketchy ☆
Um...
OH, MISTER TAKISHIMA.
ARE YOU TRYING TO SAY SOMETHING, MISTER TAKISHIMA?
GRRR GRRR
HUH?
HE'S NOT HAVING FUN, ISN'T THAT RIGHT?
I'M GOING TO GO CHECK ON HIM...
If you don't mind.
YOU CAN'T, MISS HIKARI.
GRAB

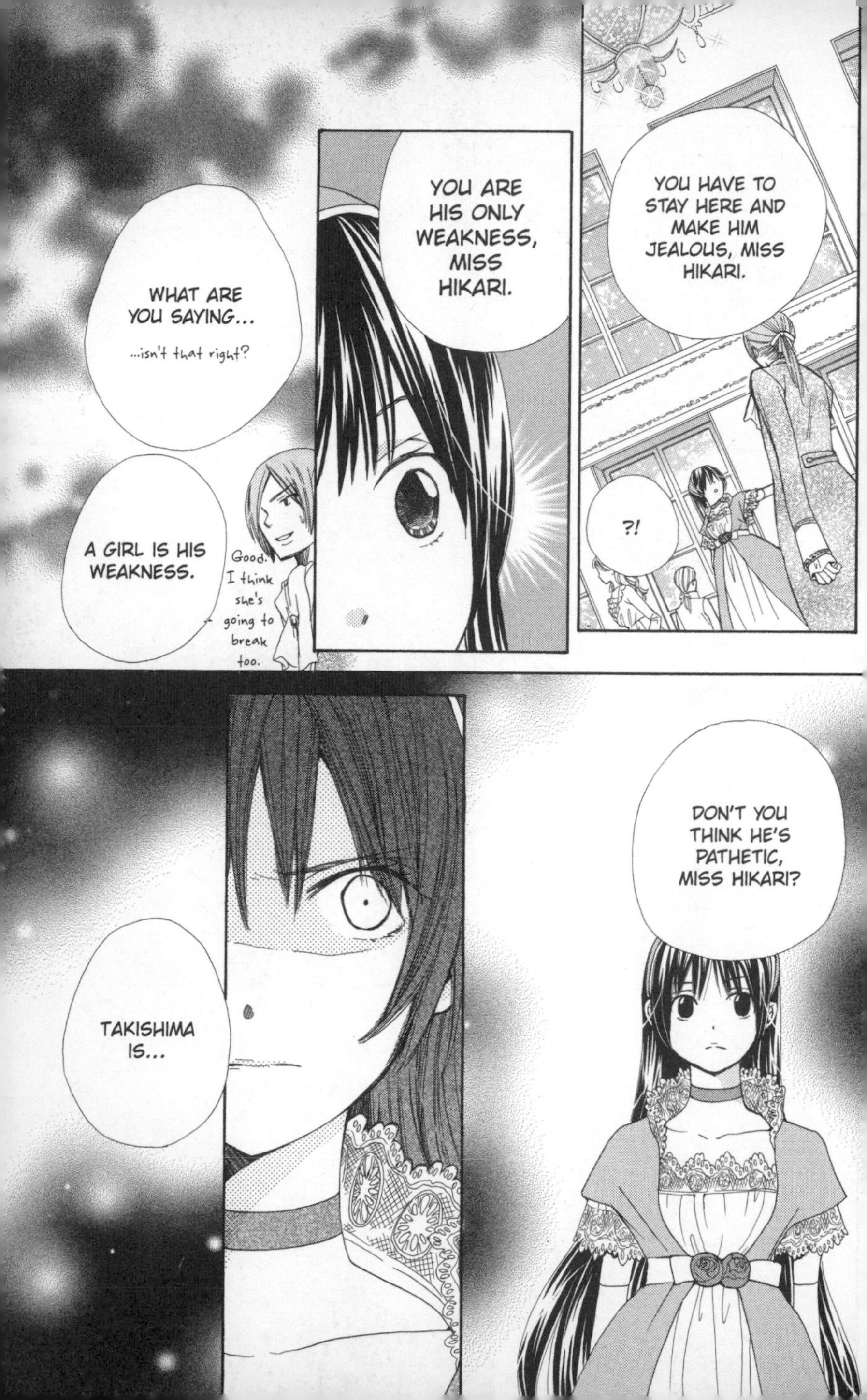
YOU HAVE TO STAY HERE AND MAKE HIM JEALOUS, MISS HIKARI.
?!
YOU ARE HIS ONLY WEAKNESS, MISS HIKARI.
WHAT ARE YOU SAYING...
...isn't that right?
A GIRL IS HIS WEAKNESS.
Good. I think she's going to break too.
DON'T YOU THINK HE'S PATHETIC, MISS HIKARI?
TAKISHIMA IS...

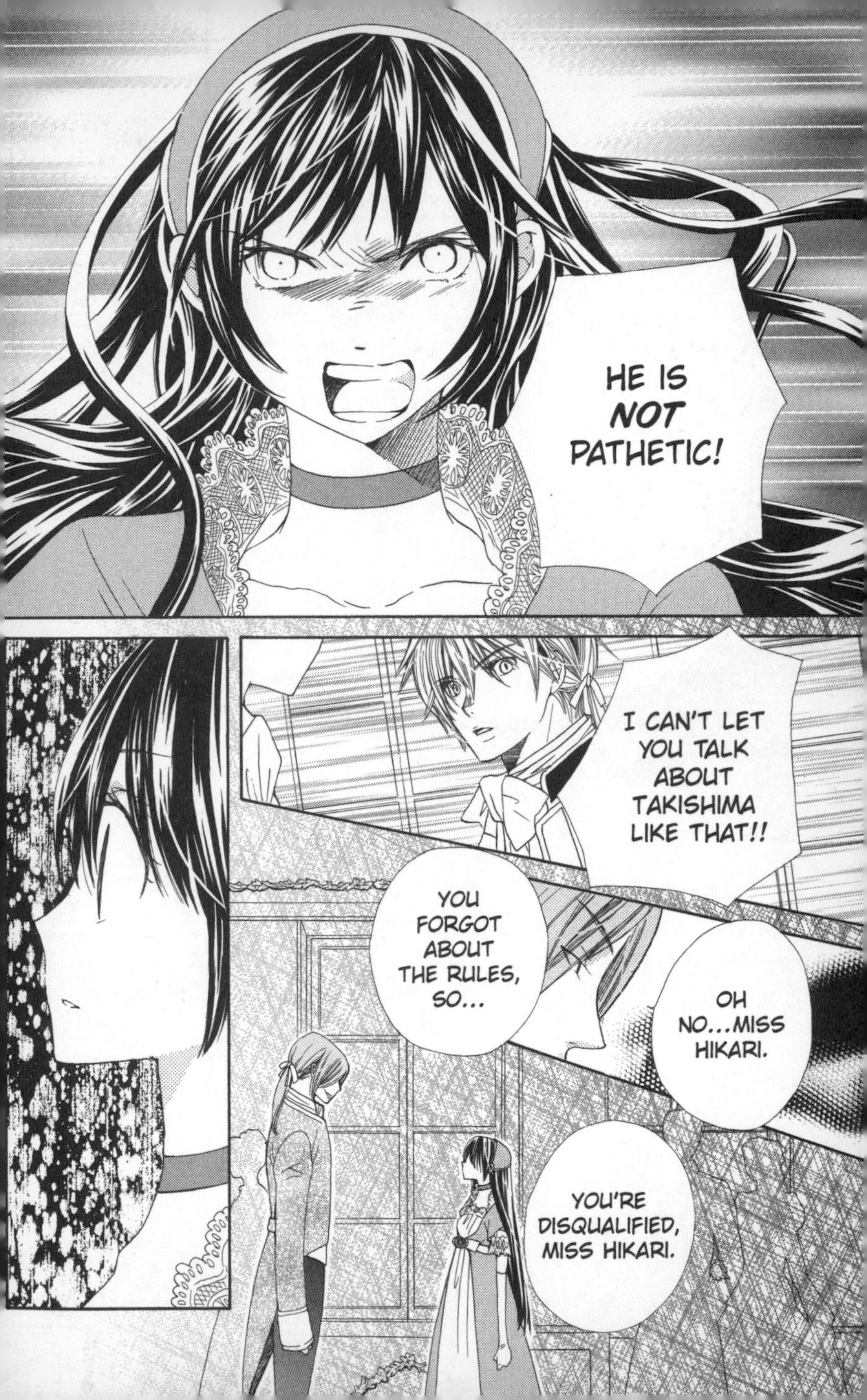
HE IS *NOT* PATHETIC!
I CAN'T LET YOU TALK ABOUT TAKISHIMA LIKE THAT!!
OH NO...MISS HIKARI.
YOU FORGOT ABOUT THE RULES, SO...
YOU'RE DISQUALIFIED, MISS HIKARI.

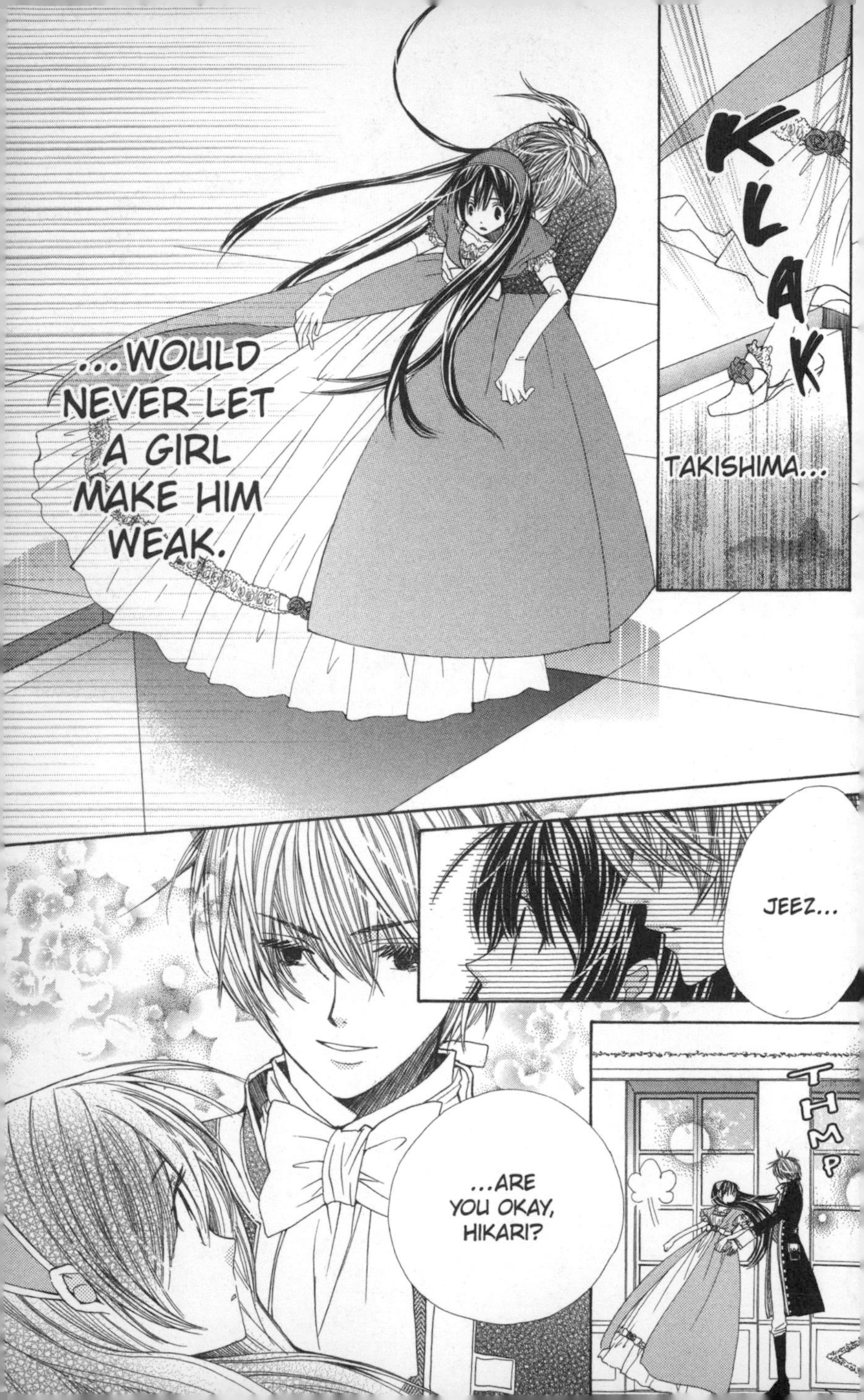
KLAK
TAKISHIMA...
...WOULD NEVER LET A GIRL MAKE HIM WEAK.
JEEZ...
THMP
...ARE YOU OKAY, HIKARI?

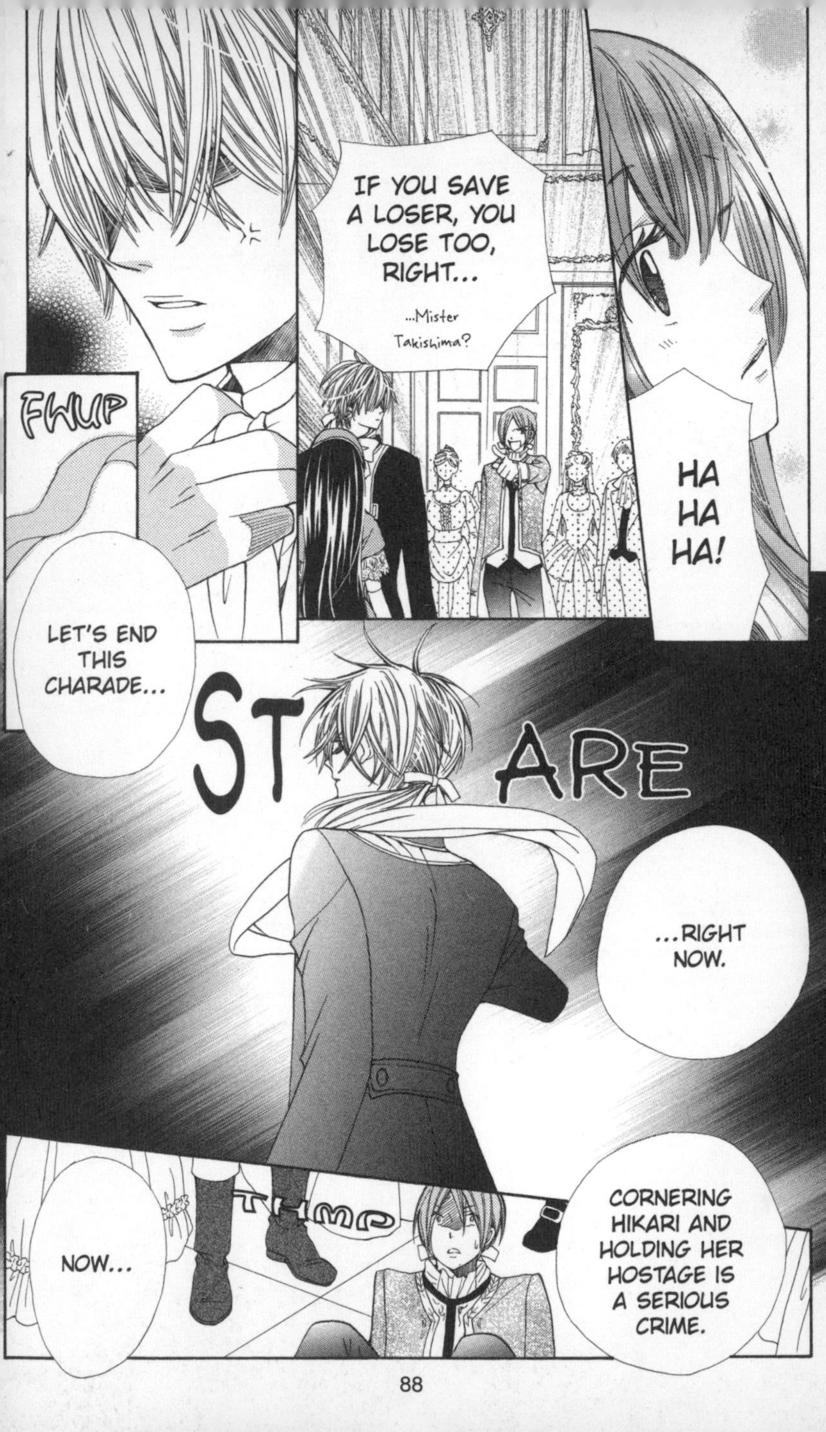
HA HA HA!
IF YOU SAVE A LOSER, YOU LOSE TOO, RIGHT...
...Mister Takishima?
FWUP
LET'S END THIS CHARADE...
STARE
...RIGHT NOW.
CORNERING HIKARI AND HOLDING HER HOSTAGE IS A SERIOUS CRIME.
THMP
NOW...

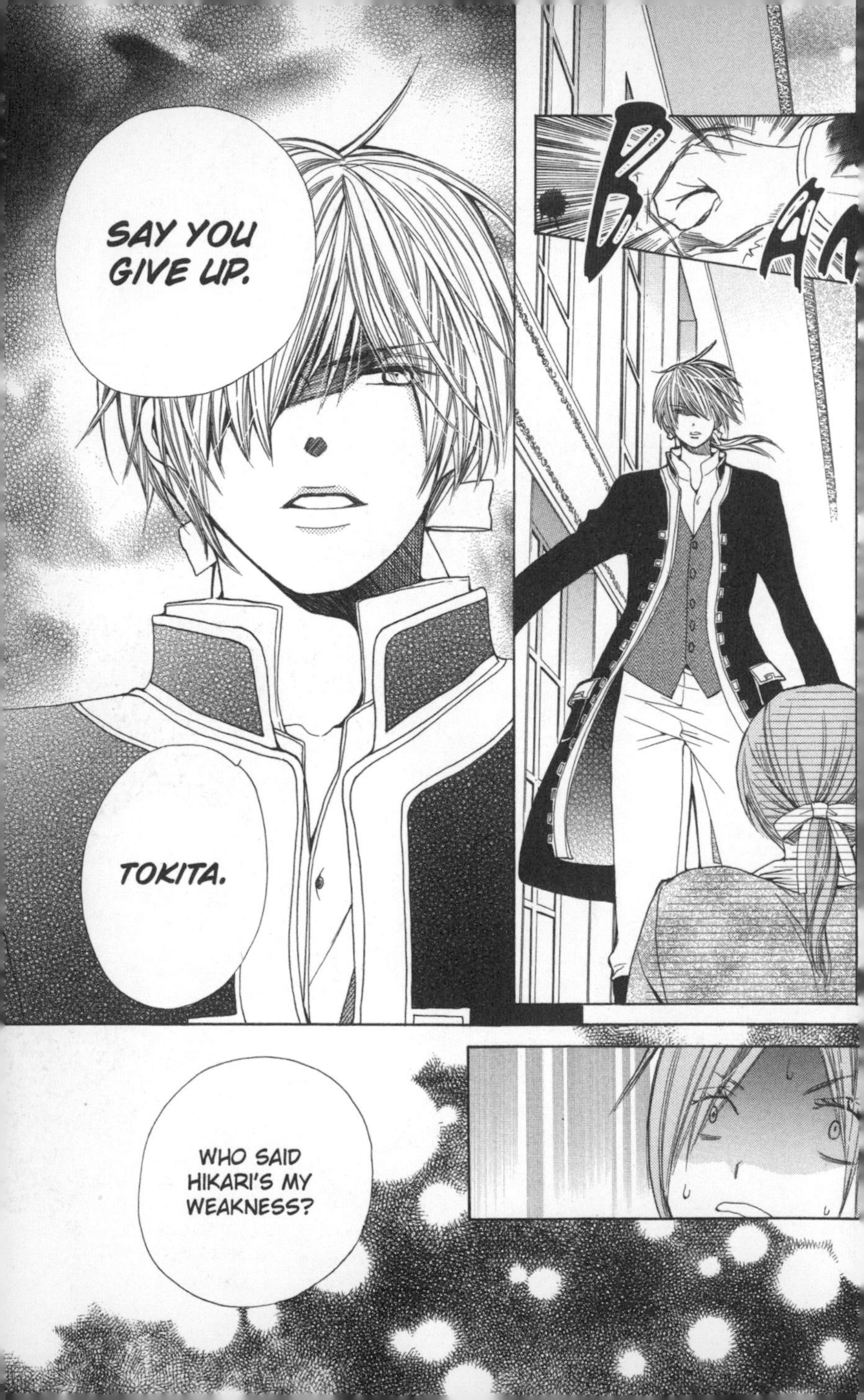
BAA
SAY YOU GIVE UP.
TOKITA.
WHO SAID HIKARI'S MY WEAKNESS?

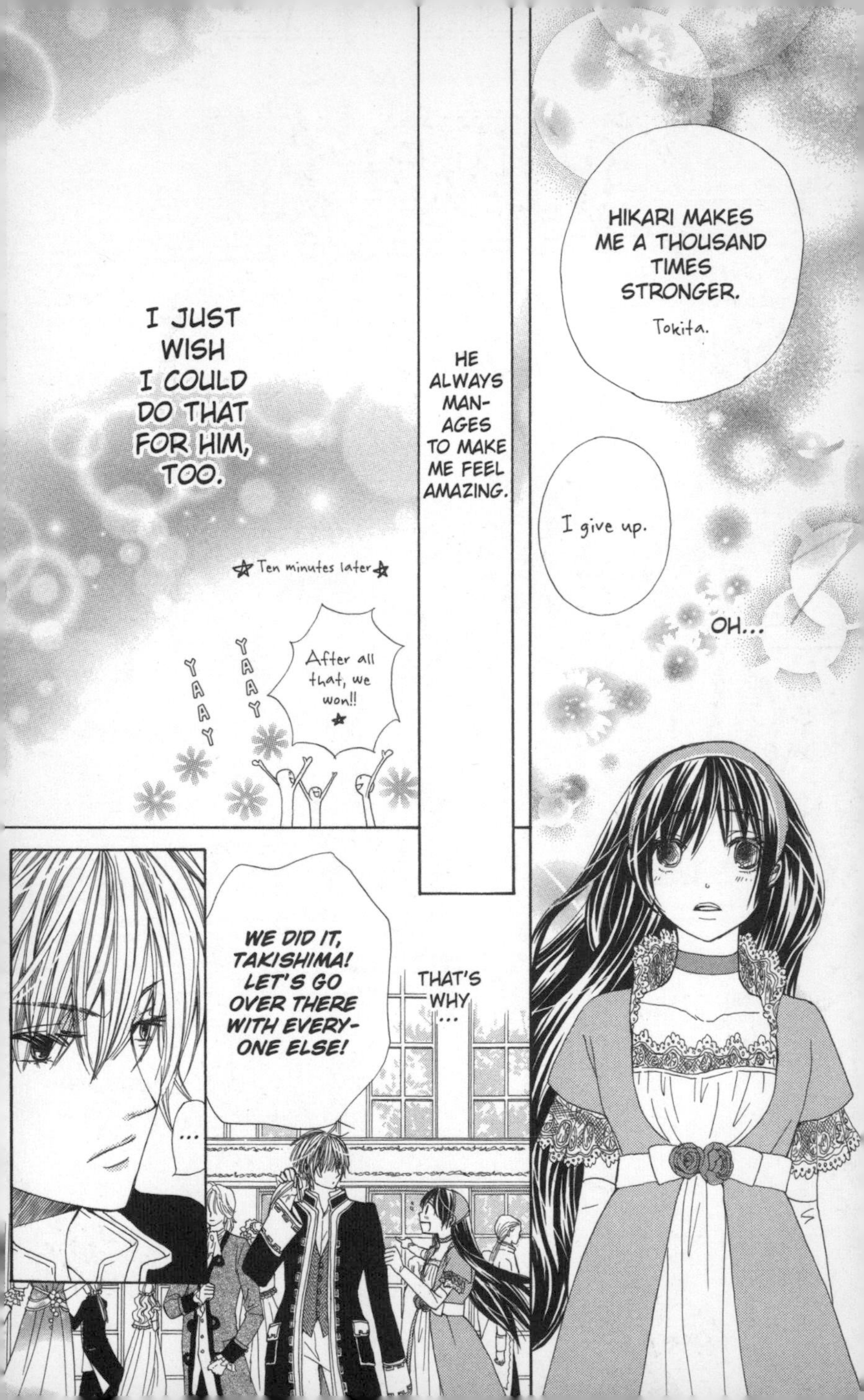

HIKARI MAKES ME A THOUSAND TIMES STRONGER.
Tokita.
I give up.
OH...
HE ALWAYS MAN-AGES TO MAKE ME FEEL AMAZING.
I JUST WISH I COULD DO THAT FOR HIM, TOO.
Ten minutes later
After all that, we won!!
YAAAY
YAAY
WE DID IT, TAKISHIMA! LET'S GO OVER THERE WITH EVERY-ONE ELSE!
THAT'S WHY...
...

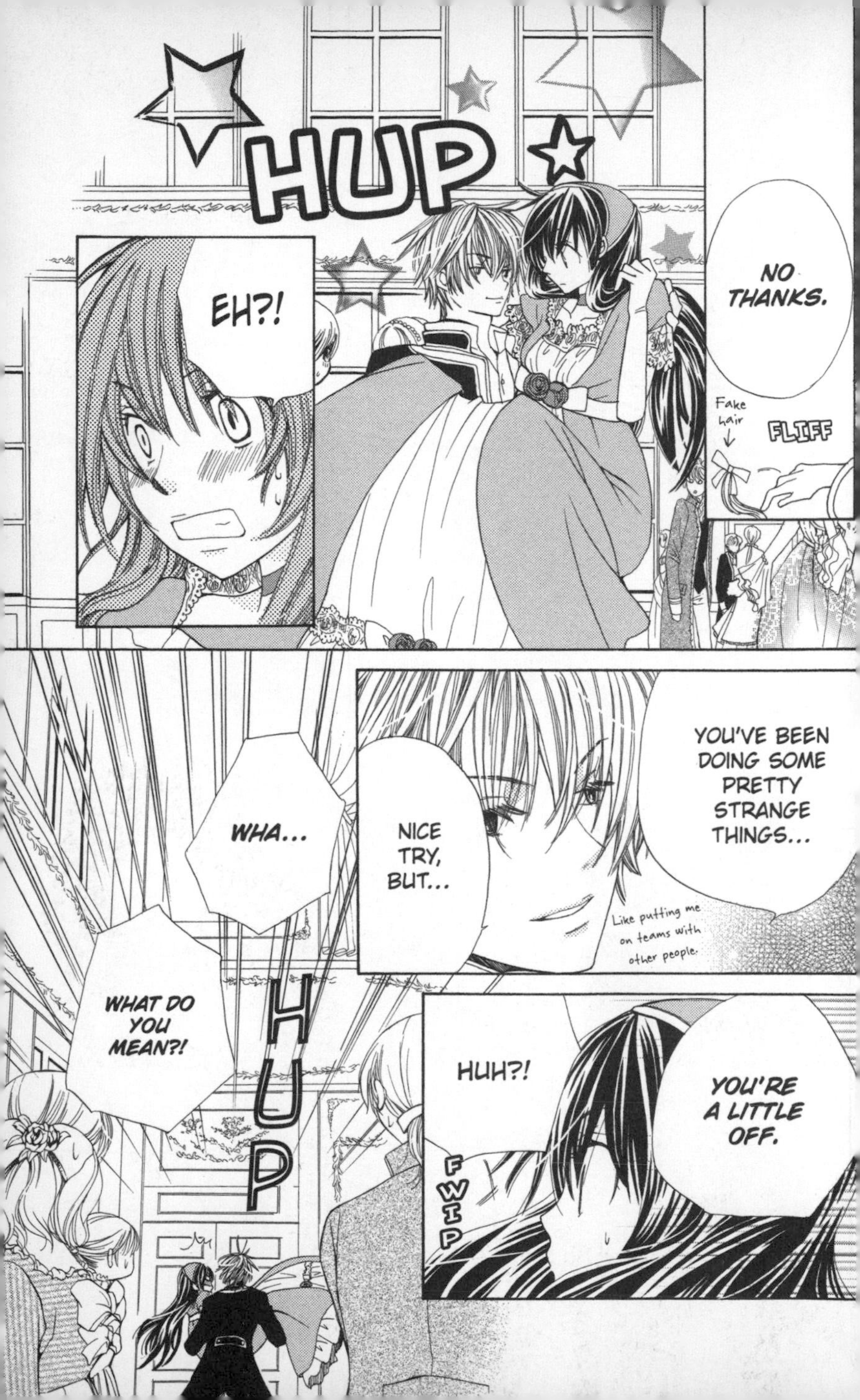
NO THANKS.
Fake hair
FLIFF
HUP
EH?!
YOU'VE BEEN DOING SOME PRETTY STRANGE THINGS...
Like putting me on teams with other people.
NICE TRY, BUT...
YOU'RE A LITTLE OFF.
HUH?!
FWIP
WHA...
WHAT DO YOU MEAN?!
HUP

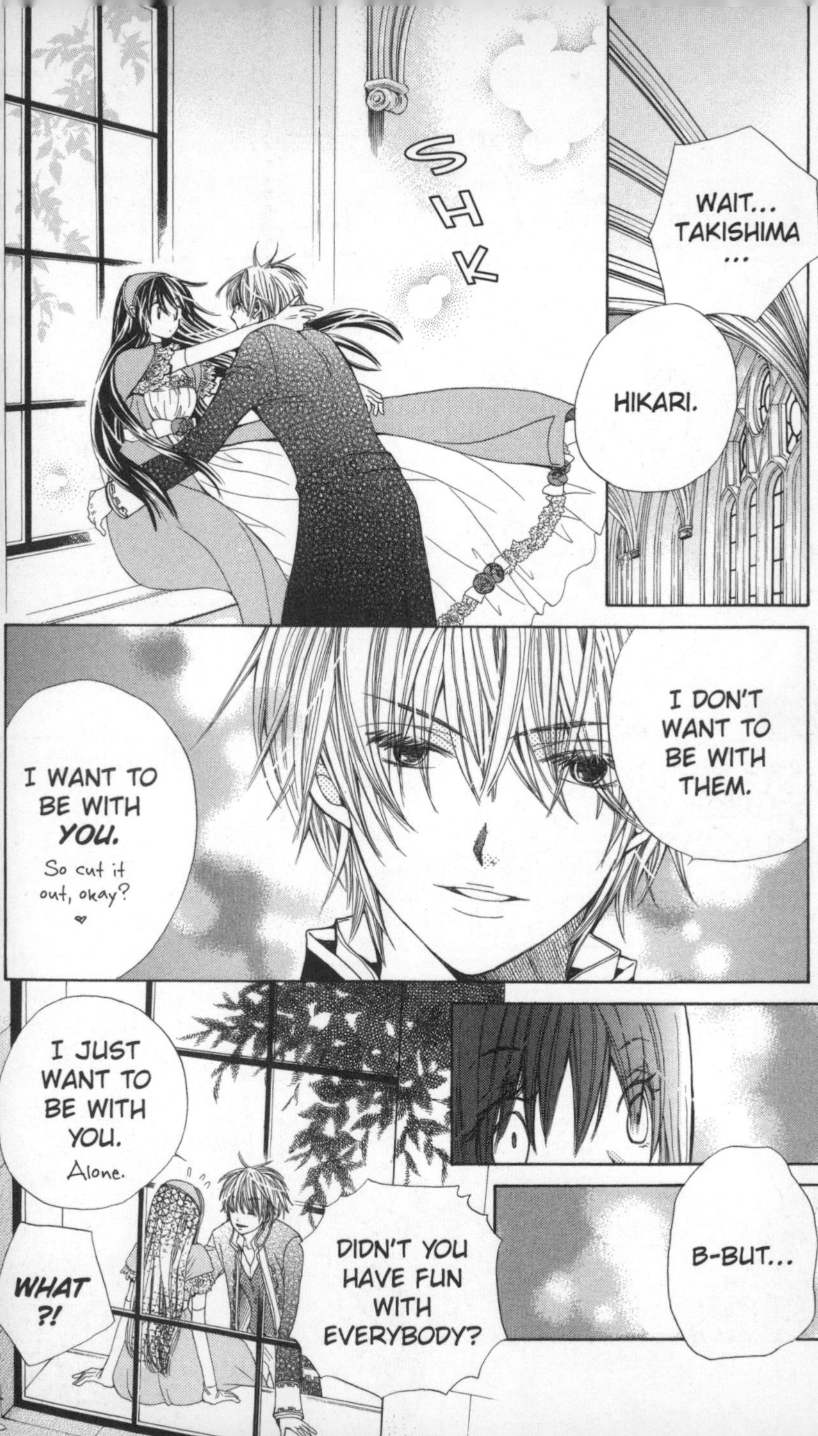
WAIT... TAKISHIMA ...
HIKARI.
SHK
I DON'T WANT TO BE WITH THEM.
I WANT TO BE WITH YOU.
So cut it out, okay? ♥
B-BUT...
DIDN'T YOU HAVE FUN WITH EVERYBODY?
I JUST WANT TO BE WITH YOU.
Alone.
WHAT?!

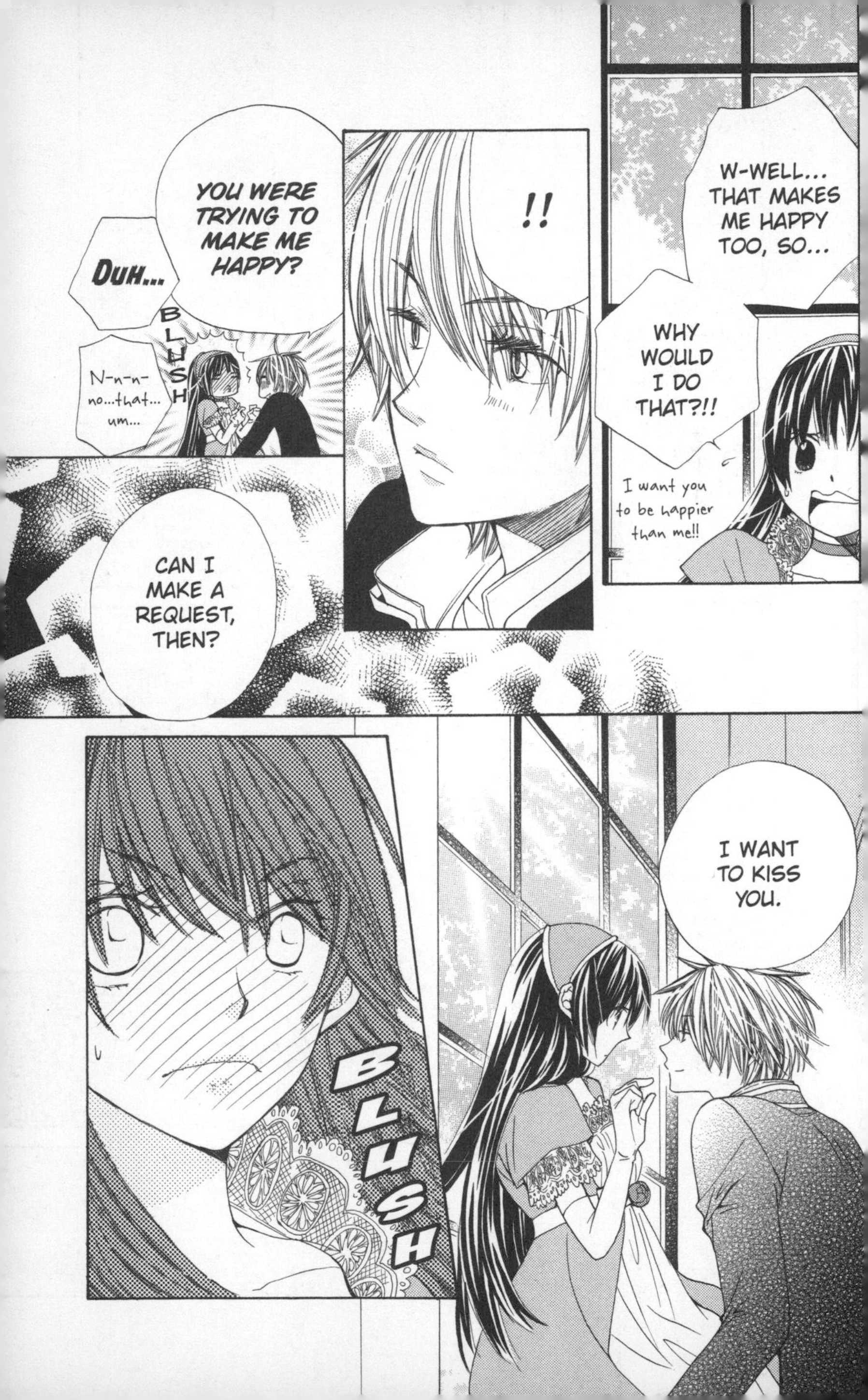
W-WELL... THAT MAKES ME HAPPY TOO, SO...
WHY WOULD I DO THAT?!!
I want you to be happier than me!!
!!
YOU WERE TRYING TO MAKE ME HAPPY?
DUH...
BLUSH
N-n-n-no...that... um...
CAN I MAKE A REQUEST, THEN?
I WANT TO KISS YOU.
BLUSH

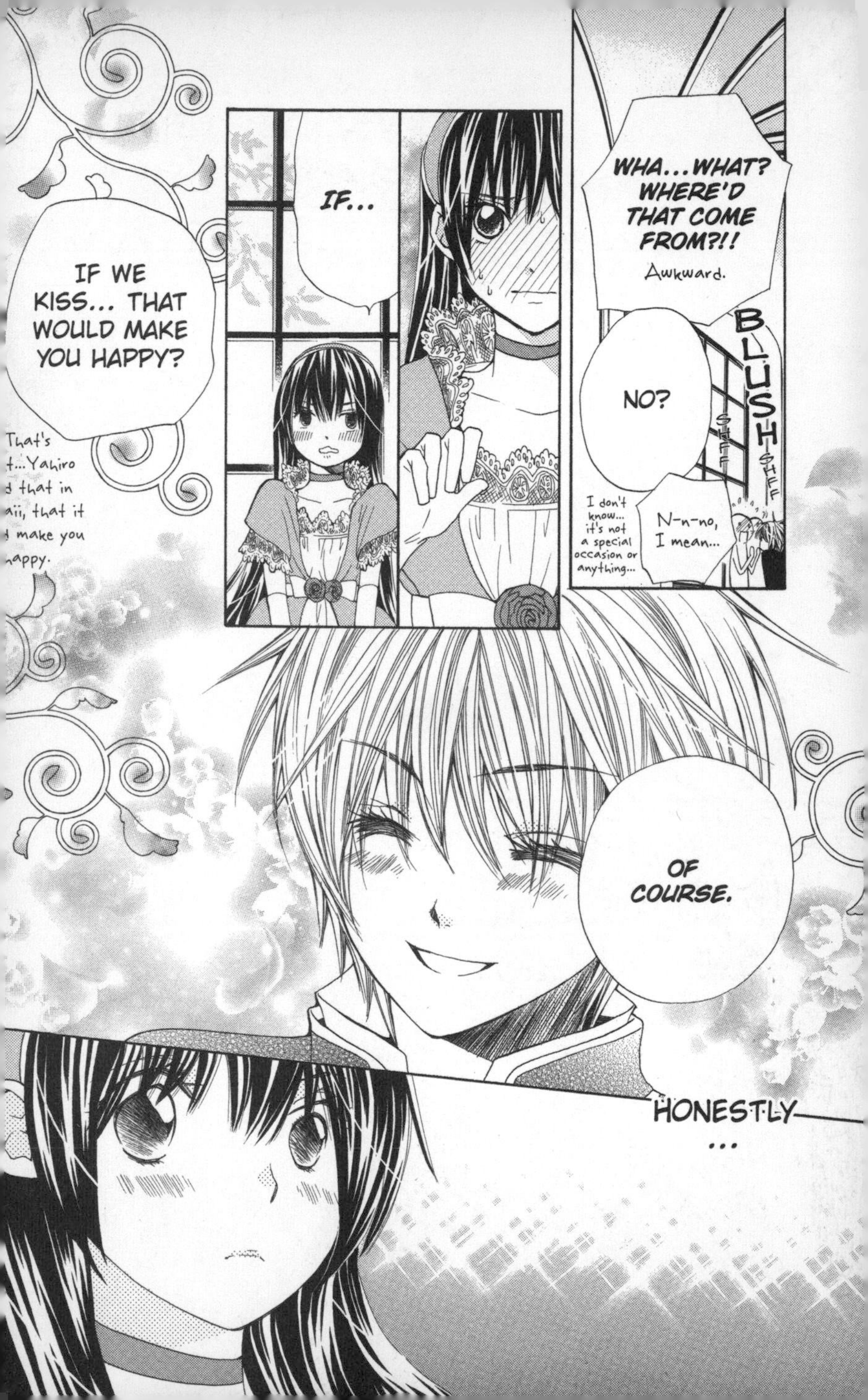

WHA...WHAT? WHERE'D THAT COME FROM?!!
Awkward.
BLUSH
NO?
SHFF SHEFF
N-n-no, I mean...
I don't know... it's not a special occasion or anything...
IF...
IF WE KISS... THAT WOULD MAKE YOU HAPPY?
That's
t...Yahiro
d that in
aii, that it
d make you
happy.
OF COURSE.
HONESTLY...

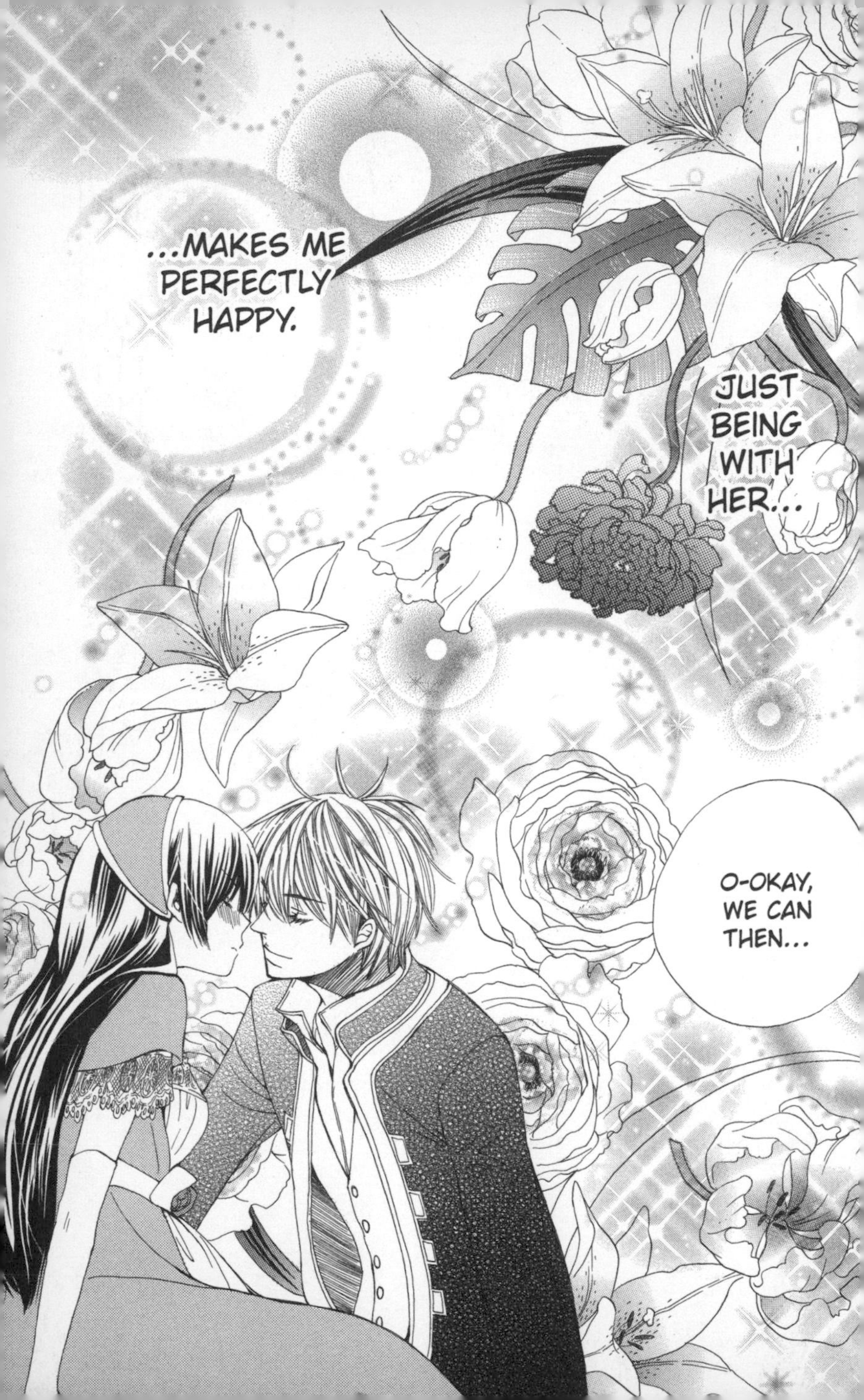
JUST BEING WITH HER...
...MAKES ME PERFECTLY HAPPY.
O-OKAY, WE CAN THEN...

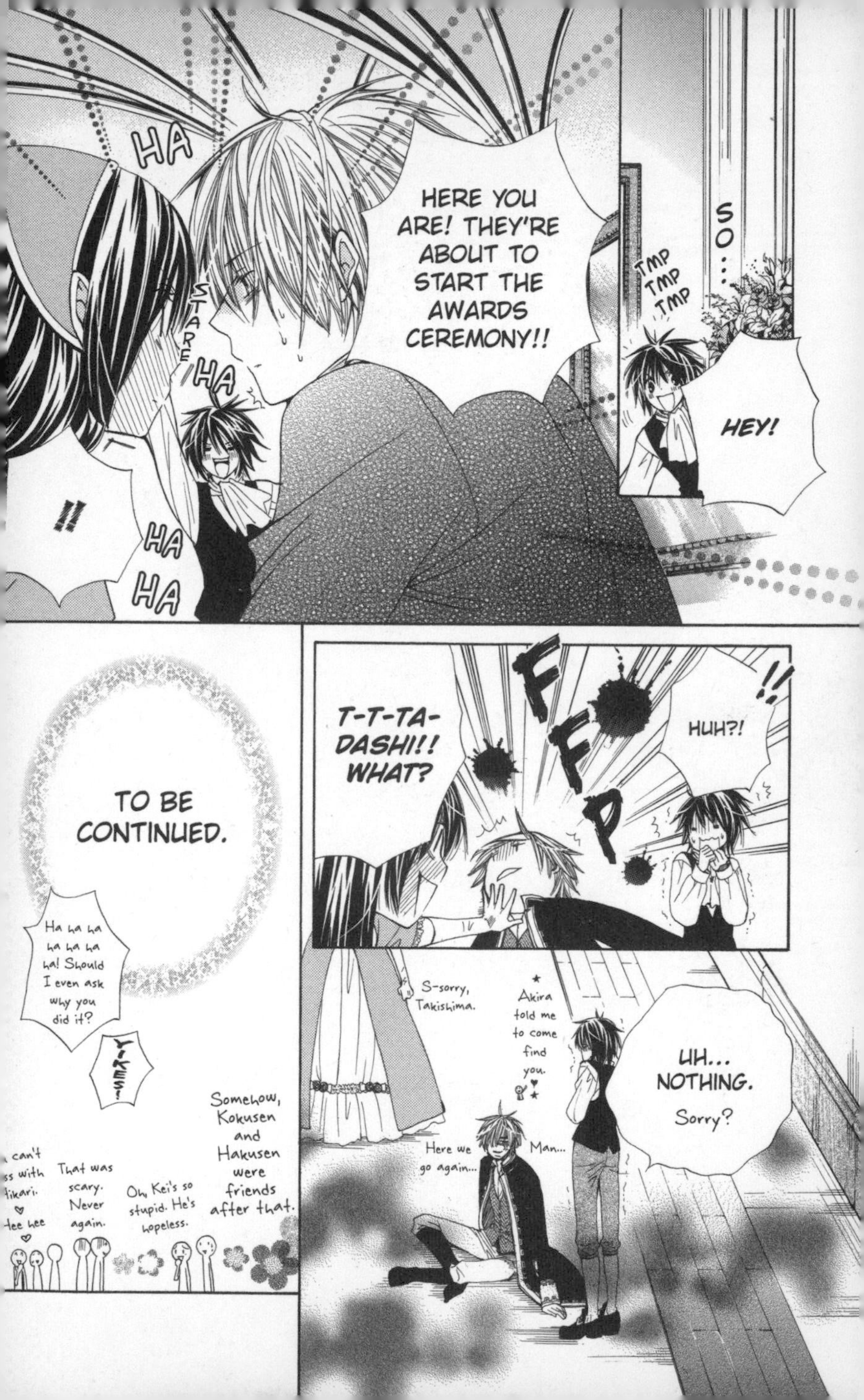
SO...
TMP TMP TMP
HEY!
HERE YOU ARE! THEY'RE ABOUT TO START THE AWARDS CEREMONY!!
HA
STARE
HA
!!
HA HA
!!
HUH?!
FFP
T-T-TA-DASHI!! WHAT?
UH... NOTHING.
Sorry?
Akira told me to come find you.
Man...
S-sorry, Takishima.
Here we go again...
TO BE CONTINUED.
Ha ha ha ha ha ha ha! Should I even ask why you did it?
YIKES!
Somehow, Kokusen and Hakusen were friends after that.
Oh, Kei's so stupid. He's hopeless.
That was scary. Never again.

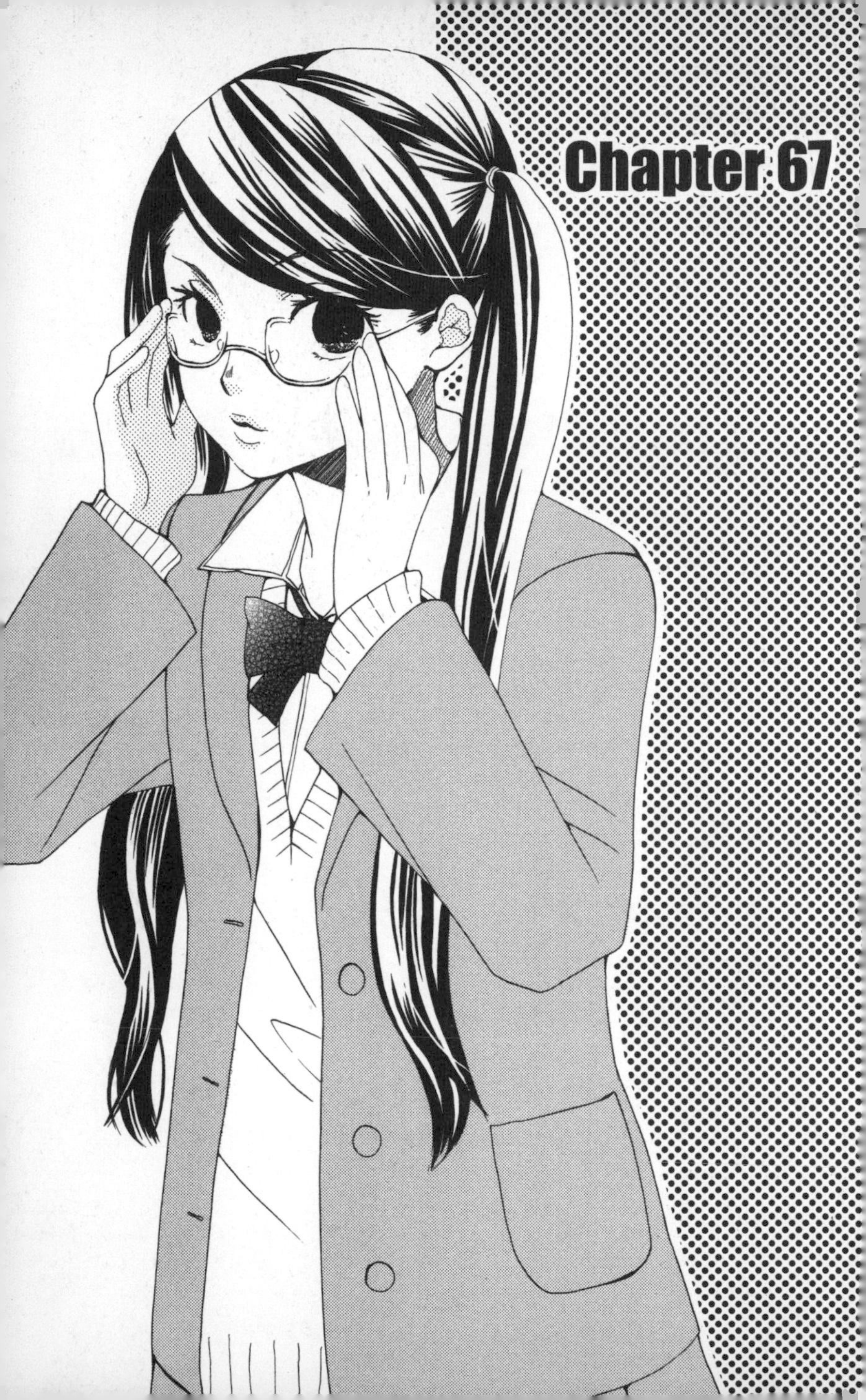
Chapter 67

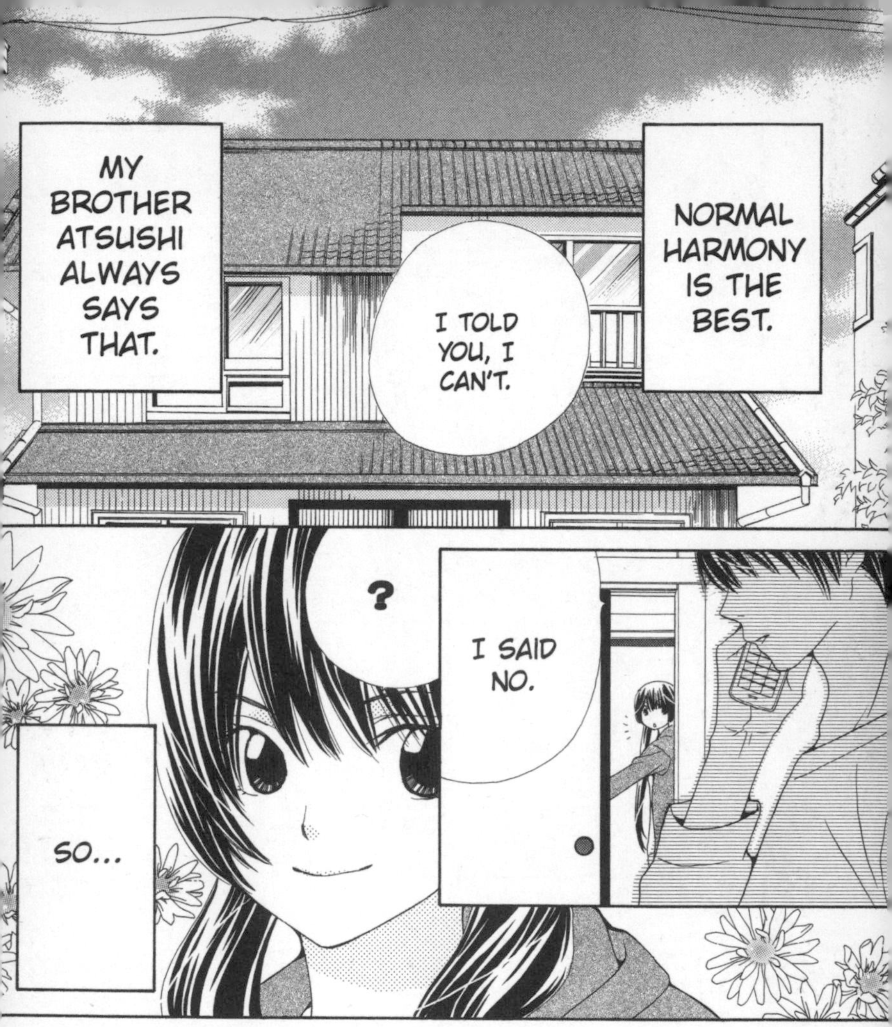
NORMAL HARMONY IS THE BEST.
I TOLD YOU, I CAN'T.
MY BROTHER ATSUSHI ALWAYS SAYS THAT.
I SAID NO.
?
SO...

· CHARACTERS ·

I WANT TO TALK ABOUT CHARACTERS.

IN THE ORIGINAL VERSION OF S.A, KEI WAS ALWAYS IN SECOND PLACE. HIKARI WAS ALWAYS FIRST AND SHE LIVED IN A LUXURIOUS MANSION. IF I HAD KEPT IT LIKE THAT, I'M PRETTY SURE IT WOULD BE A TOTALLY DIFFERENT STORY. OH, AND TADASHI LOVED GIRLS AND HE HAD A REALLY BAD RELATIONSHIP WITH AKIRA. JUN WAS ORIGINALLY A PLANT-LOVER, BUT RYU AND MEGUMI WEREN'T DIFFERENT AT ALL. OH WELL.

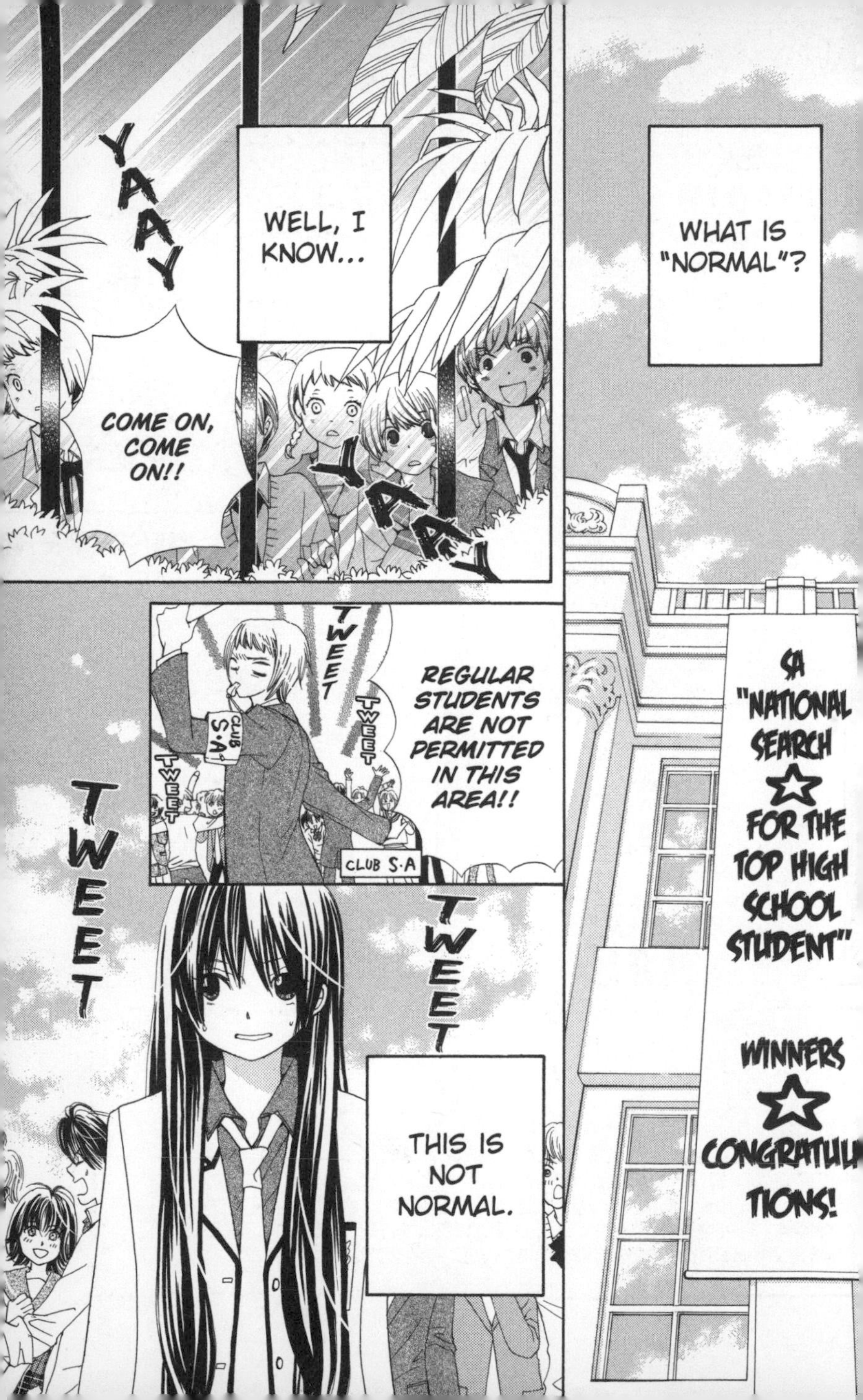

WHAT IS "NORMAL"?
SA "NATIONAL SEARCH ☆ FOR THE TOP HIGH SCHOOL STUDENT" WINNERS ☆ CONGRATUL
TIONS!
WELL, I KNOW...
YAAY
YAAY
COME ON, COME ON!!
TWEET
TWEET
CLUB S·A
REGULAR STUDENTS ARE NOT PERMITTED IN THIS AREA!!
TWEET
CLUB S·A
TWEET
TWEET
THIS IS NOT NORMAL.

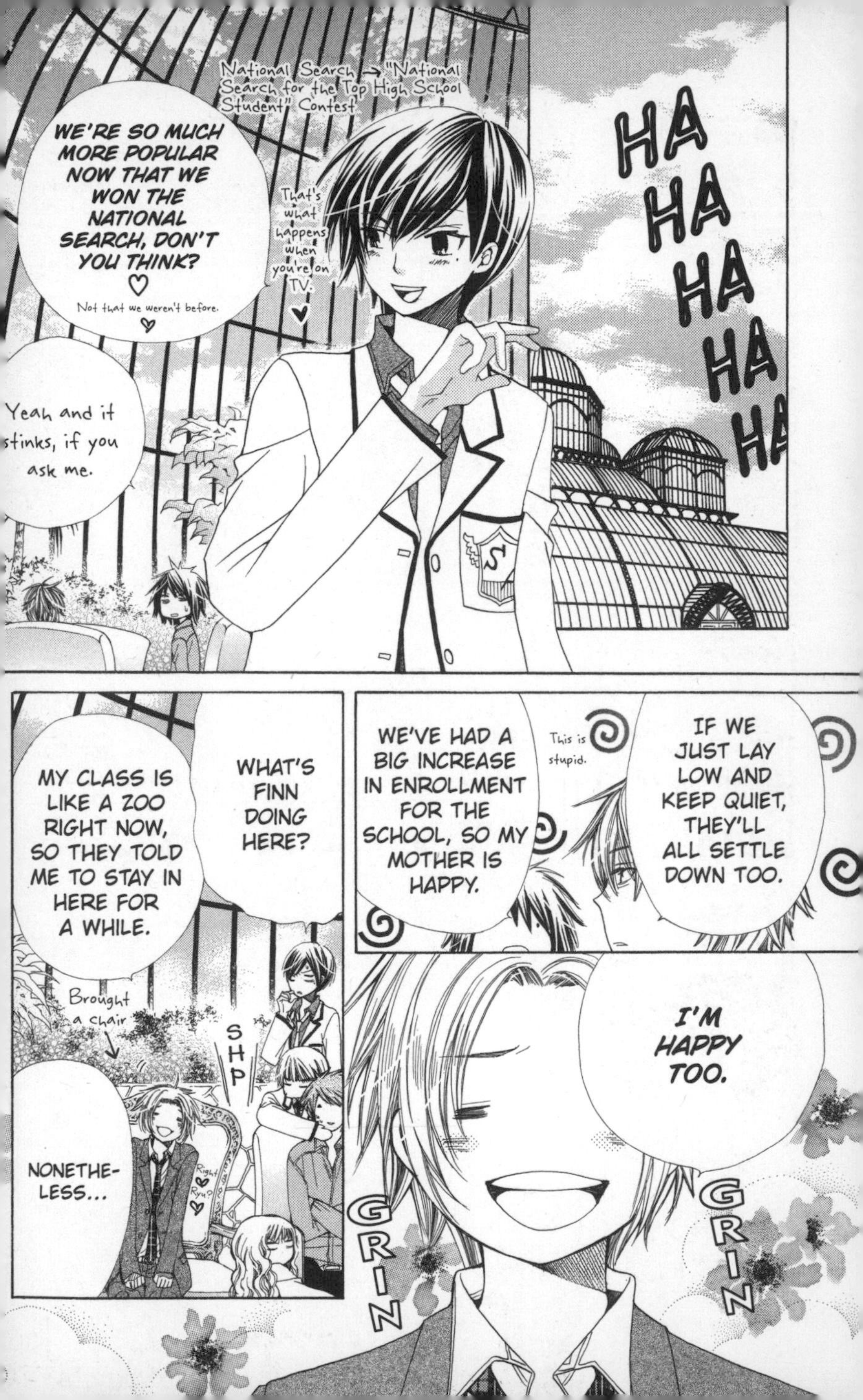
HA HA HA HA HA HA
National Search → "National Search for the Top High School Student" Contest
That's what happens when you're on TV.
WE'RE SO MUCH MORE POPULAR NOW THAT WE WON THE NATIONAL SEARCH, DON'T YOU THINK? ♡
Not that we weren't before. ♡
Yeah and it stinks, if you ask me.
IF WE JUST LAY LOW AND KEEP QUIET, THEY'LL ALL SETTLE DOWN TOO.
This is stupid.
WE'VE HAD A BIG INCREASE IN ENROLLMENT FOR THE SCHOOL, SO MY MOTHER IS HAPPY.
I'M HAPPY TOO.
GRIN
GRIN
WHAT'S FINN DOING HERE?
MY CLASS IS LIKE A ZOO RIGHT NOW, SO THEY TOLD ME TO STAY IN HERE FOR A WHILE.
Brought a chair
SHP
NONETHELESS...
Right Ryu?

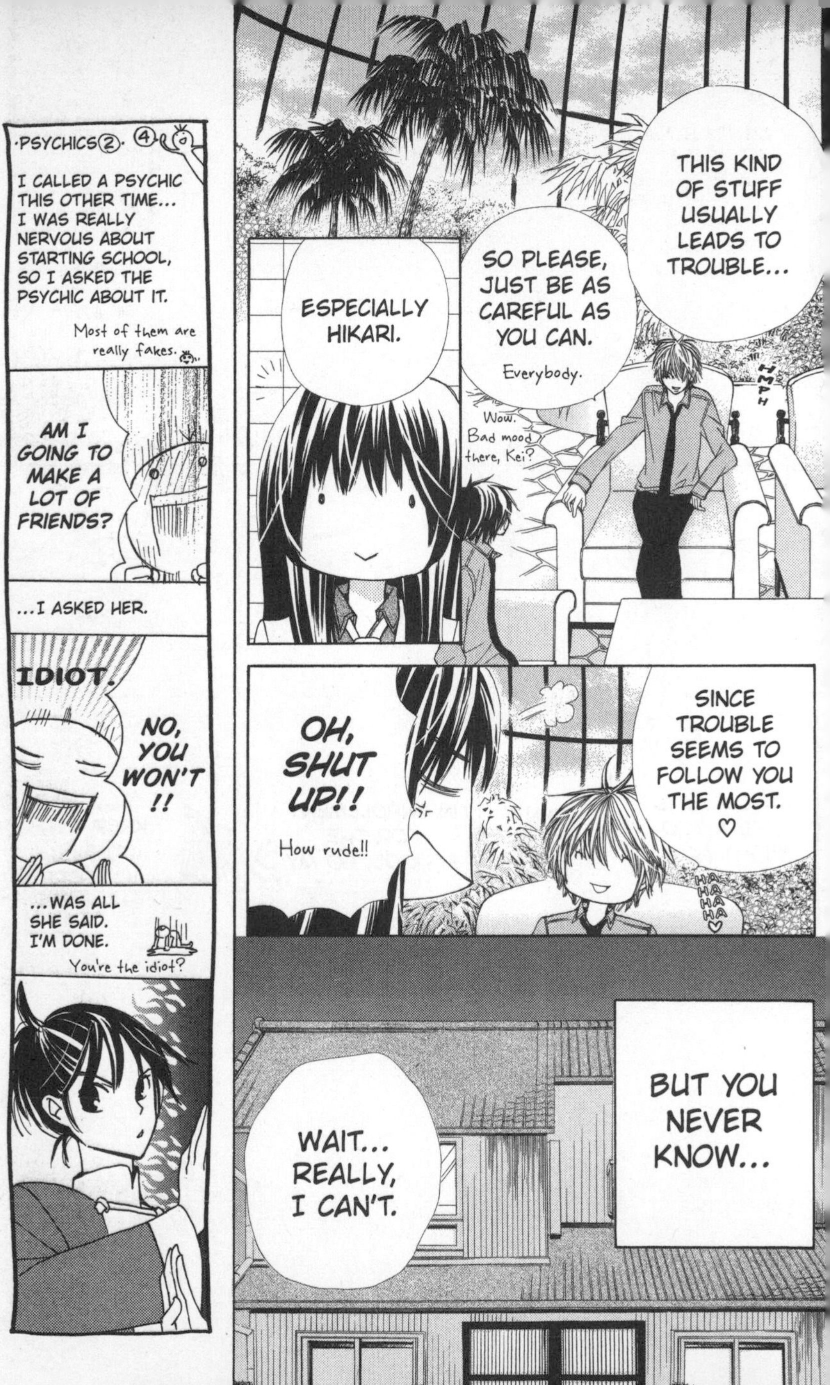
THIS KIND OF STUFF USUALLY LEADS TO TROUBLE...
SO PLEASE, JUST BE AS CAREFUL AS YOU CAN.
Everybody.
HMPH
Wow. Bad mood there, Kei?
ESPECIALLY HIKARI.
SINCE TROUBLE SEEMS TO FOLLOW YOU THE MOST. ♡
HA HA HA HA ♡
OH, SHUT UP!!
How rude!!
BUT YOU NEVER KNOW...
WAIT... REALLY, I CAN'T.
·PSYCHICS ②· ④
I CALLED A PSYCHIC THIS OTHER TIME... I WAS REALLY NERVOUS ABOUT STARTING SCHOOL, SO I ASKED THE PSYCHIC ABOUT IT.
Most of them are really fakes.
AM I GOING TO MAKE A LOT OF FRIENDS?
...I ASKED HER.
IDIOT.
NO, YOU WON'T !!
...WAS ALL SHE SAID. I'M DONE.
You're the idiot?

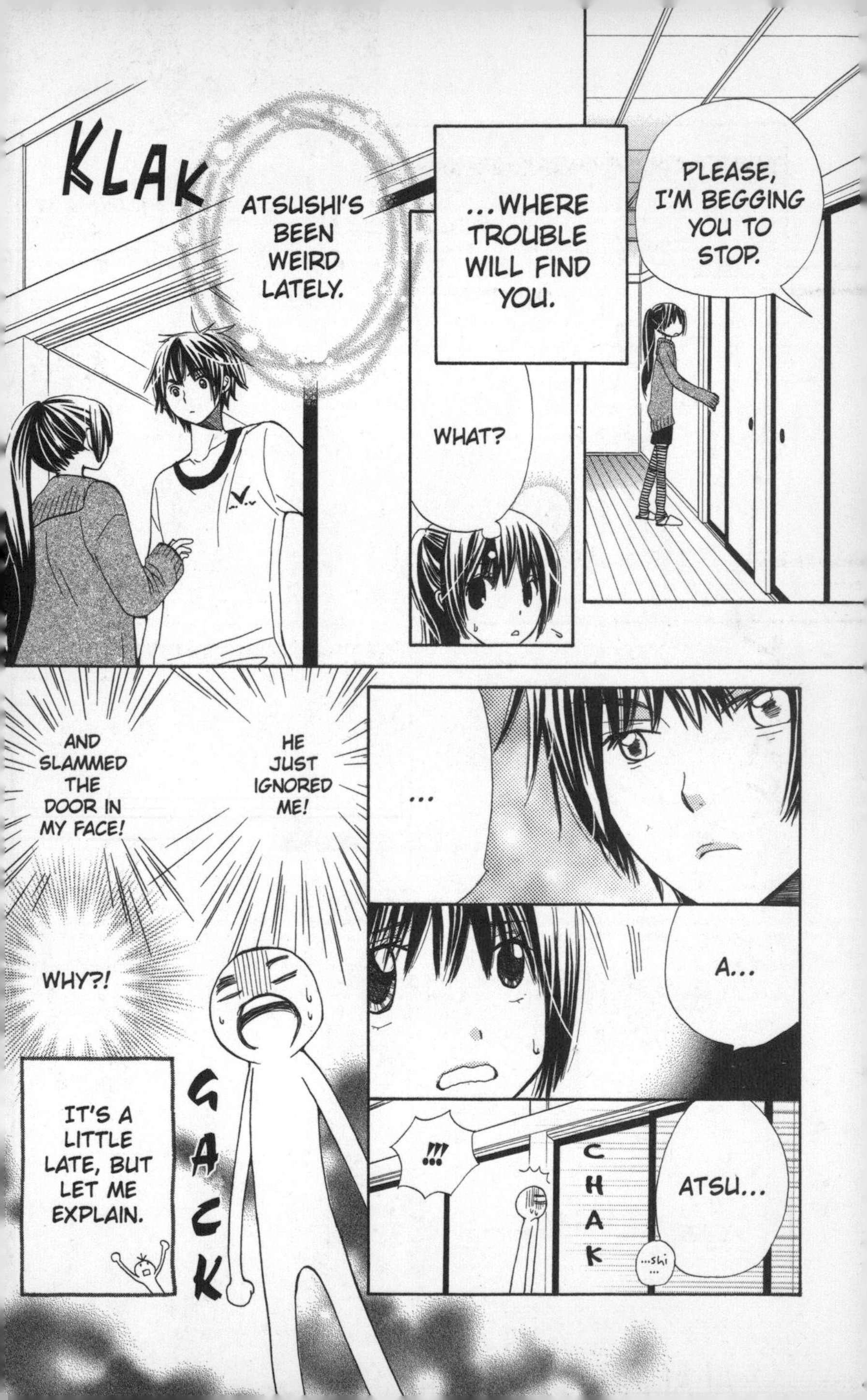
PLEASE, I'M BEGGING YOU TO STOP.
...WHERE TROUBLE WILL FIND YOU.
WHAT?
KLAK
ATSUSHI'S BEEN WEIRD LATELY.
...
A...
ATSU...
...shi ...
CHAK
!!!
HE JUST IGNORED ME!
AND SLAMMED THE DOOR IN MY FACE!
WHY?!
GACK
IT'S A LITTLE LATE, BUT LET ME EXPLAIN.

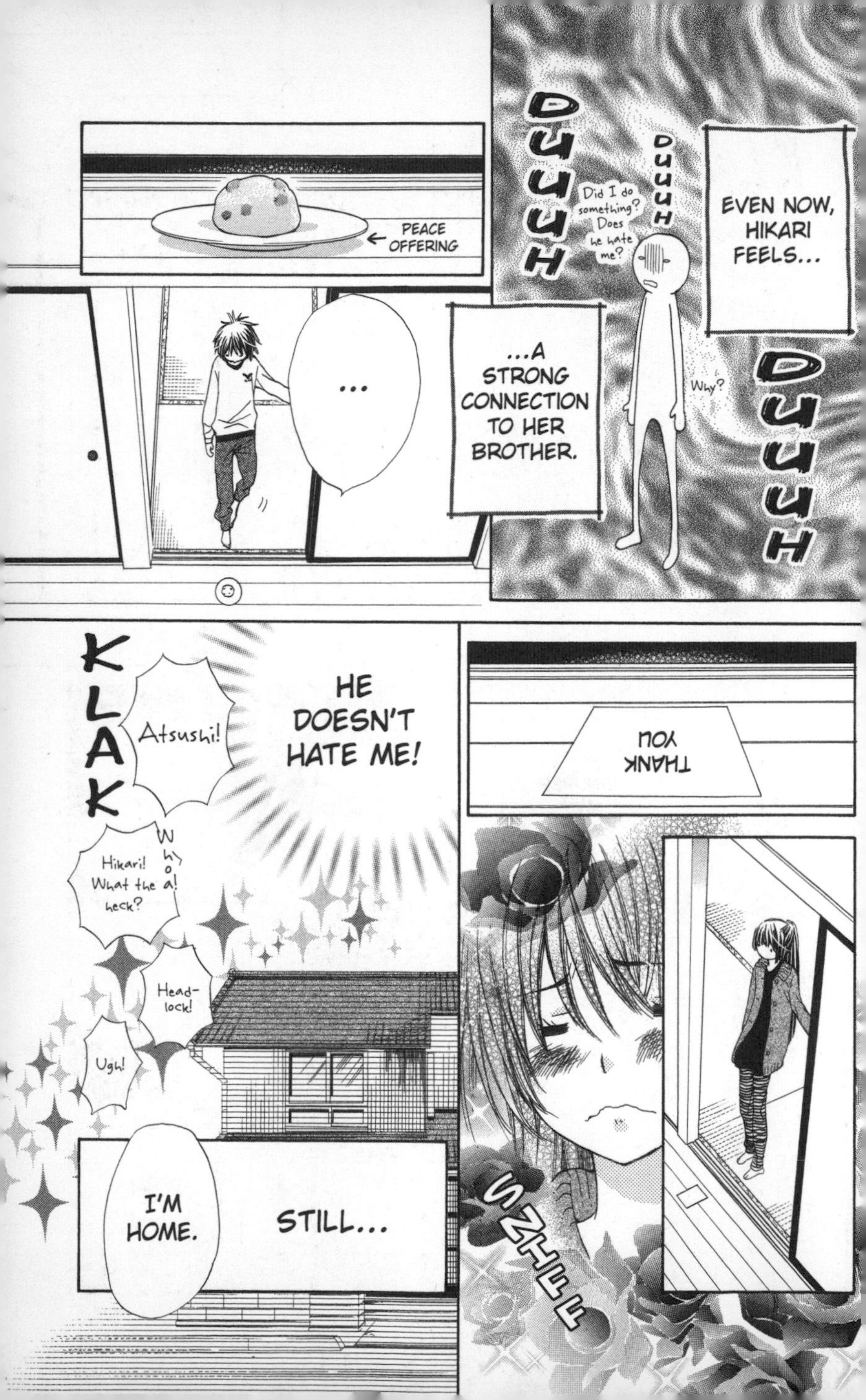
EVEN NOW, HIKARI FEELS...
DUUUH
Duuuh
Did I do something? Does he hate me?
Why?
DUUUH
...A STRONG CONNECTION TO HER BROTHER.
PEACE OFFERING
...
THANK YOU
SNIFF
HE DOESN'T HATE ME!
KLAK
Atsushi!
Whoa!
Hikari! What the heck?
Head-lock!
Ugh!
STILL...
I'M HOME.

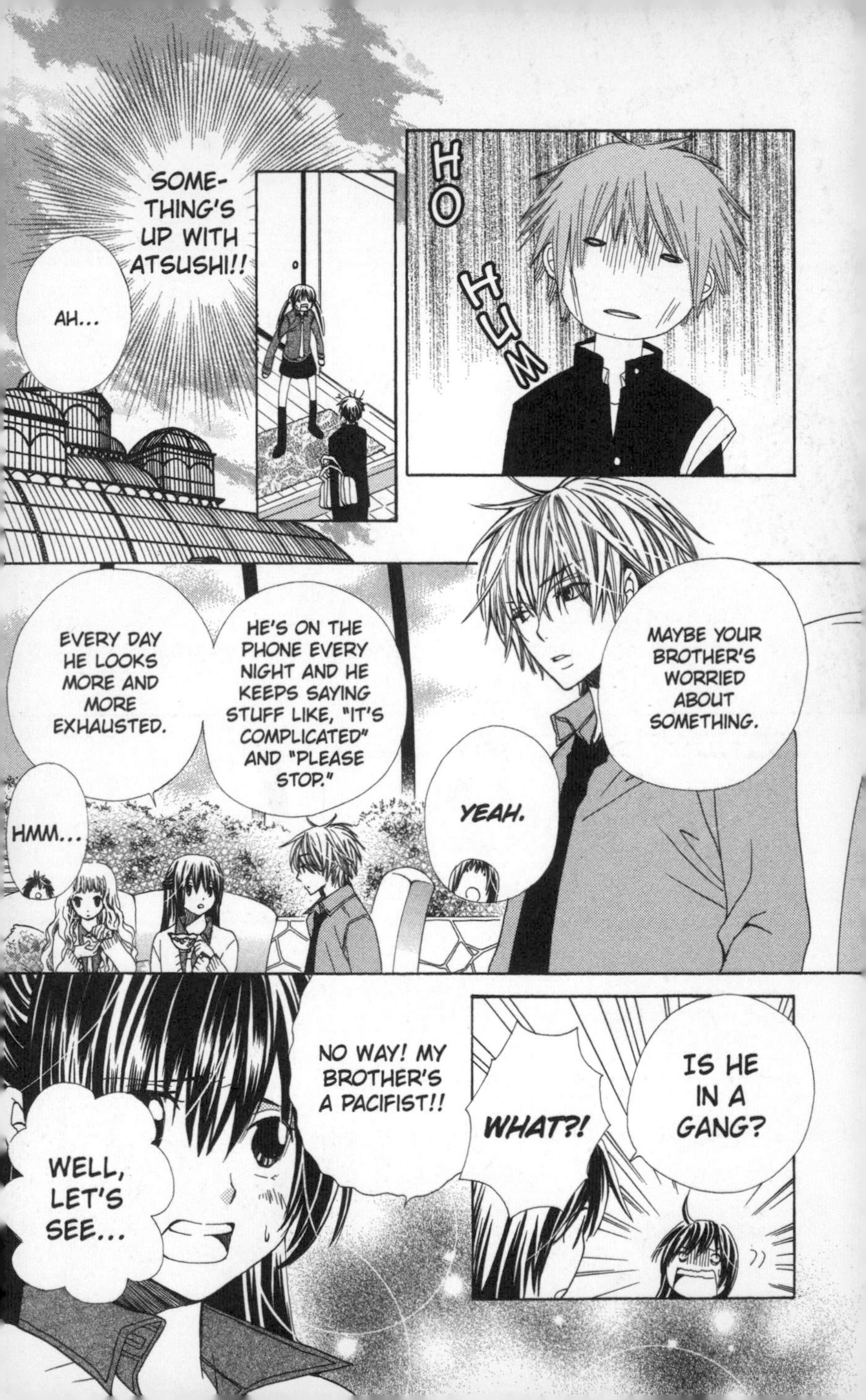
HO HUM
SOME-THING'S UP WITH ATSUSHI!!
AH...
MAYBE YOUR BROTHER'S WORRIED ABOUT SOMETHING.
YEAH.
HE'S ON THE PHONE EVERY NIGHT AND HE KEEPS SAYING STUFF LIKE, "IT'S COMPLICATED" AND "PLEASE STOP."
EVERY DAY HE LOOKS MORE AND MORE EXHAUSTED.
HMM...
IS HE IN A GANG?
WHAT?!
NO WAY! MY BROTHER'S A PACIFIST!!
WELL, LET'S SEE...

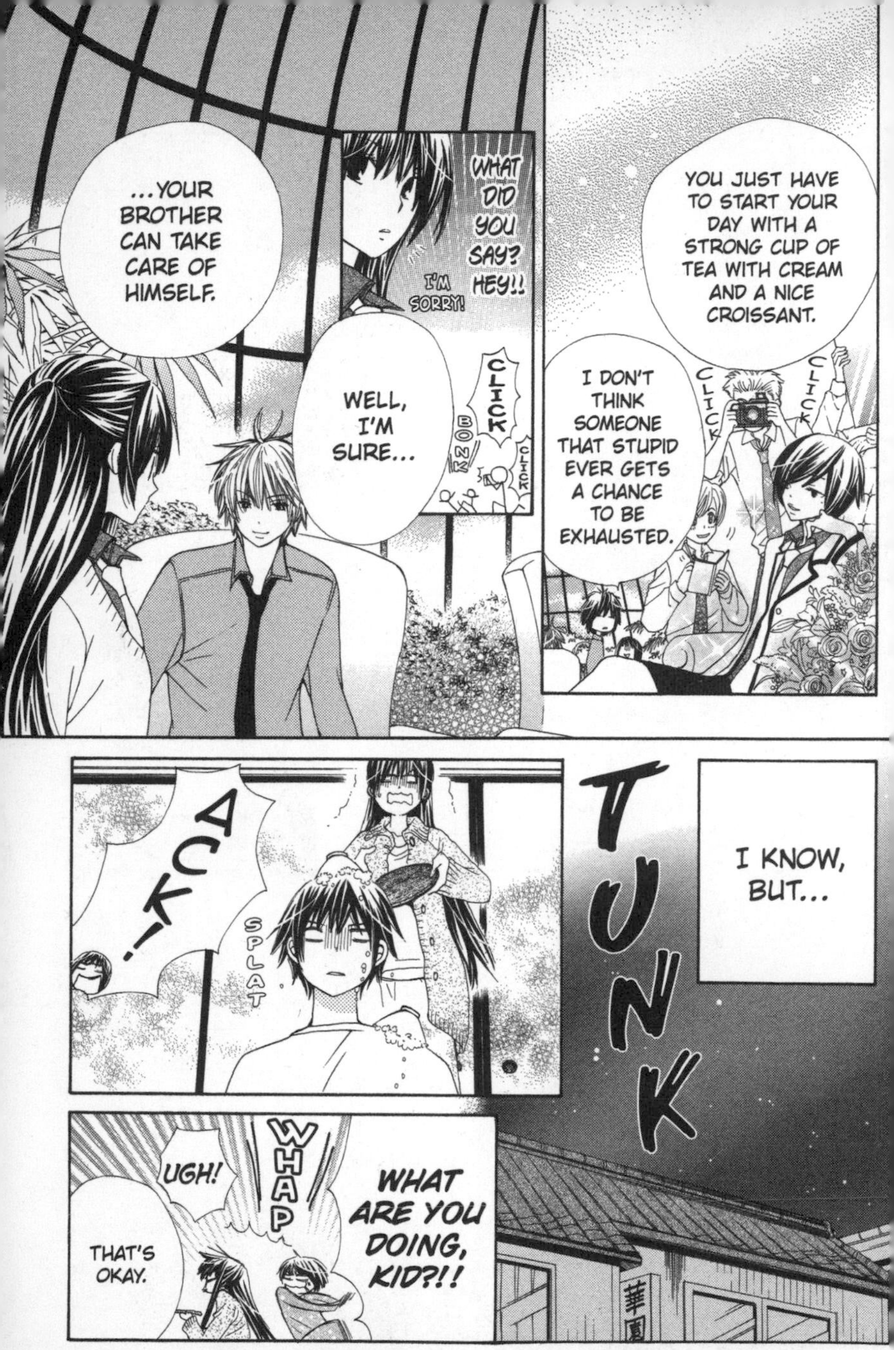
YOU JUST HAVE TO START YOUR DAY WITH A STRONG CUP OF TEA WITH CREAM AND A NICE CROISSANT.
CLICK
CLICK
I DON'T THINK SOMEONE THAT STUPID EVER GETS A CHANCE TO BE EXHAUSTED.
WHAT DID YOU SAY? HEY!!
I'M SORRY!
CLICK
BONK
CLICK
WELL, I'M SURE...
...YOUR BROTHER CAN TAKE CARE OF HIMSELF.
I KNOW, BUT...
TUNK
ACK!
SPLAT
WHAT ARE YOU DOING, KID?!!
WHAP
UGH!
THAT'S OKAY.

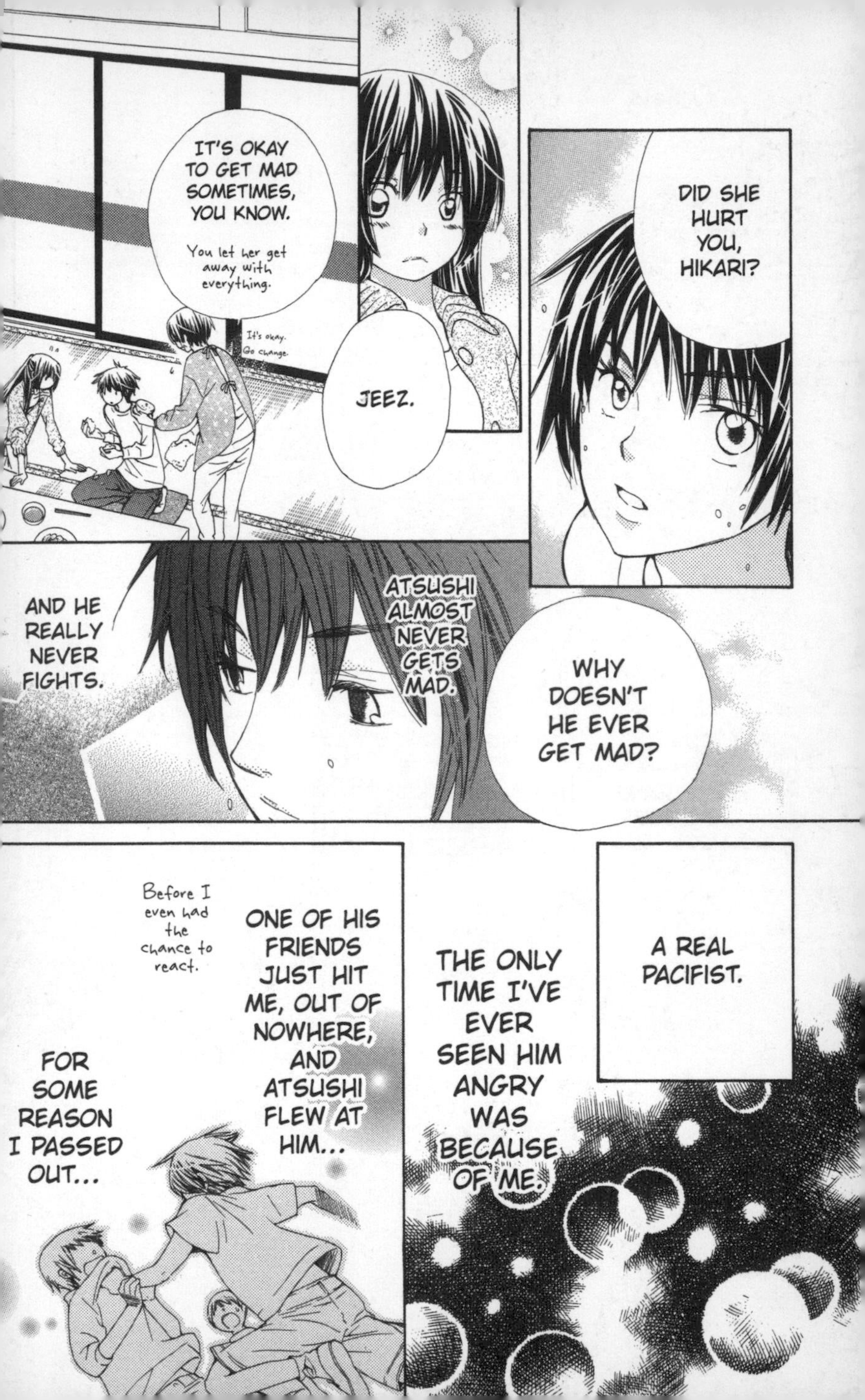
DID SHE HURT YOU, HIKARI?
JEEZ.
IT'S OKAY TO GET MAD SOMETIMES, YOU KNOW.
You let her get away with everything.
It's okay. Go change.
WHY DOESN'T HE EVER GET MAD?
ATSUSHI ALMOST NEVER GETS MAD.
AND HE REALLY NEVER FIGHTS.
A REAL PACIFIST.
THE ONLY TIME I'VE EVER SEEN HIM ANGRY WAS BECAUSE OF ME.
ONE OF HIS FRIENDS JUST HIT ME, OUT OF NOWHERE, AND ATSUSHI FLEW AT HIM...
Before I even had the chance to react.
FOR SOME REASON I PASSED OUT...

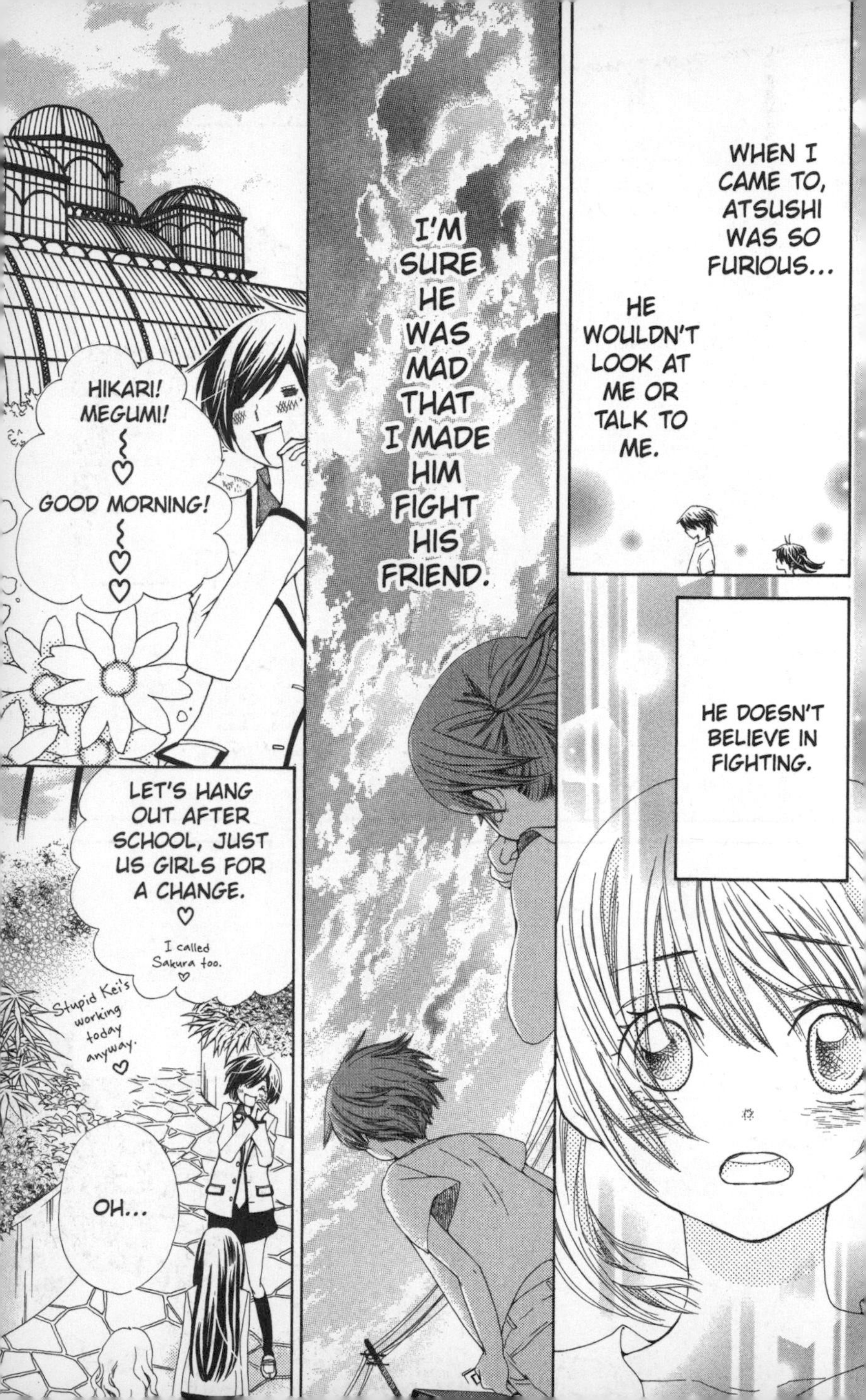
WHEN I CAME TO, ATSUSHI WAS SO FURIOUS...
HE WOULDN'T LOOK AT ME OR TALK TO ME.
HE DOESN'T BELIEVE IN FIGHTING.
I'M SURE HE WAS MAD THAT I MADE HIM FIGHT HIS FRIEND.
HIKARI! MEGUMI! ♡ GOOD MORNING! ♡♡
LET'S HANG OUT AFTER SCHOOL, JUST US GIRLS FOR A CHANGE. ♡
I called Sakura too. ♡
Stupid Kei's working today anyway. ♡
OH...

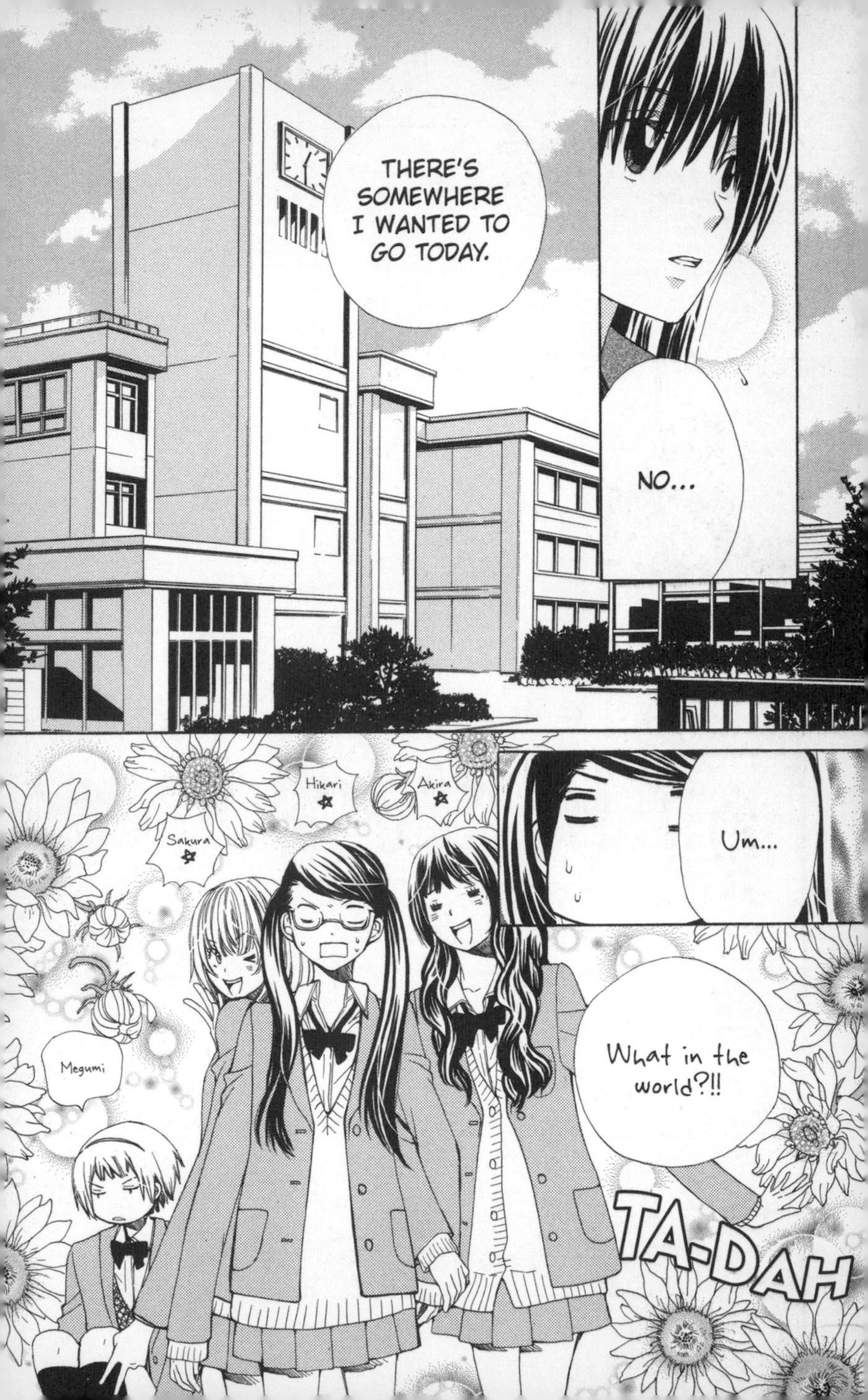
THERE'S SOMEWHERE I WANTED TO GO TODAY.
NO...
Um...
What in the world?!!
Akira
Hikari
Sakura
Megumi
TA-DAH

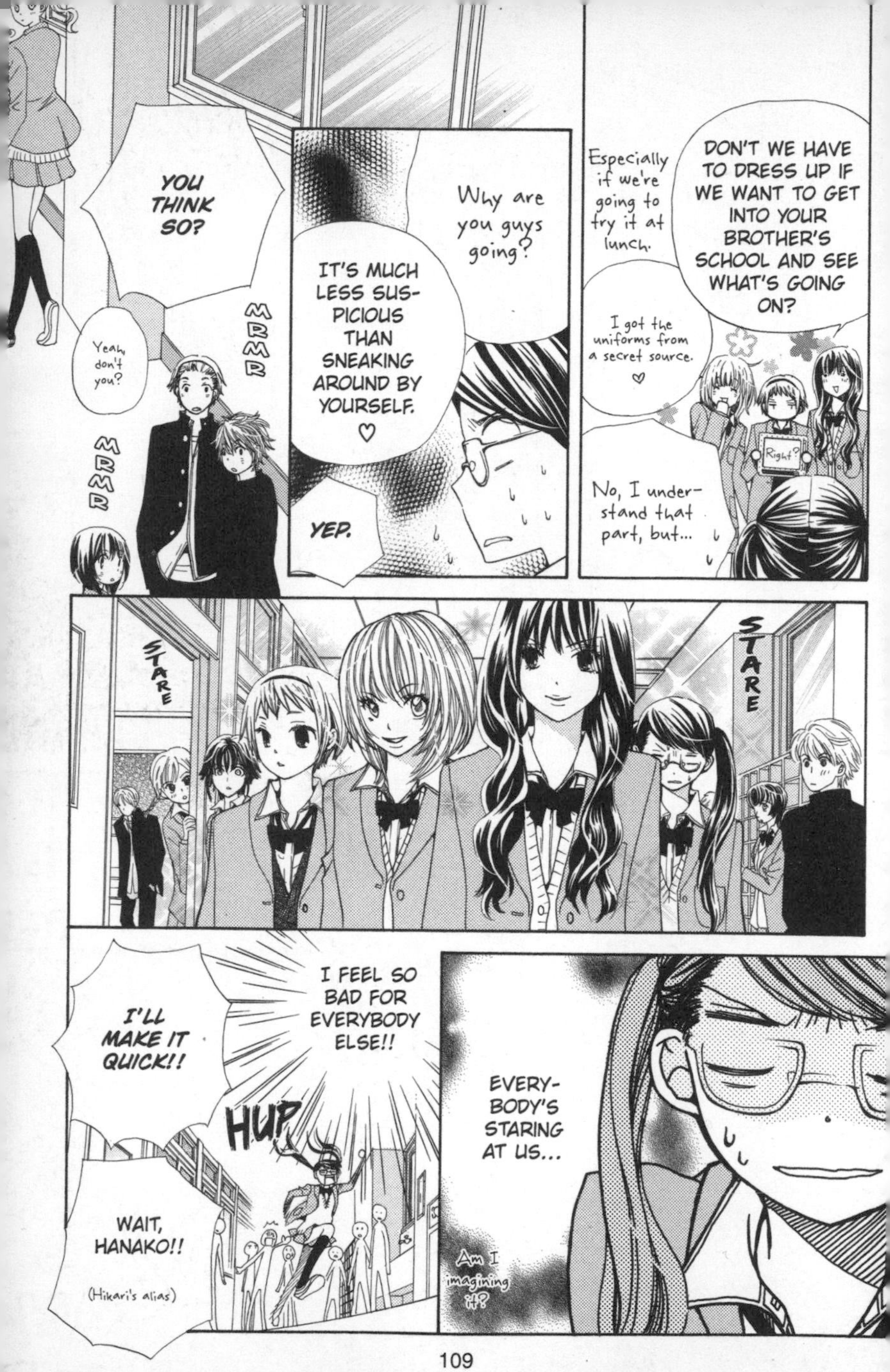
DON'T WE HAVE TO DRESS UP IF WE WANT TO GET INTO YOUR BROTHER'S SCHOOL AND SEE WHAT'S GOING ON?
Especially if we're going to try it at lunch.
I got the uniforms from a secret source. ♡
Right?
No, I understand that part, but...
Why are you guys going?
IT'S MUCH LESS SUSPICIOUS THAN SNEAKING AROUND BY YOURSELF. ♡
YEP.
YOU THINK SO?
MRMR
Yeah, don't you?
MRMR
STARE
STARE
EVERYBODY'S STARING AT US...
Am I imagining it?
I FEEL SO BAD FOR EVERYBODY ELSE!!
I'LL MAKE IT QUICK!!
HUP
WAIT, HANAKO!!
(Hikari's alias)

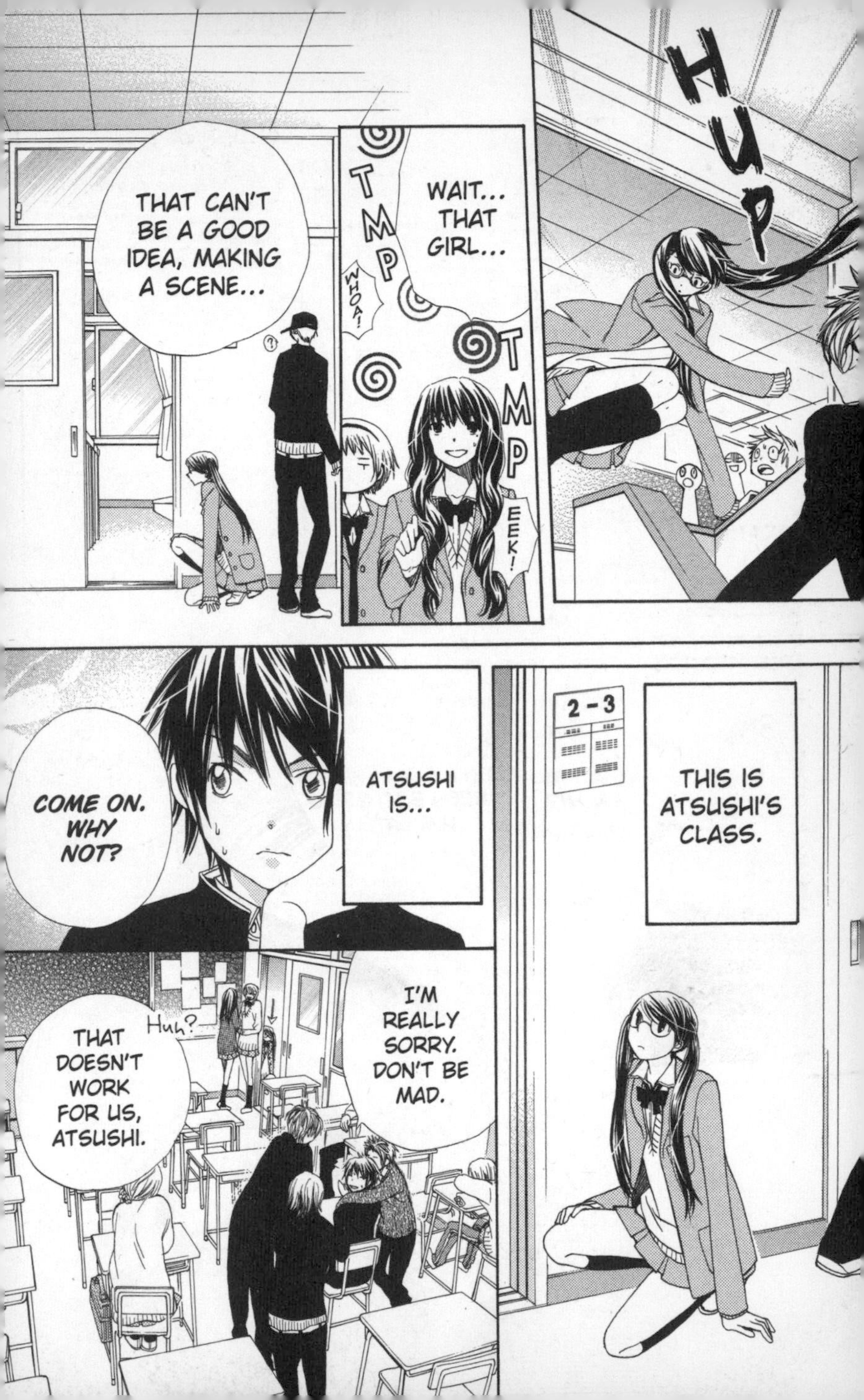
HUP
WAIT... THAT GIRL...
TMP
WHOA!
TMP
EEK!
THAT CAN'T BE A GOOD IDEA, MAKING A SCENE...
?
2-3
THIS IS ATSUSHI'S CLASS.
ATSUSHI IS...
COME ON. WHY NOT?
I'M REALLY SORRY. DON'T BE MAD.
Huh?
THAT DOESN'T WORK FOR US, ATSUSHI.

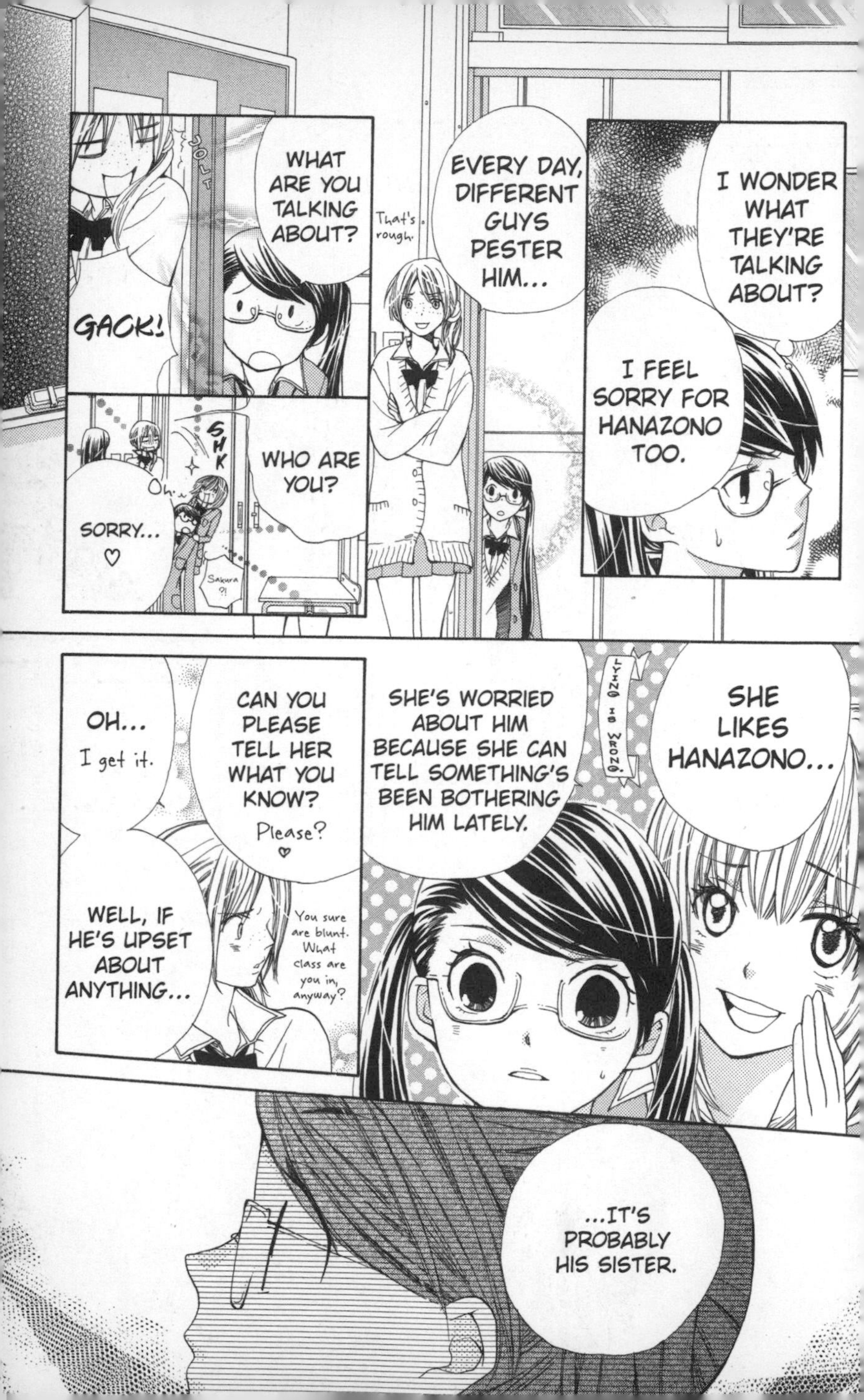
I WONDER WHAT THEY'RE TALKING ABOUT?
I FEEL SORRY FOR HANAZONO TOO.
EVERY DAY, DIFFERENT GUYS PESTER HIM...
That's rough.
WHAT ARE YOU TALKING ABOUT?
JOLT
GACK!
WHO ARE YOU?
SHK
Oh...
SORRY... ♡
Sakura ?!
SHE LIKES HANAZONO...
LYING IS WRONG.
SHE'S WORRIED ABOUT HIM BECAUSE SHE CAN TELL SOMETHING'S BEEN BOTHERING HIM LATELY.
CAN YOU PLEASE TELL HER WHAT YOU KNOW?
Please? ♡
OH...
I get it.
You sure are blunt. What class are you in, anyway?
WELL, IF HE'S UPSET ABOUT ANYTHING...
...IT'S PROBABLY HIS SISTER.

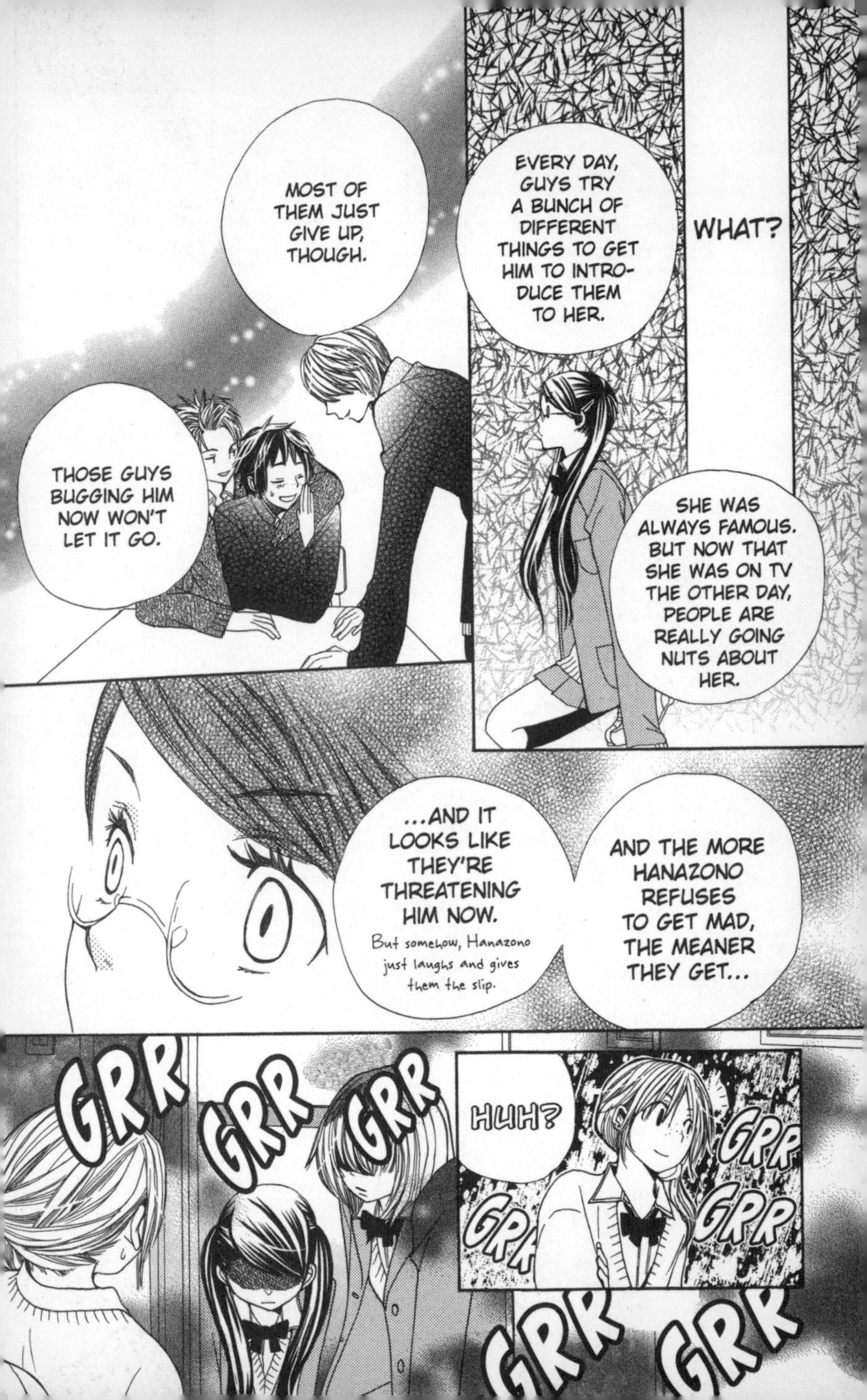
WHAT?
SHE WAS ALWAYS FAMOUS. BUT NOW THAT SHE WAS ON TV THE OTHER DAY, PEOPLE ARE REALLY GOING NUTS ABOUT HER.
EVERY DAY, GUYS TRY A BUNCH OF DIFFERENT THINGS TO GET HIM TO INTRO-DUCE THEM TO HER.
MOST OF THEM JUST GIVE UP, THOUGH.
THOSE GUYS BUGGING HIM NOW WON'T LET IT GO.
AND THE MORE HANAZONO REFUSES TO GET MAD, THE MEANER THEY GET...
...AND IT LOOKS LIKE THEY'RE THREATENING HIM NOW.
But somehow, Hanazono just laughs and gives them the slip.
GRR
GRR
GRR
HUH?
GRR
GRR
GRR
GRR
GRR
GRR
GRR

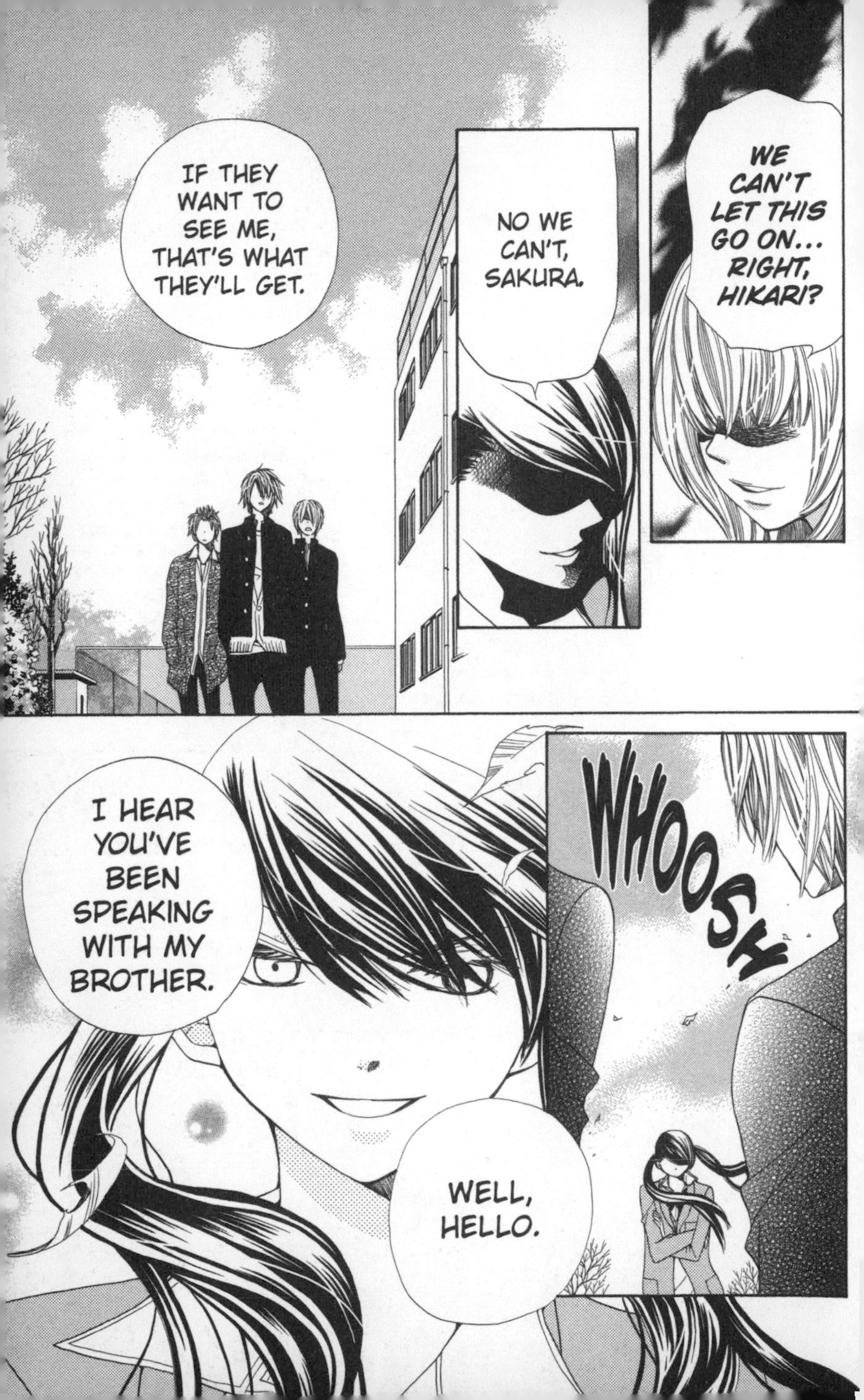

WE CAN'T LET THIS GO ON... RIGHT, HIKARI?
NO WE CAN'T, SAKURA.
IF THEY WANT TO SEE ME, THAT'S WHAT THEY'LL GET.
WHOOSH
WELL, HELLO.
I HEAR YOU'VE BEEN SPEAKING WITH MY BROTHER.

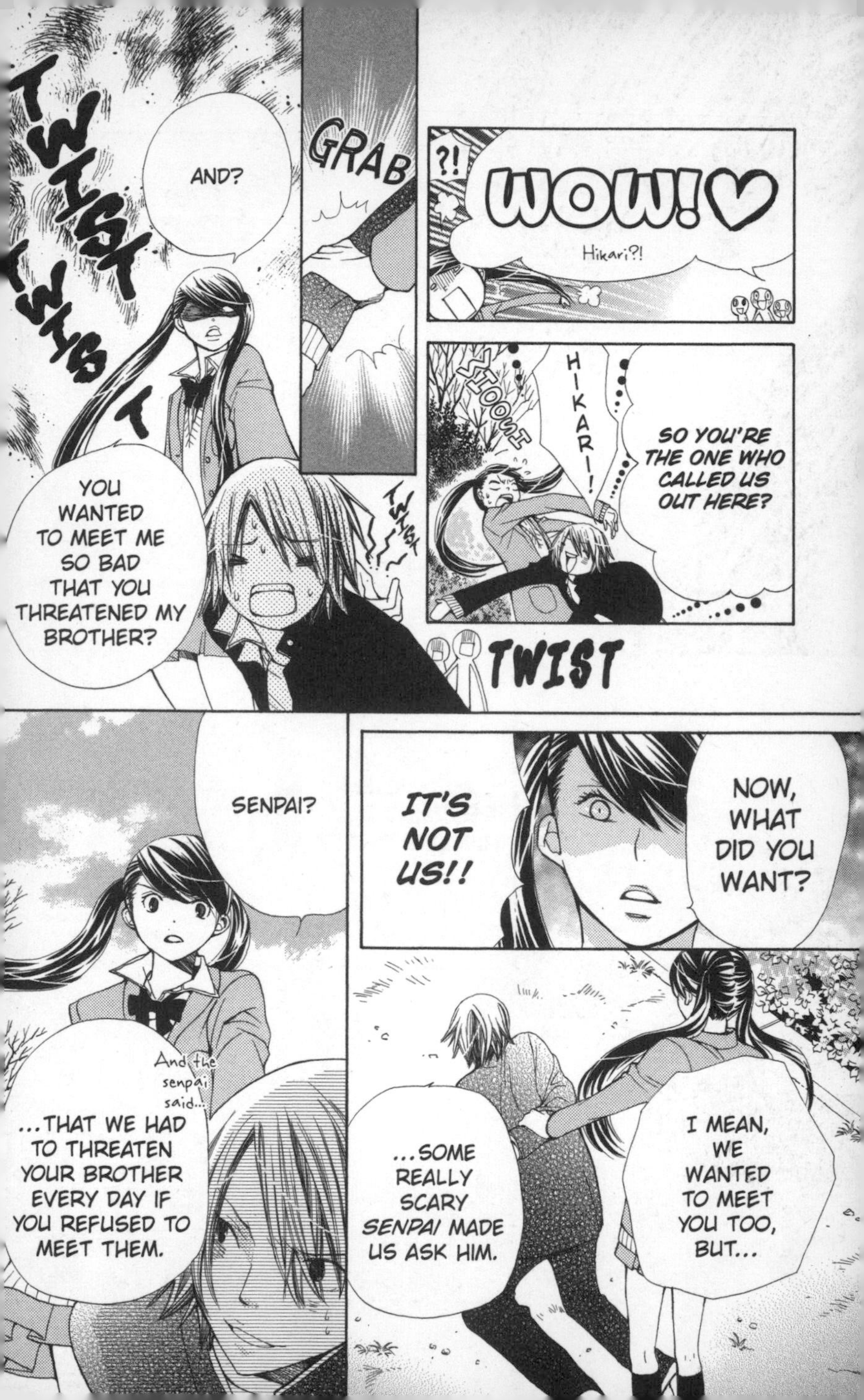
?!
WOW!♥
Hikari?!
HIKARI!!
WHOOSH
SO YOU'RE THE ONE WHO CALLED US OUT HERE?
TWIST
GRAB
TWIST
TWIST
AND?
TWIST
YOU WANTED TO MEET ME SO BAD THAT YOU THREATENED MY BROTHER?
NOW, WHAT DID YOU WANT?
IT'S NOT US!!
I MEAN, WE WANTED TO MEET YOU TOO, BUT...
...SOME REALLY SCARY SENPAI MADE US ASK HIM.
SENPAI?
And the senpai said...
...THAT WE HAD TO THREATEN YOUR BROTHER EVERY DAY IF YOU REFUSED TO MEET THEM.

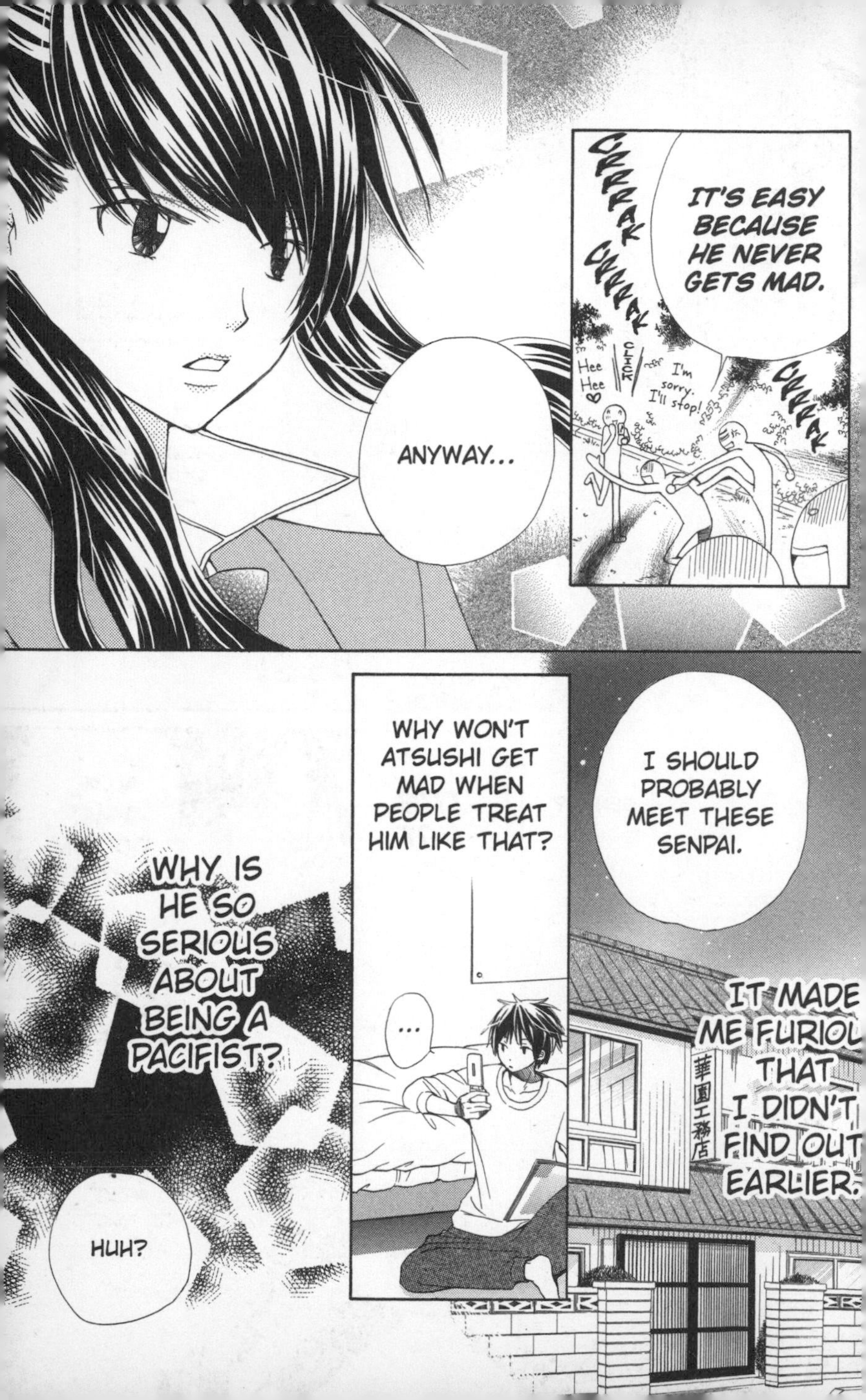
IT'S EASY BECAUSE HE NEVER GETS MAD.
CRRRAK
CRRRAK
CLICK
Hee Hee
I'm sorry. I'll stop!
CRRRAK
ANYWAY...
I SHOULD PROBABLY MEET THESE SENPAI.
IT MADE ME FURIOU THAT I DIDN'T FIND OUT EARLIER.
華園工務店
WHY WON'T ATSUSHI GET MAD WHEN PEOPLE TREAT HIM LIKE THAT?
...
WHY IS HE SO SERIOUS ABOUT BEING A PACIFIST?
HUH?

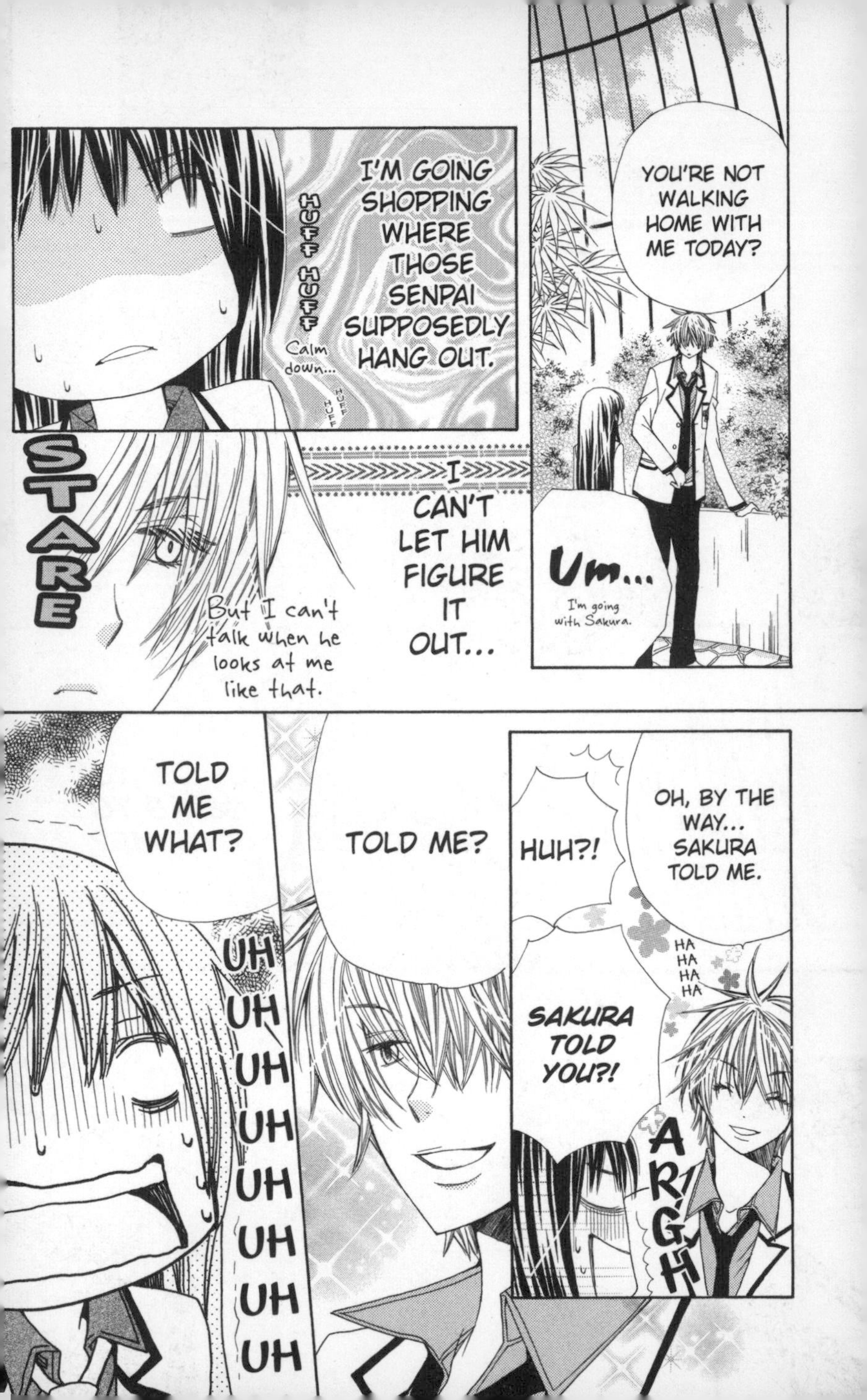
YOU'RE NOT WALKING HOME WITH ME TODAY?
Um...
I'm going with Sakura.
I'M GOING SHOPPING WHERE THOSE SENPAI SUPPOSEDLY HANG OUT.
HUFF HUFF
Calm down...
HUFF HUFF
STARE
I CAN'T LET HIM FIGURE IT OUT...
But I can't talk when he looks at me like that.
OH, BY THE WAY... SAKURA TOLD ME.
HA HA HA HA
HUH?!
SAKURA TOLD YOU?!
ARGH
TOLD ME?
TOLD ME WHAT?
UH UH UH UH UH UH UH UH UH

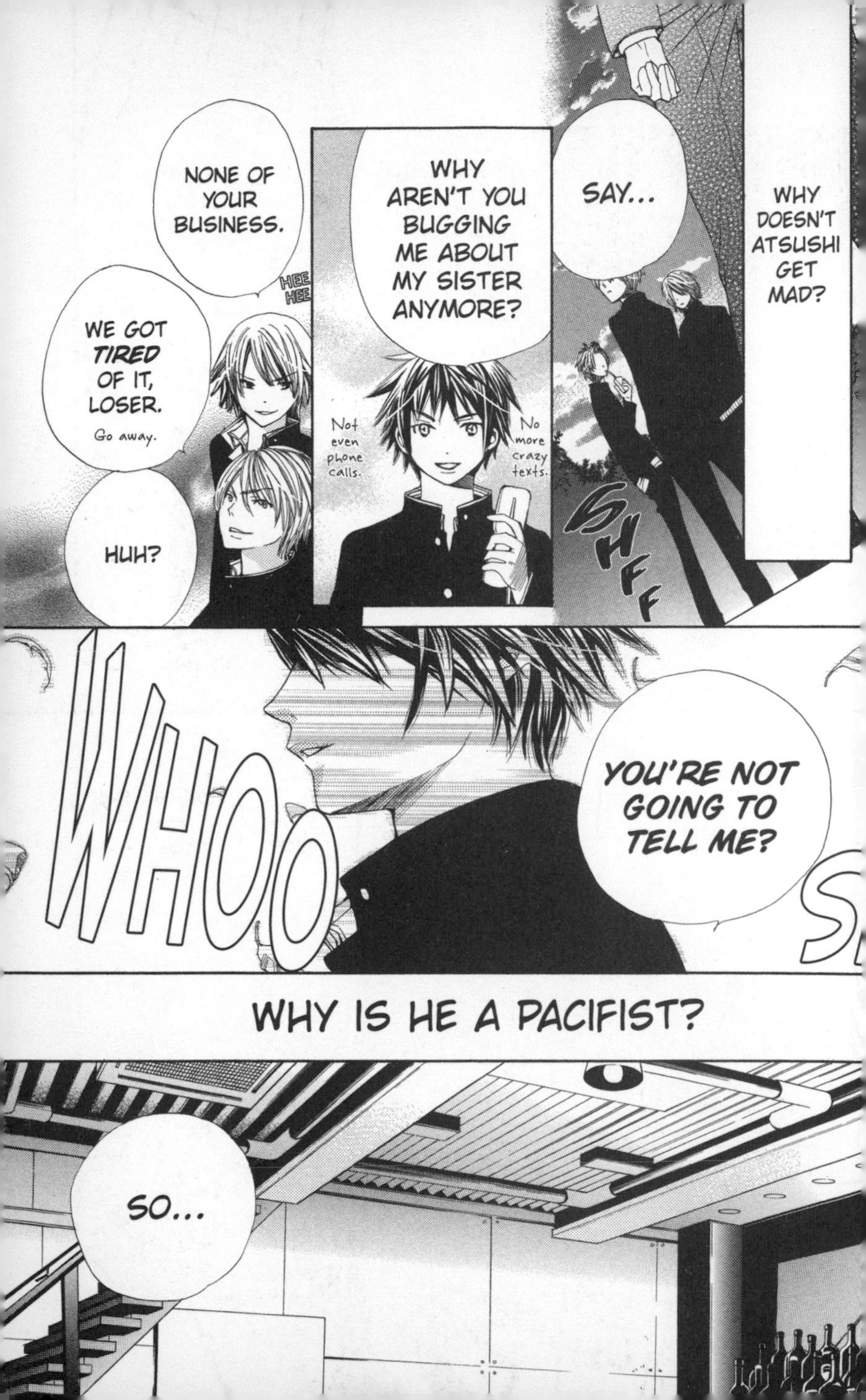
WHY DOESN'T ATSUSHI GET MAD?
SAY...
SHFF
WHY AREN'T YOU BUGGING ME ABOUT MY SISTER ANYMORE?
No more crazy texts.
Not even phone calls.
NONE OF YOUR BUSINESS.
HEE HEE
WE GOT *TIRED* OF IT, LOSER.
Go away.
HUH?
YOU'RE NOT GOING TO TELL ME?
WHOOO
WHY IS HE A PACIFIST?
SO...

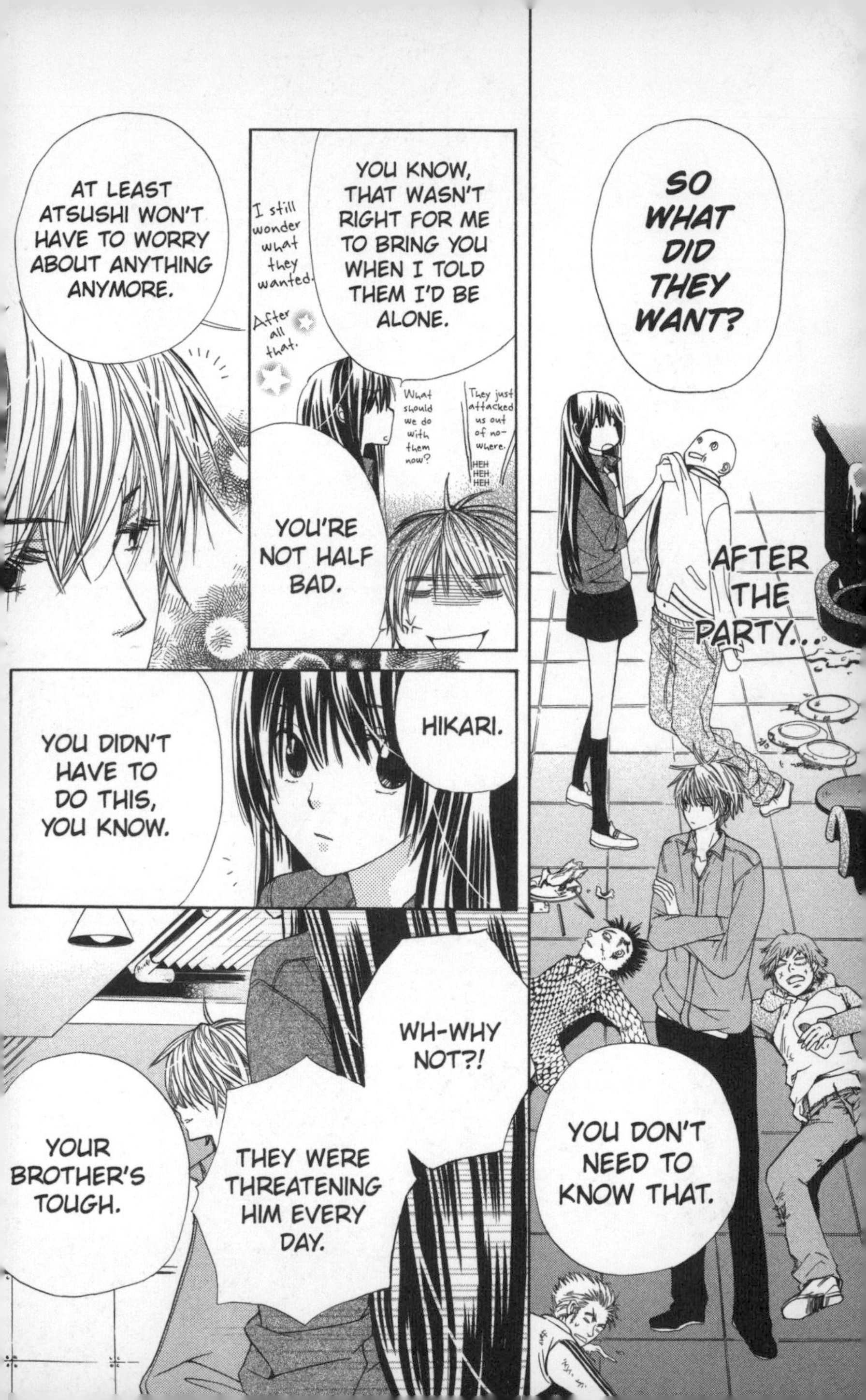
SO WHAT DID THEY WANT?
AFTER THE PARTY...
YOU DON'T NEED TO KNOW THAT.
YOU KNOW, THAT WASN'T RIGHT FOR ME TO BRING YOU WHEN I TOLD THEM I'D BE ALONE.
I still wonder what they wanted.
After all that.
They just attacked us out of no-where.
HEH HEH HEH
What should we do with them now?
YOU'RE NOT HALF BAD.
AT LEAST ATSUSHI WON'T HAVE TO WORRY ABOUT ANYTHING ANYMORE.
HIKARI.
YOU DIDN'T HAVE TO DO THIS, YOU KNOW.
WH-WHY NOT?!
THEY WERE THREATENING HIM EVERY DAY.
YOUR BROTHER'S TOUGH.

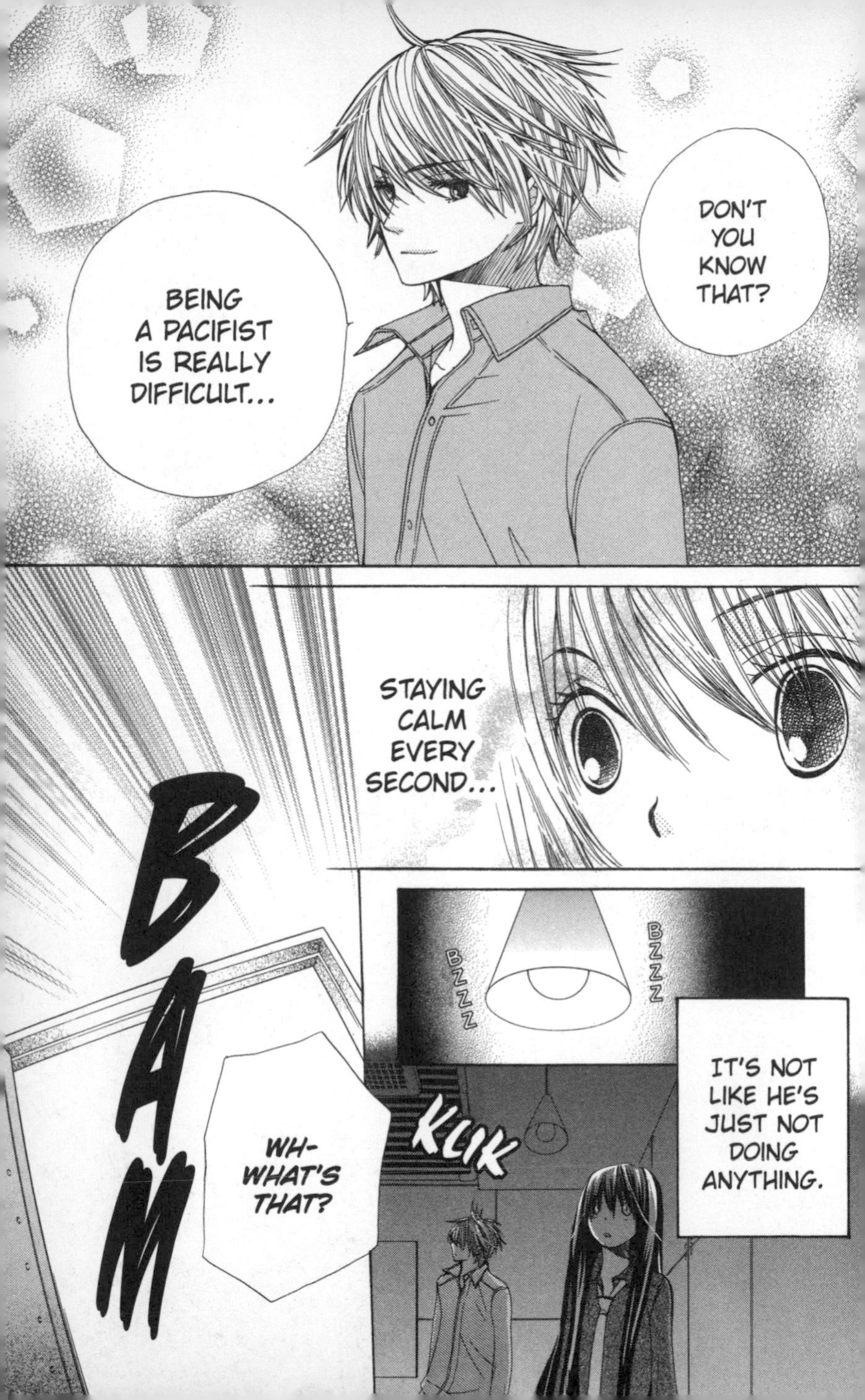
DON'T YOU KNOW THAT?
BEING A PACIFIST IS REALLY DIFFICULT...
STAYING CALM EVERY SECOND...
BZZZ
BZZZ
IT'S NOT LIKE HE'S JUST NOT DOING ANYTHING.
KLIK
BAM
WH-WHAT'S THAT?

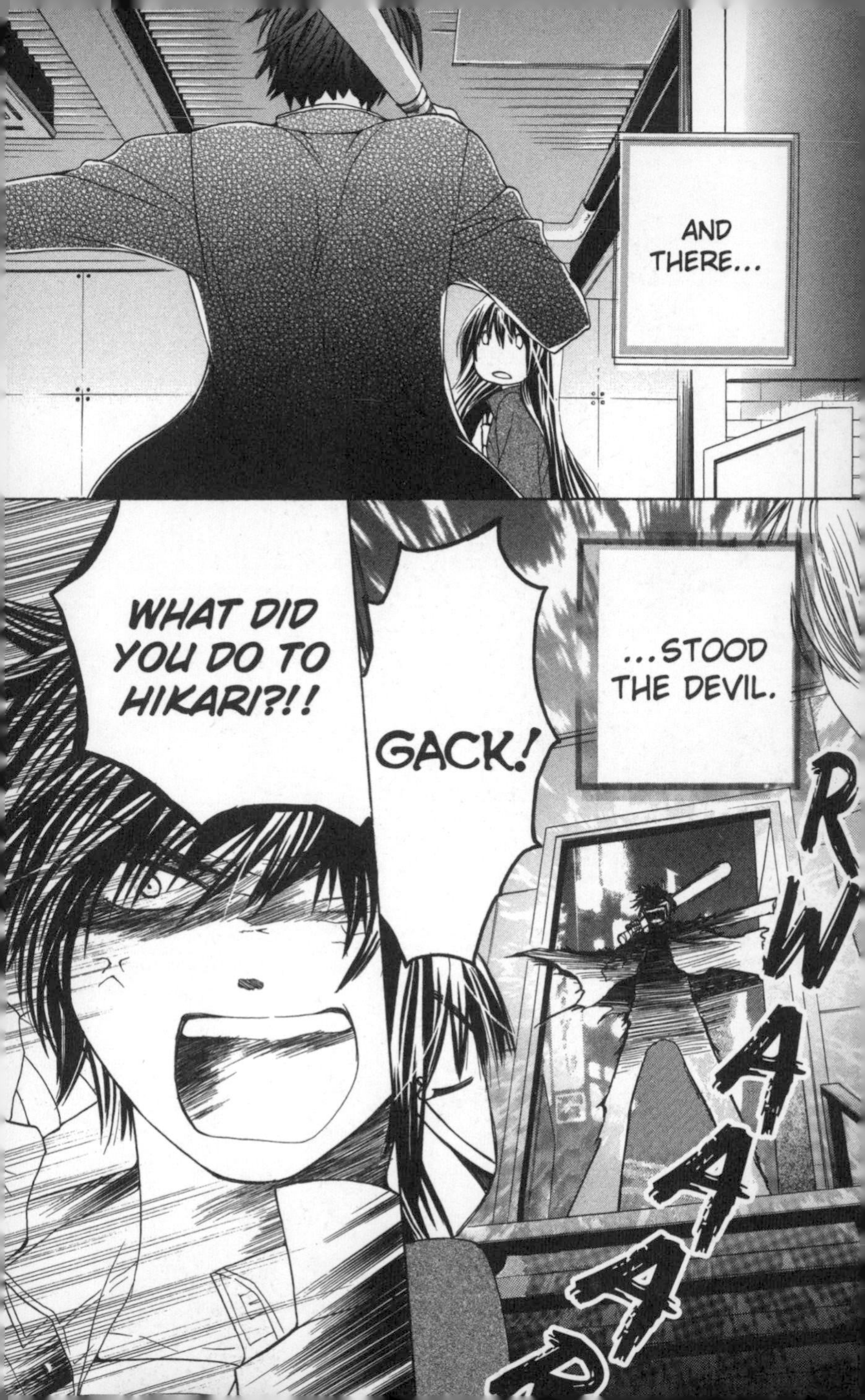
AND THERE...
...STOOD THE DEVIL.
WHAT DID YOU DO TO HIKARI?!!
GACK!
RWAAAA

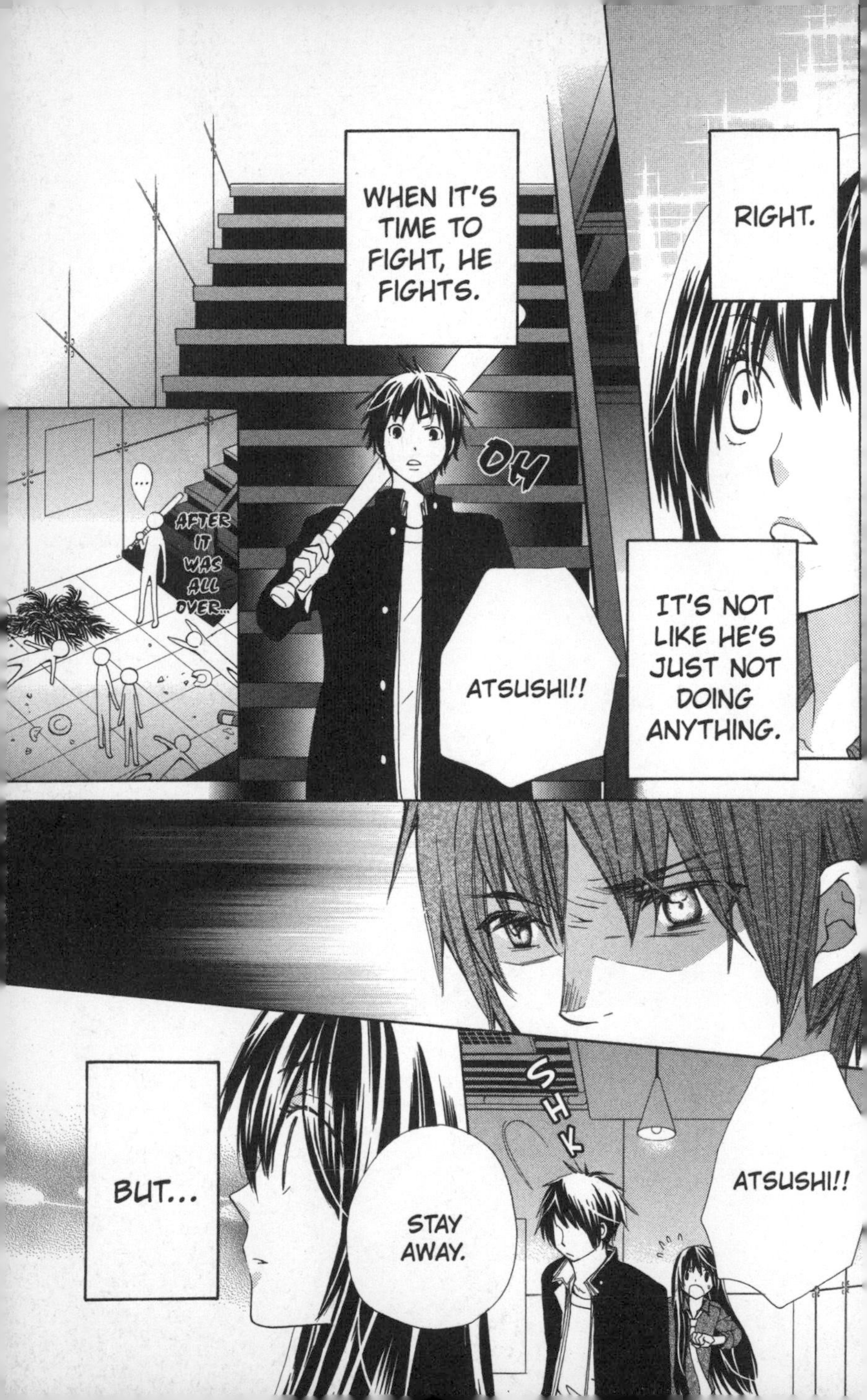
RIGHT.
IT'S NOT LIKE HE'S JUST NOT DOING ANYTHING.
WHEN IT'S TIME TO FIGHT, HE FIGHTS.
OH
ATSUSHI!!
...
AFTER IT WAS ALL OVER...
ATSUSHI!!
SHK
STAY AWAY.
BUT...

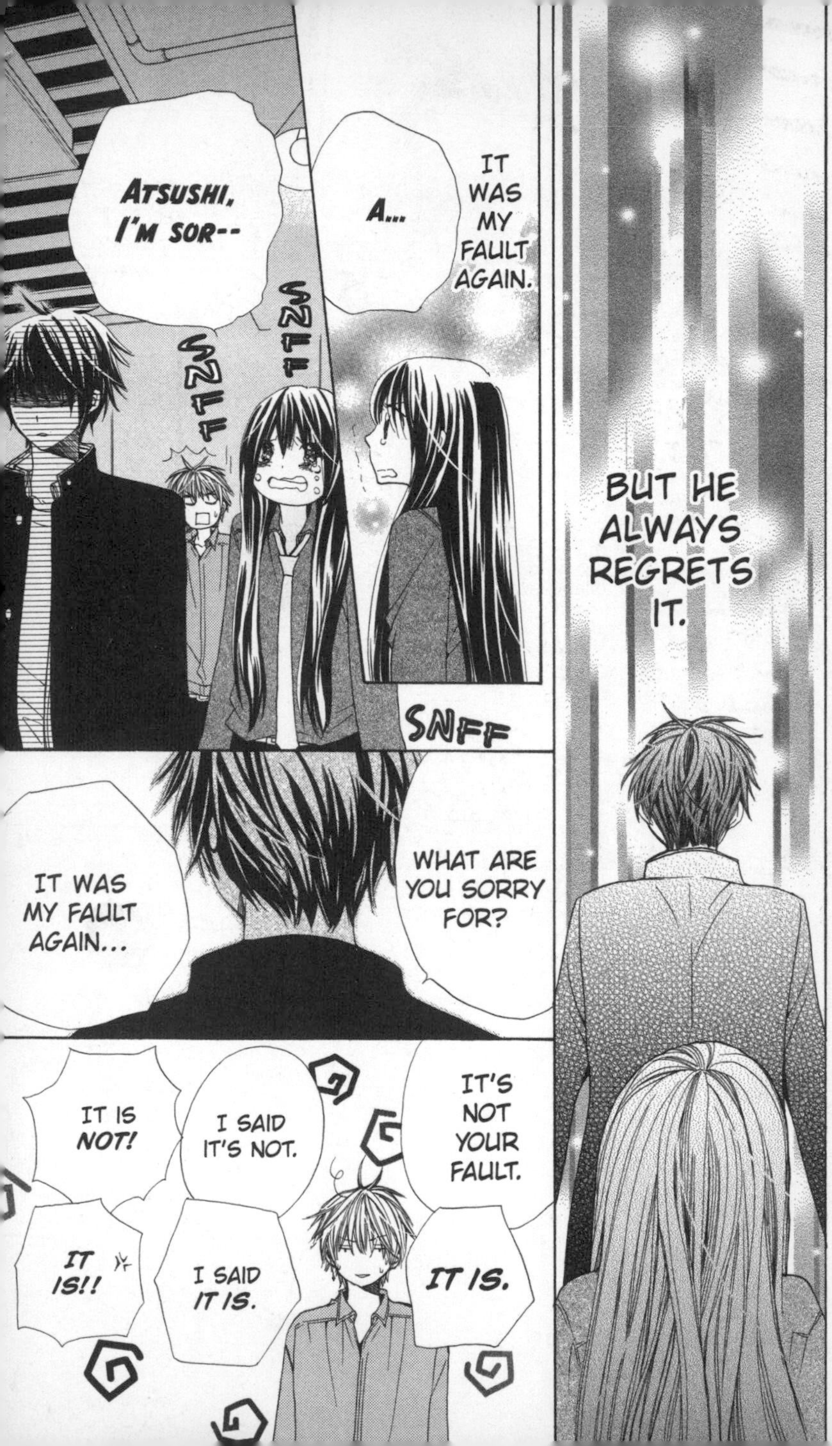
BUT HE ALWAYS REGRETS IT.
A...
IT WAS MY FAULT AGAIN.
SNFF
ATSUSHI, I'M SOR--
SNFF
SNFF
WHAT ARE YOU SORRY FOR?
IT WAS MY FAULT AGAIN...
IT'S NOT YOUR FAULT.
I SAID IT'S NOT.
IT IS *NOT!*
IT IS.
I SAID *IT IS.*
IT IS!!

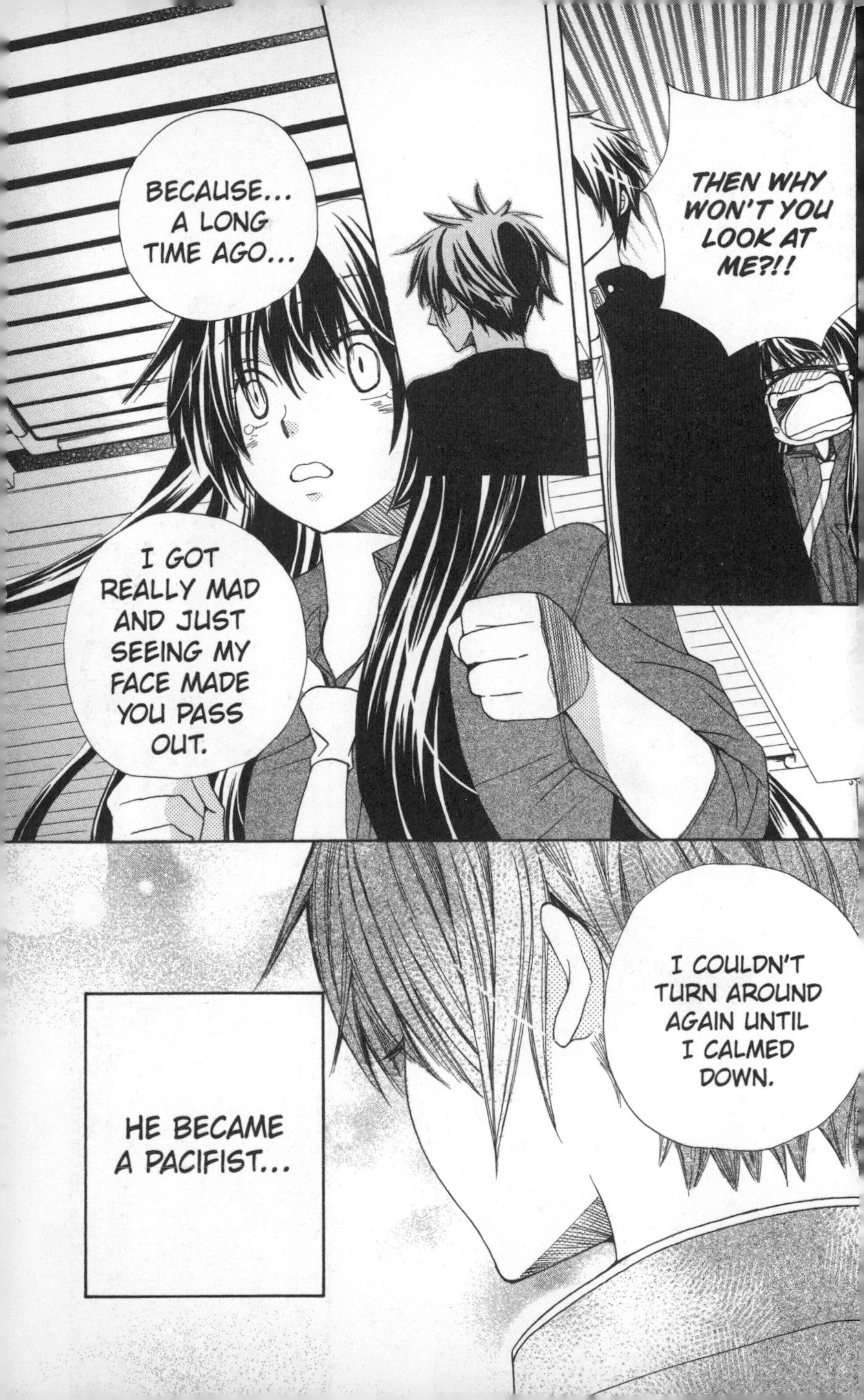
THEN WHY WON'T YOU LOOK AT ME?!!
BECAUSE... A LONG TIME AGO...
I GOT REALLY MAD AND JUST SEEING MY FACE MADE YOU PASS OUT.
I COULDN'T TURN AROUND AGAIN UNTIL I CALMED DOWN.
HE BECAME A PACIFIST...

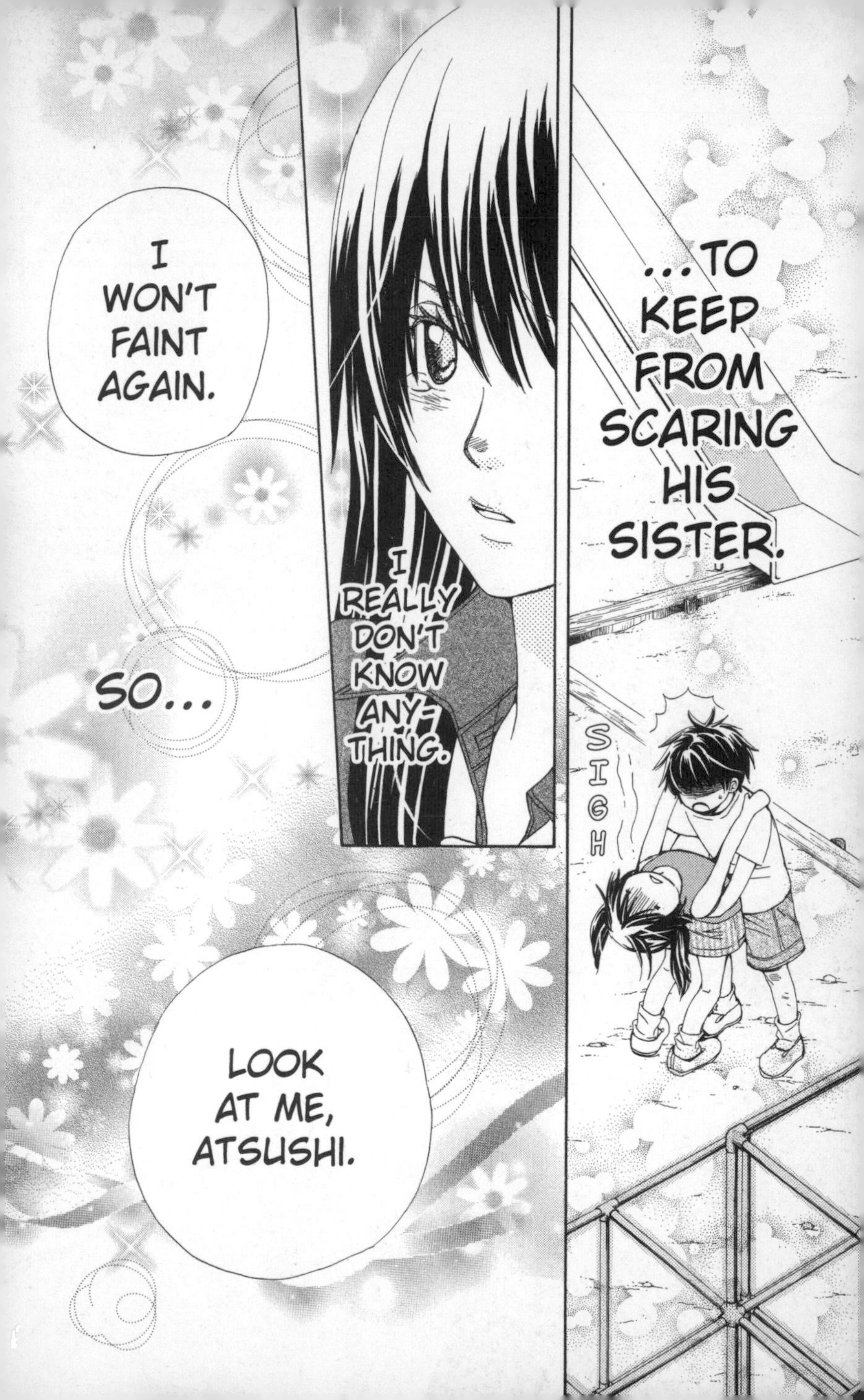
... TO KEEP FROM SCARING HIS SISTER.
SIGH
I REALLY DON'T KNOW ANY-THING.
I WON'T FAINT AGAIN.
SO...
LOOK AT ME, ATSUSHI.

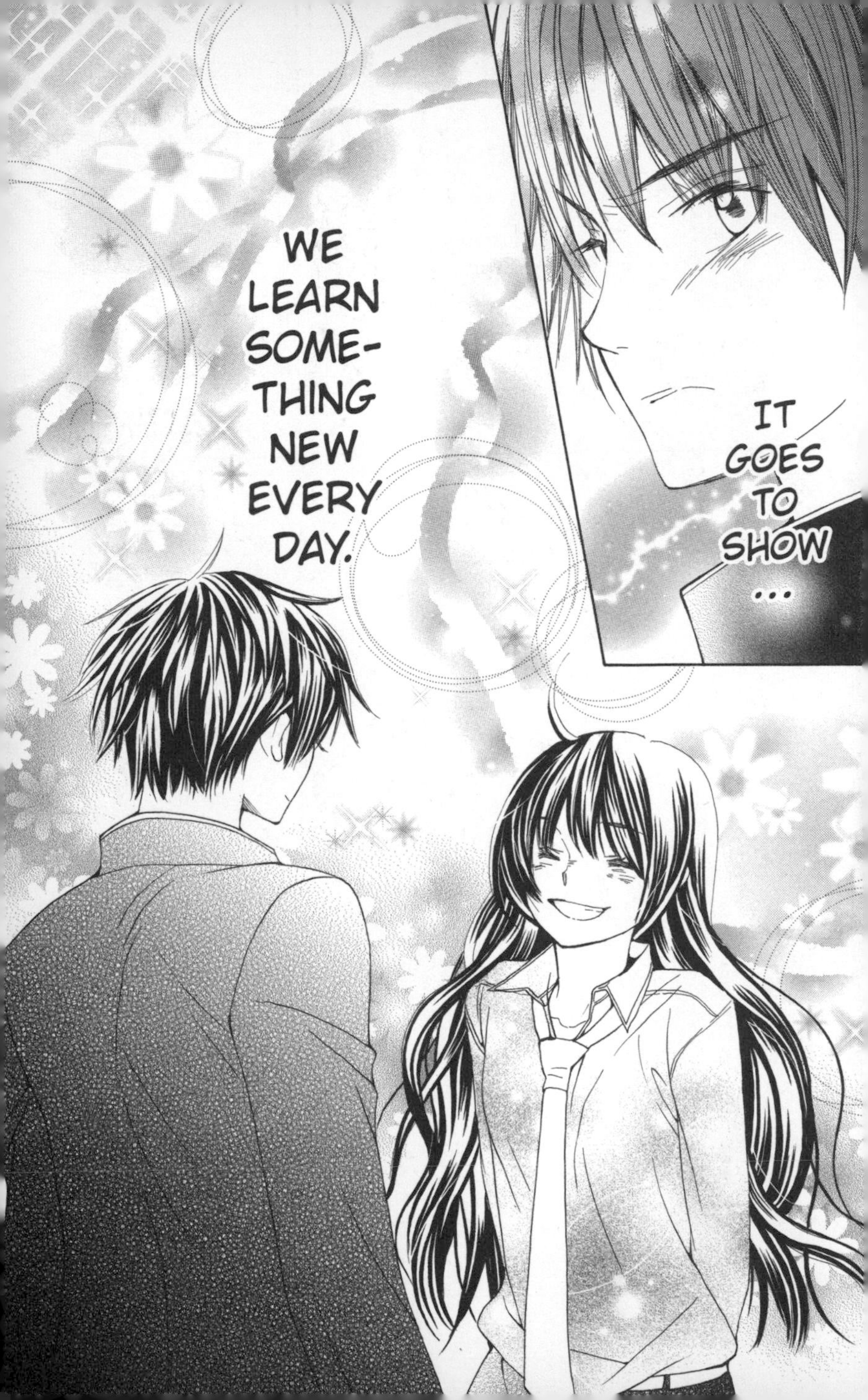
IT GOES TO SHOW ...
WE LEARN SOMETHING NEW EVERY DAY.

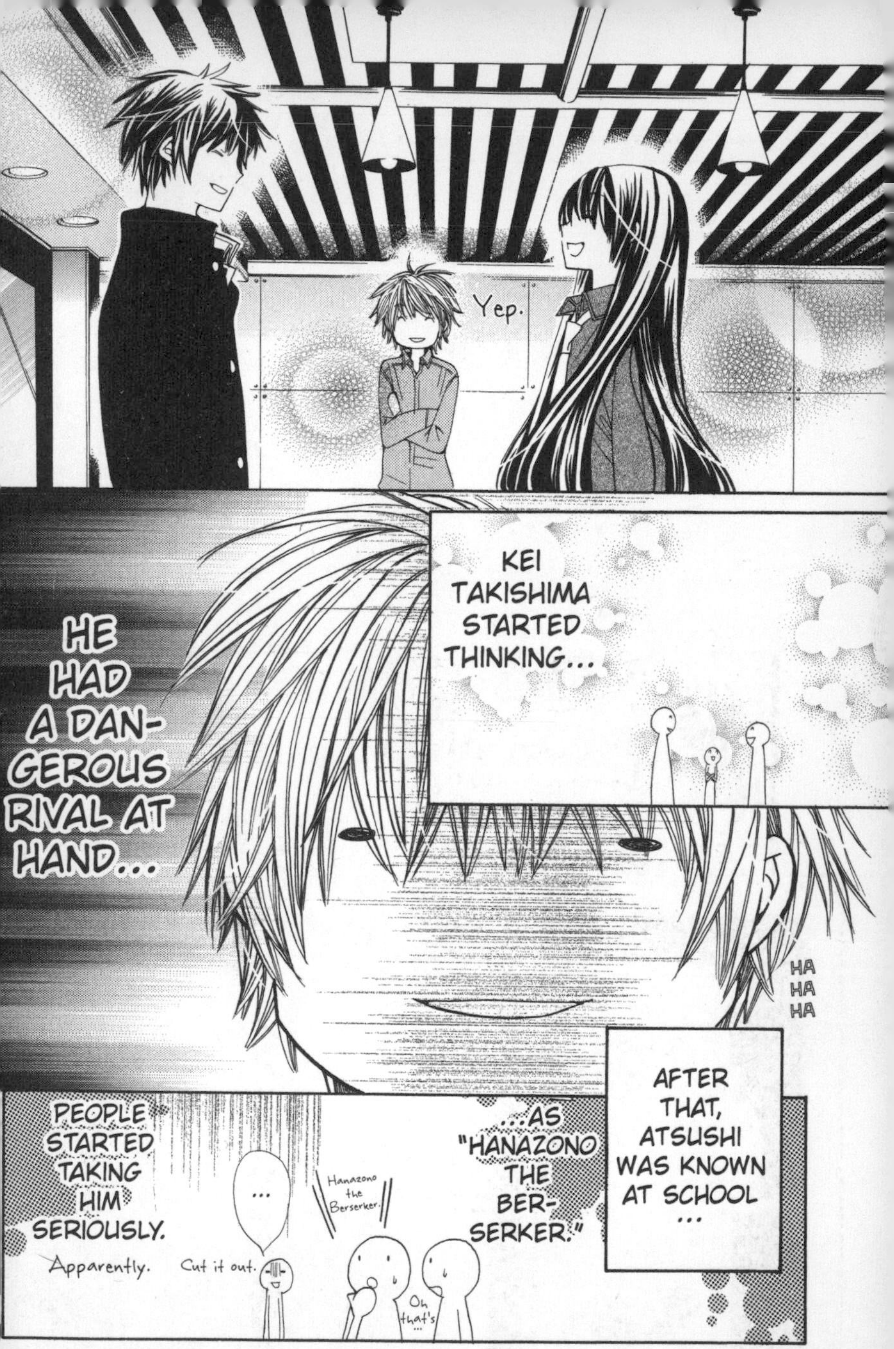
Yep.
KEI TAKISHIMA STARTED THINKING...
HE HAD A DAN-GEROUS RIVAL AT HAND...
HA HA HA
AFTER THAT, ATSUSHI WAS KNOWN AT SCHOOL ...
...AS "HANAZONO THE BER-SERKER."
Oh that's...
Hanazono the Berserker
...
Cut it out.
PEOPLE STARTED TAKING HIM SERIOUSLY.
Apparently.

Chapter 68

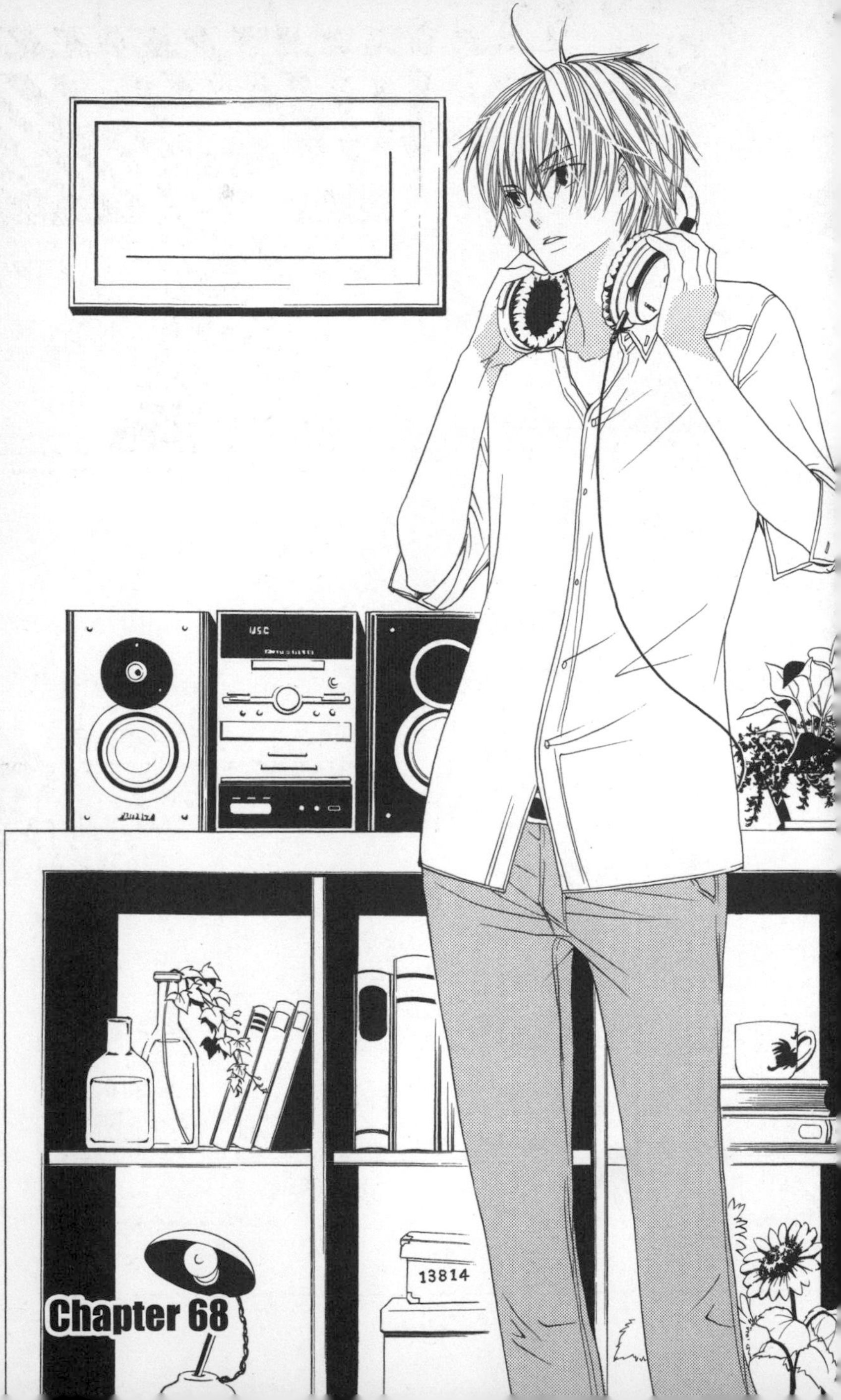
USC
13814

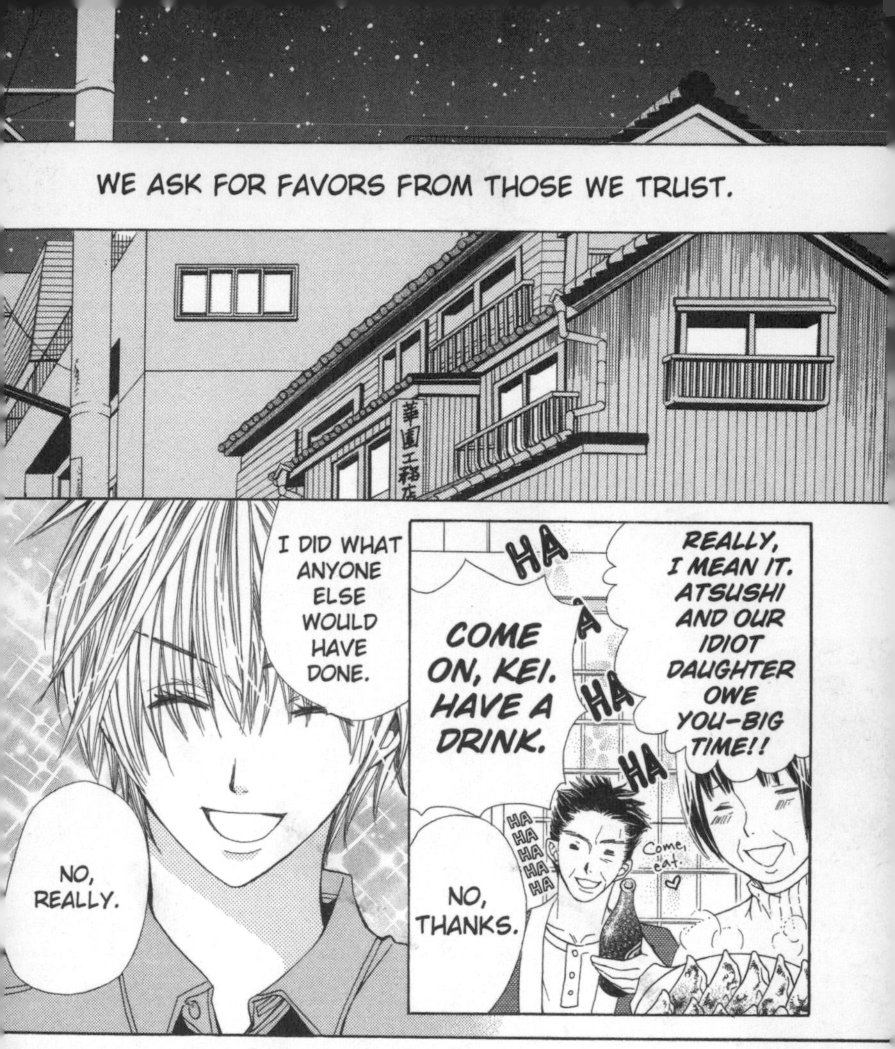
WE ASK FOR FAVORS FROM THOSE WE TRUST.
REALLY, I MEAN IT. ATSUSHI AND OUR IDIOT DAUGHTER OWE YOU-BIG TIME!!
HA A HA HA
COME ON, KEI. HAVE A DRINK.
HA HA HA HA HA
Come, eat.
NO, THANKS.
I DID WHAT ANYONE ELSE WOULD HAVE DONE.
NO, REALLY.

CHARACTERS ②

CONTINUING ON THE SUBJECT OF CHARACTERS...
I WANT TO INTRODUCE RYU'S BIG SISTER SOMETIME. AND I'M NOT SURE IF I CAN DRAW IT, BUT I WANT TO WORK IN SOMETHING ABOUT WHY RYU NEVER WEARS A TIE, IF I CAN. *HUFF. HUFF.*
AND SOMETHING ABOUT MEGUMI AND JUN'S FAMILY... NOW THAT WE'RE IN VOL. 12, I WISH I COULD TELL YOU A LOT MORE ABOUT ALL OF THE S.A CHARACTERS. IT'S REALLY FRUSTRATING FOR SOMEONE WHO'S SO NEW AT THIS. I'LL DO THE BEST I CAN.

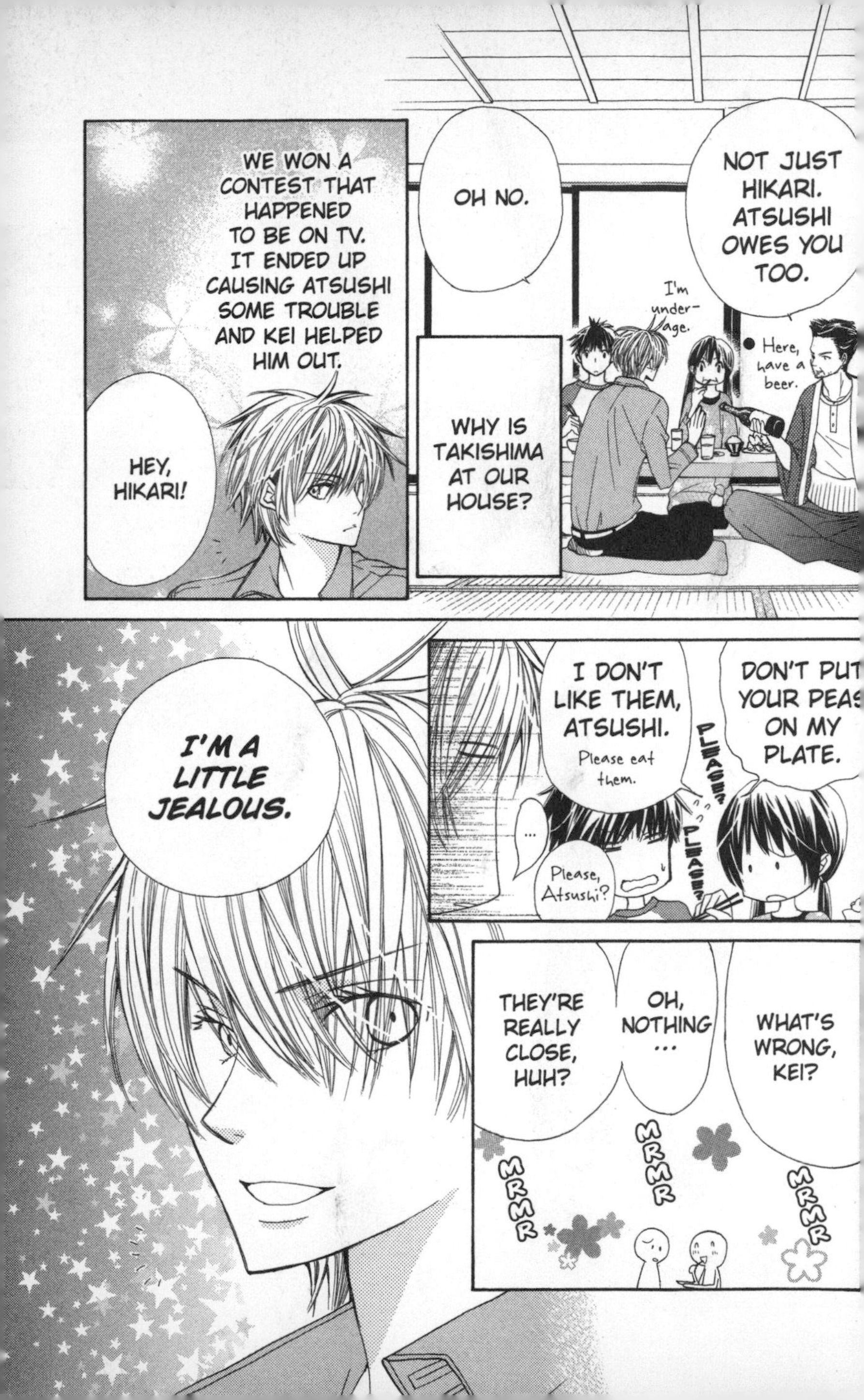
NOT JUST HIKARI. ATSUSHI OWES YOU TOO.
Here, have a beer.
I'm under-age.
OH NO.
WHY IS TAKISHIMA AT OUR HOUSE?
WE WON A CONTEST THAT HAPPENED TO BE ON TV. IT ENDED UP CAUSING ATSUSHI SOME TROUBLE AND KEI HELPED HIM OUT.
HEY, HIKARI!
DON'T PUT YOUR PEAS ON MY PLATE.
I DON'T LIKE THEM, ATSUSHI.
Please eat them.
PLEASE? PLEASE?
...
Please, Atsushi?
WHAT'S WRONG, KEI?
OH, NOTHING...
THEY'RE REALLY CLOSE, HUH?
MRMR
MRMR
MRMR
I'M A LITTLE JEALOUS.

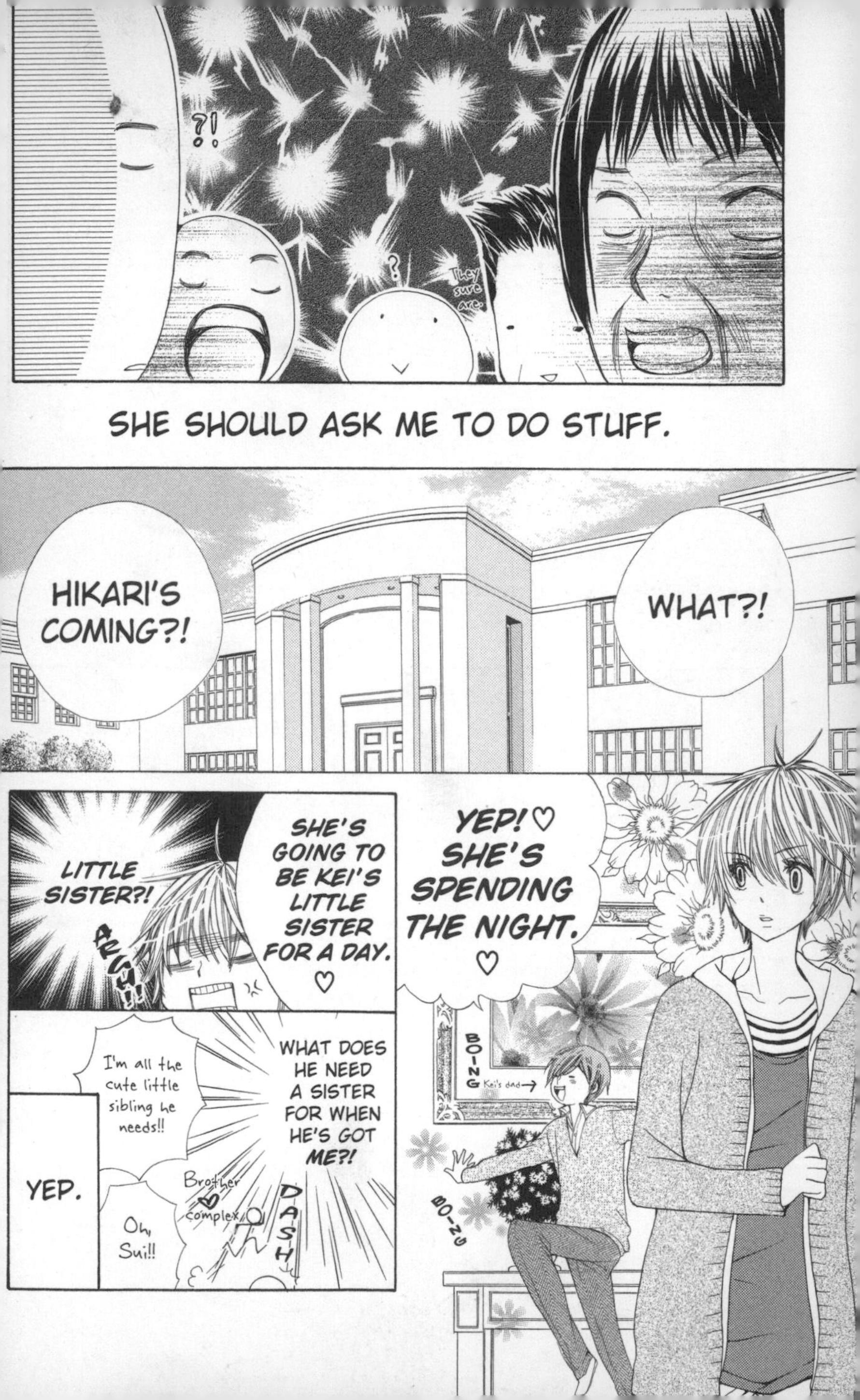
?!
?
They sure are.
SHE SHOULD ASK ME TO DO STUFF.
WHAT?!
HIKARI'S COMING?!
YEP! ♡ SHE'S SPENDING THE NIGHT. ♡
BOING
Kei's dad →
BOING
SHE'S GOING TO BE KEI'S LITTLE SISTER FOR A DAY. ♡
LITTLE SISTER?!
ARGH!!
WHAT DOES HE NEED A SISTER FOR WHEN HE'S GOT ME?!
I'm all the cute little sibling he needs!!
Brother ♡ complex
DASH
Oh, Sui!!
YEP.

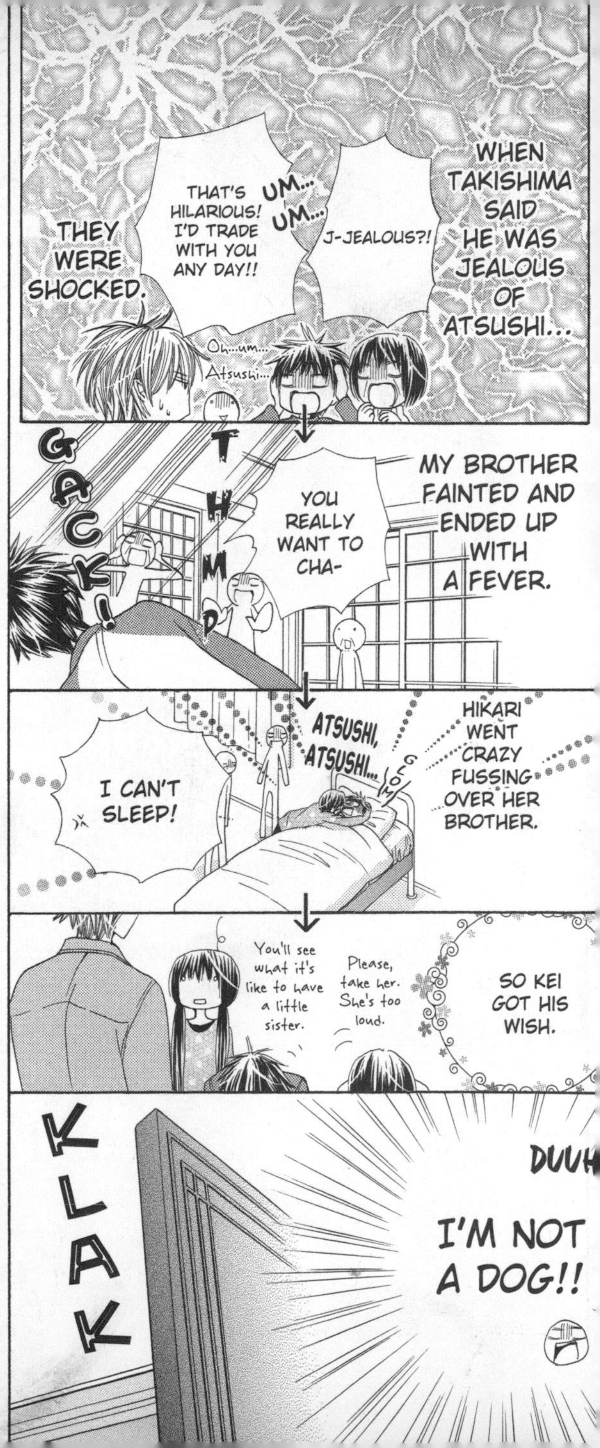
WHEN TAKISHIMA SAID HE WAS JEALOUS OF ATSUSHI...
J-JEALOUS?!
UM... UM...
THAT'S HILARIOUS! I'D TRADE WITH YOU ANY DAY!!
THEY WERE SHOCKED.
Oh...um... Atsushi...
MY BROTHER FAINTED AND ENDED UP WITH A FEVER.
YOU REALLY WANT TO CHA-
THUD
GACK!
HIKARI WENT CRAZY FUSSING OVER HER BROTHER.
ATSUSHI, ATSUSHI...
I CAN'T SLEEP!
SO KEI GOT HIS WISH.
Please, take her. She's too loud.
You'll see what it's like to have a little sister.
DUUH
I'M NOT A DOG!!
KLAK

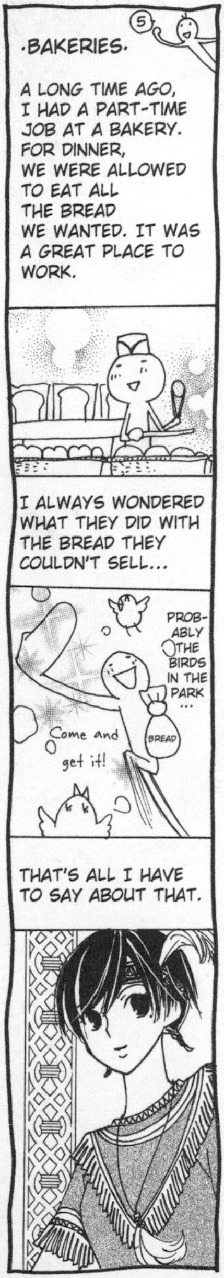
5
·BAKERIES·
A LONG TIME AGO, I HAD A PART-TIME JOB AT A BAKERY. FOR DINNER, WE WERE ALLOWED TO EAT ALL THE BREAD WE WANTED. IT WAS A GREAT PLACE TO WORK.
I ALWAYS WONDERED WHAT THEY DID WITH THE BREAD THEY COULDN'T SELL...
PROBABLY THE BIRDS IN THE PARK...
Come and get it!
BREAD
THAT'S ALL I HAVE TO SAY ABOUT THAT.

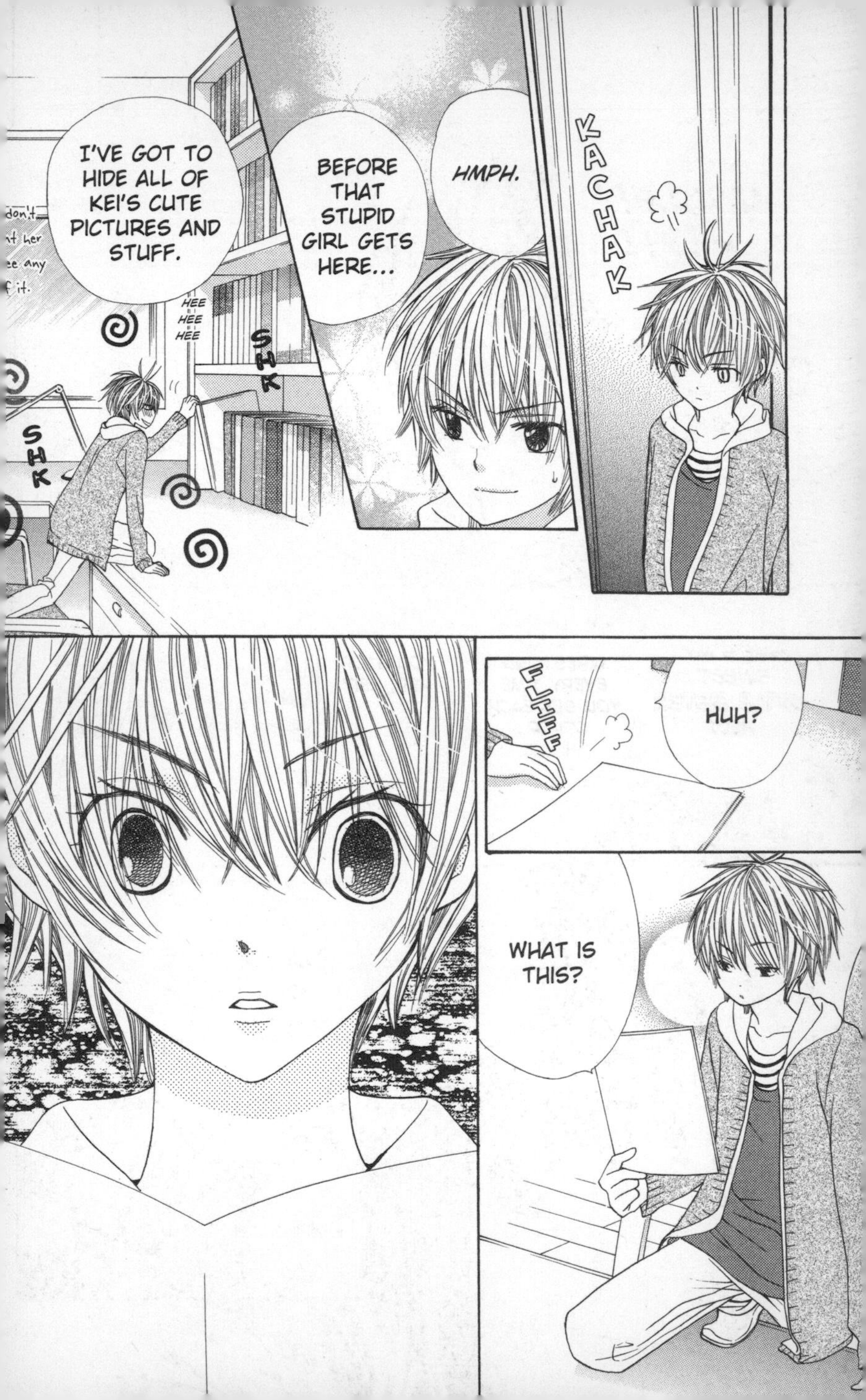
KACHAK
HMPH.
BEFORE THAT STUPID GIRL GETS HERE...
I'VE GOT TO HIDE ALL OF KEI'S CUTE PICTURES AND STUFF.
HEE HEE HEE
SHK
SHK
FLIFF
HUH?
WHAT IS THIS?

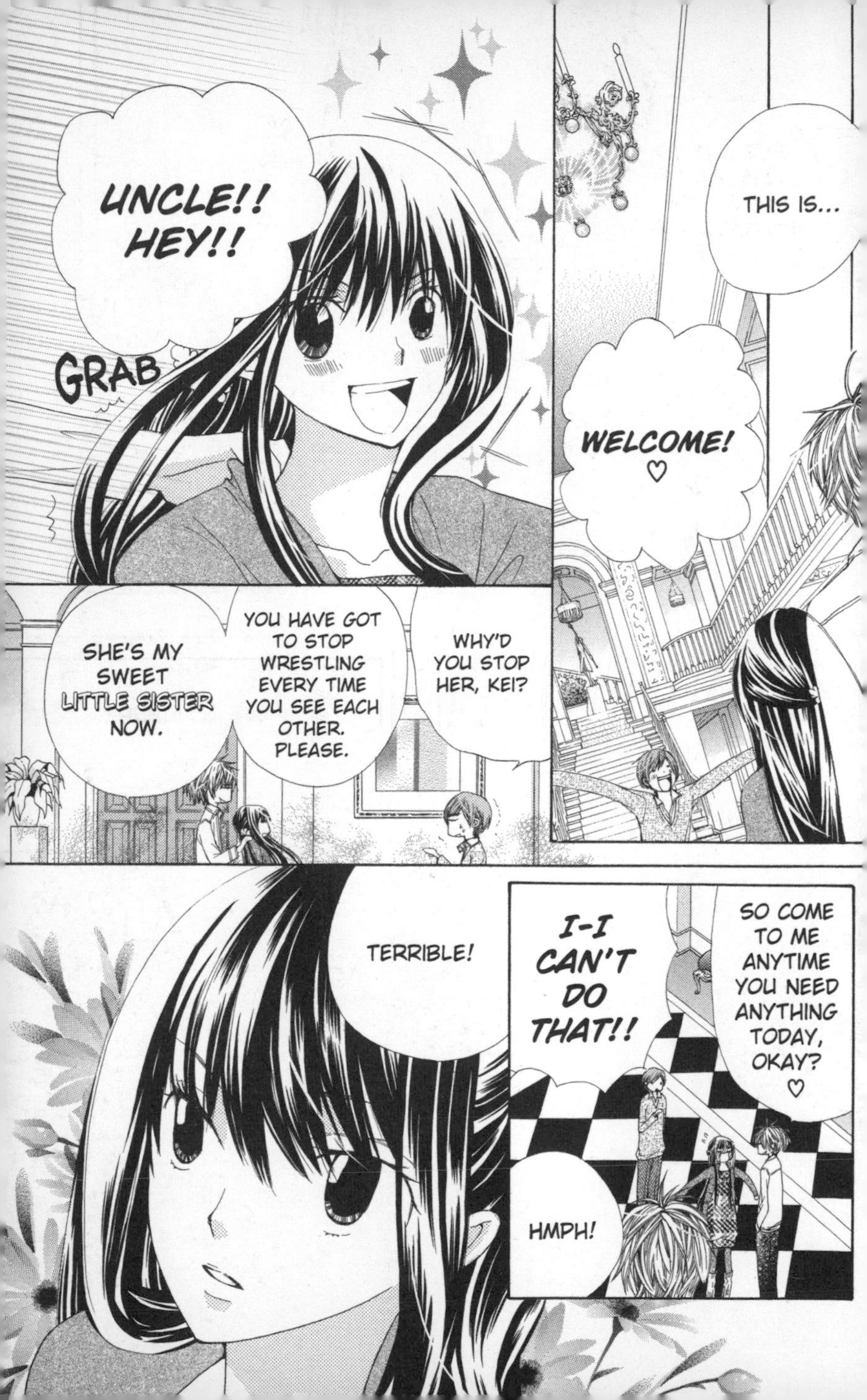
THIS IS...
WELCOME! ♡
UNCLE!! HEY!!
GRAB
WHY'D YOU STOP HER, KEI?
YOU HAVE GOT TO STOP WRESTLING EVERY TIME YOU SEE EACH OTHER. PLEASE.
SHE'S MY SWEET LITTLE SISTER NOW.
SO COME TO ME ANYTIME YOU NEED ANYTHING TODAY, OKAY? ♡
I-I CAN'T DO THAT!!
HMPH!
TERRIBLE!

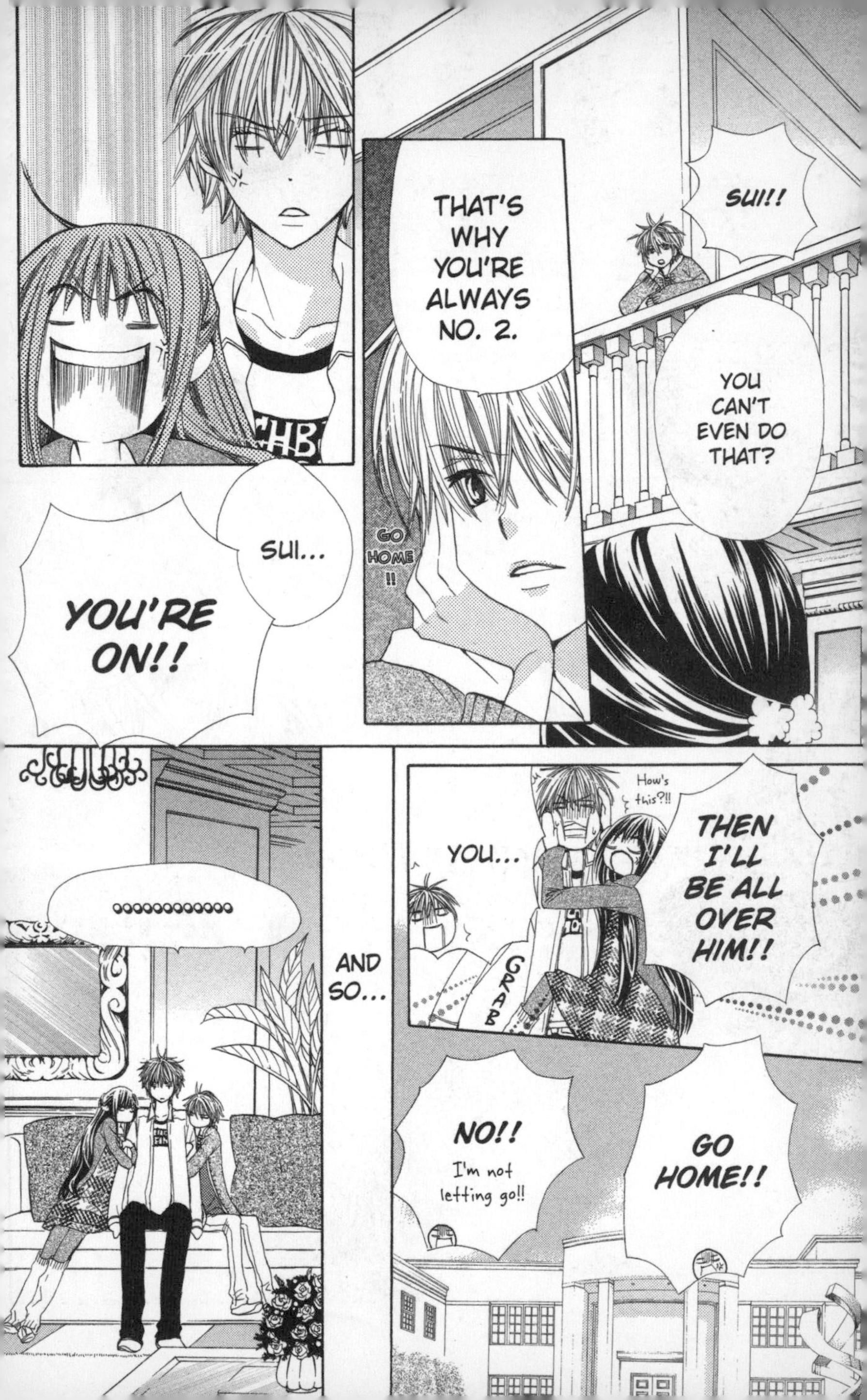

SUI!!
YOU CAN'T EVEN DO THAT?
THAT'S WHY YOU'RE ALWAYS NO. 2.
GO HOME!!
SUI...
YOU'RE ON!!
THEN I'LL BE ALL OVER HIM!!
How's this?!!
YOU...
GRAB
GO HOME!!
NO!!
I'm not letting go!!
AND SO...
....

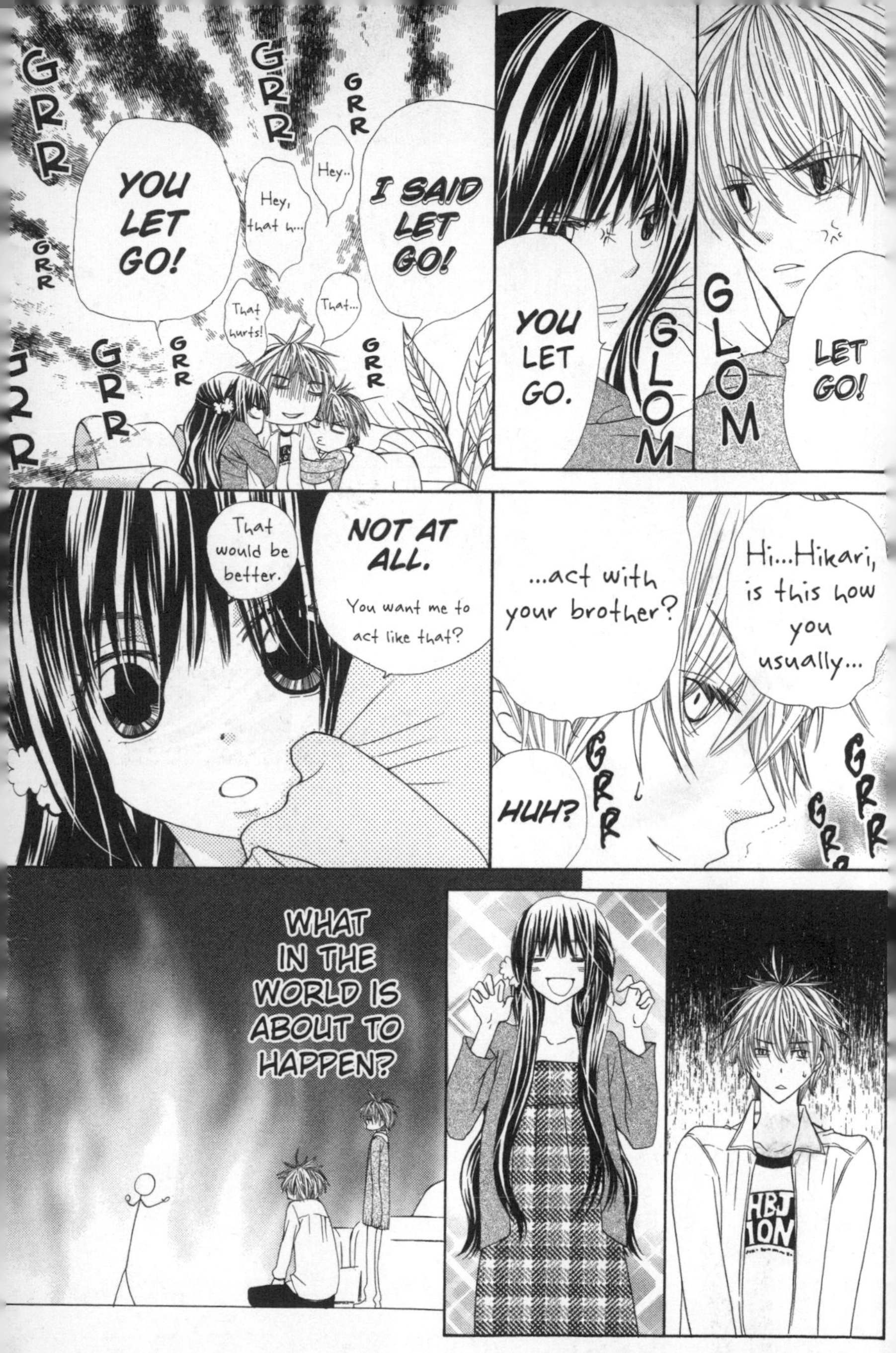
LET GO!
GLOM
YOU LET GO.
GLOM
GRR
I SAID LET GO!
Hey...
GRR
Hey, that h...
YOU LET GO!
GRR
That...
That hurts!
GRR
GRR
GRR
GRR
Hi...Hikari, is this how you usually...
...act with your brother?
GRR
GRR
HUH?
NOT AT ALL.
You want me to act like that?
That would be better.
WHAT IN THE WORLD IS ABOUT TO HAPPEN?

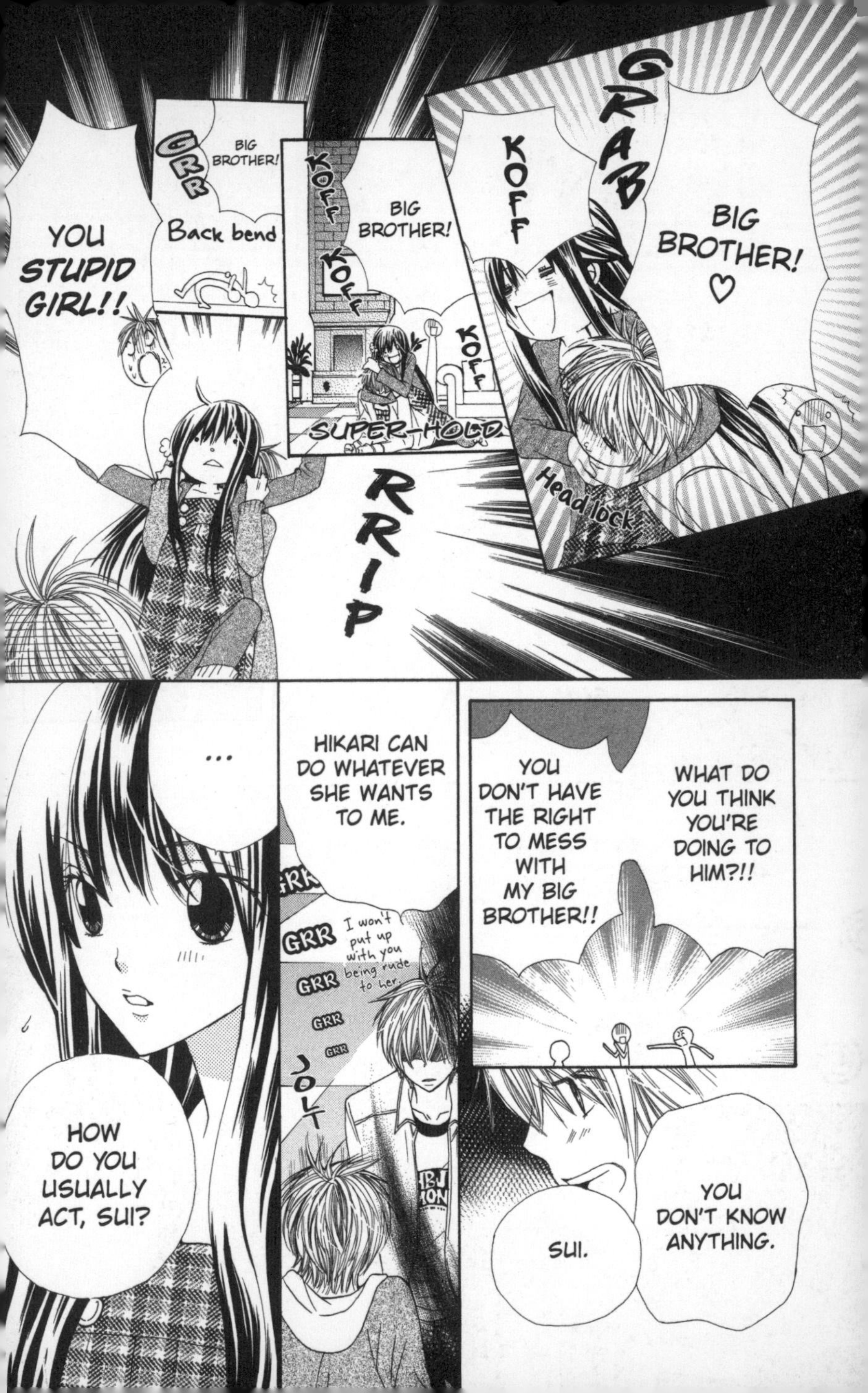
GRAB
KOFF
BIG BROTHER! ♡
Head lock
KOFF KOFF
BIG BROTHER!
KOFF
SUPER-HOLD
BIG BROTHER!
GRR
Back bend
YOU STUPID GIRL!!
RRIP
WHAT DO YOU THINK YOU'RE DOING TO HIM?!!
YOU DON'T HAVE THE RIGHT TO MESS WITH MY BIG BROTHER!!
YOU DON'T KNOW ANYTHING.
SUI.
HIKARI CAN DO WHATEVER SHE WANTS TO ME.
GRR GRR GRR GRR GRR
I won't put up with you being rude to her.
JOLT
...
HOW DO YOU USUALLY ACT, SUI?

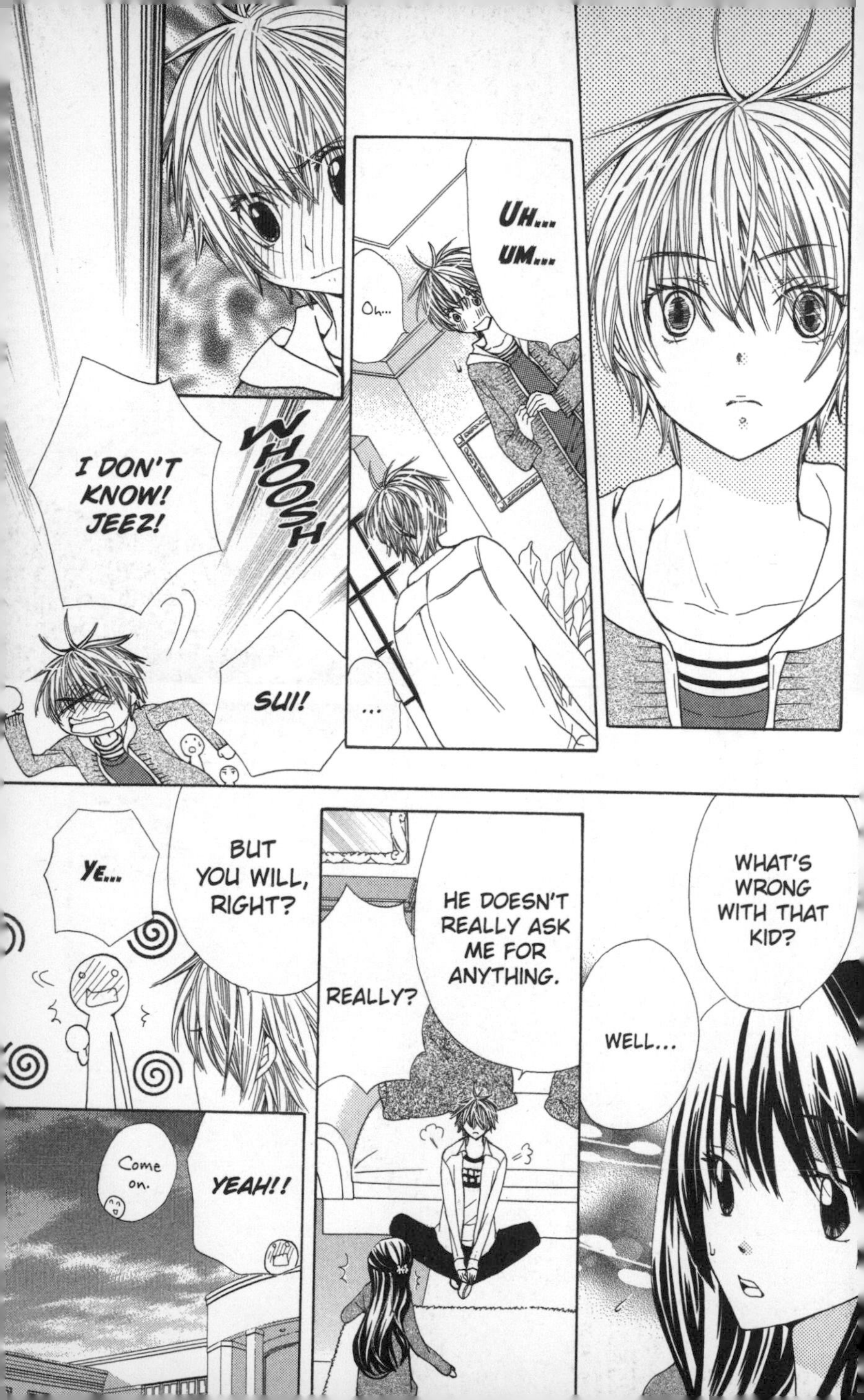
UH... UM...
Oh...
...
WHOOSH
I DON'T KNOW! JEEZ!
SUI!
WHAT'S WRONG WITH THAT KID?
WELL...
HE DOESN'T REALLY ASK ME FOR ANYTHING.
REALLY?
BUT YOU WILL, RIGHT?
YE...
YEAH!!
Come on.

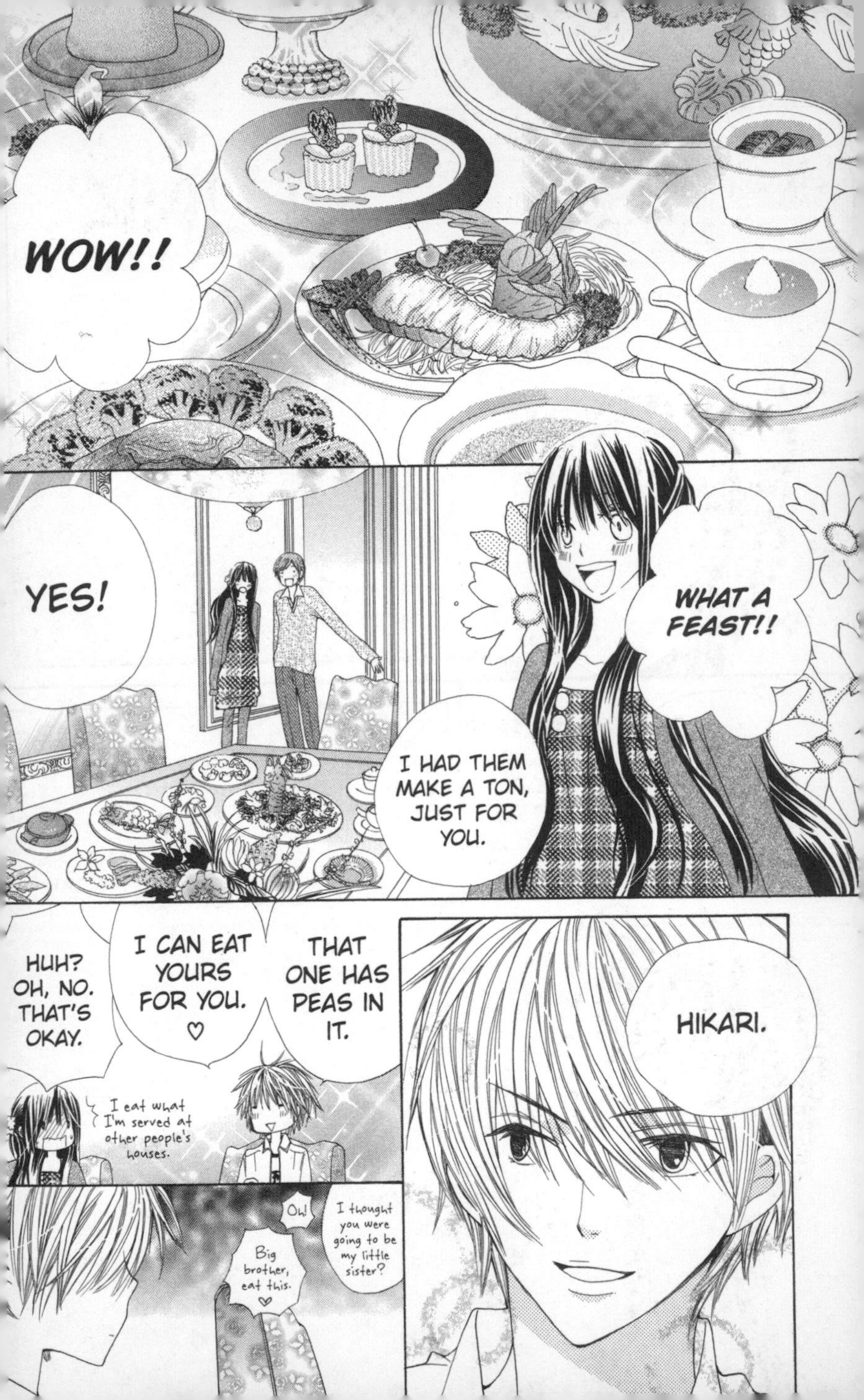
WOW!!
WHAT A FEAST!!
I HAD THEM MAKE A TON, JUST FOR YOU.
YES!
HIKARI.
THAT ONE HAS PEAS IN IT.
I CAN EAT YOURS FOR YOU. ♡
HUH? OH, NO. THAT'S OKAY.
I eat what I'm served at other people's houses.
I thought you were going to be my little sister?
Oh!
Big brother, eat this. ♡

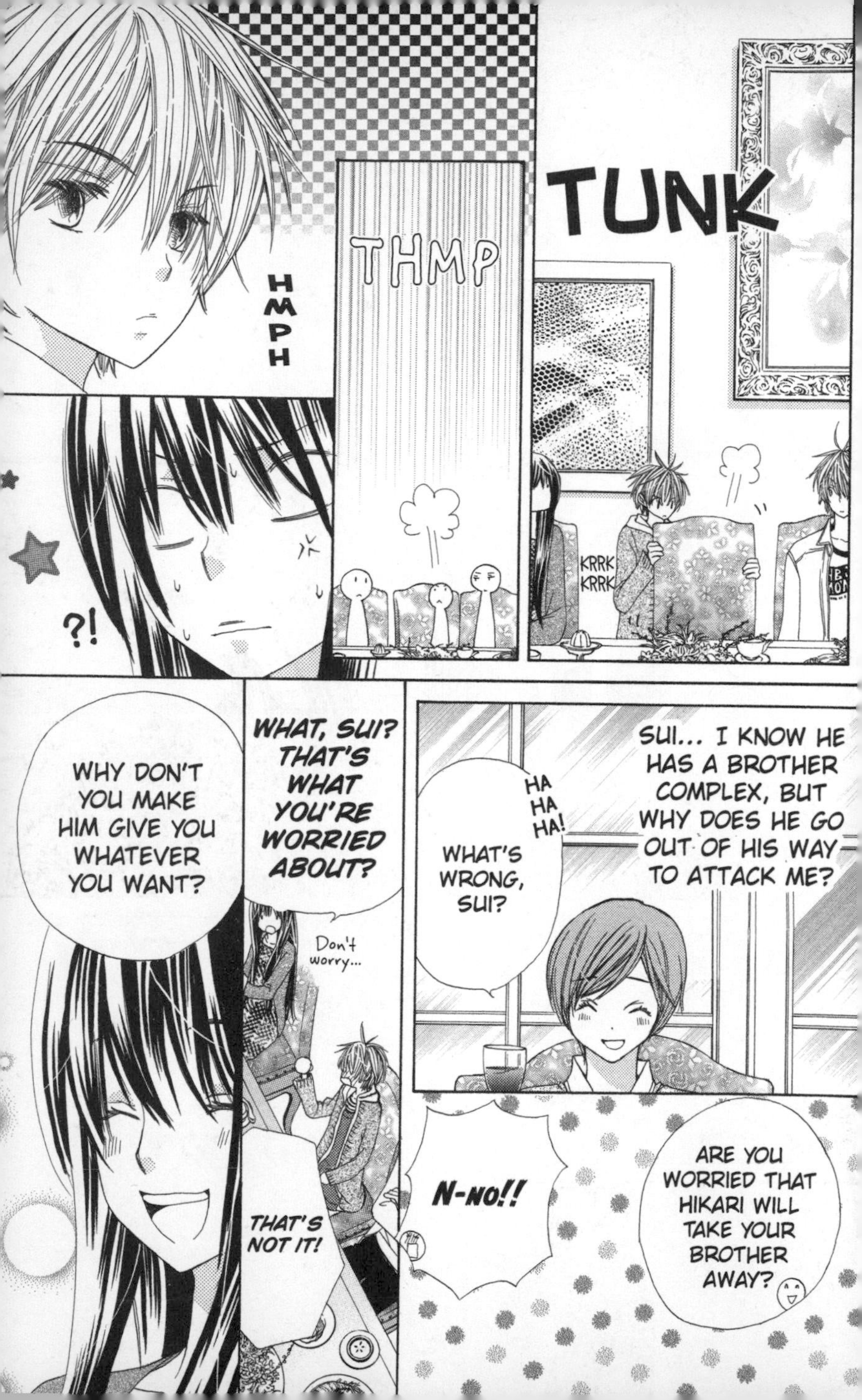
TUNK
KRRK KRRK
THMP
HMPH
?!
SUI... I KNOW HE HAS A BROTHER COMPLEX, BUT WHY DOES HE GO OUT OF HIS WAY TO ATTACK ME?
HA HA HA!
WHAT'S WRONG, SUI?
ARE YOU WORRIED THAT HIKARI WILL TAKE YOUR BROTHER AWAY?
N-NO!!
WHAT, SUI? THAT'S WHAT YOU'RE WORRIED ABOUT?
Don't worry...
THAT'S NOT IT!
WHY DON'T YOU MAKE HIM GIVE YOU WHATEVER YOU WANT?

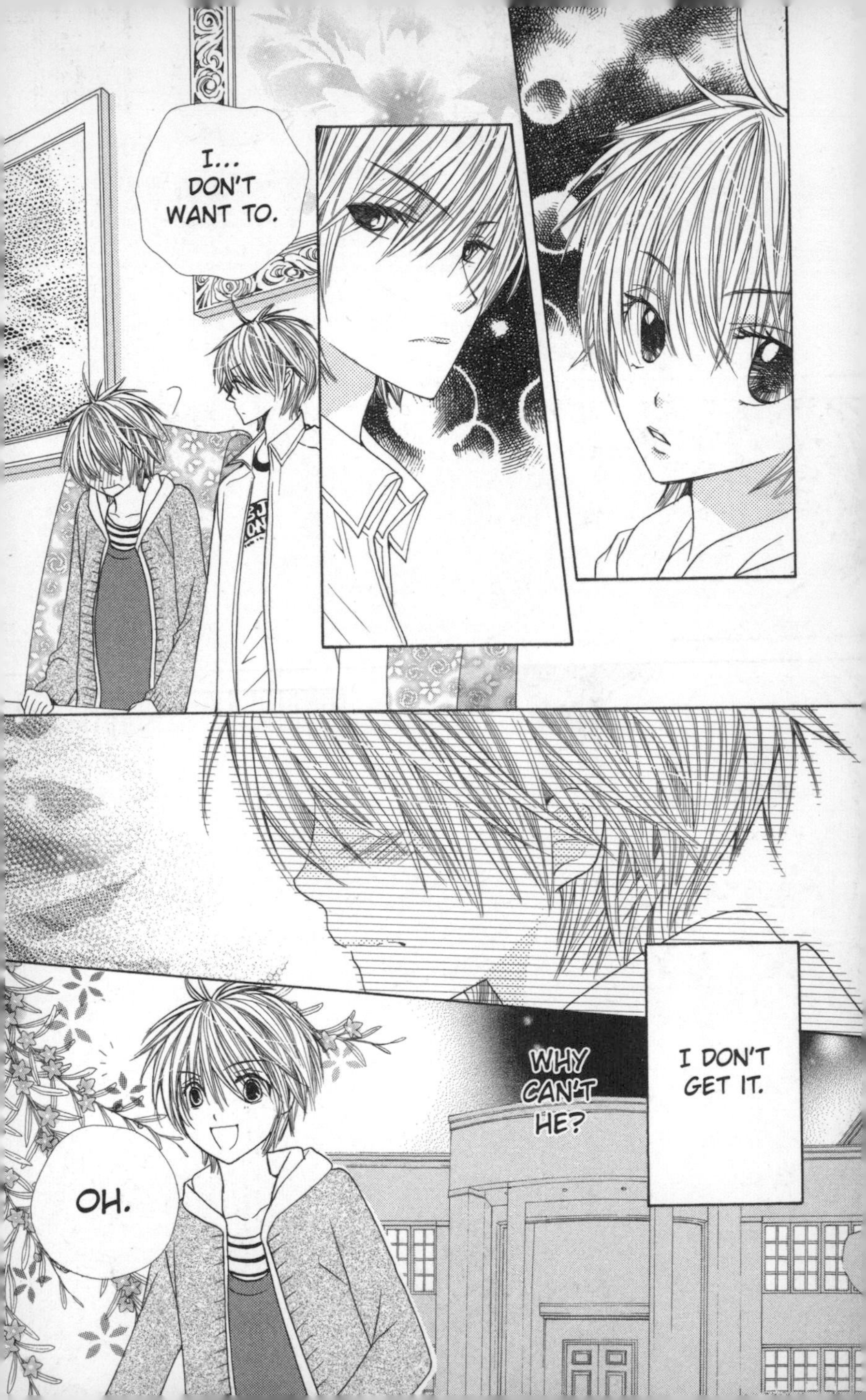
I... DON'T WANT TO.
I DON'T GET IT.
WHY CAN'T HE?
OH.

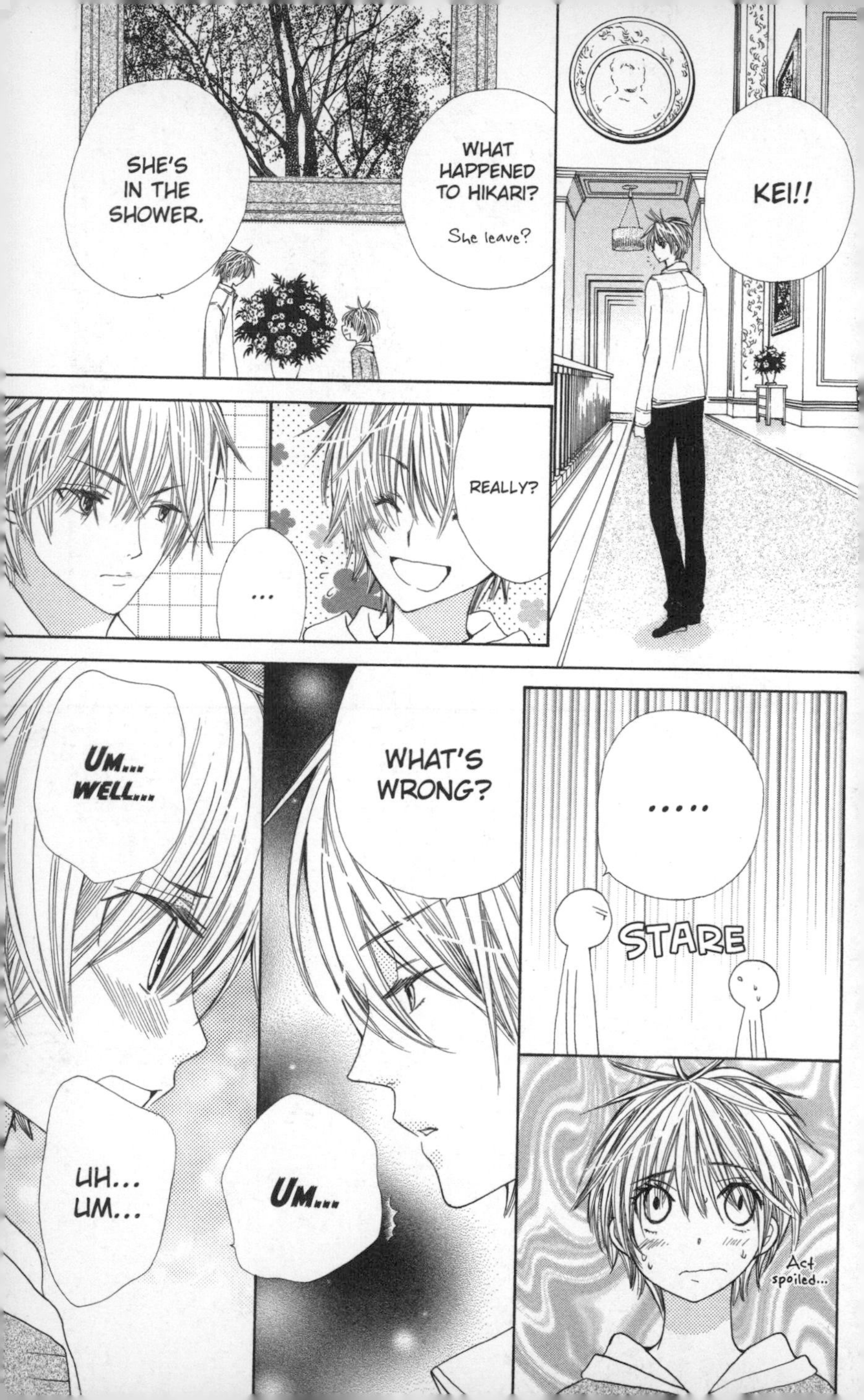
KEI!!
WHAT HAPPENED TO HIKARI?
She leave?
SHE'S IN THE SHOWER.
REALLY?
...
.....
STARE
Act spoiled...
WHAT'S WRONG?
UM...
UM... WELL...
UH... UM...

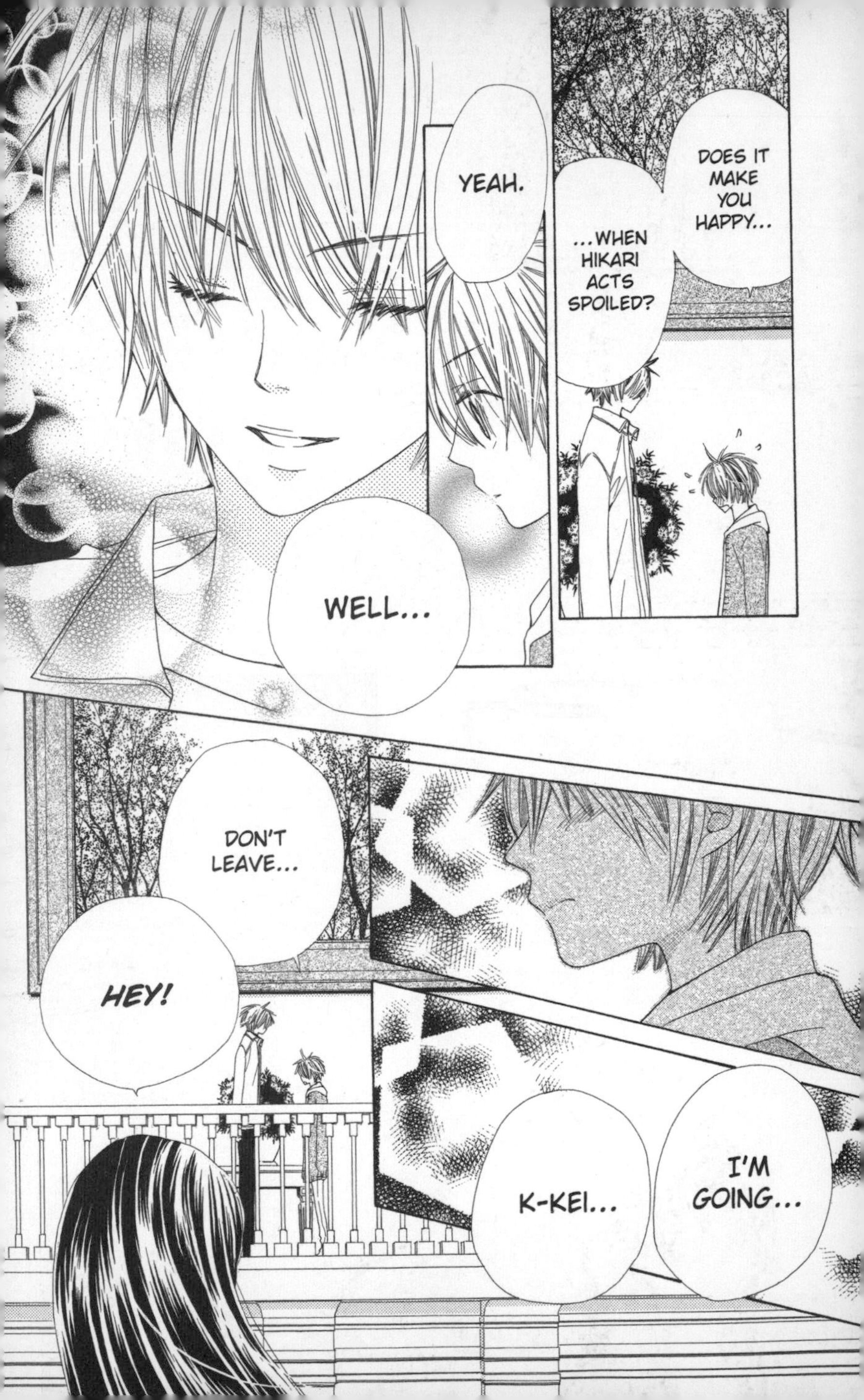
DOES IT MAKE YOU HAPPY...
...WHEN HIKARI ACTS SPOILED?
YEAH.
WELL...
I'M GOING...
K-KEI...
DON'T LEAVE...
HEY!

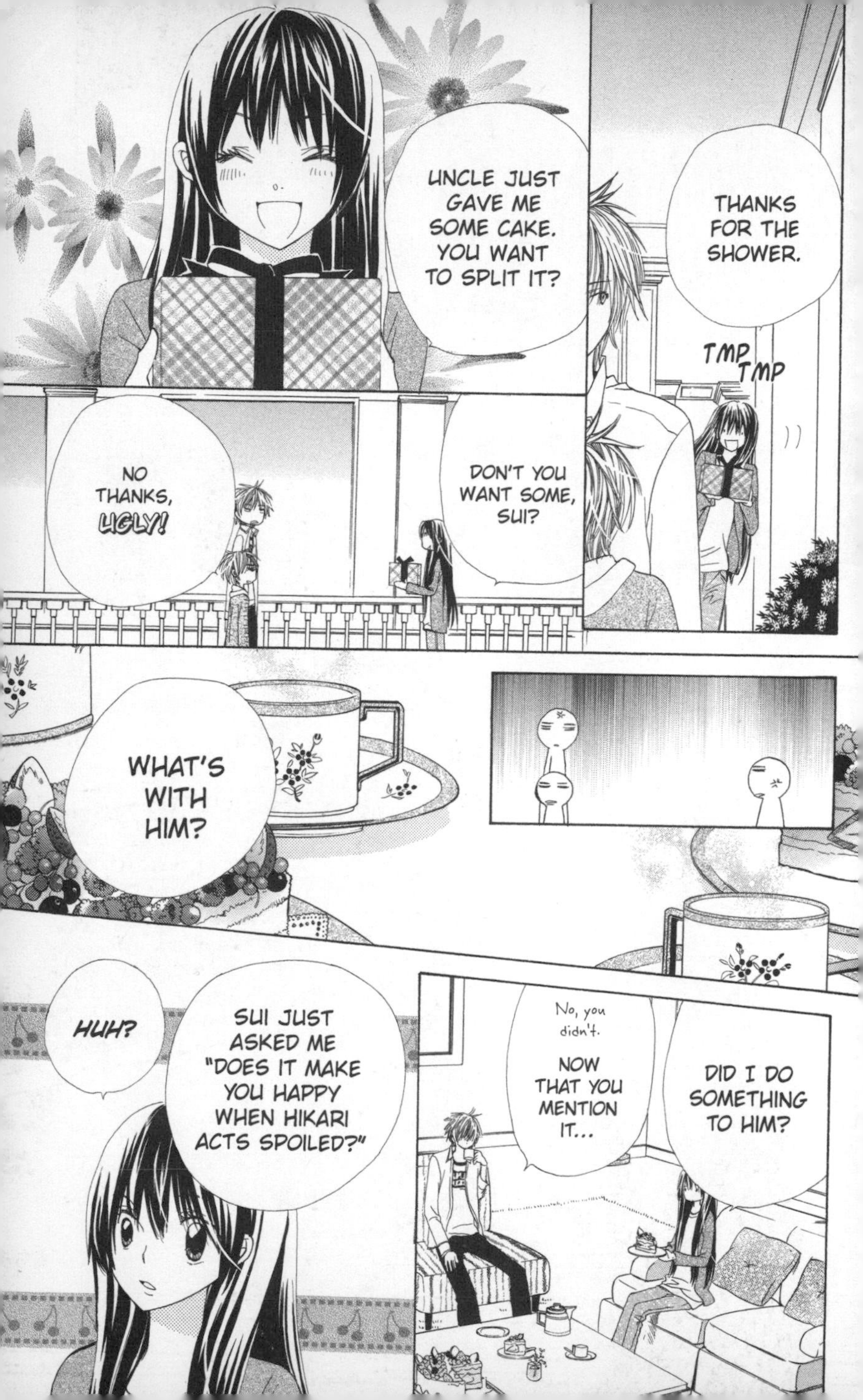
THANKS FOR THE SHOWER.
TMP TMP
UNCLE JUST GAVE ME SOME CAKE. YOU WANT TO SPLIT IT?
DON'T YOU WANT SOME, SUI?
NO THANKS, UGLY!
WHAT'S WITH HIM?
DID I DO SOMETHING TO HIM?
No, you didn't.
NOW THAT YOU MENTION IT...
SUI JUST ASKED ME "DOES IT MAKE YOU HAPPY WHEN HIKARI ACTS SPOILED?"
HUH?

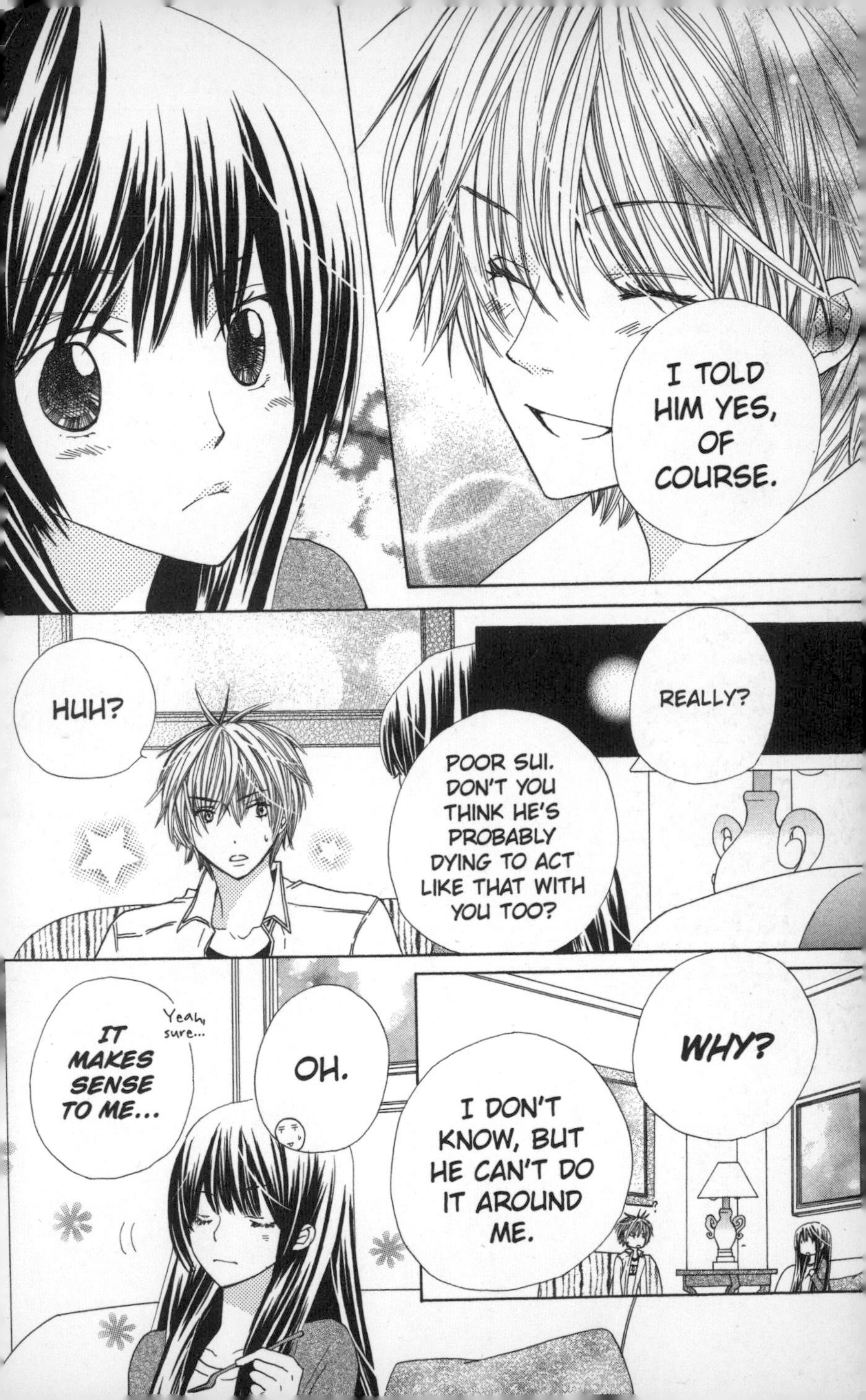
I TOLD HIM YES, OF COURSE.
REALLY?
POOR SUI. DON'T YOU THINK HE'S PROBABLY DYING TO ACT LIKE THAT WITH YOU TOO?
HUH?
WHY?
I DON'T KNOW, BUT HE CAN'T DO IT AROUND ME.
OH.
IT MAKES SENSE TO ME...
Yeah, sure...

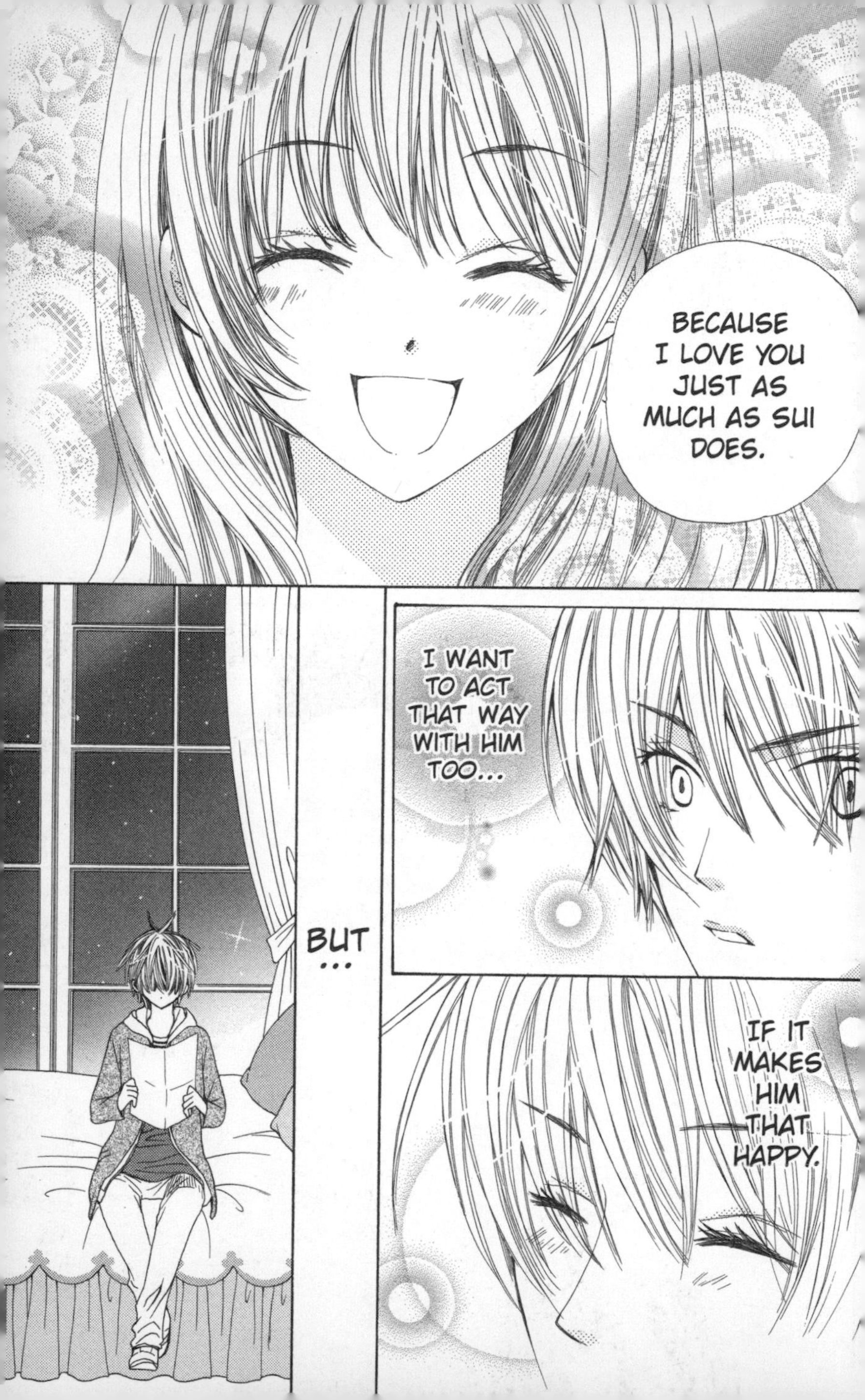
BECAUSE I LOVE YOU JUST AS MUCH AS SUI DOES.
I WANT TO ACT THAT WAY WITH HIM TOO...
IF IT MAKES HIM THAT HAPPY.
BUT...

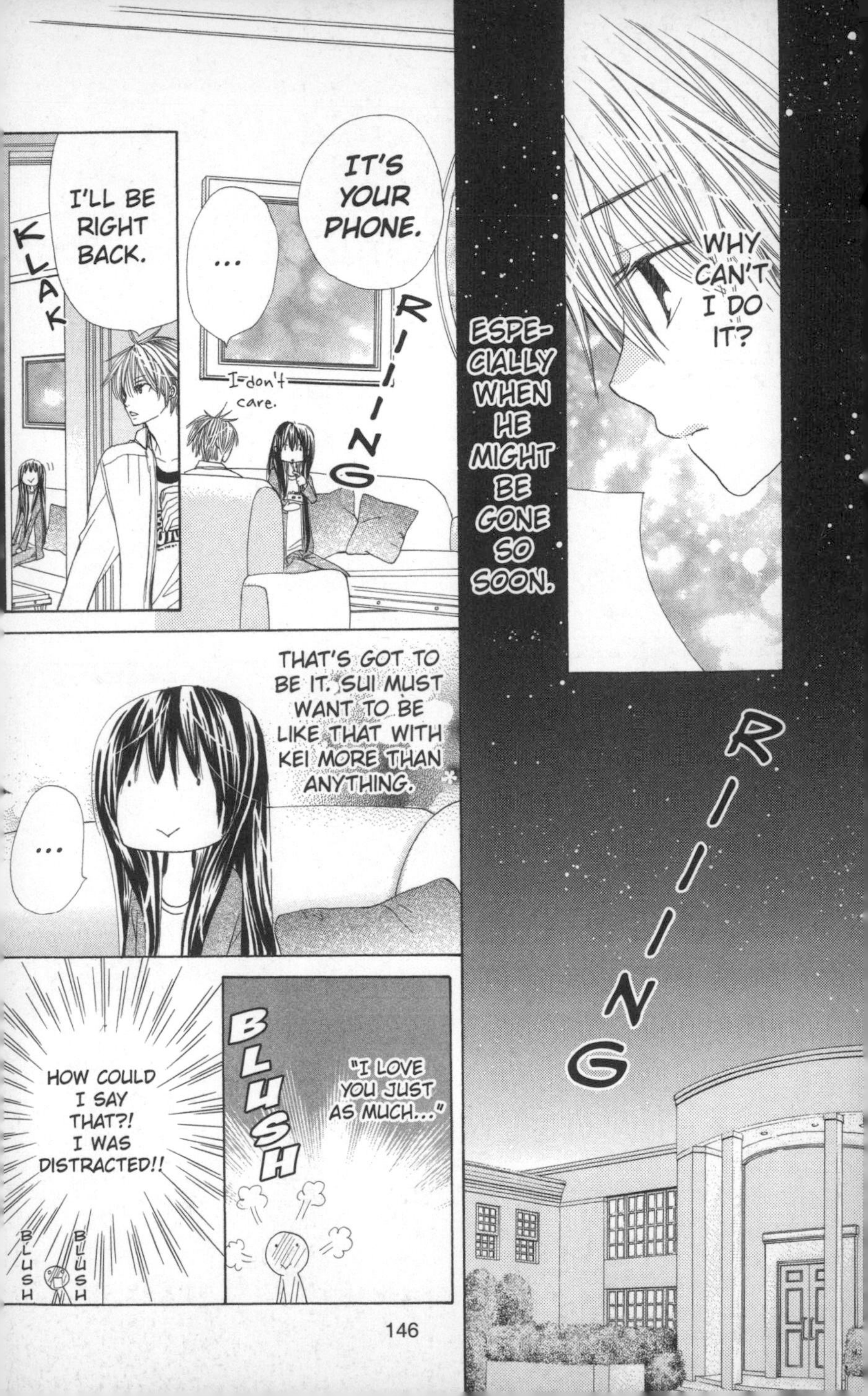
WHY CAN'T I DO IT?
ESPE-CIALLY WHEN HE MIGHT BE GONE SO SOON.
RIIIING
IT'S YOUR PHONE.
RIIIING
...
I don't care.
I'LL BE RIGHT BACK.
KLAK
THAT'S GOT TO BE IT. SUI MUST WANT TO BE LIKE THAT WITH KEI MORE THAN ANYTHING.
...
BLUSH
"I LOVE YOU JUST AS MUCH..."
HOW COULD I SAY THAT?! I WAS DISTRACTED!!
BLUSH
BLUSH

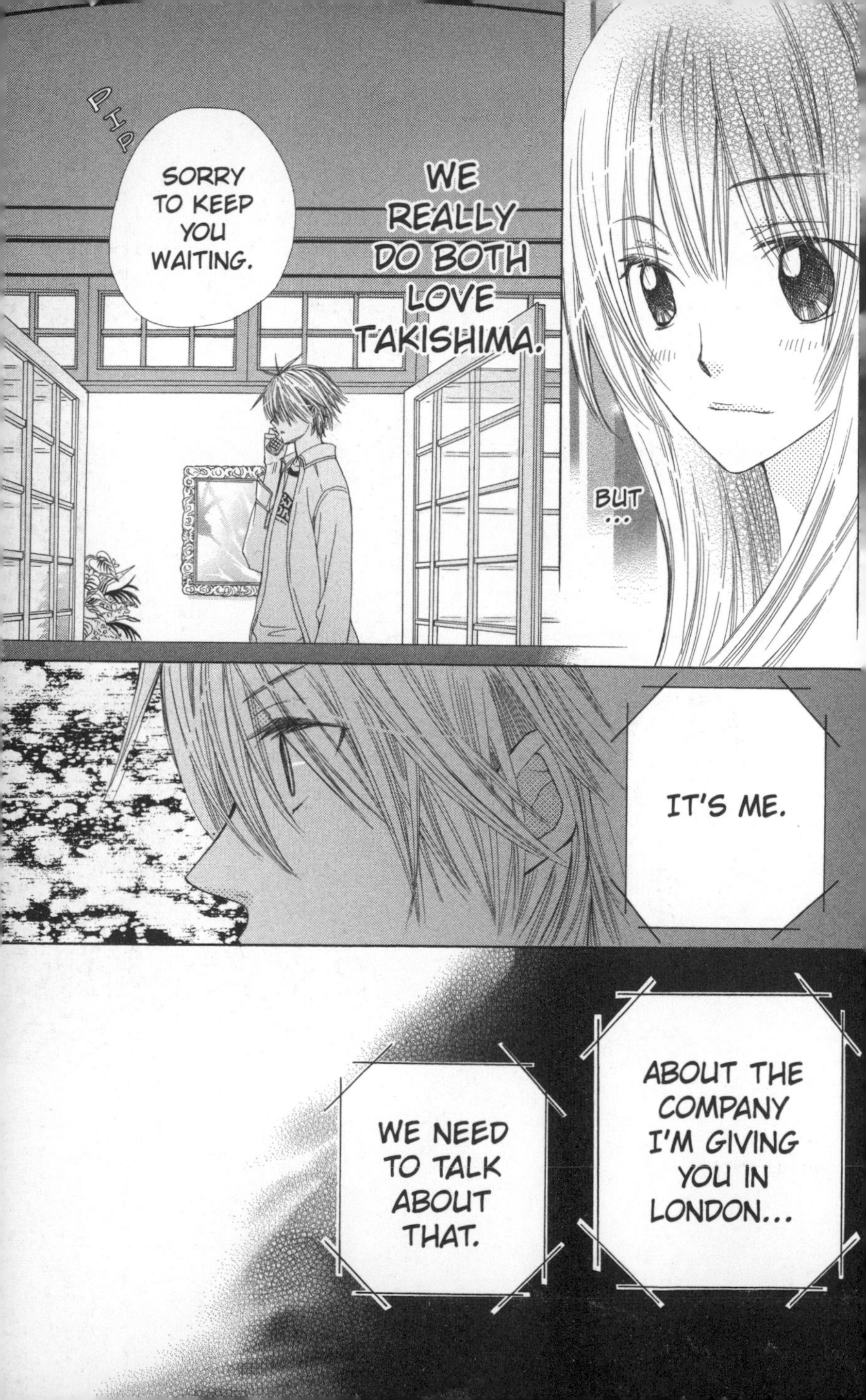
WE REALLY DO BOTH LOVE TAKISHIMA.
BUT...
pip
SORRY TO KEEP YOU WAITING.
IT'S ME.
ABOUT THE COMPANY I'M GIVING YOU IN LONDON...
WE NEED TO TALK ABOUT THAT.

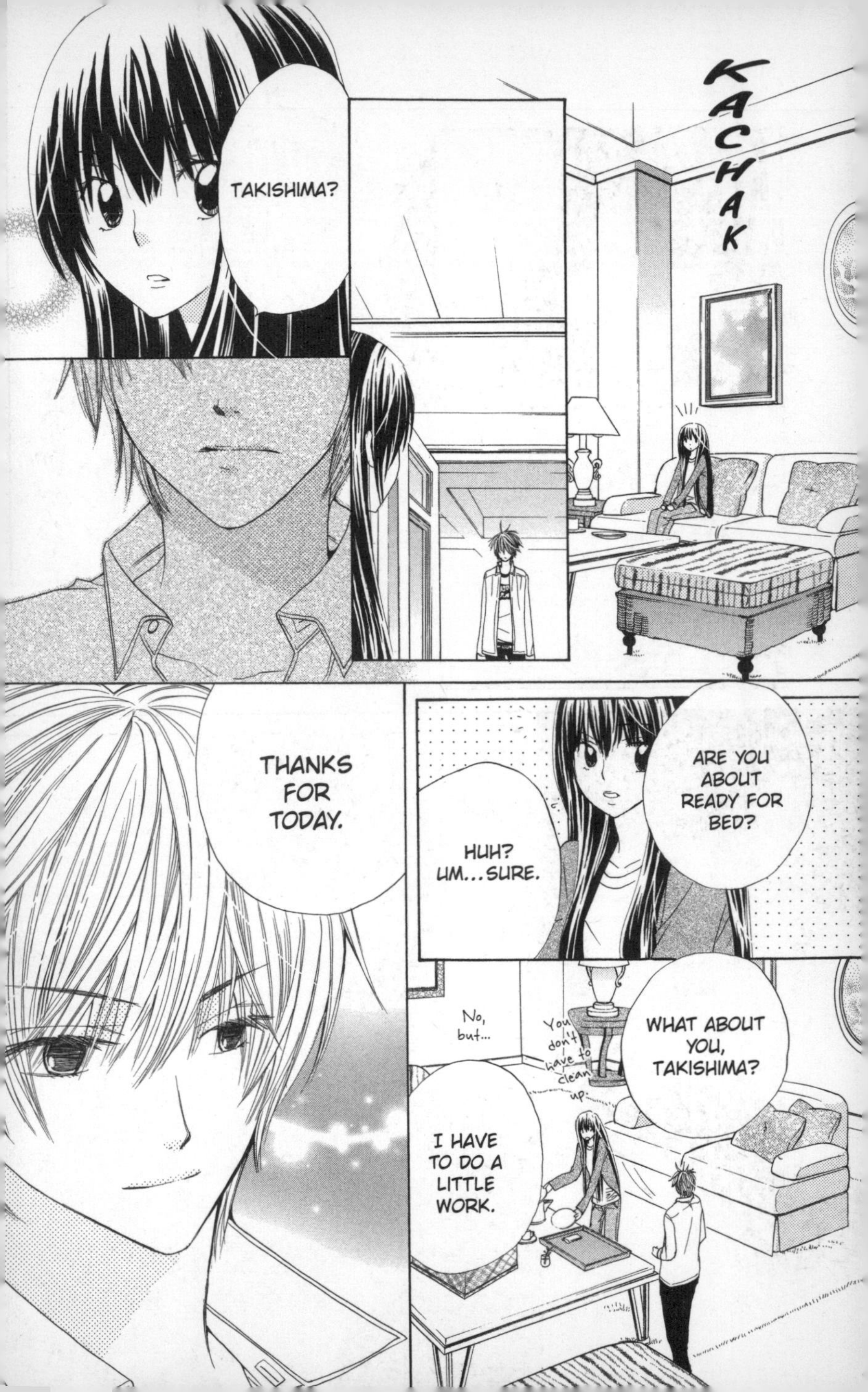
KACHAK
TAKISHIMA?
ARE YOU ABOUT READY FOR BED?
HUH? UM... SURE.
WHAT ABOUT YOU, TAKISHIMA?
You don't have to clean up...
No, but...
I HAVE TO DO A LITTLE WORK.
THANKS FOR TODAY.

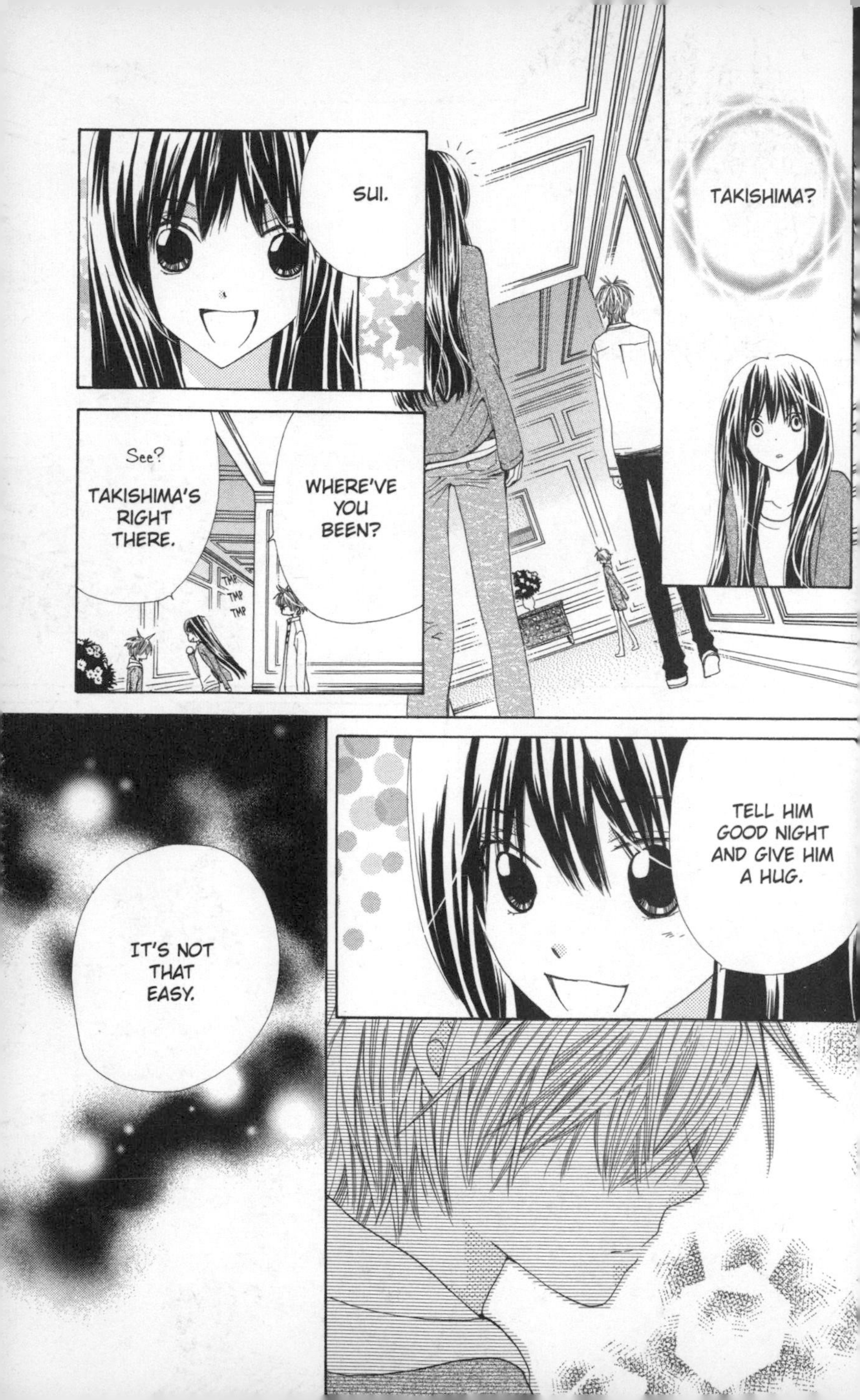
TAKISHIMA?
SUI.
WHERE'VE YOU BEEN?
See?
TAKISHIMA'S RIGHT THERE.
TMP TMP TMP
TELL HIM GOOD NIGHT AND GIVE HIM A HUG.
IT'S NOT THAT EASY.

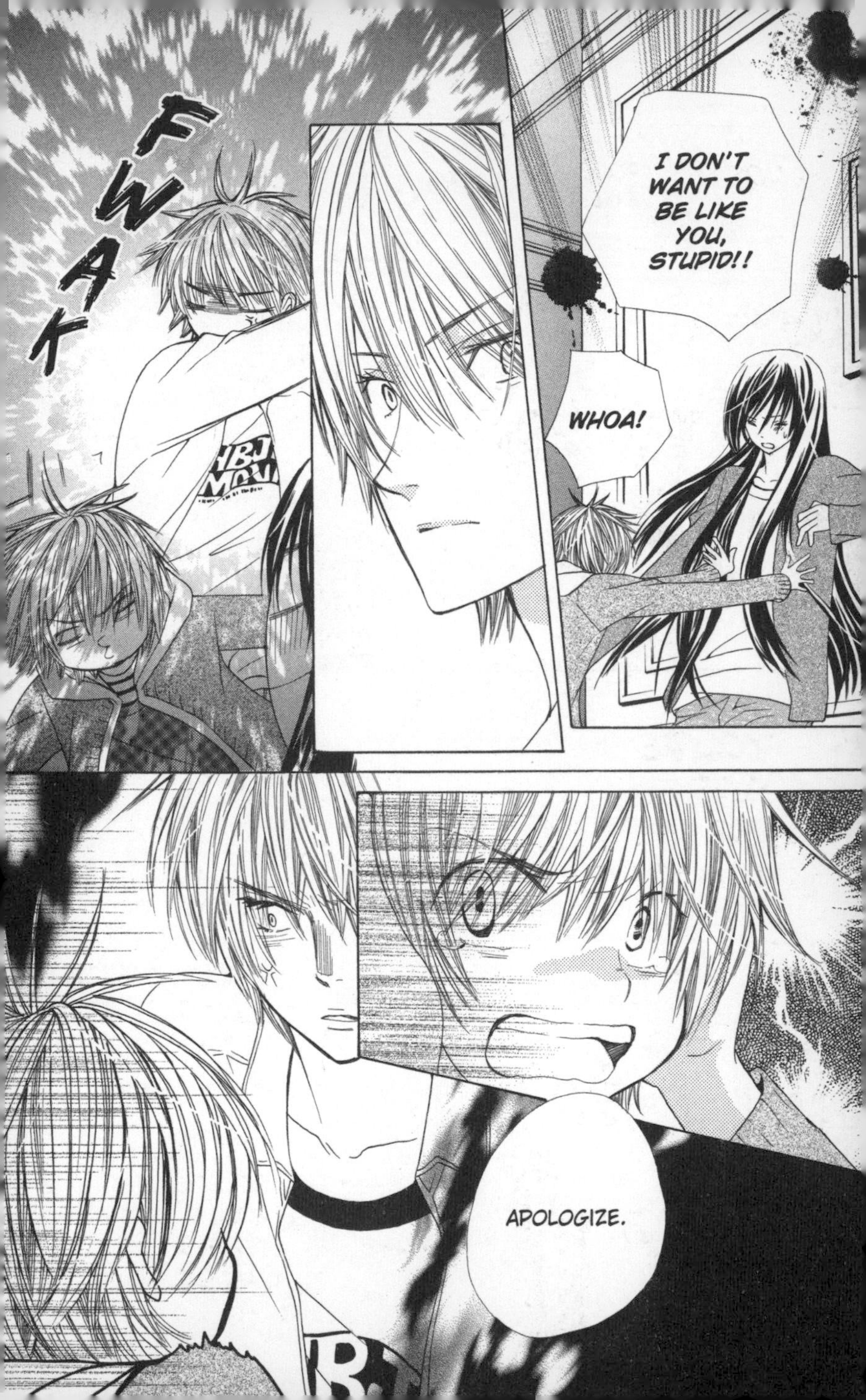
I DON'T WANT TO BE LIKE YOU, STUPID!!
WHOA!
FWAK
APOLOGIZE.

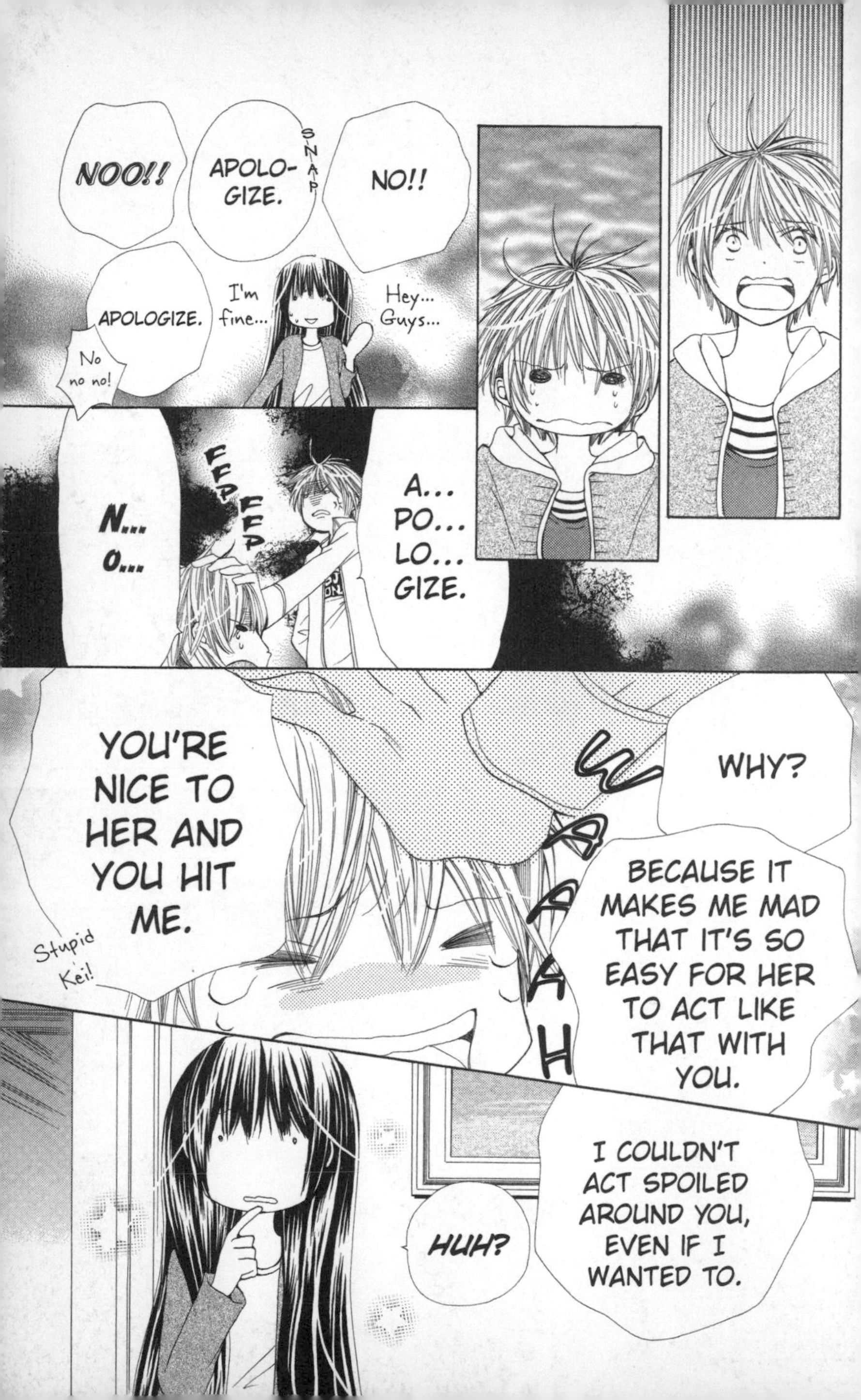
NO!!
SNAP
APOLO-GIZE.
NOO!!
Hey... Guys...
I'm fine...
APOLOGIZE.
No no no!
A... PO... LO... GIZE.
FFP FFP
N... O...
WHY?
WAAAAH
BECAUSE IT MAKES ME MAD THAT IT'S SO EASY FOR HER TO ACT LIKE THAT WITH YOU.
YOU'RE NICE TO HER AND YOU HIT ME.
Stupid Kei!
I COULDN'T ACT SPOILED AROUND YOU, EVEN IF I WANTED TO.
HUH?

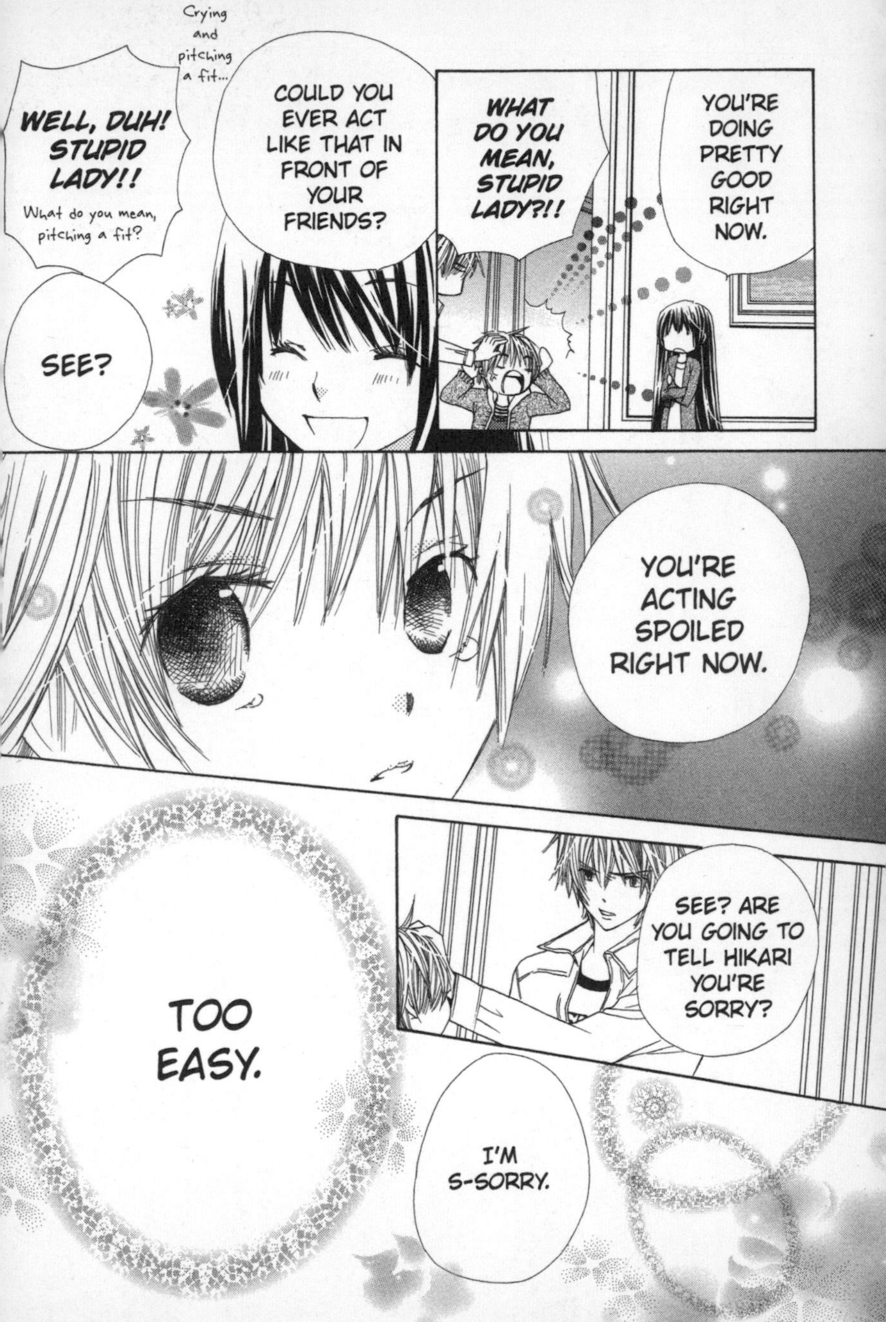
YOU'RE DOING PRETTY GOOD RIGHT NOW.
WHAT DO YOU MEAN, STUPID LADY?!!
COULD YOU EVER ACT LIKE THAT IN FRONT OF YOUR FRIENDS?
Crying and pitching a fit...
WELL, DUH! STUPID LADY!!
What do you mean, pitching a fit?
SEE?
YOU'RE ACTING SPOILED RIGHT NOW.
SEE? ARE YOU GOING TO TELL HIKARI YOU'RE SORRY?
I'M S-SORRY.
TOO EASY.

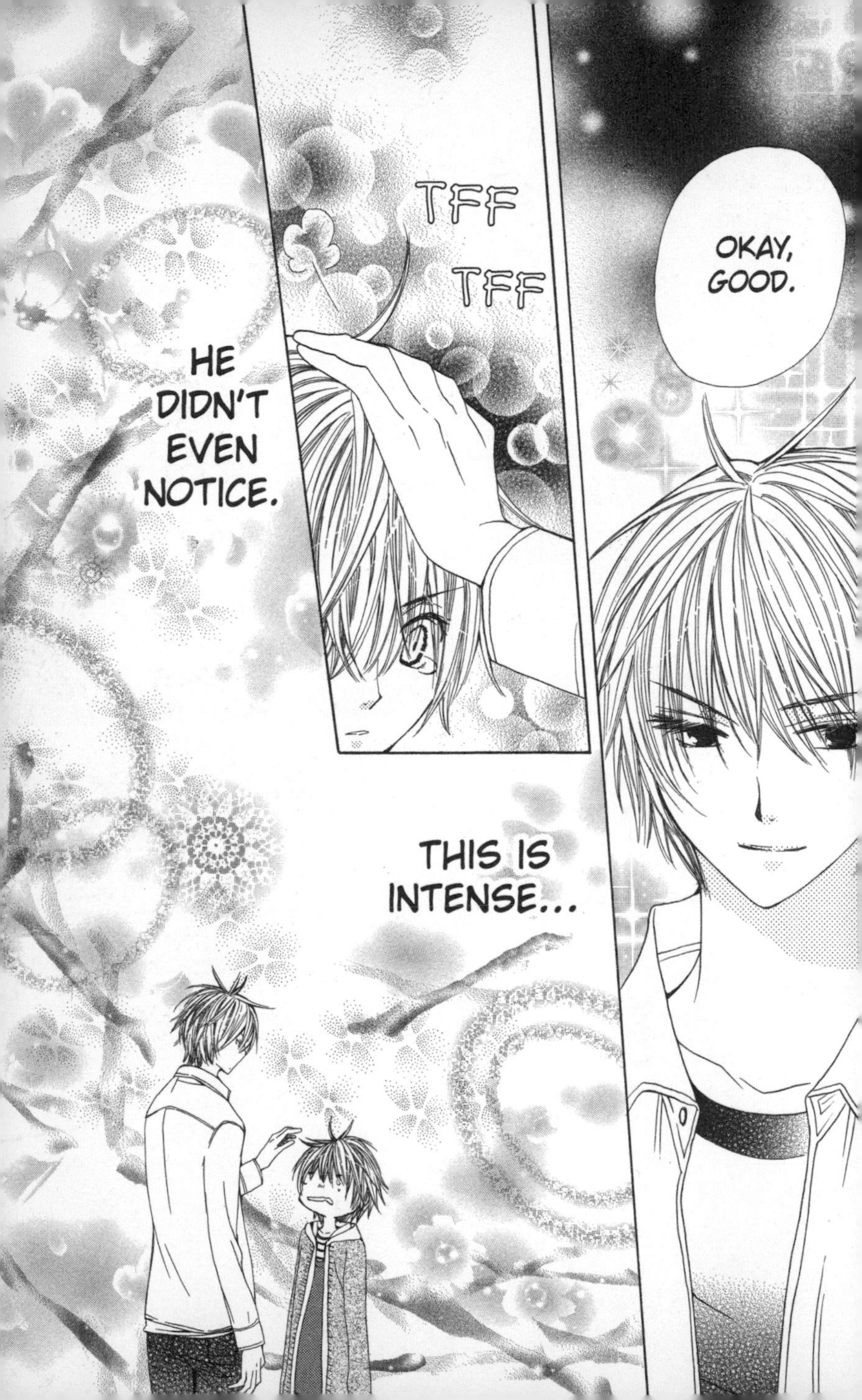
OKAY, GOOD.
TFF TFF
HE DIDN'T EVEN NOTICE.
THIS IS INTENSE...

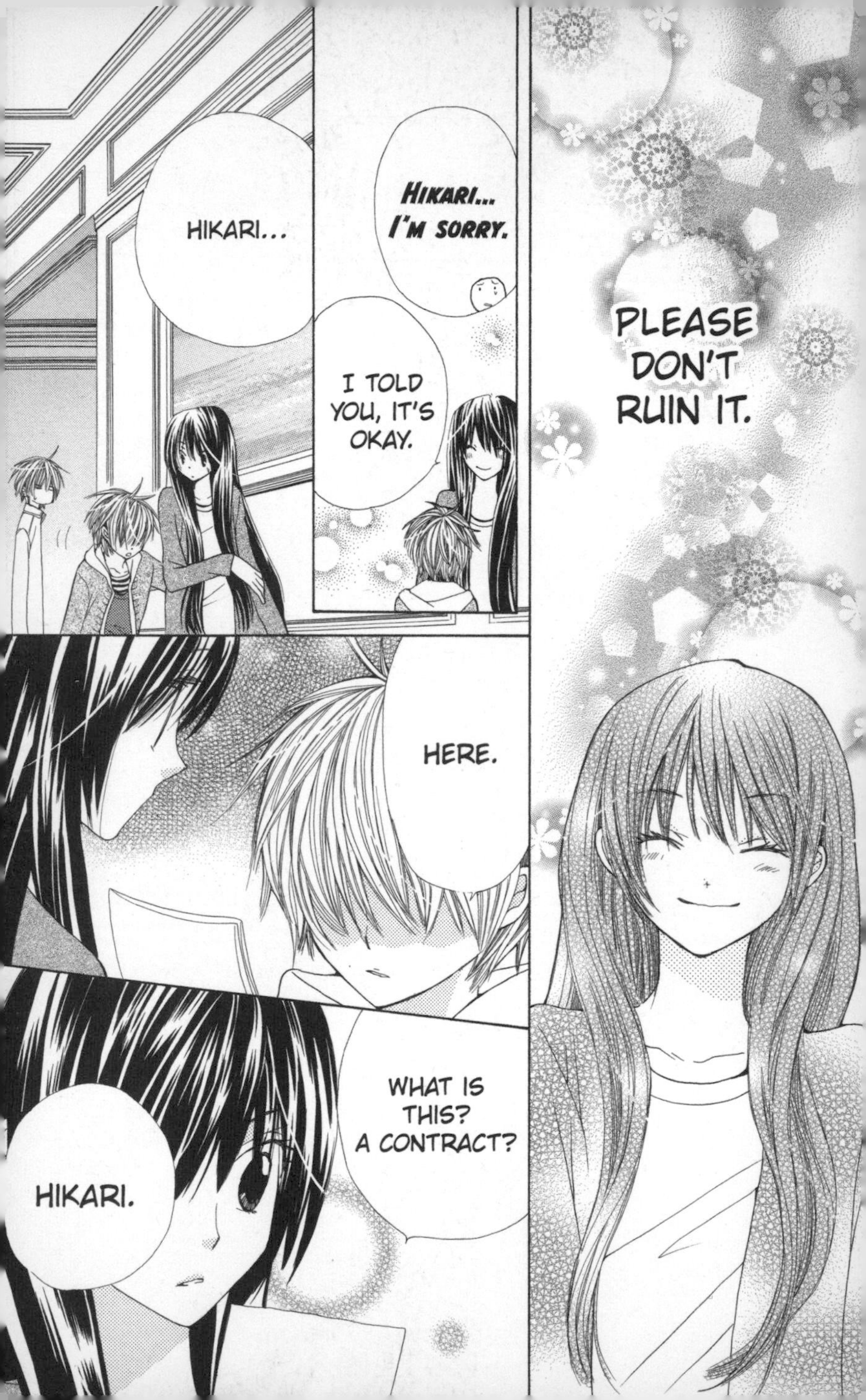
PLEASE DON'T RUIN IT.
HIKARI... I'M SORRY.
I TOLD YOU, IT'S OKAY.
HIKARI...
HERE.
WHAT IS THIS? A CONTRACT?
HIKARI.

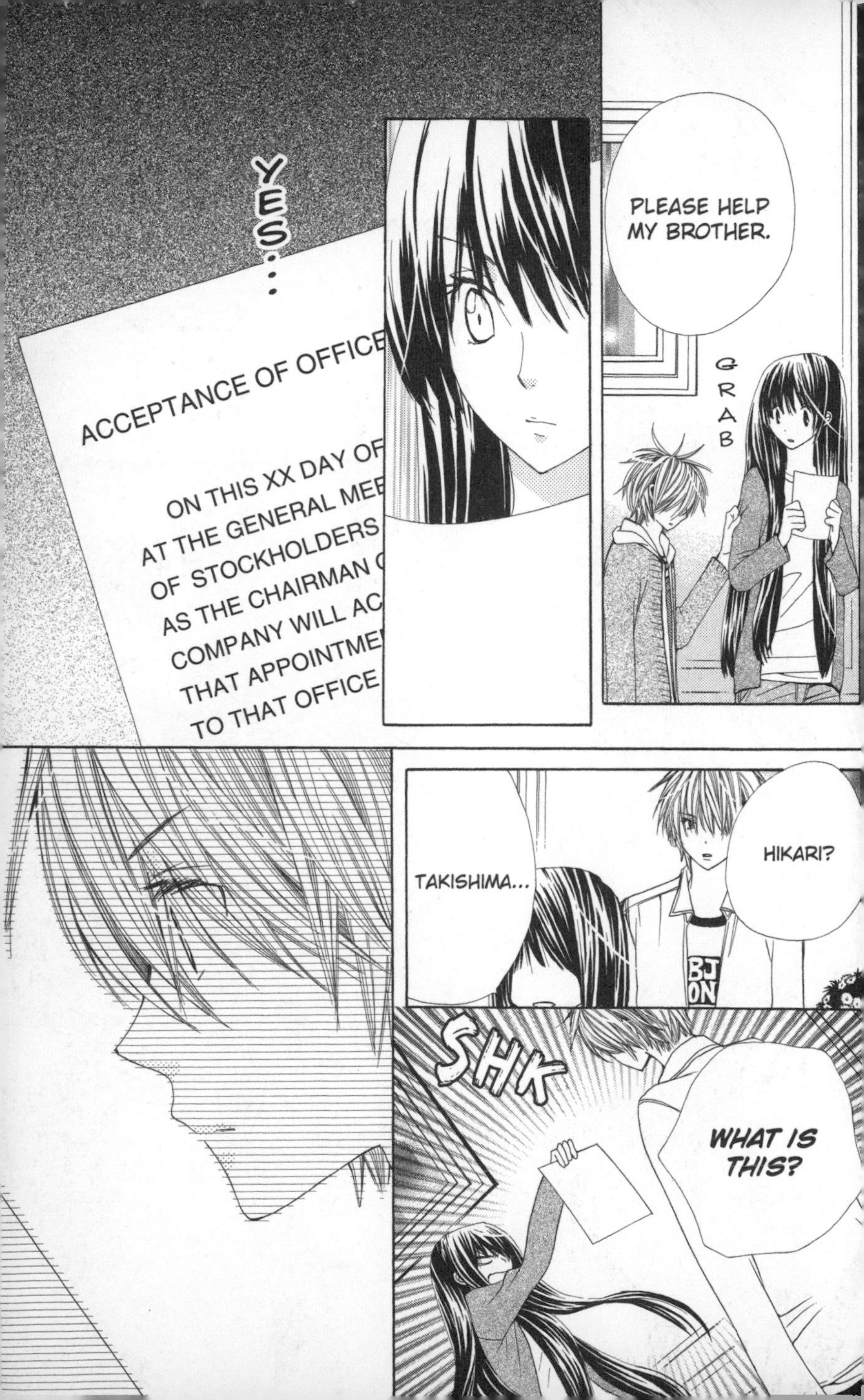
PLEASE HELP MY BROTHER.
GRAB
YES...
ACCEPTANCE OF OFFICE
ON THIS XX DAY OF
AT THE GENERAL MEE
OF STOCKHOLDERS
AS THE CHAIRMAN C
COMPANY WILL AC
THAT APPOINTMEN
TO THAT OFFICE
HIKARI?
TAKISHIMA...
BJ
ON
SHK
WHAT IS THIS?

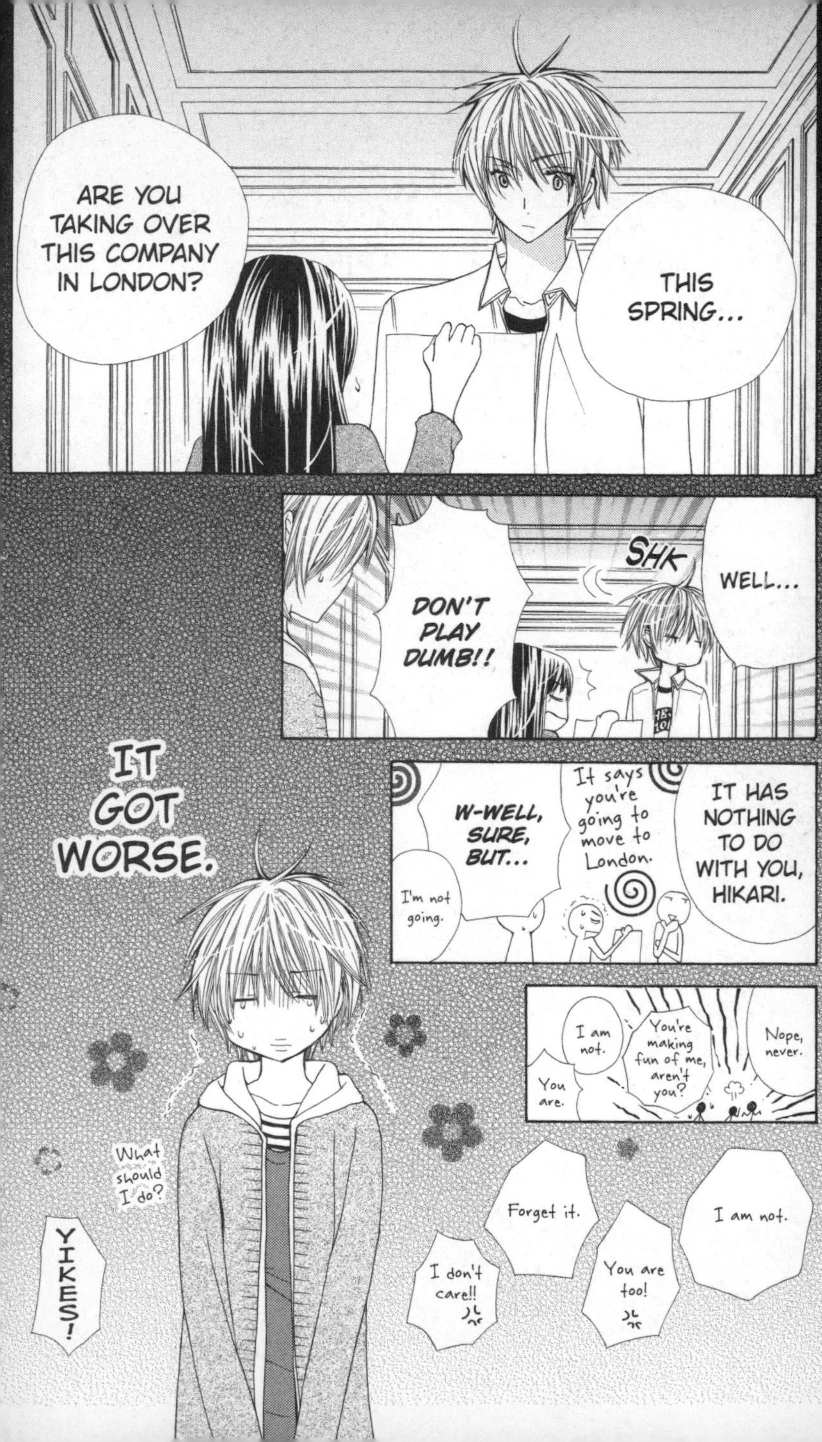
ARE YOU TAKING OVER THIS COMPANY IN LONDON?
THIS SPRING...
WELL...
SHK
DON'T PLAY DUMB!!
IT HAS NOTHING TO DO WITH YOU, HIKARI.
It says you're going to move to London.
W-WELL, SURE, BUT...
I'm not going.
Nope, never.
You're making fun of me, aren't you?
I am not.
You are.
I am not.
You are too!
Forget it.
I don't care!!
IT GOT WORSE.
What should I do?
YIKES!

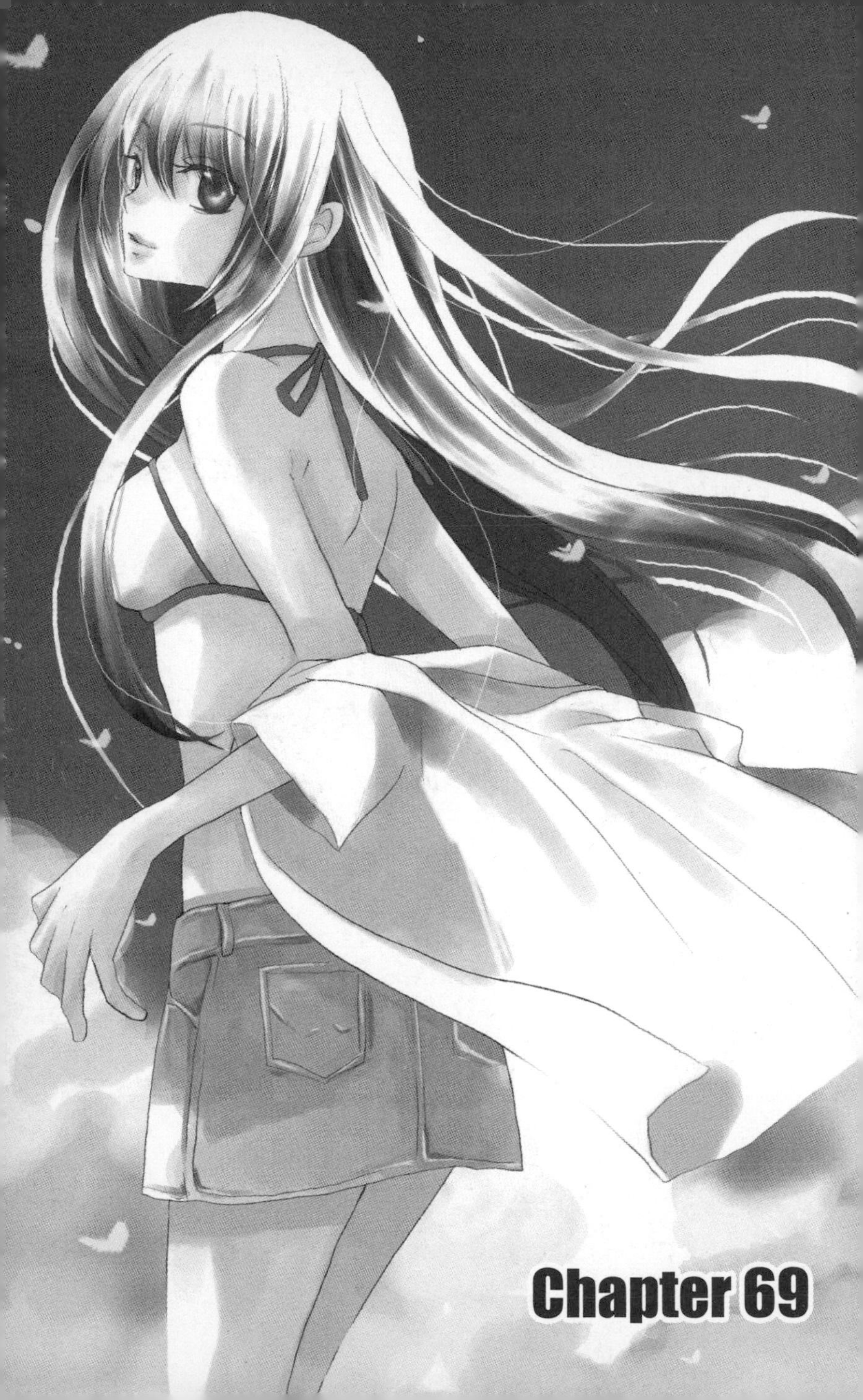

Chapter 69

Special
A

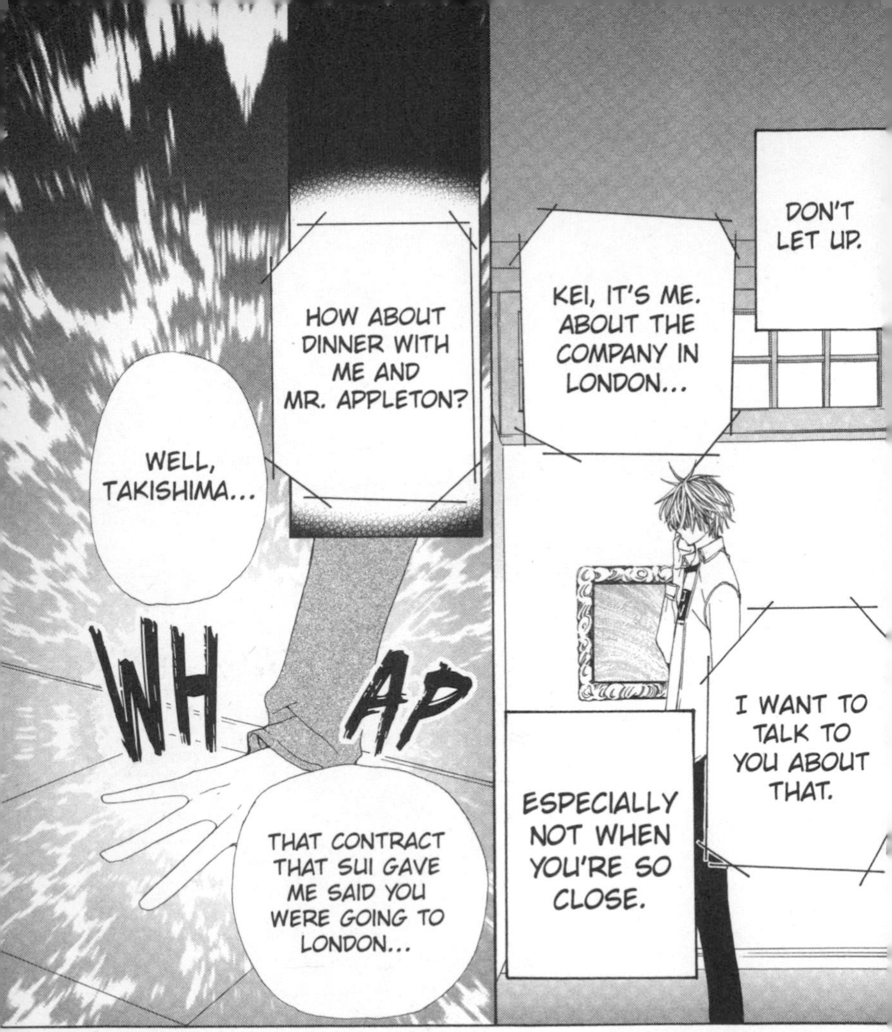
DON'T LET UP.
KEI, IT'S ME. ABOUT THE COMPANY IN LONDON...
I WANT TO TALK TO YOU ABOUT THAT.
ESPECIALLY NOT WHEN YOU'RE SO CLOSE.
HOW ABOUT DINNER WITH ME AND MR. APPLETON?
WELL, TAKISHIMA...
WHAP
THAT CONTRACT THAT SUI GAVE ME SAID YOU WERE GOING TO LONDON...

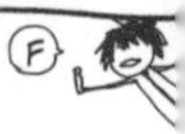

• THIS AND THAT •

I'M SORRY, I'M WAY BEHIND IN ANSWERING YOUR LETTERS.
I DIDN'T EVEN GET MY NEW YEAR'S CARDS OUT... I'LL EVENTUALLY RESPOND TO ALL OF THEM. PLEASE, BE PATIENT WITH ME. I'M SORRY!

YOUR SUPPORT DRIVES ME MORE THAN ANYTHING. AND TO EVERYONE WHO WRITES TO ME, MY CHEERFUL ASSISTANTS, MY FRIENDS...THANK YOU SO MUCH! AND THANK YOU TO MY EDITOR AND MY FAMILY, FOR WHOM I CAUSE A LOT OF TROUBLE! AND TO EVERYONE WORKING ON THE ANIMATION, AND THE ACTORS, I'M REALLY LOOKING FORWARD TO THE FINAL PRODUCT!! SEE YA!!!

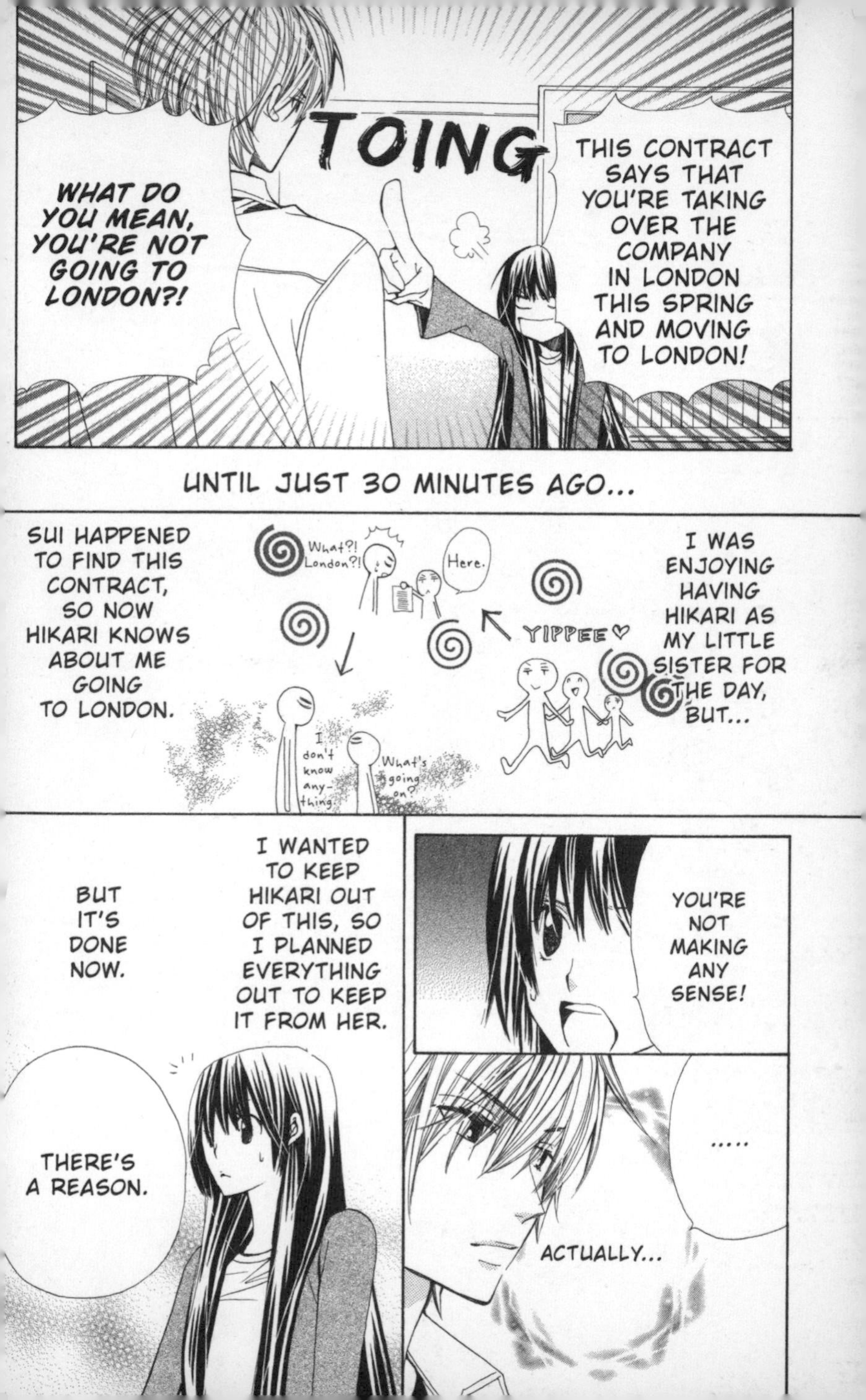
THIS CONTRACT SAYS THAT YOU'RE TAKING OVER THE COMPANY IN LONDON THIS SPRING AND MOVING TO LONDON!
TOING
WHAT DO YOU MEAN, YOU'RE NOT GOING TO LONDON?!
UNTIL JUST 30 MINUTES AGO...
I WAS ENJOYING HAVING HIKARI AS MY LITTLE SISTER FOR THE DAY, BUT...
YIPPEE♡
Here.
What?! London?!
SUI HAPPENED TO FIND THIS CONTRACT, SO NOW HIKARI KNOWS ABOUT ME GOING TO LONDON.
What's going on?
I don't know any-thing.
YOU'RE NOT MAKING ANY SENSE!
.....
ACTUALLY...
I WANTED TO KEEP HIKARI OUT OF THIS, SO I PLANNED EVERYTHING OUT TO KEEP IT FROM HER.
BUT IT'S DONE NOW.
THERE'S A REASON.

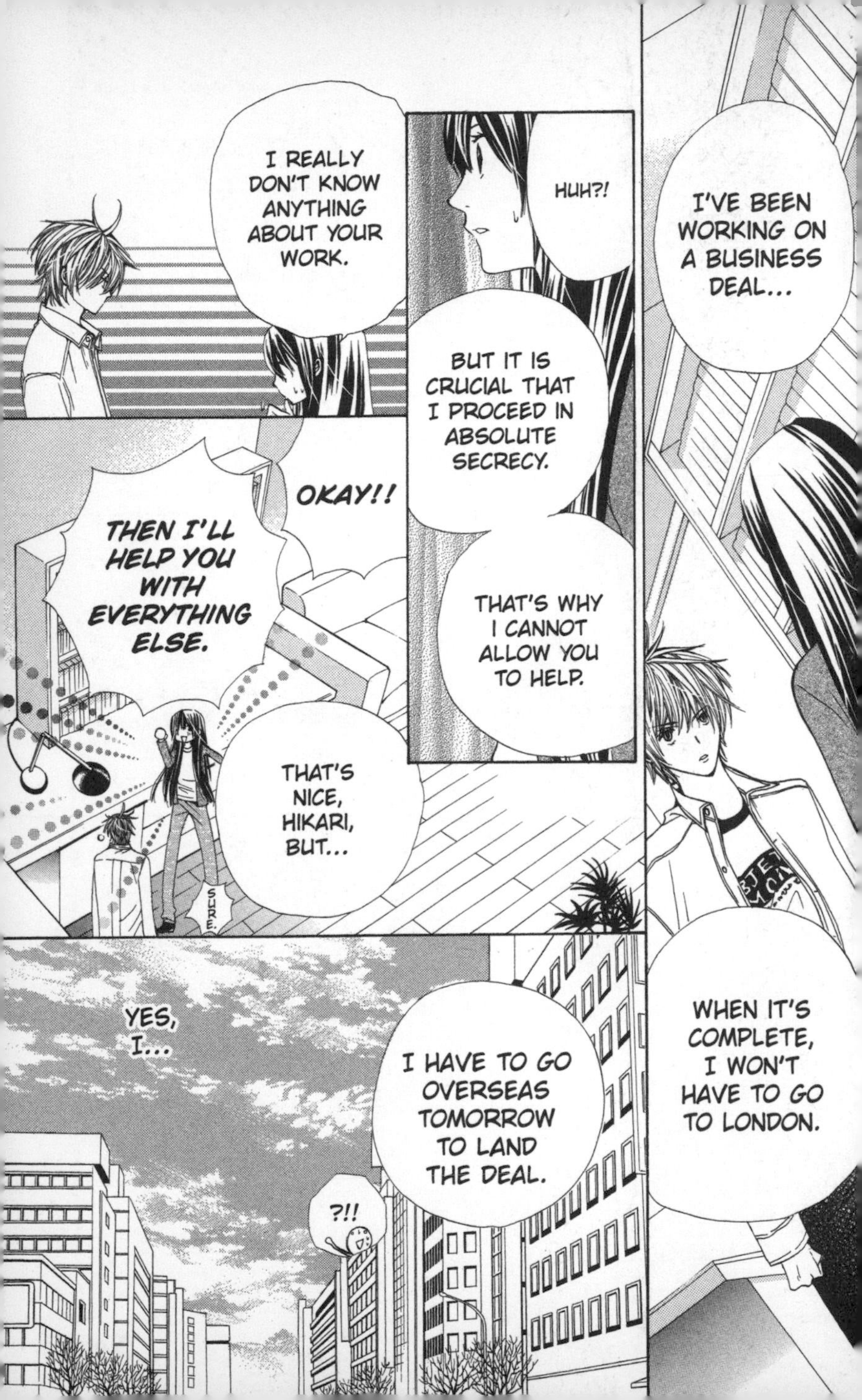

I'VE BEEN WORKING ON A BUSINESS DEAL...
HUH?!
BUT IT IS CRUCIAL THAT I PROCEED IN ABSOLUTE SECRECY.
THAT'S WHY I CANNOT ALLOW YOU TO HELP.
I REALLY DON'T KNOW ANYTHING ABOUT YOUR WORK.
OKAY!!
THEN I'LL HELP YOU WITH EVERYTHING ELSE.
THAT'S NICE, HIKARI, BUT...
SURE.
YES, I...
I HAVE TO GO OVERSEAS TOMORROW TO LAND THE DEAL.
WHEN IT'S COMPLETE, I WON'T HAVE TO GO TO LONDON.
?!!

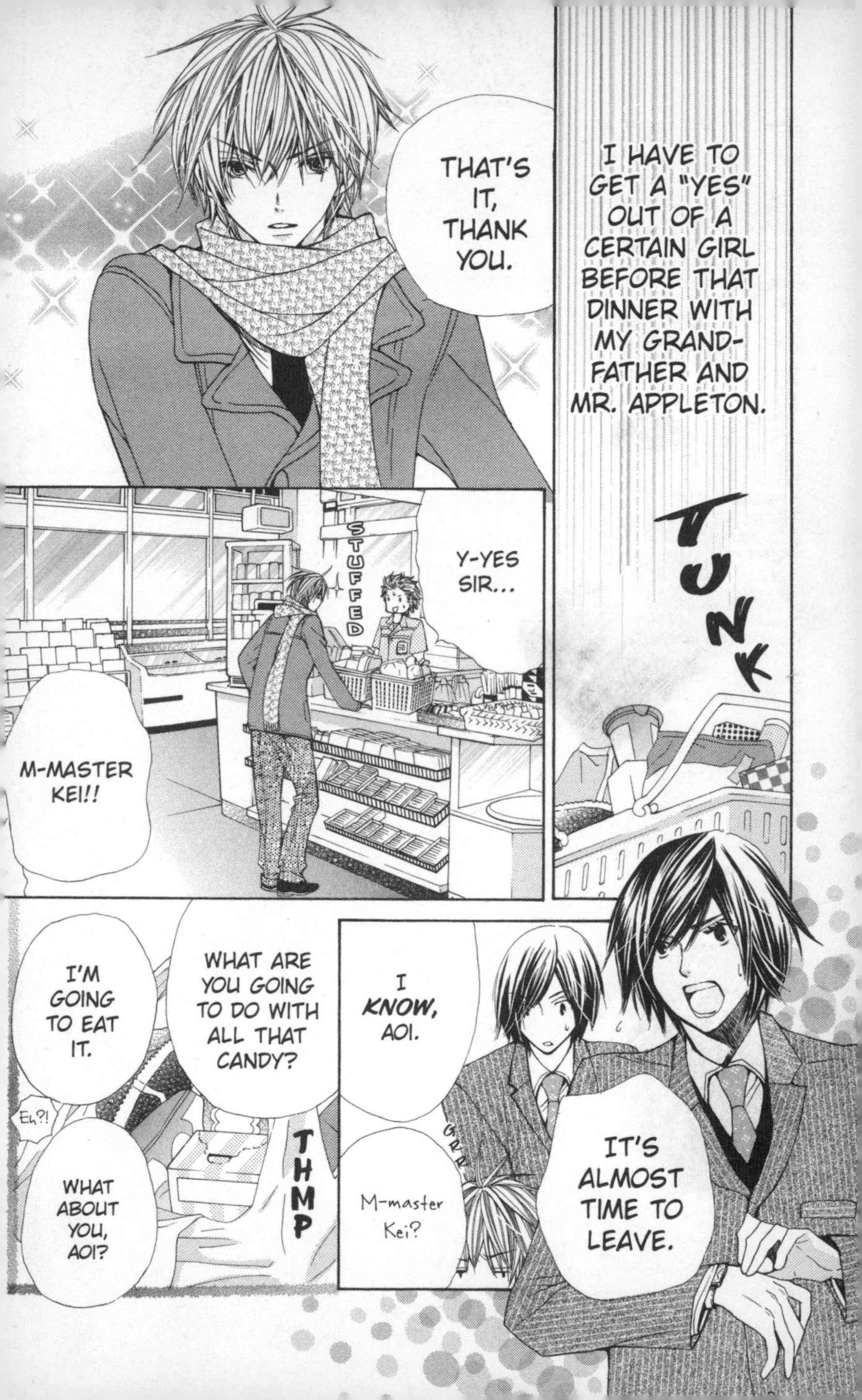
I HAVE TO GET A "YES" OUT OF A CERTAIN GIRL BEFORE THAT DINNER WITH MY GRAND-FATHER AND MR. APPLETON.
TUNK
THAT'S IT, THANK YOU.
STUFFED
Y-YES SIR...
M-MASTER KEI!!
IT'S ALMOST TIME TO LEAVE.
GRR
I *KNOW*, AOI.
M-master Kei?
THMP
WHAT ARE YOU GOING TO DO WITH ALL THAT CANDY?
I'M GOING TO EAT IT.
Eh?!
WHAT ABOUT YOU, AOI?

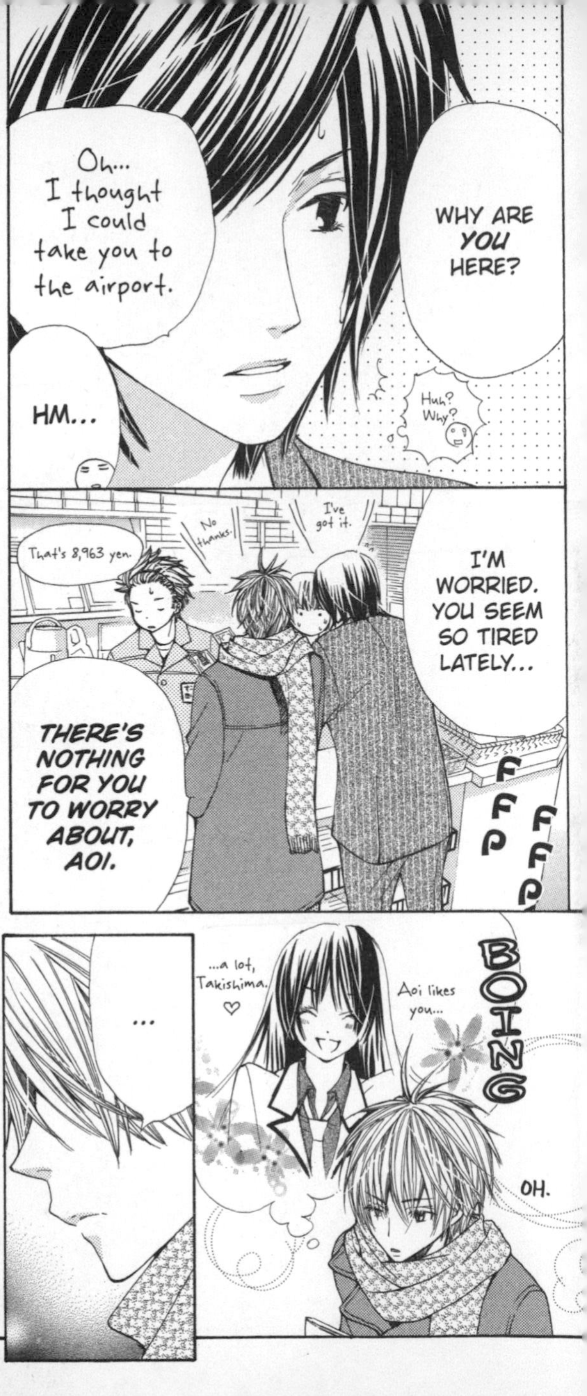
WHY ARE YOU HERE?
Huh? Why?
Oh... I thought I could take you to the airport.
HM...
I'M WORRIED. YOU SEEM SO TIRED LATELY...
FFP FFP
I've got it.
No thanks.
That's 8,963 yen.
THERE'S NOTHING FOR YOU TO WORRY ABOUT, AOI.
BOING
Aoi likes you...
...a lot, Takishima. ♡
OH.
...

6

○THIS AND THAT○

• THANK YOU FOR STICKING WITH ME THROUGH THE BOOK AND THIS LAST QUARTER PAGE. AFTER 12 VOLUMES, IT'S GETTING HARDER TO THINK UP THINGS TO WRITE ABOUT. HA HA!

• THIS TIME THE THEME WAS NATIVE COSTUMES. THE EDITOR ACTUALLY ADDED ON THE "SNOW CHILD" REQUEST. IT WAS SO MUCH FUN! THANK YOU SO MUCH!

• WELL, OKAY. THANK YOU SO VERY MUCH FOR READING THIS FAR!! I HOPE WE MEET AGAIN IN VOLUME 13!!

IF YOU'D LIKE TO, PLEASE SEND US YOUR THOUGHTS.

MAKI MINAMI
C/O VIZ MEDIA
SA EDITOR
P.O. BOX 77010
SAN FRANCISCO,
CA 94107

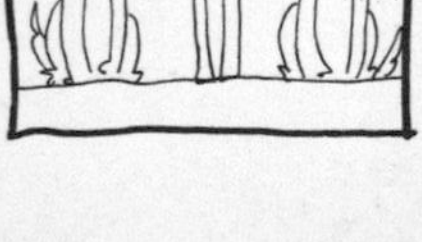
WITH ALL...
...MY HEART.

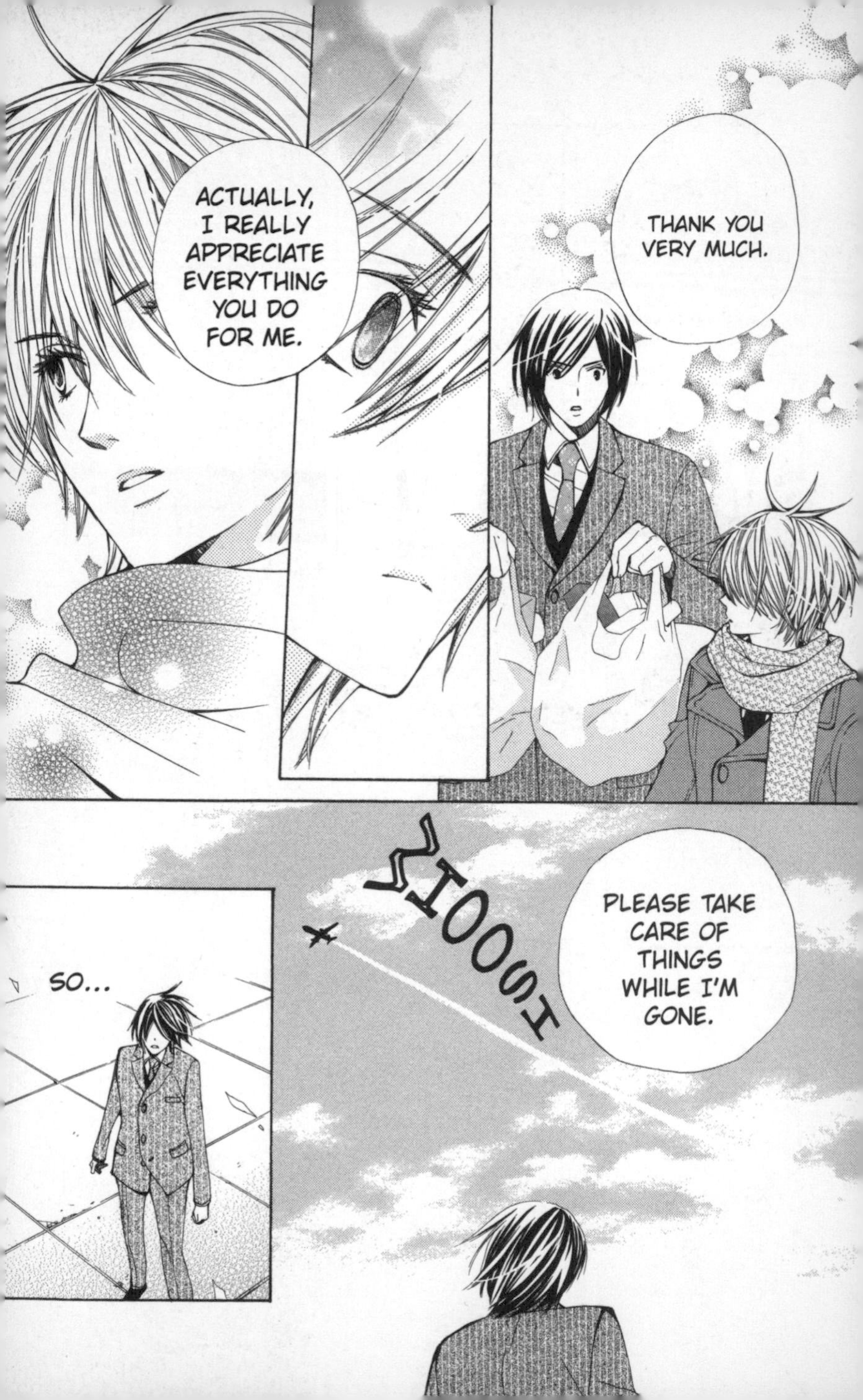
THANK YOU VERY MUCH.
ACTUALLY, I REALLY APPRECIATE EVERYTHING YOU DO FOR ME.
WHOOSH
PLEASE TAKE CARE OF THINGS WHILE I'M GONE.
SO...

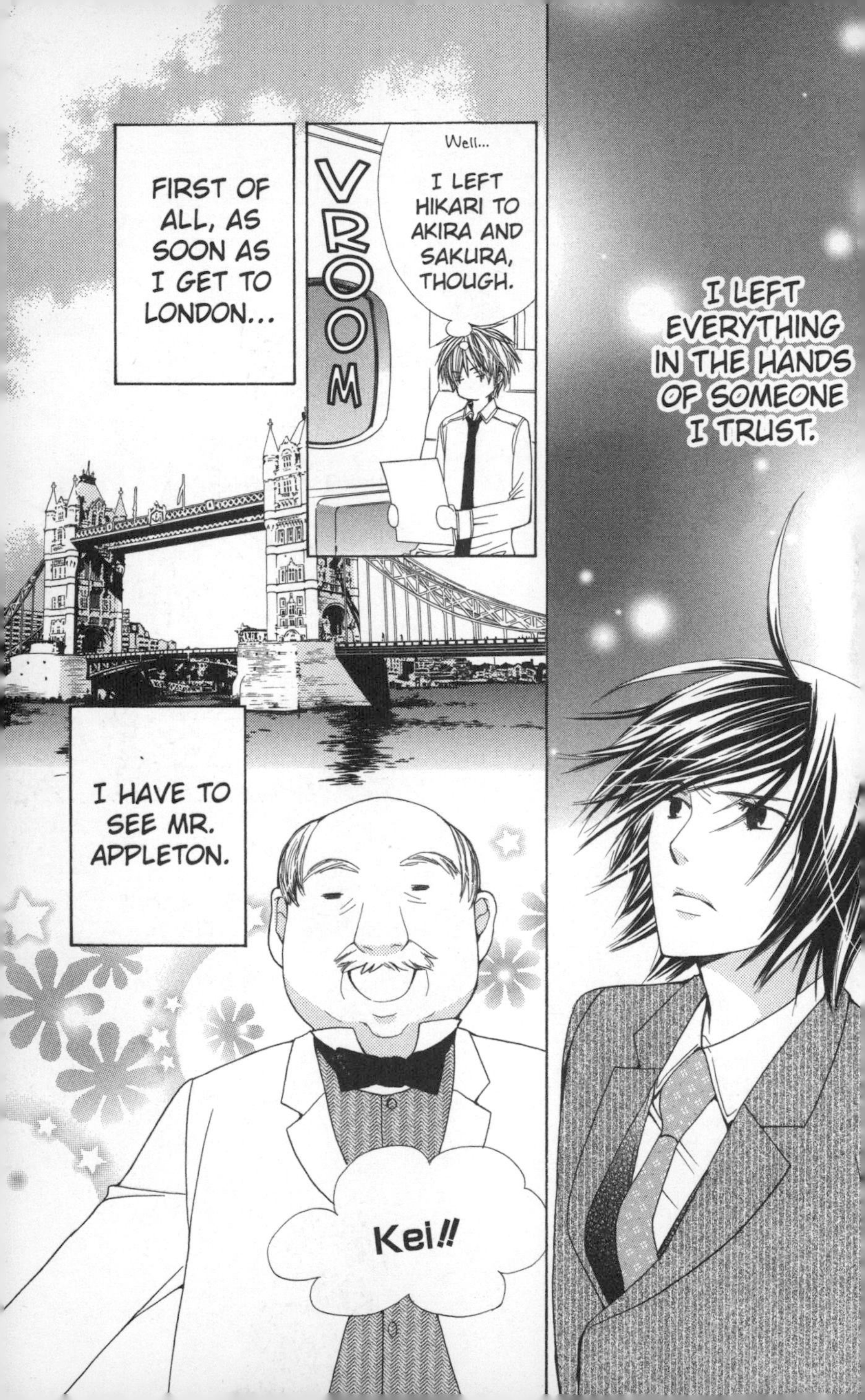
I LEFT EVERYTHING IN THE HANDS OF SOMEONE I TRUST.
VROOM
Well...
I LEFT HIKARI TO AKIRA AND SAKURA, THOUGH.
FIRST OF ALL, AS SOON AS I GET TO LONDON...
I HAVE TO SEE MR. APPLETON.
Kei!!

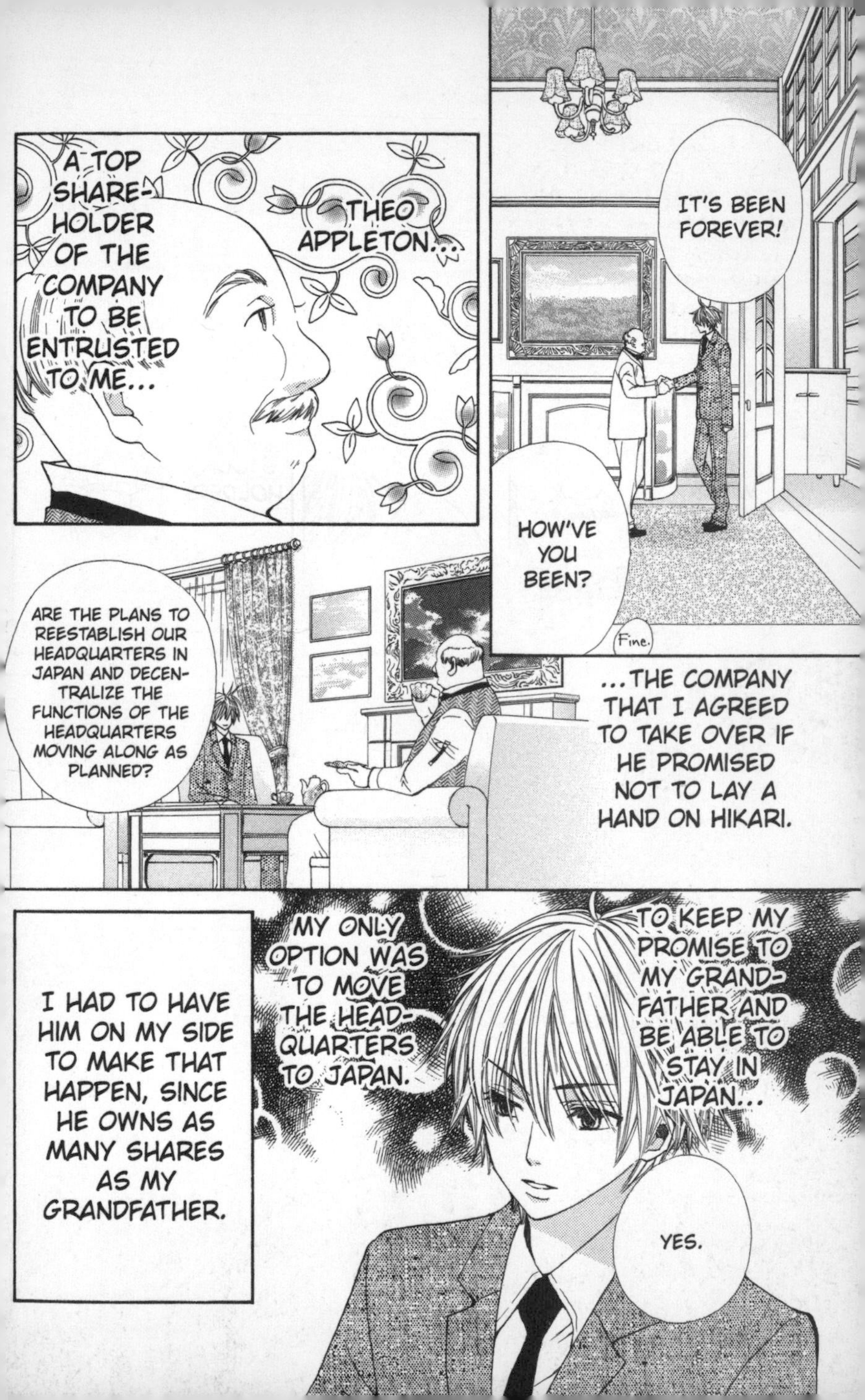
IT'S BEEN FOREVER!
HOW'VE YOU BEEN?
Fine.
A TOP SHARE-HOLDER OF THE COMPANY TO BE ENTRUSTED TO ME...
THEO APPLETON...
...THE COMPANY THAT I AGREED TO TAKE OVER IF HE PROMISED NOT TO LAY A HAND ON HIKARI.
ARE THE PLANS TO REESTABLISH OUR HEADQUARTERS IN JAPAN AND DECEN-TRALIZE THE FUNCTIONS OF THE HEADQUARTERS MOVING ALONG AS PLANNED?
TO KEEP MY PROMISE TO MY GRAND-FATHER AND BE ABLE TO STAY IN JAPAN...
YES.
MY ONLY OPTION WAS TO MOVE THE HEAD-QUARTERS TO JAPAN.
I HAD TO HAVE HIM ON MY SIDE TO MAKE THAT HAPPEN, SINCE HE OWNS AS MANY SHARES AS MY GRANDFATHER.

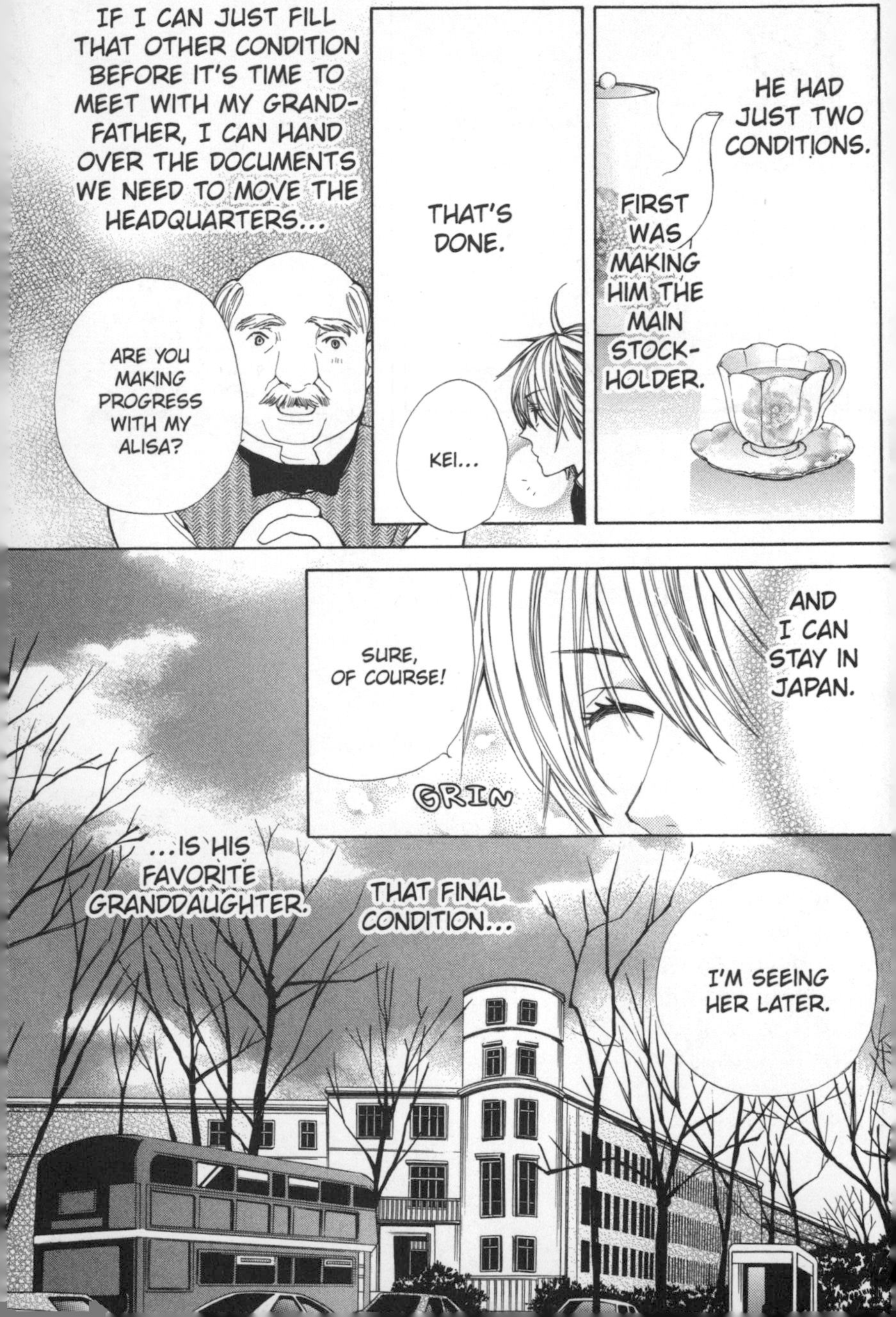
HE HAD JUST TWO CONDITIONS.
FIRST WAS MAKING HIM THE MAIN STOCK-HOLDER.
THAT'S DONE.
KEI...
IF I CAN JUST FILL THAT OTHER CONDITION BEFORE IT'S TIME TO MEET WITH MY GRAND-FATHER, I CAN HAND OVER THE DOCUMENTS WE NEED TO MOVE THE HEADQUARTERS...
ARE YOU MAKING PROGRESS WITH MY ALISA?
AND I CAN STAY IN JAPAN.
SURE, OF COURSE!
GRIN
I'M SEEING HER LATER.
THAT FINAL CONDITION...
...IS HIS FAVORITE GRANDDAUGHTER.

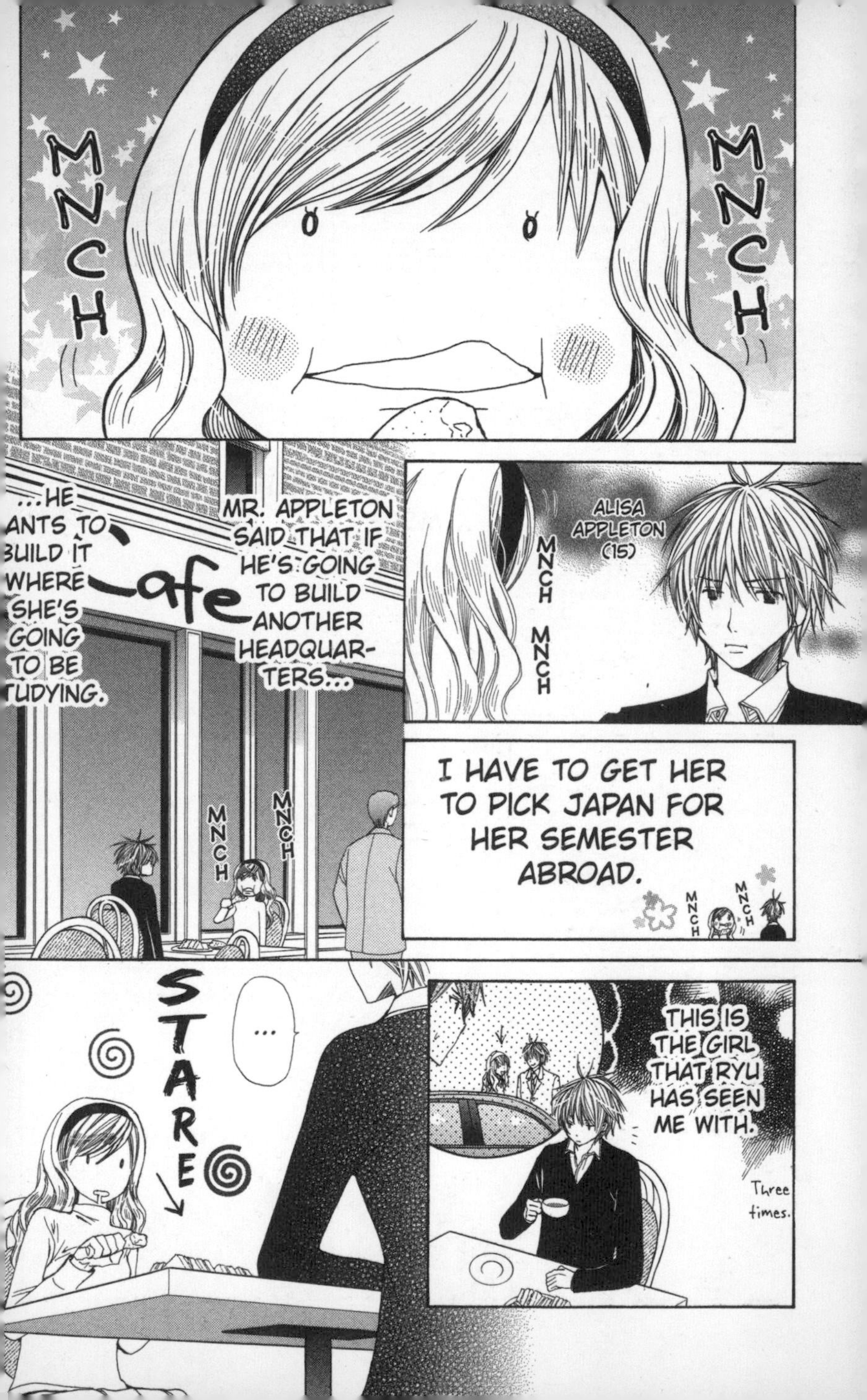
MNCH
MNCH
ALISA APPLETON (15)
MNCH MNCH
I HAVE TO GET HER TO PICK JAPAN FOR HER SEMESTER ABROAD.
MNCH MNCH
MR. APPLETON SAID THAT IF HE'S GOING TO BUILD ANOTHER HEADQUAR-TERS...
...HE ANTS TO UILD IT WHERE SHE'S GOING TO BE TUDYING.
MNCH
MNCH
THIS IS THE GIRL THAT RYU HAS SEEN ME WITH.
Three times.
...
STARE

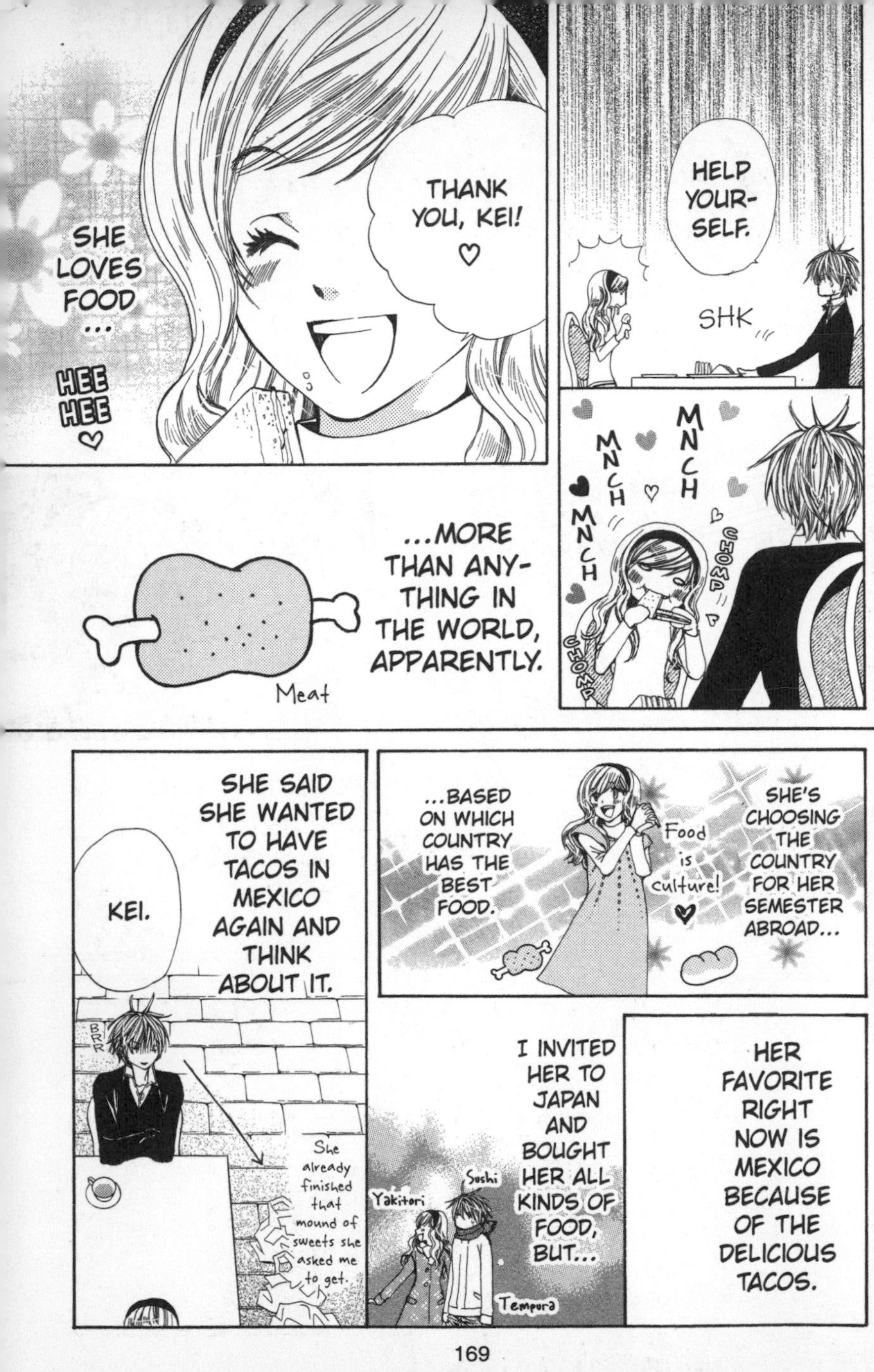
HELP YOUR-SELF.
SHK
MNCH MNCH MNCH
CHOMP CHOMP
THANK YOU, KEI! ♡
SHE LOVES FOOD...
HEE HEE ♡
...MORE THAN ANY-THING IN THE WORLD, APPARENTLY.
Meat
SHE'S CHOOSING THE COUNTRY FOR HER SEMESTER ABROAD...
...BASED ON WHICH COUNTRY HAS THE BEST FOOD.
Food is culture! ♥
HER FAVORITE RIGHT NOW IS MEXICO BECAUSE OF THE DELICIOUS TACOS.
I INVITED HER TO JAPAN AND BOUGHT HER ALL KINDS OF FOOD, BUT...
Sushi
Yakitori
Tempura
SHE SAID SHE WANTED TO HAVE TACOS IN MEXICO AGAIN AND THINK ABOUT IT.
KEI.
BRR
She already finished that mound of sweets she asked me to get.

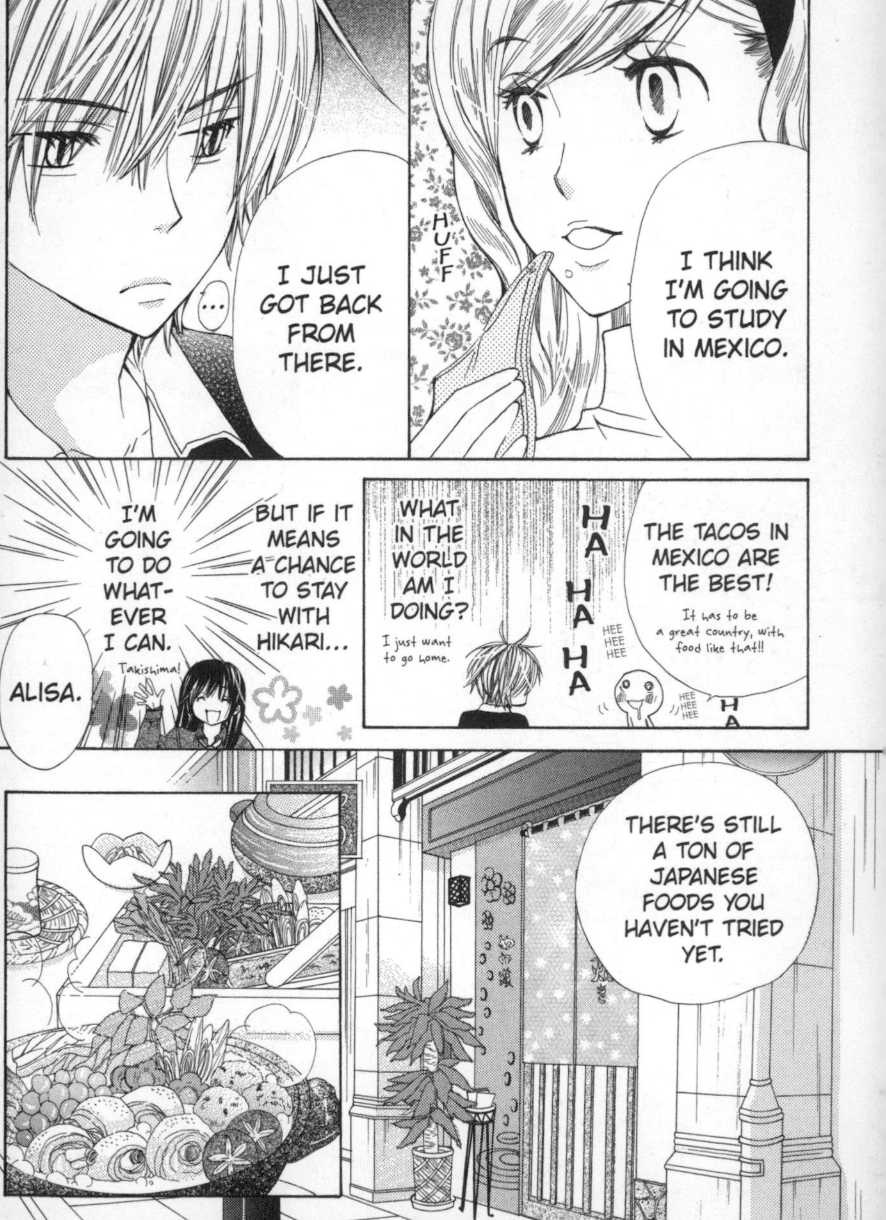
I THINK I'M GOING TO STUDY IN MEXICO.
HUFF
I JUST GOT BACK FROM THERE.
...
THE TACOS IN MEXICO ARE THE BEST!
It has to be a great country, with food like that!!
HA HA HA
HEE HEE HEE
HEE HEE HEE
HA
WHAT IN THE WORLD AM I DOING?
I just want to go home.
BUT IF IT MEANS A CHANCE TO STAY WITH HIKARI...
I'M GOING TO DO WHAT-EVER I CAN.
Takishima!
ALISA.
THERE'S STILL A TON OF JAPANESE FOODS YOU HAVEN'T TRIED YET.

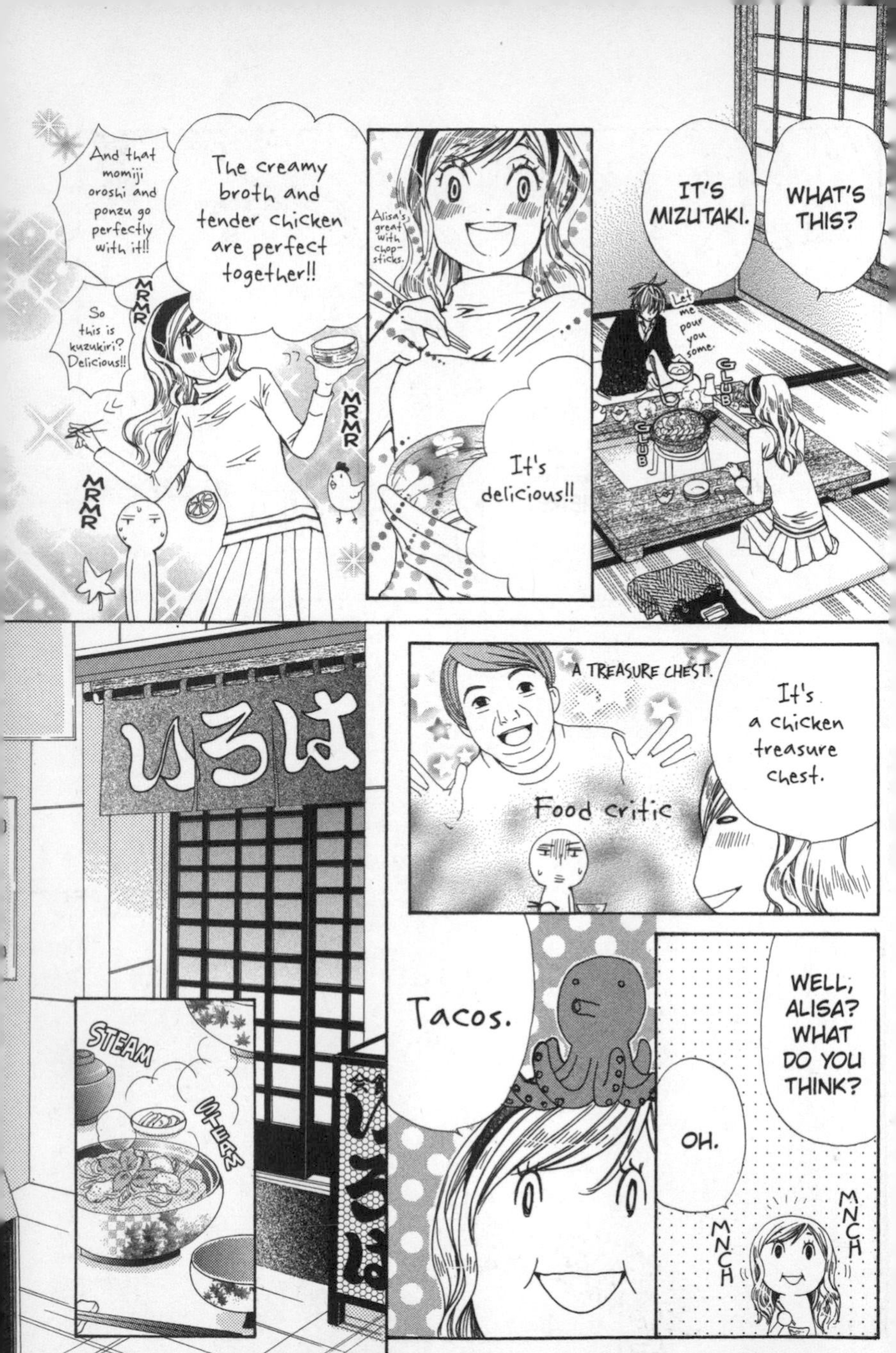
WHAT'S THIS?
IT'S MIZUTAKI.
Let me pour you some.
CLUB
CLUB
Alisa's great with chopsticks.
It's delicious!!
The creamy broth and tender chicken are perfect together!!
And that momiji oroshi and ponzu go perfectly with it!!
MRMR
So this is kuzukiri? Delicious!!
MRMR
MRMR
It's a chicken treasure chest.
A TREASURE CHEST.
Food critic
WELL, ALISA? WHAT DO YOU THINK?
OH.
MNCH
MNCH
Tacos.
いろは
STEAM
STEAM

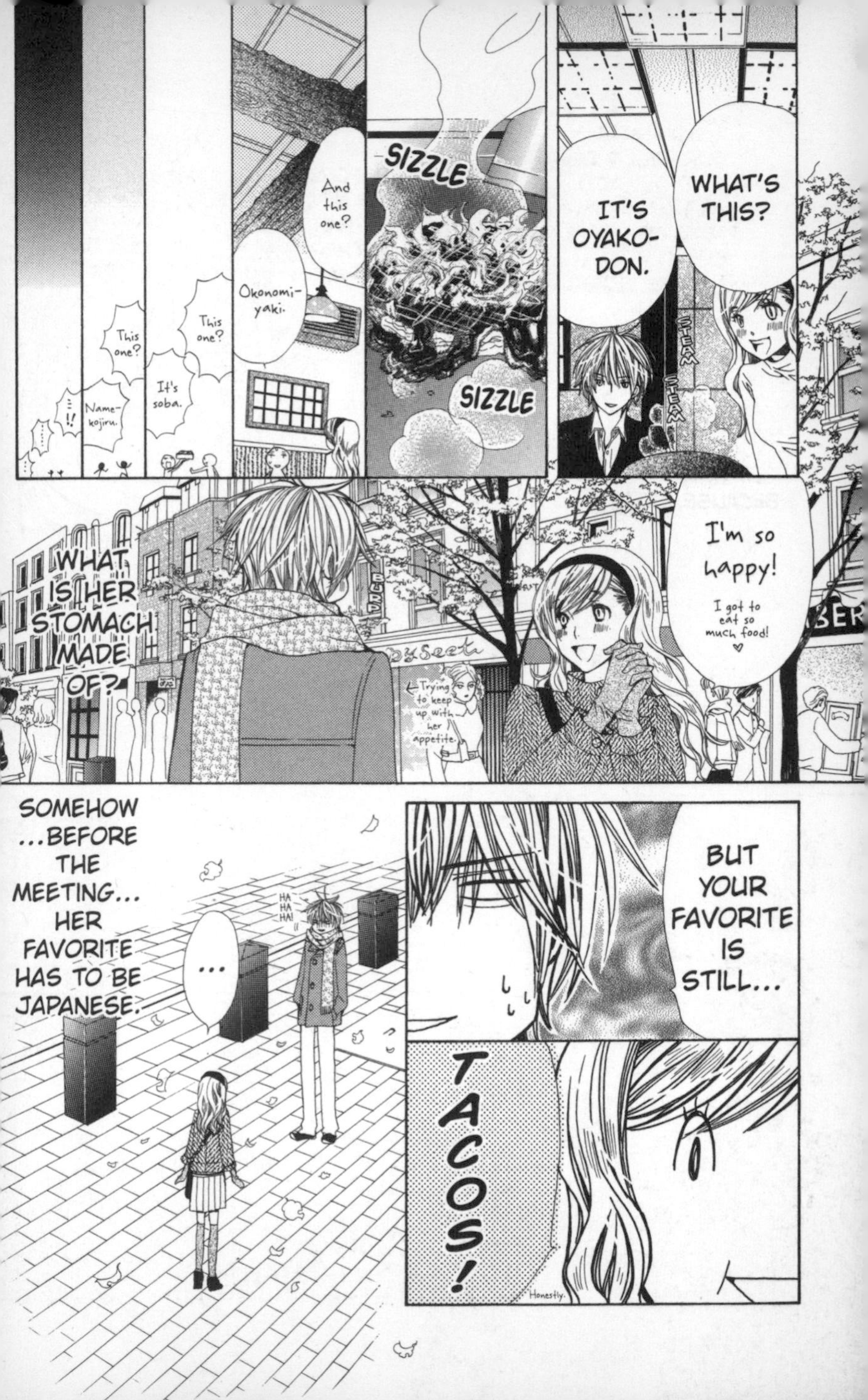

WHAT'S THIS?
IT'S OYAKO-DON.
STEAM
STEAM
SIZZLE
SIZZLE
And this one?
Okonomi-yaki.
This one?
It's soba.
This one?
Name-kojiru.
...!!
......
I'm so happy!
I got to eat so much food! ♥
Trying to keep up with her appetite.
WHAT IS HER STOMACH MADE OF?
BUT YOUR FAVORITE IS STILL...
TACOS!
Honestly.
SOMEHOW ...BEFORE THE MEETING... HER FAVORITE HAS TO BE JAPANESE.
HA HA HA!
...

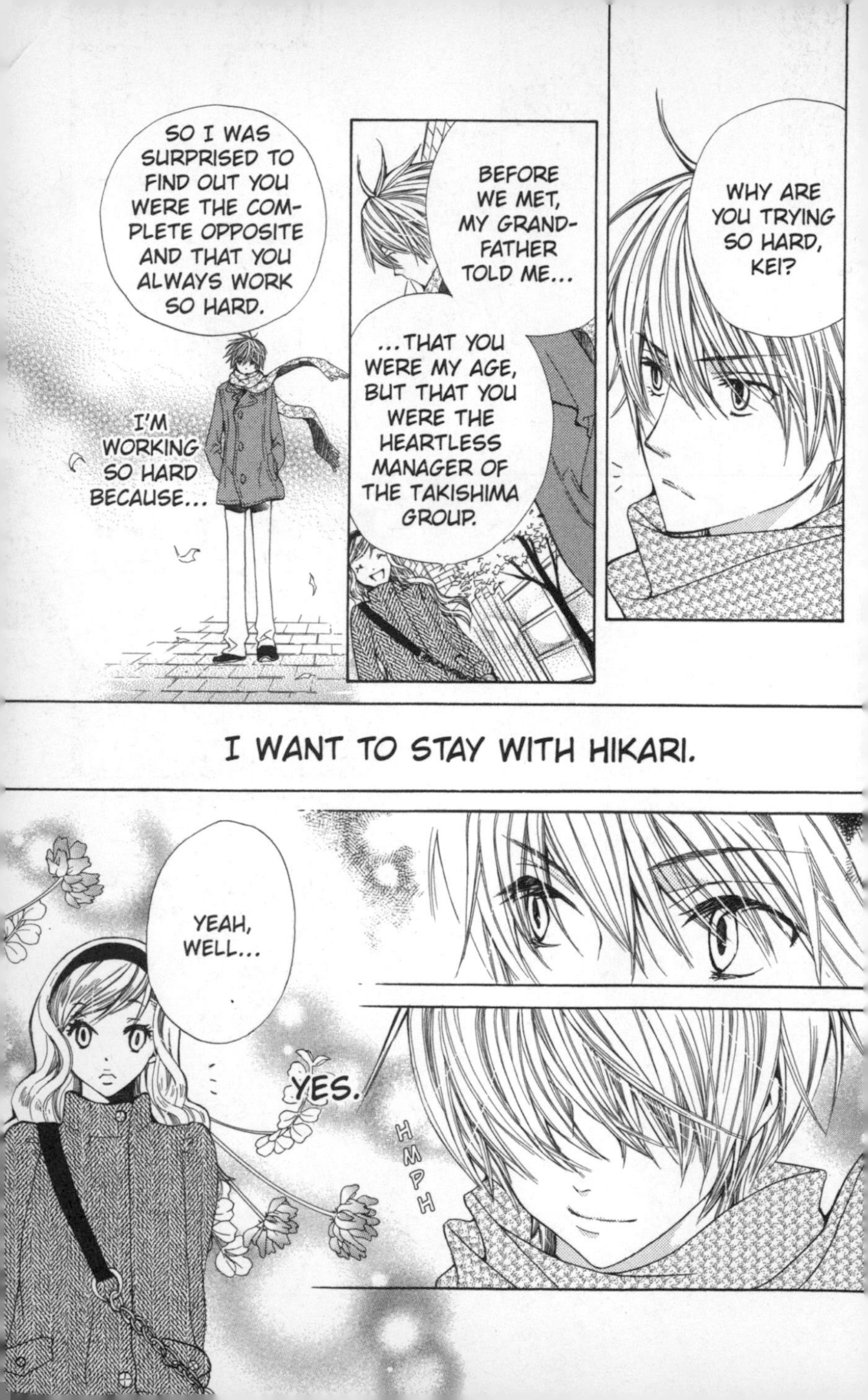
WHY ARE YOU TRYING SO HARD, KEI?
BEFORE WE MET, MY GRAND-FATHER TOLD ME...
...THAT YOU WERE MY AGE, BUT THAT YOU WERE THE HEARTLESS MANAGER OF THE TAKISHIMA GROUP.
SO I WAS SURPRISED TO FIND OUT YOU WERE THE COM-PLETE OPPOSITE AND THAT YOU ALWAYS WORK SO HARD.
I'M WORKING SO HARD BECAUSE...
I WANT TO STAY WITH HIKARI.
HMPH
YEAH, WELL...
YES.

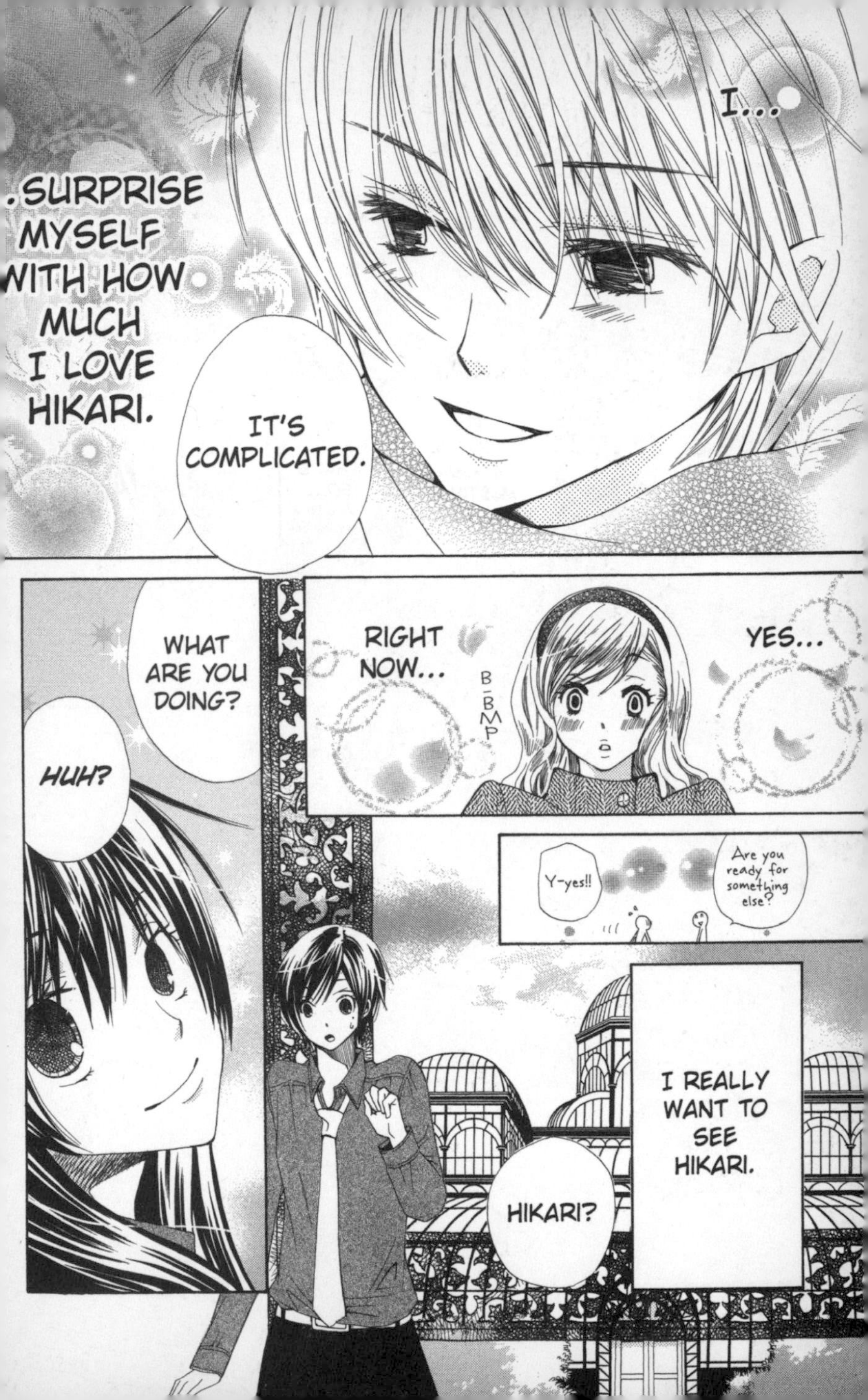
I...
IT'S COMPLICATED.
...SURPRISE MYSELF WITH HOW MUCH I LOVE HIKARI.
YES...
B-BMP
RIGHT NOW...
Are you ready for something else?
Y-yes!!
I REALLY WANT TO SEE HIKARI.
HIKARI?
WHAT ARE YOU DOING?
HUH?

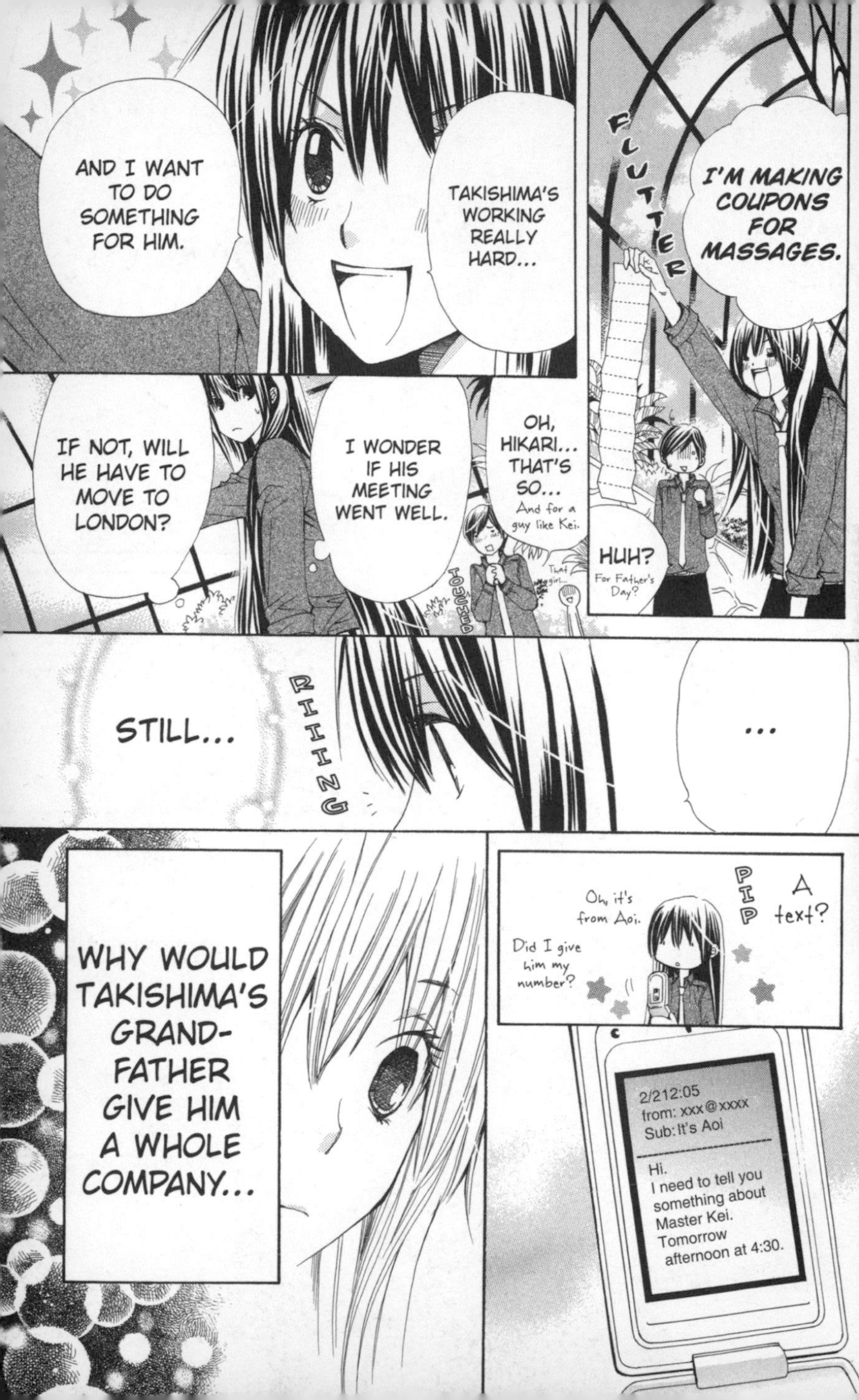
I'M MAKING COUPONS FOR MASSAGES.
FLUTTER
HUH?
For Father's Day?
TAKISHIMA'S WORKING REALLY HARD...
AND I WANT TO DO SOMETHING FOR HIM.
OH, HIKARI... THAT'S SO...
And for a guy like Kei.
That girl...
TOUCHED
I WONDER IF HIS MEETING WENT WELL.
IF NOT, WILL HE HAVE TO MOVE TO LONDON?
...
RIIIING
STILL...
A text?
PIP
Oh, it's from Aoi.
Did I give him my number?
2/212:05
from: xxx@xxxx
Sub: It's Aoi
Hi.
I need to tell you something about Master Kei. Tomorrow afternoon at 4:30.
WHY WOULD TAKISHIMA'S GRANDFATHER GIVE HIM A WHOLE COMPANY...

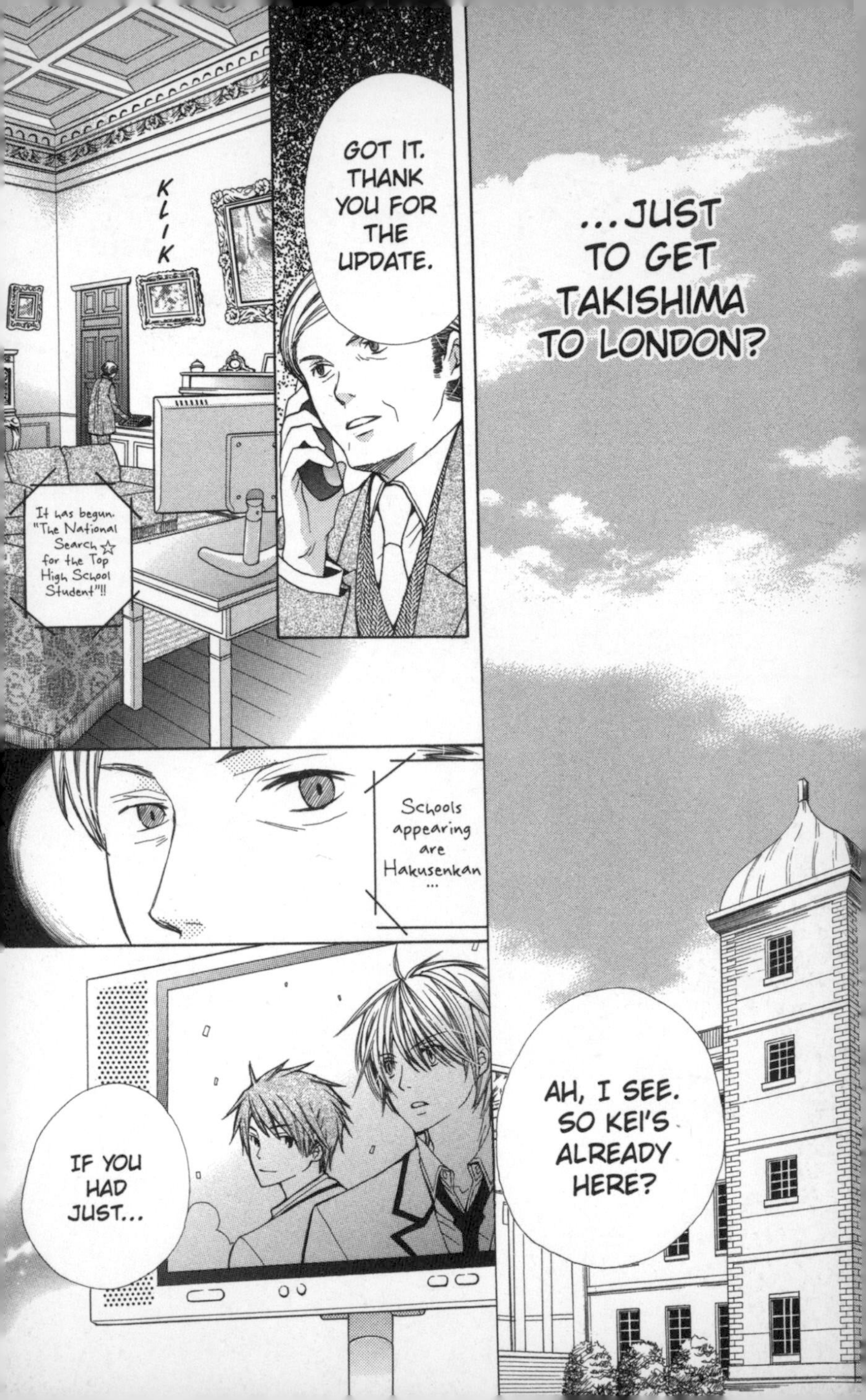
...JUST TO GET TAKISHIMA TO LONDON?
AH, I SEE. SO KEI'S ALREADY HERE?
GOT IT. THANK YOU FOR THE UPDATE.
KLIK
It has begun. "The National Search ☆ for the Top High School Student"!!
Schools appearing are Hakusenkan ...
IF YOU HAD JUST...

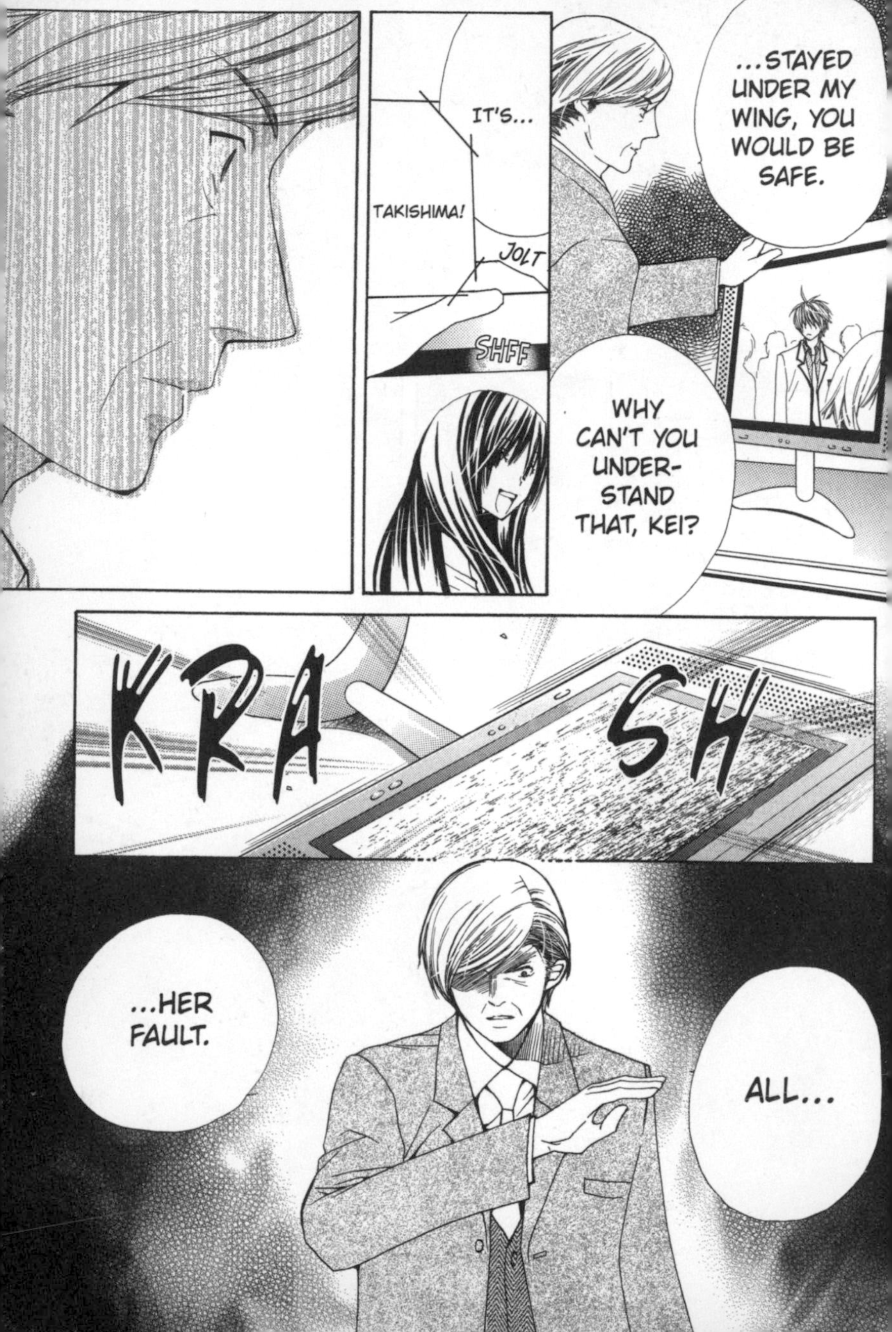
...STAYED UNDER MY WING, YOU WOULD BE SAFE.
WHY CAN'T YOU UNDER-STAND THAT, KEI?
IT'S...
TAKISHIMA!
JOLT
SHFF
KRASH
ALL...
...HER FAULT.

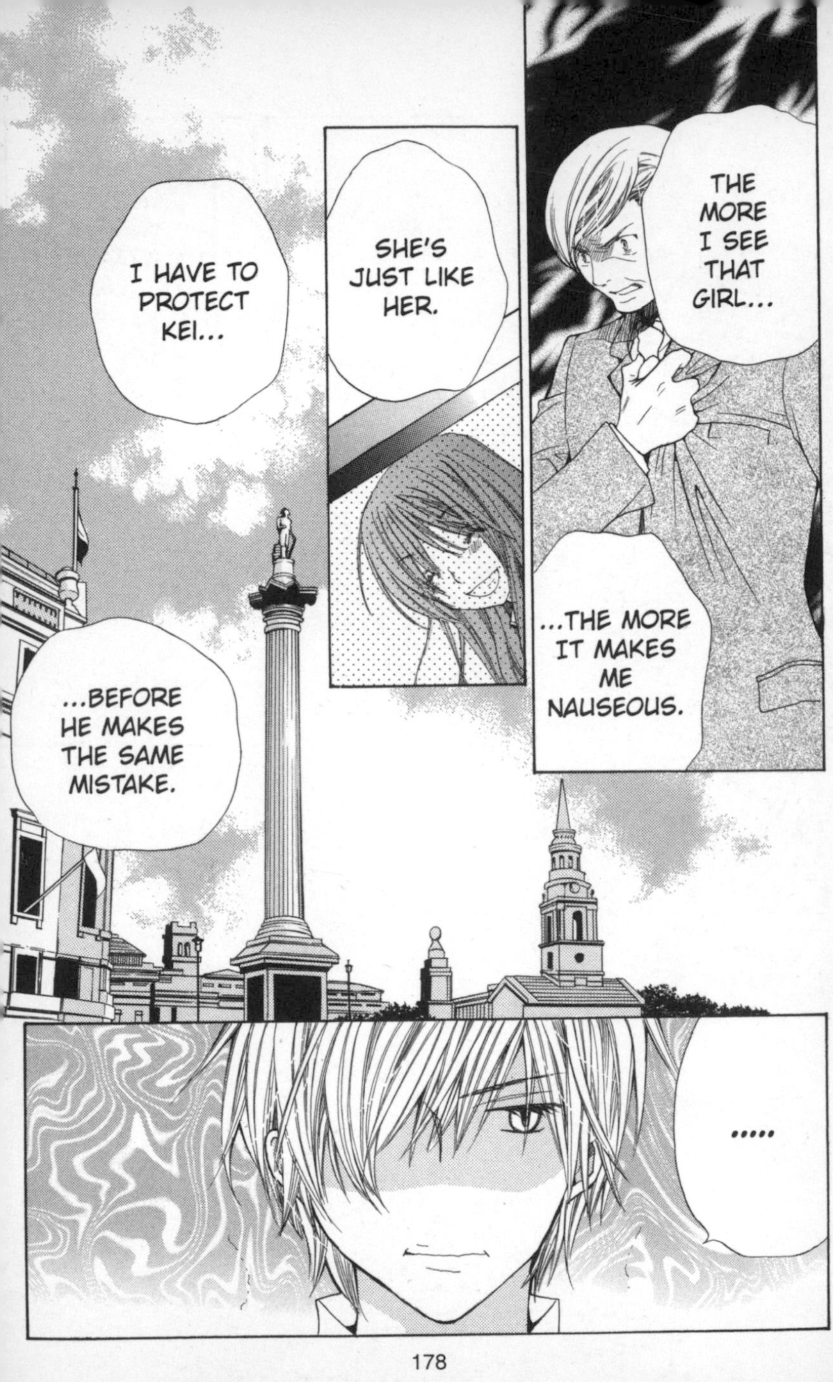
THE MORE I SEE THAT GIRL...
...THE MORE IT MAKES ME NAUSEOUS.
SHE'S JUST LIKE HER.
I HAVE TO PROTECT KEI...
...BEFORE HE MAKES THE SAME MISTAKE.
......

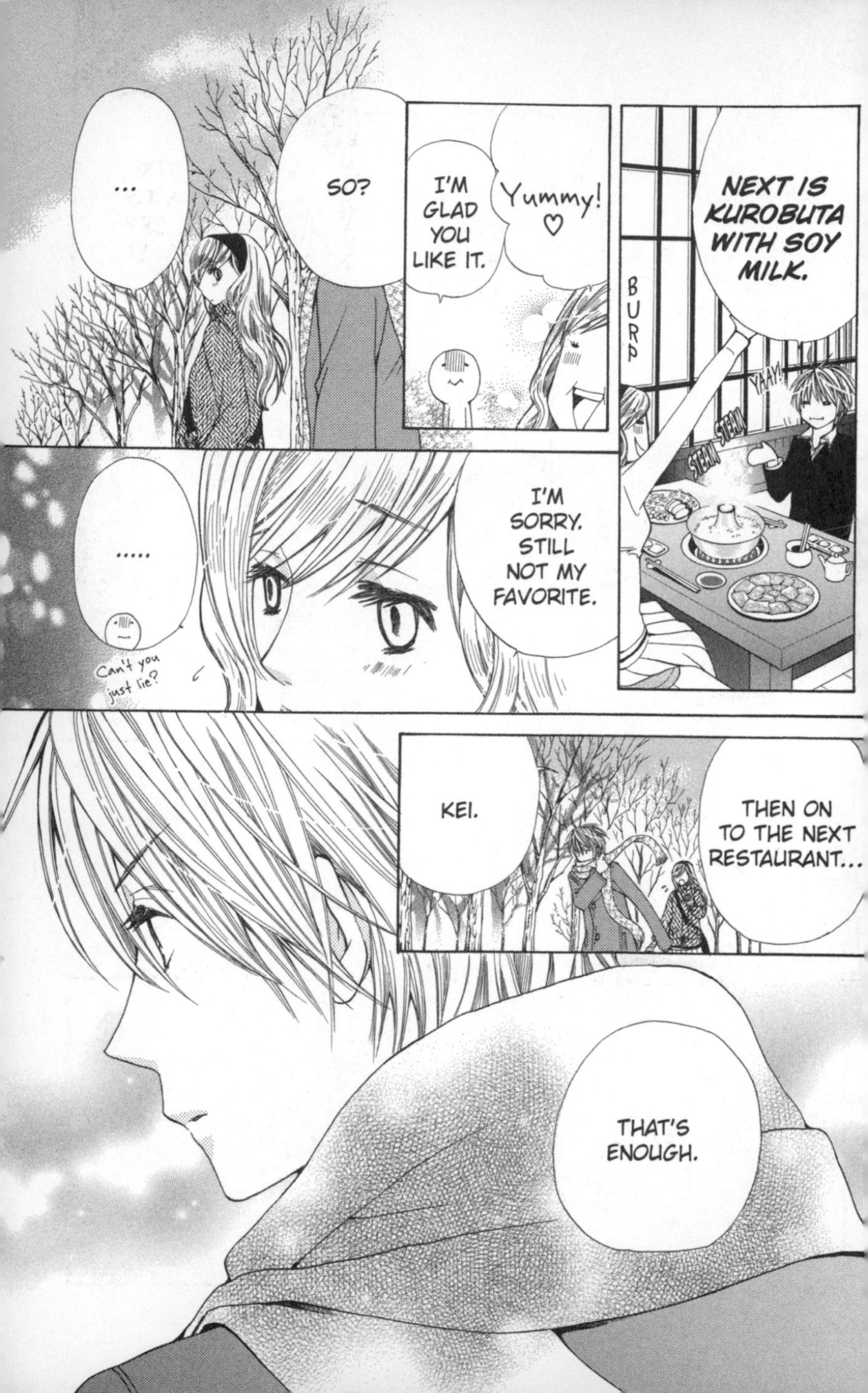
NEXT IS KUROBUTA WITH SOY MILK.
BURP
YAAY!
STEAM STEAM STEAM
Yummy! ♡
I'M GLAD YOU LIKE IT.
SO?
...
I'M SORRY. STILL NOT MY FAVORITE.
.....
Can't you just lie?
THEN ON TO THE NEXT RESTAURANT...
KEI.
THAT'S ENOUGH.

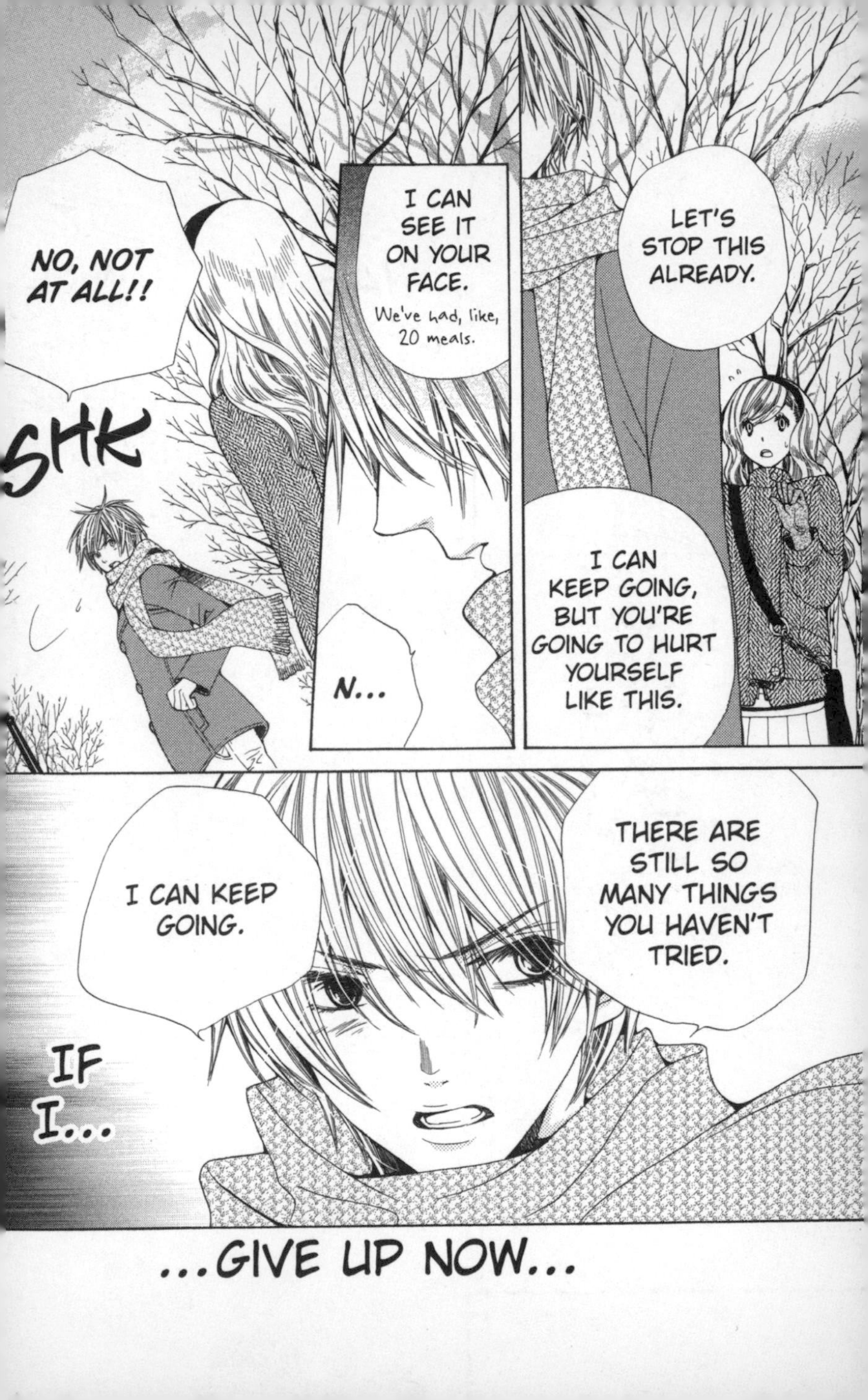
LET'S STOP THIS ALREADY.
I CAN KEEP GOING, BUT YOU'RE GOING TO HURT YOURSELF LIKE THIS.
I CAN SEE IT ON YOUR FACE.
We've had, like, 20 meals.
N...
NO, NOT AT ALL!!
SHK
THERE ARE STILL SO MANY THINGS YOU HAVEN'T TRIED.
I CAN KEEP GOING.
IF I...
...GIVE UP NOW...

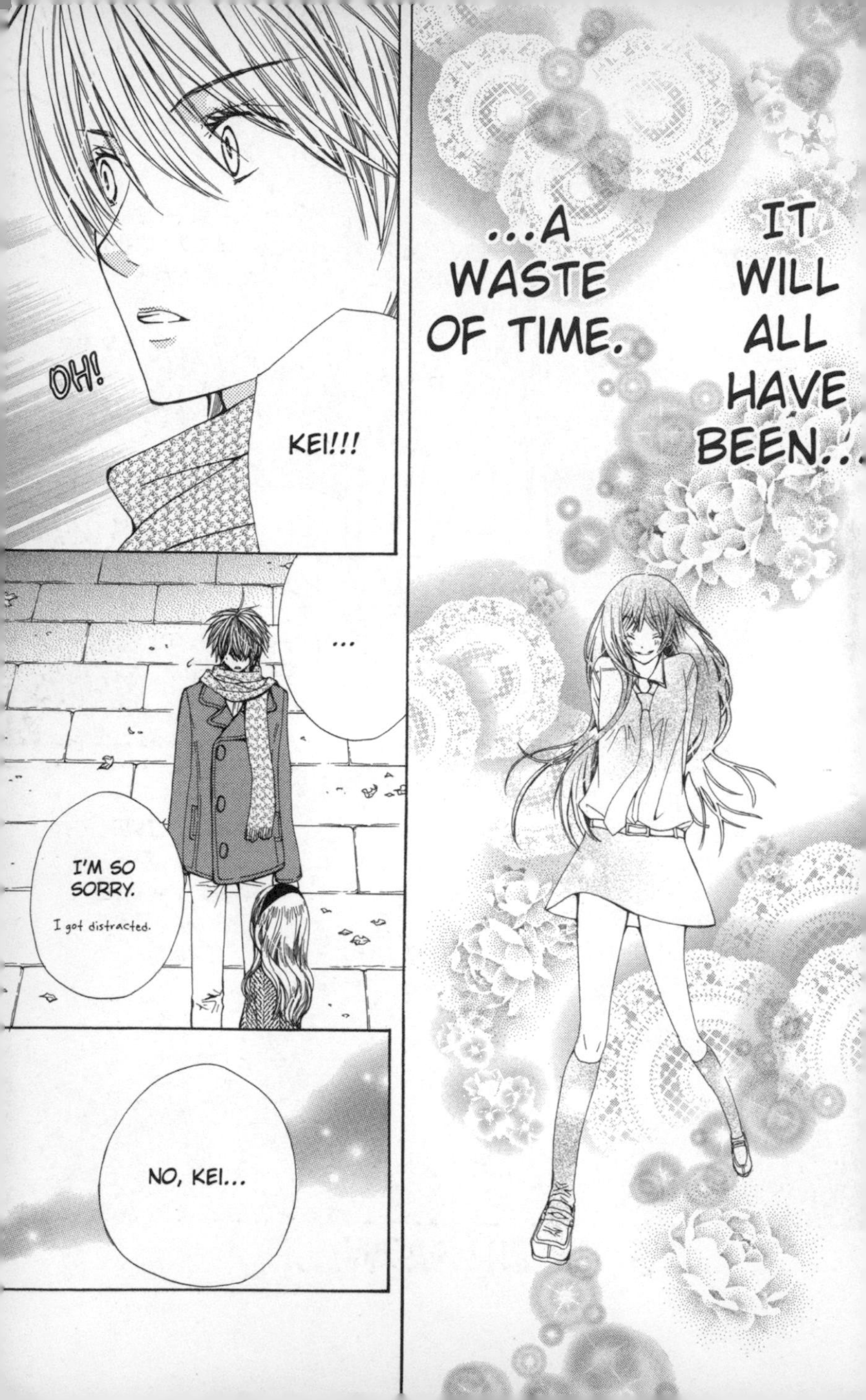
IT WILL ALL HAVE BEEN...
...A WASTE OF TIME.
KEI!!!
OH!
...
I'M SO SORRY.
I got distracted.
NO, KEI...

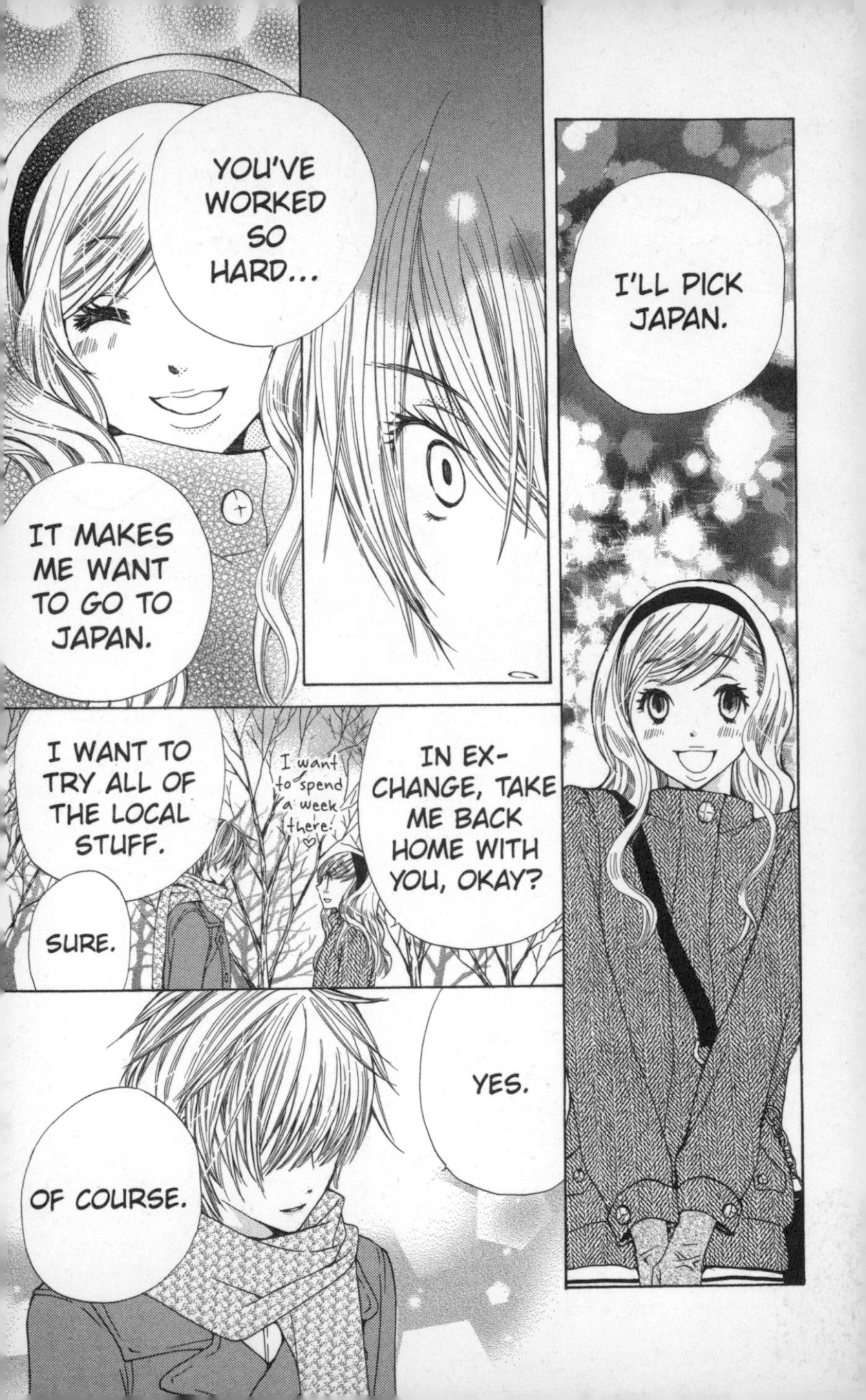
YOU'VE WORKED SO HARD...
IT MAKES ME WANT TO GO TO JAPAN.
I'LL PICK JAPAN.
IN EX-CHANGE, TAKE ME BACK HOME WITH YOU, OKAY?
I WANT TO TRY ALL OF THE LOCAL STUFF.
I want to spend a week there!
SURE.
YES.
OF COURSE.

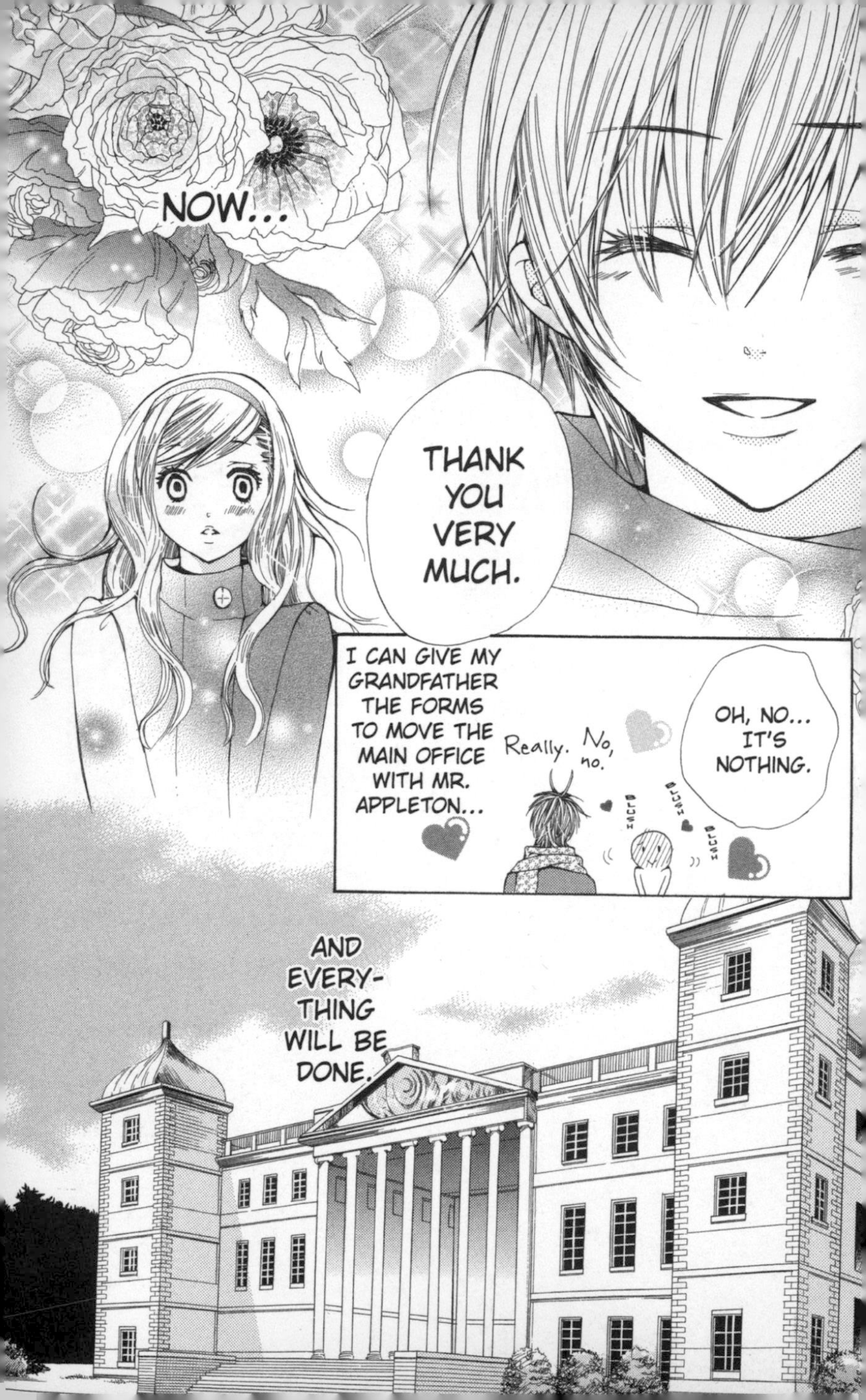
NOW...
THANK YOU VERY MUCH.
OH, NO... IT'S NOTHING.
No, no.
Really.
BLUSH
BLUSH
BLUSH
I CAN GIVE MY GRANDFATHER THE FORMS TO MOVE THE MAIN OFFICE WITH MR. APPLETON...
AND EVERY-THING WILL BE DONE.

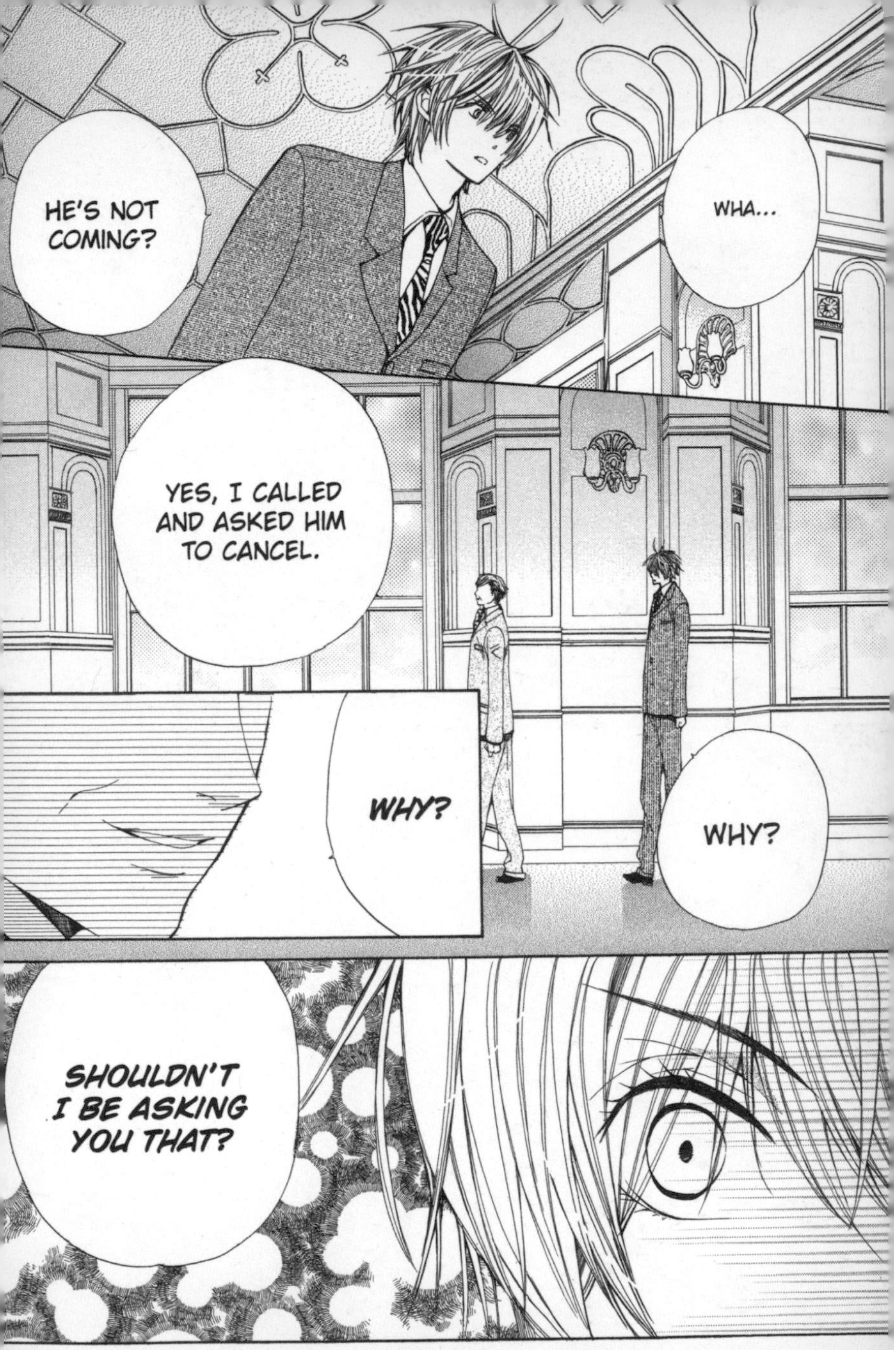
WHA...
HE'S NOT COMING?
YES, I CALLED AND ASKED HIM TO CANCEL.
WHY?
WHY?
SHOULDN'T I BE ASKING YOU THAT?

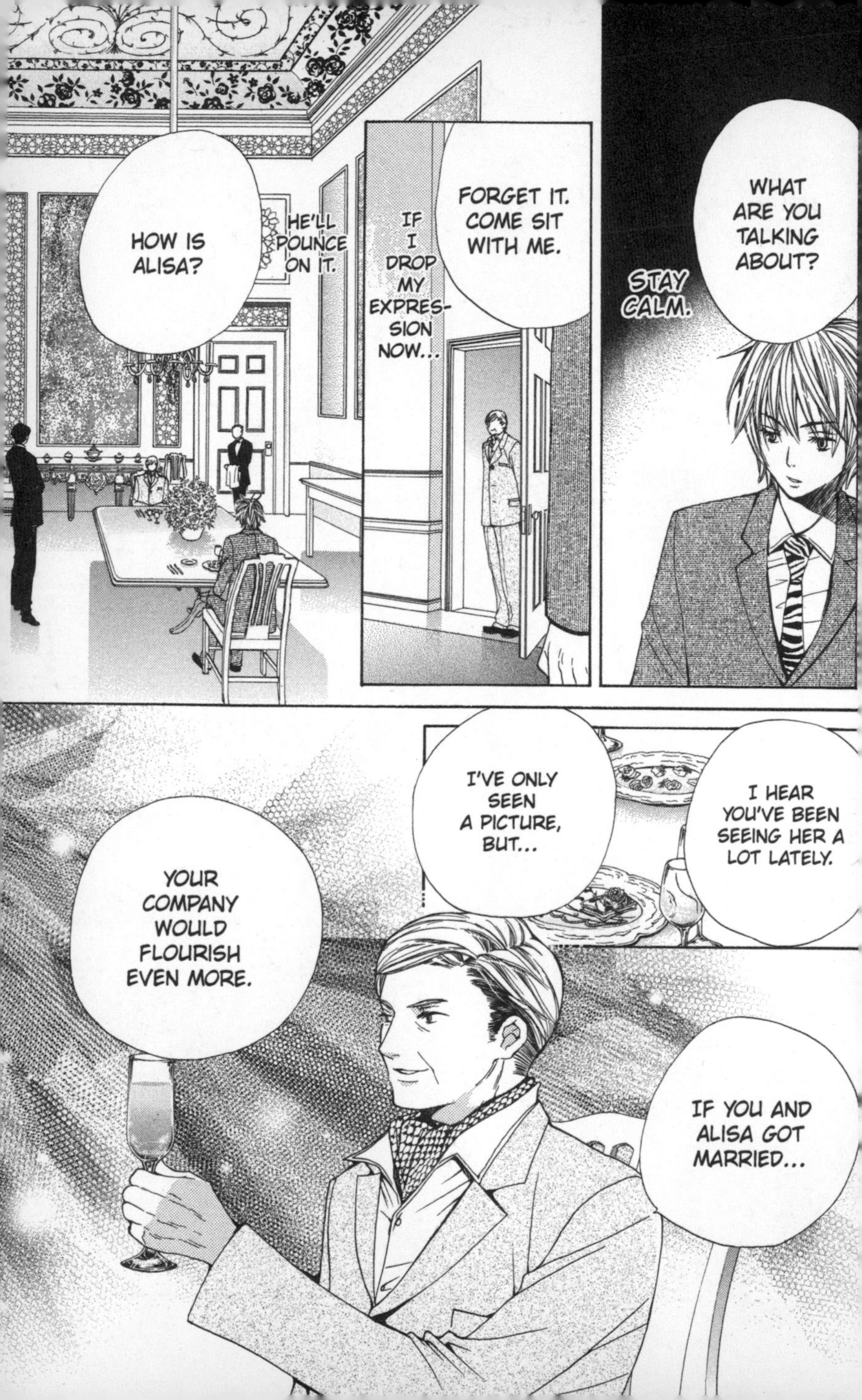
WHAT ARE YOU TALKING ABOUT?
STAY CALM.
FORGET IT. COME SIT WITH ME.
IF I DROP MY EXPRESSION NOW...
HE'LL POUNCE ON IT.
HOW IS ALISA?
I HEAR YOU'VE BEEN SEEING HER A LOT LATELY.
I'VE ONLY SEEN A PICTURE, BUT...
IF YOU AND ALISA GOT MARRIED...
YOUR COMPANY WOULD FLOURISH EVEN MORE.

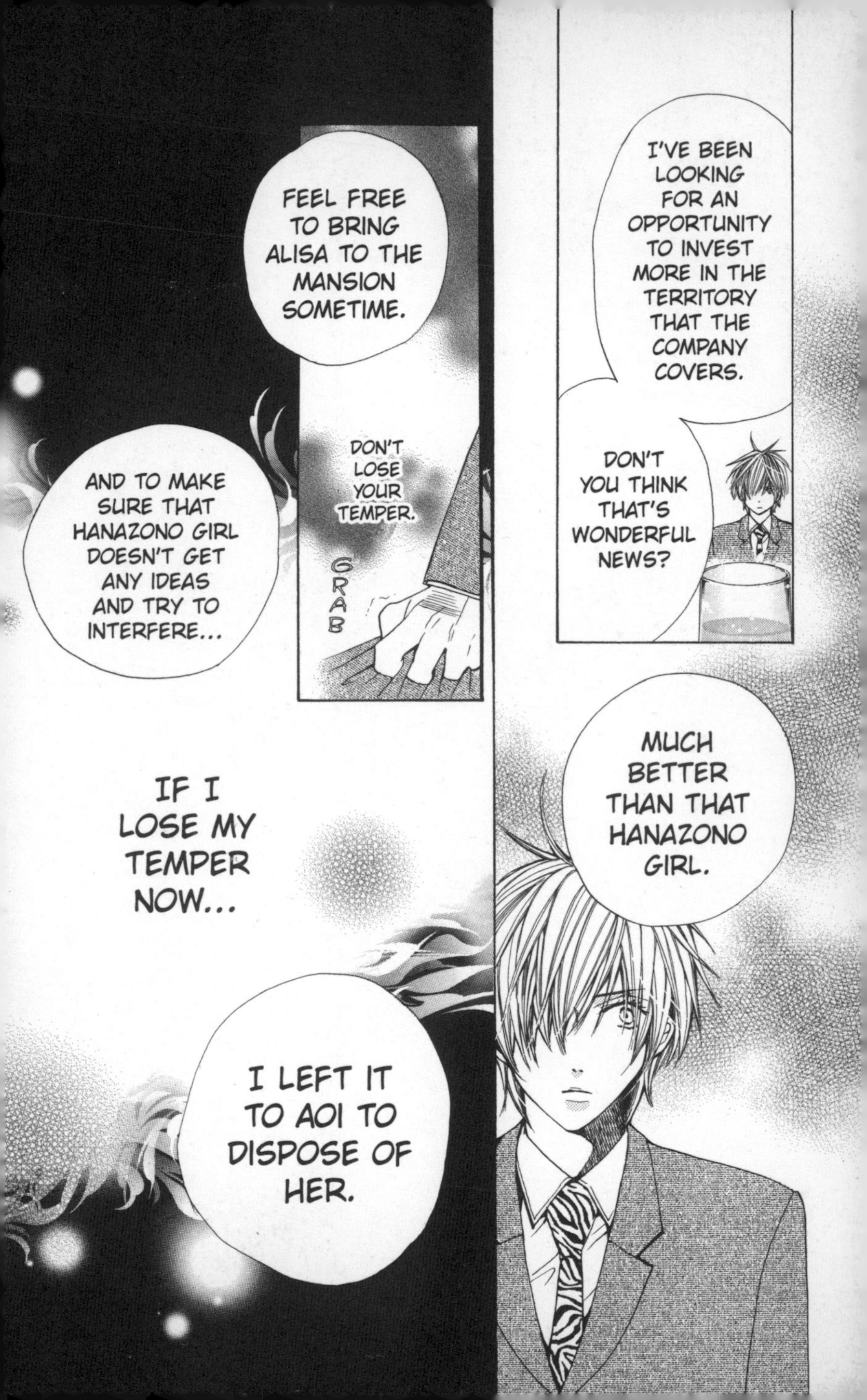
I'VE BEEN LOOKING FOR AN OPPORTUNITY TO INVEST MORE IN THE TERRITORY THAT THE COMPANY COVERS.
DON'T YOU THINK THAT'S WONDERFUL NEWS?
MUCH BETTER THAN THAT HANAZONO GIRL.
FEEL FREE TO BRING ALISA TO THE MANSION SOMETIME.
DON'T LOSE YOUR TEMPER.
GRAB
AND TO MAKE SURE THAT HANAZONO GIRL DOESN'T GET ANY IDEAS AND TRY TO INTERFERE...
IF I LOSE MY TEMPER NOW...
I LEFT IT TO AOI TO DISPOSE OF HER.

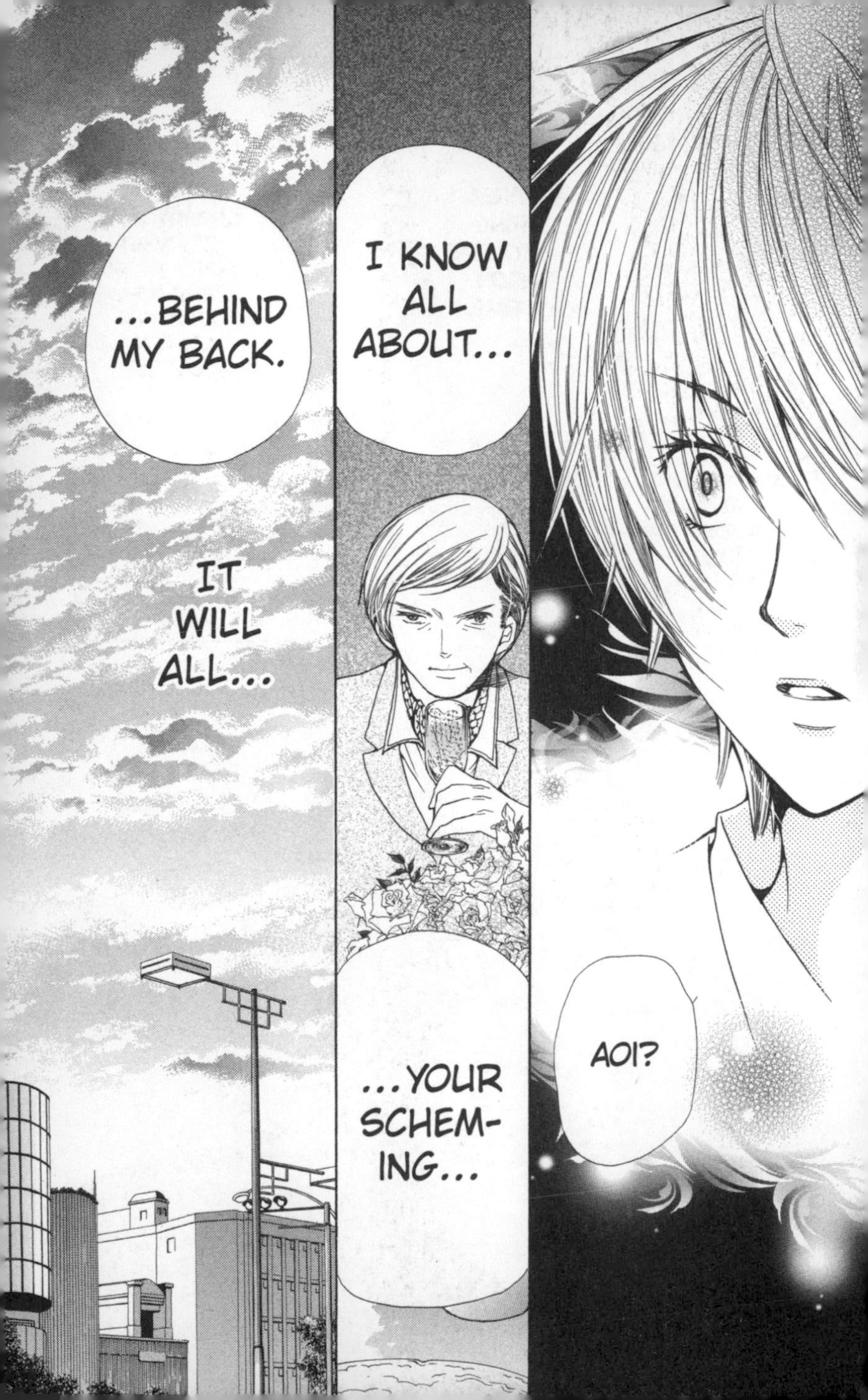
AOI?
I KNOW ALL ABOUT...
...YOUR SCHEM-ING...
...BEHIND MY BACK.
IT WILL ALL...

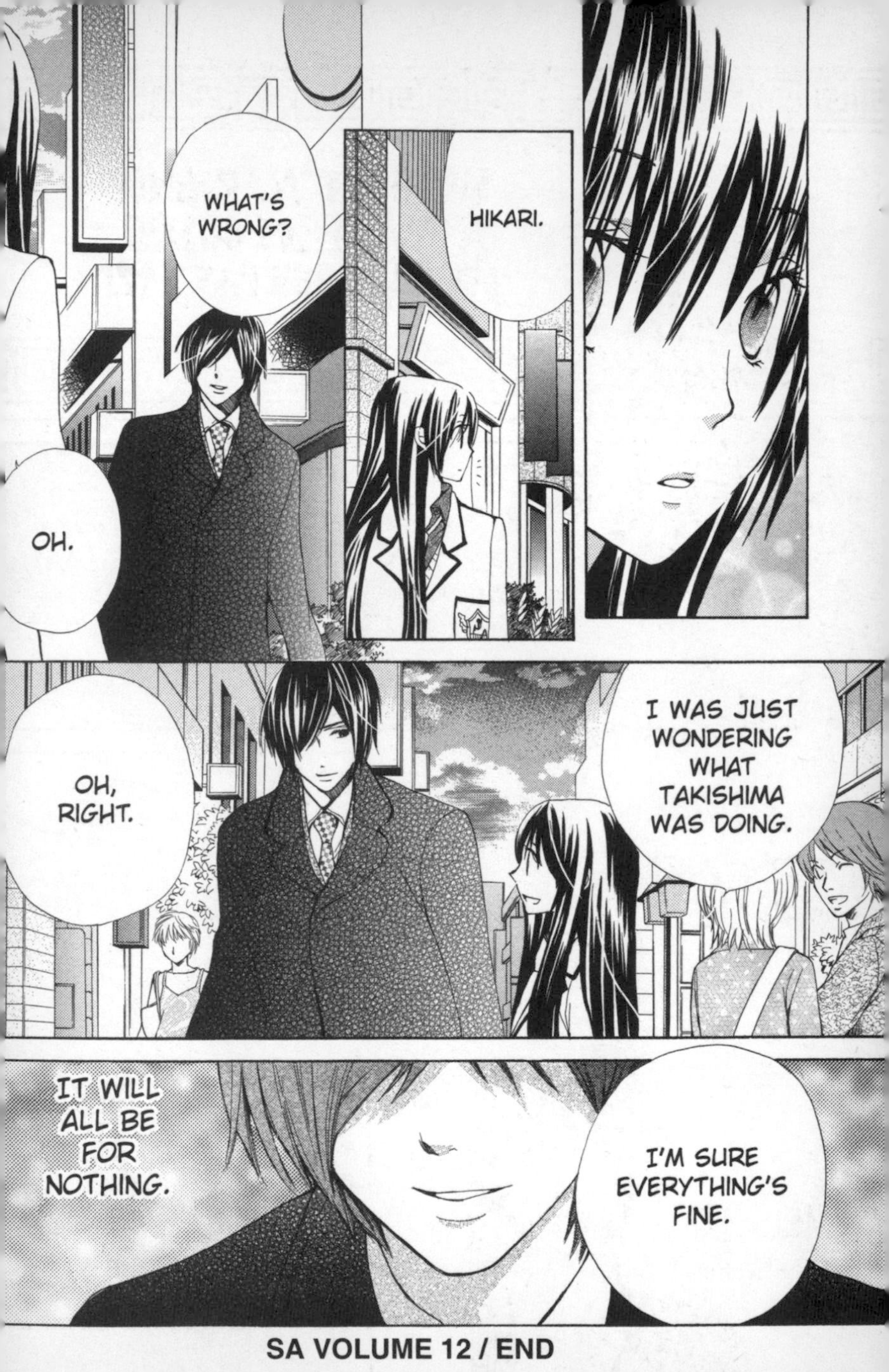
HIKARI.
WHAT'S WRONG?
OH.
I WAS JUST WONDERING WHAT TAKISHIMA WAS DOING.
OH, RIGHT.
I'M SURE EVERYTHING'S FINE.
IT WILL ALL BE FOR NOTHING.

SA VOLUME 12 / END

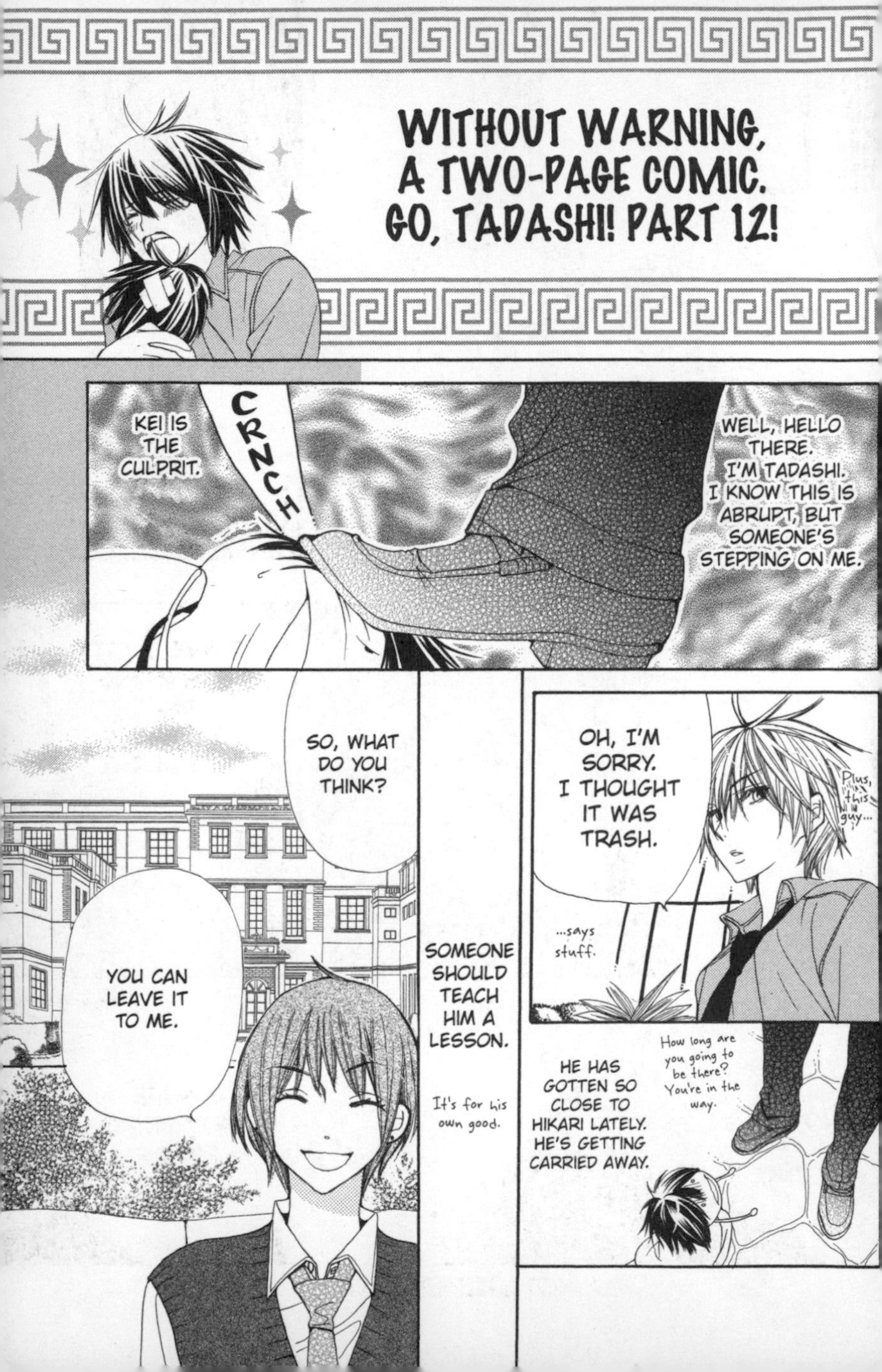
WITHOUT WARNING, A TWO-PAGE COMIC. GO, TADASHI!! PART 12!
WELL, HELLO THERE. I'M TADASHI. I KNOW THIS IS ABRUPT, BUT SOMEONE'S STEPPING ON ME.
CRNCH
KEI IS THE CULPRIT.
OH, I'M SORRY. I THOUGHT IT WAS TRASH.
Plus, this guy...
...says stuff.
How long are you going to be there? You're in the way.
HE HAS GOTTEN SO CLOSE TO HIKARI LATELY. HE'S GETTING CARRIED AWAY.
SOMEONE SHOULD TEACH HIM A LESSON.
It's for his own good.
SO, WHAT DO YOU THINK?
YOU CAN LEAVE IT TO ME.

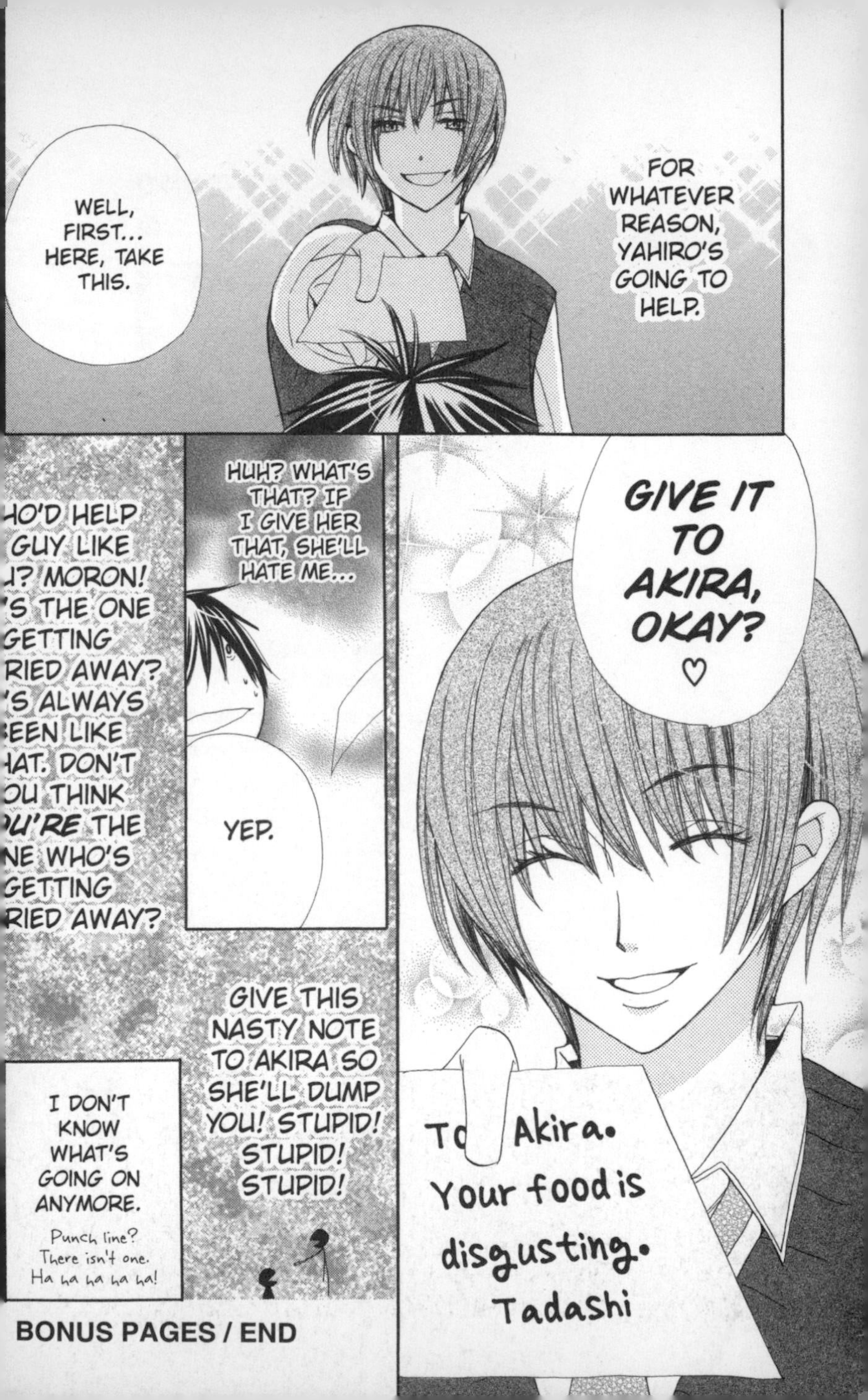
FOR WHATEVER REASON, YAHIRO'S GOING TO HELP.
WELL, FIRST... HERE, TAKE THIS.
GIVE IT TO AKIRA, OKAY? ♡
To Akira. Your food is disgusting. Tadashi
HUH? WHAT'S THAT? IF I GIVE HER THAT, SHE'LL HATE ME...
YEP.
HO'D HELP GUY LIKE U? MORON! 'S THE ONE GETTING RIED AWAY? 'S ALWAYS EEN LIKE HAT. DON'T OU THINK *U'RE* THE NE WHO'S GETTING RIED AWAY?
GIVE THIS NASTY NOTE TO AKIRA SO SHE'LL DUMP YOU! STUPID! STUPID! STUPID!
I DON'T KNOW WHAT'S GOING ON ANYMORE.
Punch line? There isn't one. Ha ha ha ha ha!

BONUS PAGES / END

Maki Minami is from Saitama
Prefecture in Japan. She debuted
in 2001 with *Kanata no Ao*
(Faraway Blue). Her other works
include *Kimi wa Girlfriend*
(You're My Girlfriend), *Mainichi
ga Takaramono* (Every Day Is a
Treasure) and *Yuki Atataka*
(Warm Winter). *S•A* was serialized in
Japan's *Hana to Yume* magazine and
made into an anime in 2008.

S・A

Vol. 12
The Shojo Beat Manga Edition

STORY & ART BY
MAKI MINAMI

English Adaptation/Amanda Hubbard
Translation/JN Productions
Touch-up Art & Lettering/Hudson Yards
Design/Deirdre Shiozawa
Editor/Jonathan Tarbox

VP, Production/Alvin Lu
VP, Publishing Licensing/Rika Inouye
VP, Sales & Product Marketing/Gonzalo Ferreyra
VP, Creative/Linda Espinosa
Publisher/Hyoe Narita

S•A -Special A- by Maki Minami © Maki Minami 2008. All rights reserved.
First published in Japan in 2008 by HAKUSENSHA, Inc., Tokyo. English
language translation rights arranged with HAKUSENSHA, Inc., Tokyo.
The stories, characters and incidents mentioned in this publication are entirely
fictional.

Printed in Canada

Published by VIZ Media, LLC
P.O. Box 77010
San Francisco, CA 94107

Shojo Beat Manga Edition
10 9 8 7 6 5 4 3 2 1
First printing, September 2009